Reformation Principle
and Practice

Reformation Principle and Practice

ESSAYS IN HONOUR OF

ARTHUR GEOFFREY DICKENS

EDITED BY

PETER NEWMAN BROOKS

Scolar Press · London

Published 1980 by Scolar Press
90/91 Great Russell Street
London WC1B 3PY

BRITISH LIBRARY CATALOGUING IN PUBLICATION DATA
Reformation principle and practice.
1. Reformation – Addresses, essays, lectures
I. Brooks, Peter Newman II. Dickens, Arthur Geoffrey
270.6   BR305.2

ISBN 0 85967 579 3

Designed by Humphrey Stone
Set in Monotype Ehrhardt
and printed in Great Britain
by Western Printing Services Ltd
Bristol

Frontispiece: Photo-portrait of Professor Arthur Geoffrey Dickens,
C.M.G., F.B.A., D.LIT., sometime Director of the Institute
of Historical Research in the University of London
(*Photo : Edward Leigh*)

Contents

Contents

Preface

If this book of essays has itself some claim to be regarded as a modest contribution to Reformation studies, its overall theme is primarily intended to portray the life-long professional interest of one whose achievement in the discipline has made him arguably the leading English authority in an area long dominated by German and American scholarship. For the particular contribution Arthur Geoffrey Dickens has made to the understanding of Reformation – whether in England or on the continent of Europe, whether Catholic or Protestant – demands the traditional recognition of those who respect him as colleague, follow him as mentor and value him as friend. It is therefore singularly appropriate that such a volume should be published to celebrate Professor Dickens's seventieth birthday. The event signals not merely the appreciation of those American, English and European scholars who have contributed to the work, but also symbolizes the great army of admirers who owe so much to the energy and skill with which a truly Olympian figure has inspired and encouraged innumerable young historians during a long, dedicated and most distinguished career.

A Yorkshireman, whose proudest moment must have been the recognition accorded by the University of his native city of Hull when he was presented for the degree of Doctor of Letters *honoris causa*, A. G. Dickens spent an active undergraduate career as *Demy* of Magdalen College, Oxford. After covering himself with glory in the Final Honour School of Modern History, he became, in 1933, Fellow and Tutor of Keble College, lecturing in sixteenth-century English history in the University of Oxford. When but thirty-nine years of age, Geoffrey Dickens returned to Hull as G. F. Grant Professor. It was here that teaching and an unrivalled knowledge of northern archives during two decades resulted in what many still regard as his most enduring work of scholarship, *Lollards and Protestants in the Diocese of York* (1959). Notable articles had of course been written long before; but it is in the Preface to this work that Dickens readily acknowledges a debt to Dr A. L. Rowse who 'by forceful precept and inspiring, if inimitable, example, urged me to write books.' Meriting the classification *magnum opus*, it was to prove a seminal study both expounding the interplay of the many forces that went to make up the Henrician Reformation, and appreciating to the full the historian's need of particularist regional studies to push forward research frontiers. A veritable sortie into the unknown, in short, the volume effectively focussed the nature and purpose of historical research, whilst as a localized study it provided English Reformation scholars with a completely fresh approach. A kind of first-fruits achievement when published, moreover, *Lollards and Protestants* gained international acclaim for one whose administrative and teaching skills had simultaneously raised him to eminence as Deputy Principal, Dean of the Arts Faculty and Pro-Vice-Chancellor of the University of Hull.

But it was first and foremost to Clio that Professor Dickens chose to cleave. In 1960 *Thomas Cromwell and the English Reformation* appeared in print. Described with characteristic modesty by its author as a 'succinct provisional reassessment', attempted 'after the appearance of Dr Elton's stimulating researches', this may be described in near Gilbertian terms as the very model of a modern brief biography. It certainly did much to establish Professor Dickens as the kind of gifted writer the student world exalts and avid general readers can never ignore for his compelling interest, accurate historical portrayal, and the sheer enjoyment his pen conveys.

Yet it was of course the publication of *The English Reformation* in 1964 that effectively invested Professor Dickens with the doctor's bonnet to widespread acclaim from the international world of learning. Enlarging Reformation horizons from localism to nationalism, the book established its author as a unique authority in a notorious and hazardous subject. With a pleasing simplicity concealing both his own profundity of mind and the infinite perplexity of the period under consideration, the Preface to this definitive study reveals a threefold purpose of magisterial instruction to the reader. First, because the historian's task must always be basic explanation, there was description of the crucial conditions obtaining between 1529 and 1559, the background of those dramatic, well-known changes in Tudor England. Secondly, careful analysis was afforded a long-neglected but central topic, the doctrinal development and regional advance of Protestantism. And thirdly, all the skills of the social historian analysed a movement that inevitably affected the ordinary men and women scholars had hitherto scorned by reserving the centre-stage spotlight exclusively for kings and prelates, monasteries and service-books. With common sense and basic humanity related to formidable learning couched in felicitous style, the book rapidly became a best-seller and remains the single reason why Professor Dickens will always be held in the highest regard by colleagues in a field where reputations are either notorious or transitory. One secret of such success is surely the discussion so distinguished an historian chose to allot conventional themes, for the reason that the familiar story of goings-on at the Tudor court could in no way cohere in their absence. Such an object lesson in the writing of history proved its own reward, the Chair of History at King's College, London, claiming Professor Dickens in 1962. Although innumerable honours followed in the next few years – principally his election as a Fellow of the British Academy in 1966 – a remarkable little study, *Martin Luther and the Reformation*, also appeared at this time showing that when London professors manage to escape to their clubs, they are not merely recovering from the burdens of University committee work. It might indeed be placed on record that the library of the Athenaeum is one of the greatest arguments in favour of continuing the exclusivity of the best in clubland – for Reformation studies would certainly have suffered if so approachable and open a man as Professor Dickens, immensely generous with his time, had not been able to use the fine resources of such an inaccessible retreat to the full.

At this stage in a rising career, the complexities of Protestant and Catholic Reformation in continental Europe would have daunted a lesser individual. But Professor Dickens well knew the direction he should take. The central problem of Reformation he once identified as 'the intellectual and social forces which got Luther's revolt off the ground'. He was also convinced that his work 'will have served its main purpose if it reveals something of the amazing diversity and depth of the changes sweeping Europe at the moment when her culture was beginning effectively to expand and reshape the destinies of the whole human race'.[1]

How appropriate that so clear-sighted and productive an historian should have gained the succession to Pollard, Galbraith, Goronwy Edwards and Wormald as Director of the Institute of Historical Research in 1967. Such a title may conjure up dizzy visions of further research – col after col *en route* for a summit achievement, so to state – but the practice has long proved altogether different. London's Institute in no way resembles Princeton, and the Director has an essentially pastoral role that figures not at all in an historian's bibliography. However, in terms of biography, or biographical memoir, this new task does demand prominence. It was certainly the case that, under the direction of Professor Dickens, the Institute provided the best of academic hospitality for both renowned scholars and routine post-graduate students busying themselves with the stuff of research. With a minimum of fuss, Yorkshire hospitality embraced those obliged to study in the metropolis, maintaining a fine reference library and extending the peace and quiet so essential for the art of written communication, as well as providing an ideal rendezvous for historians from all over the world. As the representative of British historical scholarship at home and abroad, the new Director was thus obliged to combine his own continuing researches with an arduous diplomatic assignment, particularly as the Academy itself saw fit to appoint Professor Dickens Foreign Secretary in 1969. Even so, research never once fell out of a precise personal focus, the Director's industry not merely editing the *Bulletin* for a decade, but, in addition to supervising the studies of a number of rising young scholars fascinated by his own favoured interest, enabling him annually to host the important Anglo-American

1 *Reformation and Society in Sixteenth-Century Europe*, London, 1966, p. 7.

Conference of historians at London's Senate House. That these were also years when Professor Dickens was elected to a special lectureship on Dr Ford's foundation at Oxford, and Birkbeck Lecturer at Trinity College, Cambridge, indicates both his dedication and sheer stamina.

It is invariably the case that behind such men there stands a remarkable woman. Molly Dickens supremely merits affectionate acknowledgement of this kind for reasons far removed from conventional tribute. An exceptional wife and mother of two sons, she proved ever active in affording Geoff precisely the measure of encouragement and support at home that alone enabled him to endure in an increasingly public life. The soul of discretion, a superb northern wit and constant companion at those awful jamborees and daunting receptions which regularly demand attendance from the internationally renowned, Molly's warm spirit and apt humour radiated forth on occasions which have been the downfall of lesser women. Whatever the company, Molly in fact proved the perfect complement to a husband she loved dearly and served to the last. When she died in 1978 – bravely buoyant through a mercifully short, but tragic, illness – Dickens told his closest friends that it was like suffering the shock of amputation. Present at his formal retirement party and presentation in 1977, it is the saddest loss to Professor Dickens and her own many friends that Molly is not herself able to know that this tribute includes her in its salute, for so much a lifetime's dedication abundantly deserves.

The wide-ranging interests and sheer accomplishments of A. G. D. will long inspire those privileged to know his rare and urbane genius. That they will also hearten and stimulate those who merely come across the man through his writings – *Dicens dixit* – need not be in question. When he first put pen to paper, Reformation studies were the peculiar preserve of the dogmatist. In a crucial sense, he thus liberated the discipline from a restricting clericalism that, by confining its interest to the *cognoscenti*, customarily deprived ordinary mortals of enjoying a fascination offered by few other historical periods.

A becoming modesty in Professor Dickens has all too often concealed the full measure of this singular feat. While at the Institute, he chose to describe himself as 'a part-time sexagenarian scholar' who, without the large team of researchers available to counterparts in Germany or the United States, was able to revel in his assignment by taking comfort in the undoubted fact that it was an impossible task. Impossible too it would have been but for the kind of life-support system unstintingly afforded her professor by Miss Cynthia Hawker. The PPS in the proverbial million, she had a grasp of historical technique, professional protocol and the ability to process endless trays of correspondence and *TSS* that made her indispensable to Dickens throughout a long career of unselfish, immensely loyal service.

With the *en passant* observation that 'almost every paragraph owes a debt to personal friends', Professor Dickens is apt to dismiss his writing and as if conscious that even a disclaimer of this kind lays him open to a charge of 'elaborate name-dropping', he proceeds to emphasize the 'many undeserved strokes of fortune' that bring contact with those leading Reformation research in both the Old World and the New. A typical instance of scholarly generosity and humility, the reference has a compelling relevance uniting the man and his chosen discipline. For by its nature, the Reformation of the sixteenth century presents the historian with a most hazardous subject for study, not least because the intimate nature of spiritual conviction in the human soul is invariably inaccessible to the documentary material affording scholars primary evidence in expositions of a bygone age. The sensitivity required to use such sources derives from a most subtle blend of skills. But when such three-dimensional understanding matures and marries its mind with the events, ideologies and personalities of a tumultuous period in the evolution of western society, the old strife of national and urban politics is enlivened by contact with vigorous truths altogether new to the experience of remarkable generations of preachers and pastors, polemicists and printers to give birth to Reformation. Whether this was achieved in territorial or in city states, or merely in the minds of ascetic, world-denying men and women, the movement has long intrigued the lively mind of Arthur Geoffrey Dickens. And for that simple yet profound fact, every kind of historian will ever remain indebted and deeply grateful.

New Year's Day   PETER NEWMAN BROOKS
1980

List of Abbreviations

ADB	*Allgemeine Deutsche Biographie*
A & M	*The Acts and Monuments of John Foxe*
AR	*Archiv für Reformationsgeschichte*
BL	British Library
CALC	Cathedral Archives and Library Canterbury
CQR	*Church Quarterly Review*
DNB	*Dictionary of National Biography*
DWL	Dr Williams's Library
EHR	*English Historical Review*
ESRO	East Sussex Record Office
HHA	Haina Hospitalsarchiv
JEH	*Journal of Ecclesiastical History*
JTS	*Journal of Theological Studies*
KAO	Kent Archives Office
NDB	*Neue Deutsche Biographie*
PRO	Public Record Office
PS	Parker Society
St A	Stadtarchiv Augsburg
StAM	Staatsarchiv Marburg
VCH Yorks	*Victoria County History, Yorkshire*
WA	Martin Luther *Werke*, kritische Gesamtausgabe
WA Br	Martin Luther, *Werke : Briefwechsel*
WA TR	Martin Luther, *Werke : Tischreden*
YAJ	*Yorkshire Archaeological Journal*

I

The Battle of the Books:
The Ferment of Ideas and the Beginning
of the Reformation

❦

GORDON RUPP

'Mightier than an army is the power of an idea, whose time has come' is a text on which a good many homilies about the sixteenth century might be written. But how ideas 'come' and 'go' in this sense – how, having been inert, common-place and unimportant for long enough, they suddenly find their hour, and become living, moving forces in the minds, hearts and wills of masses of human beings – is a complex mystery. Much the same is true of the spread of ideas from time to time and from place to place. For ideas are like germs; they seem often to be carried by 'carrier patients' who are perhaps more dangerous than the fanatics or the prophets. And there certainly seem to be incubation periods at the end of which the authorities awaken to danger, finding themselves ill prepared with a plague on their hands. Probably we underestimate the speed of things. The history of art shows striking examples of the way in which icono-graphic symbols, paints (like the lapis lazuli in the *Book of Kells*) and jewels could come to Ireland from Egypt or Byzantium in the seventh century, while the transcontinental litter of the Norsemen, itself precious loot, turns up in every corner of Christendom in an astonishingly short space of time. He would be bold who would devise a comparative table between high roads and cities, desert places and forest tracks. As every Grand Inquisitor knows, it is easier to kill men than destroy their ideas. You never know when thoughts may be revived; and it has been well said that only God knows when a book is dead. The Erasmus edition of Origen, the Rhenanus edition of Tertullian and Le Fèvre's edition of Hermas spoke explosively to the 1520s, as the writings of Thomas Müntzer show. On the other hand, they may revive too late. A page of Wycliffe embedded in a tract by Jerome Barlow is a case in point, for who in 1528 wanted an argument clinched by Grosseteste and FitzRalph? When in 1524 Otto Brunfels got hold of some Huss manuscripts (probably found among Hutten's papers), he reprinted them;[1] though the tract on *Anti-Christ* was in fact from Matthew of Janow, and he reprinted at the same time Wycliffe's important *Trialogus*.[2] But these are rather like unexploded shells from World War I ploughed up during World War II. By this time there were more up-to-date treatises with which to criticize the church, and a new apocalyptic literature was emerging in a work like the *Book of a Hundred Chapters*. The film producer Sam Goldwyn is said to have grumbled: 'I'm tired of all these old clichés. Go out and get me some new ones.' In this sense a case can be made for some of the

---

1 J. C. Margolin, 'Otto Brunfels dans le milieu évangelique', in *Strasbourg au coeur religieux du XVIme siècle*, ed. Livet and Rapp (Strasbourg, 1977). Cf. N. L. Zinzendorf, *Matthias Janow: Opera* (New York, 1975), p. 6, and *Tomus Tertius: Sermonum Johannis Huss ad Populum* (1525), for introductory letter of Brunfels to Luther, iii.
2 Basel, 1525. This does not appear to have sold well, and it would be interesting to know if Tyndale read it.

older historical clichés. Perhaps students still need to be told that some grasp of Christian theology is, even more than Latin or German, or a diploma in Social Studies, a prerequisite for understanding the Reformation. They need to be reminded that the painful craft of writing decent English is still honourable, for it is even more valid now than when Philip Guedalla wrote that 'historians' English is an industrial disease.' Likewise, they need to be reminded that the English Reformation neither began nor ended at the white cliffs of Dover.

It is, perhaps, a truism that a history of the Reformation could well begin with John Wycliffe; for a thorough, analytical reappraisal of his whole theology is more than overdue. Without prejudice to excellent modern studies of his political and legal notions, or the description of his philosophic teaching, it is as a theologian that he needs to be judged.[3] The recent welcome concentrated studies of fourteenth- and fifteenth-century theologians treat Wycliffe as if he were a kind of black star in the firmament.[4] Important as his philosophical realism was, it merely supported, and did not control, his theology. If it trapped him into a denial of transubstantiation, it may have eased his view of the nature of the Church, and of the relation of Christ to the Gospel. Furthermore, it gave to his view of Holy Scripture a subtlety and complexity which makes of it more than antiquarian significance in the modern hermeneutic debate; and it is shuddering to find Dr Leff and Miss Smalley dismissing such a view of the plenary inspiration of Scripture with the grossly anachronistic description 'fundamentalist'.

The wedge that was thought to have been driven in recent years between Wycliffe and the Wycliffite Bibles, and between him and the Lollard preachers, must now be re-examined;[5] and the recent distinguished studies by Dr Anne Hudson have emphasized the existence of a whole hierarchy of media whereby the doctrines and ideas of Wycliffe could be communicated from the University and articulate level to that of the common people.[6] In any case, what was put forward as a problem – how such an intricate scholasticism as that of Wycliffe could direct and stimulate a popular movement – had always to face the demonstration that this in any case is what happened in Bohemia, where his

3 H. O. Oberman in a typically profound essay, 'Fourteenth-century religious thought: a premature profile', *Speculum*, vol. liii (1978), does not mention Wycliffe. Cf. his study of the relation of Scripture and tradition in *The Harvest of Medieval Theology* (1962), pp. 372f.; while conversant with recent secondary studies altogether ignores the three important volumes of Wycliffe on Holy Scripture, thus treating him as little more than a re-hash of Bradwardine. Miss Smalley, however, finds that 'most important of all, he made people think of Scripture as a whole, and about its place in theology, as a fundamental problem.' (*Cambridge History of the Bible*, vol. ii, ed. G. W. H. Lampe, (Cambridge, 1969, p. 208.)
4 Her luminous article 'The Bible and eternity: John Wyclif's Dilemma', *Journal of the Warburg Institute*, xxvii (1964), does not attempt to discuss his theological solutions.
5 See H. Hargreaves, 'The Wycliffite Versions', in *Cambridge History of the Bible*, vol. ii, pp. 387f., and J. L. Fristedt, *The Wycliffite Bible* (Stockholm, 1953).
6 A. Hudson, *English Wycliffite Writings* (Cambridge, 1978); cf. *JTS* (1972), pp. 65f., 407f., and *JTS* (1974), pp. 129f.

teachings came as a blood transfusion into the affairs of the Czech people, and the incipient revolt in the Czech Church.

It would be fascinating to know the answers to several questions. Who, when and how it was that the marriage between a Bohemian princess and an English King set in train such a passage of men, manuscripts and ideas. The massive presence of Wycliffite manuscripts in Prague and Vienna show how far-reaching this commerce became. In the journeys of the Englishman Peter Payne, and his attempt to blend together the inheritance of the Lollards and those of the Hussites and Waldensians, for example, is a reminder that, throughout the fifteenth century, there was overall dissent.[7] In this context, the words Lollard, Hussite, Waldensian become less and less precise, since they covered an inheritance much older than they knew, of rebellion against the established Church, of anticlericalism (itself of considerable complexity), and the attempt to return to a simple, Bible-based, Christocentric obedience, a Christianity like that of the primitive Church, unplugged from power and wealth and 'great possessions'.[8]

Late-medieval Christians had more exotic literature available than the received Scriptures; and at times the Gnostic apocryphal gospels and Jewish legends of the first centuries got into dissenting conventicles. Some ideas can indeed be almost given pedigrees reaching back across central Europe and, via the Balkans, to the Gnostic ideas of the first Christian age. What among the Anabaptists is sometimes called 'Melchiorite Christology' thus has older roots. The saying that 'Our Lord passed through his mother like water through a pipe' goes back to the early Gnostic Christians. Though there have been recent attempts to play down the importance and even the coherent existence of the Brethren of the Free Spirit, there is too much evidence in too many places over too long a period to convince scholars that all is smoke without fire.[9] Admittedly it is true that historians are prone to cry 'Lo here!' whenever antinomianism raises its head, but antinomianism is endemic in Christian history, a nasty fringe of all evangelical revivals. But the way in which the text 'Be fruitful and multiply' turns up again (in Lollard investigations among others) suggests Gnostic and Adamite associations, a return to the state of Adam before the Fall, to support those who find some connection between this and the 'Earthly Paradise' of Jerome Bosch, not to mention happenings among the Anabaptists of Strasbourg and Amsterdam, and the doubtless much-maligned 'Family of Love'.

In another direction, John Colet illustrates the converting power of the encounter with books. For while Grocyn, More, Linacre and Erasmus himself

7 M. Lambert, *Medieval Heresy* (London, 1977), pp. 259, 330. Also, Gonnet and Molnar, *Les Vaudois au Moyen Age* (Turin, 1974).
8 See F. Rapp, *Réforme et Réformation à Strasbourg, 1450–1525* (Paris, 1976), book v, pp. 435–81.
9. Cf. M. Lambert, op. cit., p.107, and A. Hudson, op. cit., p. 154.

5

were affected by the Platonic revival, in Colet's case, Christian Platonism coloured the whole of his theology, in a way not otherwise found in England though it is the hall-mark of the sodalities in both Florence and Paris. Despite his brush with his bishop and the presence of Lollards at his sermons, Colet was no heretic, and it is perhaps coincidental that he was born at Wendover, on the Lollard highway through the Chiltern hills. According to Erasmus he had read the writings of Wycliffe.[10] He had, like Wycliffe, the disconcerting way of turning in an academic discussion to round on the clergy in a biting attack – his animadversion on litigiousness in his *Romans* is more extreme than the outburst of Robert Barnes on the same theme, for which Barnes got into such trouble thirty years on in Cambridge. Colet's Christian Platonism has to be seen against the background of the age of Gerson and Nicholas of Cusa, with its movement away from rationalist scholasticism, its concern for moral theology and *theologia spiritualis*, its view of Christianity not so much as a set of doctrines, but rather as a way of life, and a vision of God.

In the first place, Colet was deeply impressed by the writings of Pseudo-Dionysius the Areopagite. Believing him to have been the beloved disciple of St Paul, the apt interpreter of those doctrines which Paul had himself received when rapt into the third heaven,[11] Colet held Pseudo-Dionysius in high esteem. When he learned, as he must have done, that his friend Grocyn (in lectures Colet invited him to give on Dionysius in St Paul's Cathedral) had followed Valla in denying his apostolicity, Colet may simply have refused to believe him.[12]

There are books we read, and books we encounter, and Colet came across Dionysius when studying in France, almost certainly in Paris. For it was here that St Paul's convert on Mars hill (incorporated by tradition with St Denis of France) found his lovers from the twelfth century. There were revivals in the time of Gerson, and at the end of the fifteenth century in the Lefèvre circle.[13] Colet wrote, commented, abridged and lectured on the Dionysian writings. The excited scrawls in his manuscripts show his fascination with the writer's hierarchical view of the universe, with his angelology and with the reflection of these

---

10 C. R. Thompson, *The Colloquies of Erasmus* (Chicago, 1965), p. 305:
   OGYGIUS: An Englishman named Gratian Pullus . . .
   MENEDEMUS: Some Wycliffite, I suppose.
   OGYGIUS: I don't think so, though he had read his books. Where he got hold of them
       isn't clear.
On the identification of Colet and Pullus, cf. P. S. Allen, *Opus Epistolarum Des. Erasmi Roterodami* (Oxford, 1922), vol. iv, Ep. 999, p. 517.
11 Ficino had entitled his lectures on Romans *In epistolas D. Pauli, ascensus ad tertium coelum*. Cf. Ficino, *Opera Omni* (reprinted at Turin, 1962), pp. 54–5.
12 There are certainly such hints to be found in the letters of his friends.
13 D. Knowles, 'The influence of Pseudo-Dionysus on Western Mysticism', in Peter Brooks (ed.), *Christian Spirituality* (London, 1975). Cf. J. B. Trapp, 'John Colet, his MSS and the Pseudo-Dionysus', in R. R. Bolgar (ed.), *Classical influences on European culture, 1500–1700* (Cambridge, 1976), pp. 205ff.

things in the ministry and sacraments of the church.[14] Yet he was never a Johnny-head-in-clouds, and in his famous sermon when Wolsey was made cardinal, he outpaced Dionysius by expounding the cardinalate as an emblem of the seraphim, those flaming spirits who betoken enraptured and complete devotion – surely a most deadly irony (whether intended or not), and more damaging as a comparison than the epithet 'butcher's cur' in Roye and Barlow's rhyme.

Almost as important for Colet as Dionysius were the Florentine Platonists.[15] John Pico della Mirandola's *Heptaplus* undergirds and may have inspired Colet's *Letters on Genesis* while Ficino's translations from Plato and Plotinus, his *Theologica Platonica* and the essays of his *Epistolae*, were incessantly quoted. When it is considered how very recent were the editions and writings of these men, and how deeply they coloured Colet's mind, it is hard to think of a parallel, unless it is perhaps a younger theologian of our time being bowled over by the writings of a Teilhard de Chardin.

The manuscripts of his writings present problems, for there are some deep contradictions. But there is nevertheless a recurring and incessant Platonic idiom, the use of the dialectic of body and soul and spirit, the theme of the attractive love of God drawing men out of darkness into the light of his presence, and the notion of divine love as the rays of the sun. But even more than in the case of Ficino, the Platonism is adjectival to a genuinely Christian theology. Both in Ficino's and Colet's *Romans* and in Colet's *1 Corinthians*, a firm centrality is given to the Biblical plan of salvation, to the incarnation, and to redemption in Christ. If there is more traditional theology in him than appears on the surface (echoes of the scholastic 'doing what in one lies' – and the distinction between the book of Creation and the book of Scripture which surely comes from Raymond of Sabunde), at the heart is his devotion to Paul as the best interpreter of the mind of Christ, so that here, and in his stress on the imitation of Christ, Colet at least approaches Erasmus's *Philosophia Christi*. Erasmus may for once have been guilty of understatement in his praise, for Colet was a great 'character' possessed of both devotion and imagination, a preacher-theologian who perhaps gave a lasting mystique to the office of dean of St Paul's.[16] Among all the educational treatises of an age extending from Gerson to Brunfels, Erasmus, Vives and Ascham, there is scarcely a phrase so evocative as Colet's reference to the 'little white hands' of the boys at his school – however much most schoolmasters might raise their brows and choose to qualify the epithet of colour.

But Erasmus may have set historians on the wrong track about the real significance of Colet's lectures at Oxford. For one thing, though Colet was not a D.D., he may have been *baccalaureus Biblicus* and so competent to lecture on

---

14 Cambridge University Library, MS Gg iv 26, fols 148f.
15 With Professor Trapp, I think it possible that Colet did reach Florence.
16 In the famous pen portrait written for Justus Jonas; cf. P.S. Allen, *Opus Epistolarum Erasmi*, vol. iv, Ep. 1211, pp. 507–27.

Scripture. That his lectures proved a sensation, sending all the dons flocking to hear him, is entirely credible. Yet his innovation was by no means the fact that he lectured on the text of a book of the Bible; that would be to do sad injustice to the persistence of Biblical studies in fifteenth-century Oxford.

Nor is it at all probable that they were a 'landmark' because for the first time here were public lectures on the text of a Biblical book, using the Humanist methods of philological exegesis, set in the historical context, using the latest linguistic tools, and concentrating on the 'literal' sense.[17] Of the sacred languages, Colet knew only a not too elegant Latin. There are very few explanations of words; some of them, like *eulogia* (Greek) and *Maranatha* (Hebrew), were in languages he did not know. Also, 'literal' is itself a complexity. It might involve the distinction between the 'literal historical' and the 'literal prophetic' found when the young Luther objected to Nicholas of Lyra for turning the Old Testament, historically interpreted, into a Jewish book, whereas he preferred the 'literal prophetic' reference to Christ. It could also mean, as was the case with Aquinas, the 'authentic' sense; or for Reuchlin, the divinely intended 'inner' meaning; and it becomes even more complicated with reference to the contemporary revival of Augustine's 'Letter and Spirit' and further hermeneutical references.[18] No more than in the case of Luther, do we know how the Colet manuscripts relate to what he actually said. But they are all the evidence we have, and the attempt of Seebohm to turn Colet into a modern critic, by listing the passages where Colet discusses the historical situation, is not very successful,[19] for they are less factual than those given by Ficino in his *Romans* and mainly arise within the epistle itself. After all, the Oxford theologians did not come running to the schools to know that, in the early Church, there was tension between Jews and Gentiles and between Christians and heathen.

In fact, Colet's exegesis is what might be expected from one with deference for Origen, Dionysius and Ficino; and it is amazing how this has been missed by writers looking for something else. Again and again Colet deserts a historical explanation, as when he applies the Christian *agape* in 1 Corinthians 10–11 to the 'feast' of Holy Scripture, or when he gives a long Dionysian explanation of the universe as a hierarchy of being, which has only the slightest connection with the text of 1 Corinthians 12.[20]

This is surely not Biblical humanism, but the edifying discourse of a Christian

17 Leland Miles, *John Colet and the Platonic Tradition* (London, 1962), pp. 182f.
18 H. De Lubac, *Exégèse Médiévale* (Paris, 1963), cap. 9, sect. 2. Colet himself, in various places, defends the quadriga or four-fold exegesis.
19 The argument to the contrary is feeble indeed. Cf. E. W. Hunt, *Dean Colet and his Theology* (London, 1956), p. 92.
20 It was never apt to contrast Colet's lectures with Longland's sermons (cf. J. H. Lupton, *A Life of John Colet, D. D.* (London 1887), p. 108), or to cite the more arid utterances of theologians rather than the exegetes of the fifteenth century. From the time of Raymond Lull, Raymond of Sabunde and Nicholas of Cusa there had been other kinds of commentaries, not abounding in citations of authorities.

Platonist. What must have made it intriguing and even sensational was the personality of Colet himself, his interpretation of Scripture in terms of *theologia spiritualis*, and an imagery which, as in all Christian Platonism, has an affinity with poetry even more than with the definitions of the schools, and returns again and again to two central stresses, the love of God and the imitation of Christ.

From its union with God by the uniting ray of grace, the soul is born again and has a new existence . . . it trusts and believes in God and in its faith has the clearest vision and in its vision the clearest faith . . . it loves and longs for God and for all divine things for the sake of God.

The imitation of Christ is no outward legalist copy, but an inner conformity of the soul.

It was thus that Christ our brother acted: and his whole life, deeds and words are nothing else than a pattern, modelled and placed before men for their imitation, if they would follow whither he has ascended. For like a good teacher he portrayed in himself the true manner of living: that men, gazing upon his life, might plainly read the way in which those must live in this world, who after this life would live for ever-more.[21]

These surely were the beautiful passages which touched the hearers' hearts and wills as truly as their minds, while his learned audience must have loved his innumerable digressions, for which he had constantly to apologize.

The recent suggestion (which perhaps falls short of demonstration) that Colet spent his undergraduate days, not at Oxford, but in Cambridge, suggests we think of him not as an Oxford Reformer, but as the father of the Cambridge Platonists![22] For two of the most important Colet manuscripts were presented to the University Library at Cambridge and to the library of Emmanuel College in the seventeenth century by the two Masters Tuckney and Holdsworth, who nurtured the Emmanuel Platonists. In fact, the nearest parallel to Colet's lectures, and one which is very suggestive, is to be found in the writings of Ralph Cudworth, John Smith and, above all, Peter Sterry.

Colet, like other wealthy humanists such as Peutinger and Pirckheimer, seems to have preferred to dabble in manuscripts rather than books, in this last interval before to write, or not to write, books became the perennial dilemma of dons.[23] But with the invention of printing, a new dimension was given to the speed and multiplication of ideas. 'Either we must root out printing or printing will root us out' is one of the few wise sayings attributed to the Henrician Vicar of Croydon. Others, like John Foxe, saw it as the instrument of providence:

21 At Romans 14; cf. J. H. Lupton, *Colet Super Opera Dionysii* (1869).
22 W. R. Godfrey, 'John Colet of Cambridge', *AR*, lxv (1974), pp. 6–18. The notion would receive reinforcement in Colet's marginal comment on one of Ficino's *Epistolae* (cf. Sears Jayne, *John Colet and Marsilio Ficino* (London 1836), p. 98) where, against an attack on university professors as *philopompi*, Colet has put in the margin *Cantabrigienses*!
23 J. B. Trapp, 'Notes on MSS written by Peter Meghen', *The Book Collector* (spring 1975).

'God hath willed', he wrote, 'that his cause be advanced, not with sword or target . . . but with printing, reading and writing . . . hereby tongues be known, knowledge groweth, judgment increaseth, books are dispersed, the Scriptures are seen, the doctors be read, stories be opened, times compared, truth discerned, falsehood detected, and with finger pointed, all through the benefit of printing.'[24] This immense acceleration began a battle of books and veritable pamphlet war. Some writings achieved the widest circulation to become bestsellers; others found only a few readers and soon disappeared. The group of tracts which surrounded Henry VIII's *Assertion . . . of the Seven Sacraments against Martin Luther* is typical.

By 1521 Luther had become involved in a polemic which took away an increasing proportion of his time from the writing of edifying commentaries and treatises. Even when he was willing to ignore attacks on himself – which was sometimes the case – his friends demanded he give due attention to the matter, so that he once complained 'I had to read the thing when I'd have been better off playing bowls.' It was in German that Luther wrote best, expressing himself with a fluency and flexibility, an irony and humour and a vast amount of simple invective in three- and four-letter words. The vehemence of the language against him – the traditional abuse of heretics – led the Reformer to adopt his own brand of scurrility. 'I get carried away', he said with masterly understatement. From the outset, it was natural that the Thomists of the Dominican order – Cajetan, Alveldus and Catherinus in particular – should number themselves among his adversaries. And it was no small wonder that Luther carried over into his writing against Henry VIII those notions of 'Thomist asses' and 'Thomist pigs'.

Among these, the writings of Ambrosius Catherinus became entangled in the English Luther debate. Catherinus was an Italian Dominican, a fully-fledged lawyer, and as a theologian sufficiently *autodidactos* to get himself in trouble in after years. But he produced in 1520 an *Apologia pro veritate catholicae et apostolicae fidei ac doctrinae, adversus impia et valde pestifera Martini Lutheri Dogmata.*[25] It was this writing, and not a second tract of 1521, which had interesting repercussions. For it began by enumerating eleven 'Tricks' (*Doli*) of Luther. He accused the Reformer of manifold inconsistencies, of having changed his mind on the question of indulgences, on the nature of papal authority, and on the authority of councils. The other feature of the work was a defence of papal authority to be much quoted in the next years by both Eck and Cochlaeus. Catherinus also charged Luther with denying the visible Church and came near to a view that arguably originated with Thomas Murner, namely that Luther reduced the Church to a Platonic idea. Luther got a copy in March 1521

24 *Acts and Monuments*, ed. G. Townsend and S. R. Cattley (London, 1837–40), vol. iii, pp. 718–22, and vol. iv, pp. 252, 725.
25 F. Lauchert, *Die italienischen literarischen Gegner Luthers* (1912; reprinted 1972), pp. 30ff.

and gave it short shrift in his *Ad librum eximii magistri nostri Ambrosii catherini . . .*
responsio M. Lutheri in April.[26] This is a short work but contains some of
Luther's finest utterances about the nature of the Church. Built on the Word
and *sola fide perceptibilis*, it is known by the outward signs of the sacraments
and the preaching of the Gospel. The tract by no means merits the contempt
it received from Murner, 'Rosseus' and Fisher, but, ending with a curious
exposition of Daniel 8, contains a reminder of an early Luther preoccupied
with apocalyptic.

Catherinus had written before Luther's revolutionary manifestoes appeared
in 1520. But in his *Babylonish Captivity* written in Latin for clergy and scholars,
Luther freely admitted that he had changed his mind about many things and
threatened to develop such revolutionary ways.[27] For example, he launched
into a violent attack on the Roman Church and reduced the seven sacraments
to those three which included the Scriptural promise to make them sacraments
of the Gospel for all Christians. He insisted that all doctrines and usages must
be judged by the Scriptures, though it is part of the liberty of the children of
God to be able to discriminate between what is vital and what is of secondary
importance. It was a writing which infuriated Luther's enemies, badly scared
some of his friends, and drove some of the undecided into orthodoxy. Against
this writing, Henry VIII decided to enter the lists. From the first the English
authorities had shown concern about the new doctrines, for there was enough
dissent about to exercise Wolsey and the bishops. They began to collect copies
of Luther's works, from Rome and from ambassadors like Pace and Tunstall.
At some point, an informal commission of learned and godly men was appointed
to examine Luther's writings (the beginning of a fateful device?)[28] There is no
reason to doubt that the work was, to use Wolsey's ambivalent phrase, of the
King's 'devising'. The evidence suggests that Henry had already begun to
write about Luther in the matter of indulgences; but now at a fair speed he
dealt with the attack on the seven sacraments.[29]

When the work was finished Henry read it to a committee of divines, and
they may well have been consulted at a later stage. There is the possibility (a
dozen names could be mentioned as likely) that individuals were asked about
patristic references, Biblical texts and philological details (which included
Hebrew). But it is moderately learned (making much of such quasi-text-books
as Hugh of St Victor on the Sacraments) and written in a fluent Latin – which
Erasmus claimed to have influenced. It had obvious virtues, chiefly that it was

26 *WA*, vol. vii, pp. 705–78; *WA Br*, vol. ii, p. 295.
27 *WA*, vol. vi, pp. 497–573. *Luther's Works* (American edn), vol. 36, pp. 3ff.
28 *Letters and Papers of Henry VIII*, vol. iii, pt I, p. 1218 (3 April 1521), p. 1297 (21 May
1521).
29 Cf. N. S. Tjernagel, *Henry VIII and the Lutherans* (St Louis, 1965); E. Doernberg, *Henry
VIII and Luther* (London, 1961); G. Krodel, 'Luther, Erasmus and Henry VIII', *AR*, vol. liii,
pts 1/2 (1962), pp. 6off.; J. H. Scarisbrick, *Henry VIII* (London, 1968), pp. 110ff.

short, and moderate compared with what was to come. Those who lacked time to wade through great compilations like those of 'Rosseus' and Fisher must have found it a useful compendium of orthodox ideas. It may not have been the fact of Royal authority alone (backed by papal approval, by the title 'Defender of the Faith' and the offer of an indulgence to all who should read it) which made it something of a best-seller.

Here, from a 'godly Prince', was a work which Luther could not possibly ignore, if only for the fuss with which Duke George of Saxony was promoting the work. Luther wrote his reply in two versions, one German, the other in Latin, the one not simply a translation of the other.[30] Once again the charge of inconsistency had been levelled. But Luther while admitting, even glorying, in the fact that he had learned better ways about the value of indulgences and the basis of papal authority, now made an important distinction, drawing up two lists, one of fundamental doctrines of the Gospel, the other those extra-Scriptural institutions and practices around which practical abuses had come to centre. It was no trivial distinction or debating ploy, for it would underlie the structure of the Augsburg Confession a decade later. About the first, Luther denied that he had ever changed. Thus, in charging him with inconstancy about the Gospel, Henry had lied, just as in defending blasphemous institutions he had soiled the majesty of Christ. Luther, who had employed his considerable invective against doctors of the Church and the Pope himself, was not going to ease off at this point, though perhaps he hardly realized what a handle he was giving to his opponents by the boldness with which he spoke of dignities.

'Rosseus' was to suggest that Henry, when he read Luther's reply, laughed it off. But perhaps he was more than nettled, and since as a mighty prince he was unable 'descendre dans la rue', he sent an envoy to the Princes of Saxony, with the demand that Luther be put down. The herald was coldly treated by the Catholic Duke George, but lavishly welcomed by the canny Frederick the Wise. When the envoy therefore departed, and his head cleared, he took home nothing but evasive words. Henry nevertheless took a personal interest in the business up to the time of his final letter to Luther in 1525.

He must surely have been aware of a series of writings which now appeared, with Royal Privilege, from the press of the King's Printer, the Norman denizen, R. Pinson.[31] The first (in manuscript November 1522, published December 1523) was by Edward Powell, S.T.P., canon of Salisbury; it was vetted, the author claimed, by the theologians of Oxford. It is not a defence of the royal *Assertio*, which is mentioned in the preface and conclusion, but it defends the papal primacy and the seven sacraments in a generally stodgy way, and with many inept proofs from the Old Testament. More interesting, though they seem to have been

---

30 *WA*, 10. 2, pp. 180–222 (Latin), pp. 227–62 (German).
31 S. H. Johnston, 'The career and literary publication of Richard Pynson' (dissertation, University of Western Ontario, 1977).

worse sellers, were two tracts by one of the Queen's Spanish chaplains, Alphonsus de (or a) Villa Sancte (*sic*), a member of the Friars Observant at Greenwich, with whom the Queen, as a Franciscan tertiary, had a close and devout association. It is clear that the Queen's servants were now, at her instigation, involved in the great debate. There are intriguing references in prefaces dedicated to the Queen as Defendress of the Faith to other writings from this same source: 'De quo et si aliis meis scriptis qua sublimitatis tuae etiam jussu in Lutherum composui: nolui disceptare: nunc tamen loqui cogor.' The first tract discusses the problem of indulgences and replies to Luther on the grounds of reason, Scripture and the Fathers.[32] It is lucid, reasonable and remarkably free from overmuch contumely. The second seems to be a first sample of an analysis of the *Loci Communes* of Philip Melanchthon (1521), though it is limited to the article on Free Will.[33] The author displays a sense of humour, and writes wryly of those religious who prefer 'good hours in the garden and kitchen' to writing, and who have left controversy to the King.

At the end of 1523 a work of major size and importance appeared. This was the *Responsio* to Luther's attack on the King, written by 'William Ross'. The first version of the work was attributed to a learned Spanish theologian, Ferdinando Baravellus; and prefatory letters and the introduction – aptly described as 'humanistic whimsey' and affording the kind of imaginary setting such as More had given *Utopia* – tell how the business was conceived in a castle in Spain and how a solitary copy turned up in England, there to be printed and edited by another. Of this Baravellus version only one copy survives, in Durham University Library.

The second version is given an entirely different setting. At some time after February 1523 the original was scrapped and a new set of prefatory material named the author as 'William Rosseus', an Englishman in Italy. At the gathering sig. H there is an interpolation of some thirty leaves. These deal with the nature of the Church and refute in detail Luther's *Reply to Ambrosius Catherinus*.[34]

It is generally accepted that 'Rosseus' must be Thomas More; and the later reference by Fisher to 'More's book against Luther', and the marginal comment 'Moreus' made by John Eck on the title page of his presentation copy, must be set against the silence of Erasmus, More himself and indeed almost everybody else when it first appeared. Here are mysteries indeed, which the editor of the

---

32 Alphonsus de Villa Sancte, *Problema indulgentiarum quo Lutheri errata dissoluuntur* . . . (dated from 'our cell at Greenwich', 14 Kal. Feb. 1523).

33 *De libero arbitrio adversus Melanchtonem, authore fratre Alphonsus a Villa Sancte, minorita regularis observationis* (14 Kal., November 1523). A copy of this extremely rare tract is in the library of Emmanuel College, Cambridge, where it is bound with the other tract and with the King's Book against Luther in a volume from Sion House.

34 The interpolation is primarily concerned with the nature of the visible Church and think it possible that Murner had a hand in it.

Yale text hardly probes, perhaps because they are never likely to be solved. Why the anonymity, which does the author no credit? Why should the first edition have been scrapped and the castle in Spain turned into a villa in Italy? And if More wrote it, did he do so alone, or had he helpers?

That More was capable in learning, style and wit of writing such a treatise by himself, I have no doubt. He was now at the height of his powers and, immersed in affairs as he was, I would put hardly any intellectual achievement beyond him. On the other hand, there is a scurrility which goes beyond anything which Luther ever wrote; and many friends of Sir Thomas More would be profoundly grateful to think he was not responsible for it. Penetrating the 'whimsey', it is possible that the King or Wolsey encouraged the author really to go to town in this respect, with the kind of abuse (*festivus*) which delighted lewd scholars of the baser sort, but affronted Erasmus and deeply shocked many of the Reformers, who were, on the whole, a solemn lot. But if there were others who supplied More with ammunition – and those at home like Margaret Roper and John Clement to do the donkey work of copying out great gobbets from Luther, which there was no need at all for More to do himself – then among the possibilities must surely be Alphonsus de Villa Sancte with his 'other writings about Luther'. It is even more probable, too, that Thomas More had the counsel and assistance – putting it cautiously – of the exiled Observant Franciscan, Thomas Murner.

Murner was in England during the summer of 1523, as we learn from a letter from More to Wolsey:

Hit may further lyke your good grace to be advertised that one Thomas Murner, a Frere of Saynt Francisco which wrote a book against Luther in defence of the Kings book, was owte of Almaigne sent into England by mean of a simple person, namying himself servant unto the kingis grace, and affermyng unto Murner that the King had giveyn him in charge to desire Murner to cum over to hym in England, and by occasion whereof he is commen over and hath bene here a good while . . . Wherefore the king's Grace requireth your Grace that it may like you to cause him to have in reward one hundred pounds . . . and now, since his cumming hither he hath translated into Latin the book that he before made in Almaigne in defence of the King's book. He is a doctor of divinity, and of both laws, and a man for writing and preaching of great estimation in his country.[35]

One hundred pounds – as reward for what? It does not rouse the curiosity of Professor Headley. Yet a hundred pounds was the annual honorarium of the Speaker in the House of Commons, and the headmaster of Colet's new school was to have thirty-five pounds a year. For all his touting, nobody gave Erasmus

---

35 Professor Headley seems to take 'a good while' to mean a few days, when it must surely imply at least several weeks and perhaps months. The last date Murner is known to have been in Strasbourg is 19 January; that Faber wrote to him at Strasbourg in May does not prove Murner was there. Cf. J. M. Headley (ed.), *Complete Works of Thomas More* (New Haven, 1969), vol. v, pts I and II.

a hundred pounds at a blow, and we find Erasmus bitterly complaining to Faber that Murner left England a rich man!

The money seems to have been paid; and when Murner left, it was with a handsome testimonial from the King to the city of Strasbourg, which was not thinking in terms of the fatted calf for its returning prodigal but rather regarding him as an incorrigible troublemaker under censure for violence of the tongue. Murner did not in fact go straight home, but accompanied Henry's envoy to the Imperial Diet to be mentioned by him in a despatch to the king as 'your Friar'.[36]

Although undoubtedly a man of learning, Thomas Murner was too unstable and thin-skinned a character. He got across so many people that he may be thought of as the Karlstadt of the opposition. His verse was better than his prose, and his satire *The Great Lutheran Fool* was popular. But he was incensed by caricatures of himself as a cat in the pamphlet war then centring in Strasbourg, particularly in the opening lines of the famous *Karsthans*:

MURNER: Mrrrrrrr-ow. Murrmaw.
KARSTHANS: Listen!
STUDENT: What's up, father?
KARSTHANS: Is that somebody singing, or somebody crying?
STUDENT: Oh, it's only the cat.
KARSTHANS: But it sounds just like a man crying . . .
STUDENT: It's a Cat!
KARSTHANS: What a queer song . . .[37]

Murner had translated the *Babylonish Captivity* into German – *pour épater les bourgeois* – and promised vast numbers of tracts against Luther, of which the few he wrote became increasingly scurrilous. In 1522 he had sprung to the defence of Henry VIII with a work *Is the King of England a Liar?* The work concluded that it was Luther, and not Henry, who was prone to prevarication. This was the writing More held Murner had translated into Latin during his stay in England; but he took the MS back to Strasbourg where it was seized by Matthew Zell when a mob ransacked Murner's lodgings. From the many pleas which he addressed to the civic authorities, this was a manuscript on which Murner laid great store.

Murner actually printed about a third of the work, a hasty, ill-written fragment (*Mendacia Lutheri*), the sole copy of which is in Munich University Library.[38] In this torso, Murner only deals with ten of Luther's 'lies', though he promised to bring the total to forty or fifty. It is not, in fact, simply a translation of his German tract *Is the King of England a Liar?* for he prints only a paragraph or so of this. In contrast, it is turgid and repetitive, haggling over

36 *Letters and Papers of Henry VIII*, vol. iii, pt II, p. 3390.
37 O. Clemen (ed.), *Flugschriften aus der ersten Jahren der Reformation*, iv (1907; reprinted 1967), p. 76.
38 T. Murner, *Mendacia Lutheri* (University of Munich Library), 946, i.

small points, thus constituting perhaps the weightiest argument against Murner having had a direct hand in 'Rosseus'.[39]

It is possible that the hundred pounds was given to Murner for services not yet rendered, on the promise that he would complete the *Mendacia*. This would certainly account for the agitation he showed when his MS was lost; but he must have had consultations with the King, and with More and Fisher. Between the scrapping of *Baravellus* (which includes a date, February, 1522) and the publication of 'Rosseus' at the end of the year, there is an unaccountable delay of many months. Professor Headley suggests that Henry may have been waiting for results from his mission to the Saxon authorities, but this does not seem likely, for there is another possibility.

The increasing number of Luther's writings, and their serious reception by learned men, was beginning to embarrass Catholic polemists who had dismissed the Reformer as an egocentric half-wit. Faced with passages of learning, subtlety, wit and humour, they could only reply 'Of course, he had help!' There are references in 'Rosseus' to a 'Theseus' who might plausibly be supposed to be Philip Melanchthon.[40] But it seems that in the middle of 1523 somebody planted a thought in the mind of Henry VIII that this assistant might have been Erasmus.

Erasmus did not have a good summer at all in 1523. From the start he was still under suspicion of having written Henry's books against Luther; he told his friends that he might have helped to train Henry in writing decent Latin, but that was all. He was then violently attacked by Ulrich von Hutten for not going over whole-heartedly to Luther's side; and now came Henry's suspicion that he was the unknown collaborator who wrote the funny bits for Luther. It was no joke! In June Tunstall wrote to Erasmus congratulating him on having cleared himself, and in August Erasmus told the story to Pirckheimer: 'I don't know if I told you about the tragedy which took place in England . . . somebody put it into the King's head that I assisted Luther in his last ridiculous book.' It was all serious enough for Erasmus to have to send his *famulus* post-haste to London to sort things out, and to bring back the apology of King and cardinal and the gift of not one hundred pounds but a mere thirty florins.

For 'Rosseus' this was surely a most disconcerting happening, especially if the King and Wolsey had instigated his work behind the scenes. For More to have written such a scurrilous diatribe against a work partly written by Erasmus, is what, as the song nearly says, no humanist could face with equanimity. There was every reason to postpone publication.

If there must be speculation whether Murner consulted More, there is

39 Professor Headley has listed the many similarities of style and learning between More and Murner in 'Thomas Murner, Thomas More and the first expression of More's ecclesiology', *Studies in the Renaissance*, xiv (1967), pp. 73–92. He regards these as coincidence.
40 Cf. Headley, *Responsio*, pp. 121, 138.

little doubt that he exchanged ideas with Fisher. Edward Powell might be a rather poor sample of Oxford divinity, but in John Fisher Cambridge had a theologian of whom to be justly proud.[41] He was a humanist who used the latest Biblical tools, whether in controversy with Lefèvre about the number of disciples named Mary in the gospels, or in an able reply to Velenus who asserted that Peter never went to Rome. In his controversial writings – though he defends the schoolmen and shows considerable knowledge of them – it is to the Bible and the Fathers that he mostly turns.[42] Above all, he was a devoted admirer of Reuchlin – to whom he suggested that he might like to send to England his bright young nephew, Philip Melanchthon. And Melanchthon in Cambridge is surely an intriguing 'if' of English Reformation history.

His *Confutation* of 1523, in which he dealt with Luther's defence of the articles condemning him, is a learned, sustained and largely calm piece of controversy. He does not, like More and Murner, reproduce great gobbets of Luther but short extracts, each with one idea, which he then analyzes and refutes. There is a solid section dealing with the papal power, to which many Catholics, including More, Eck and Cochlaeus, appealed again and again.

It was not until 1525 (though he had begun it in 1523) that he published his own *Defence* of Henry VIII against Luther.[43] One may suspect that he saw some weaknesses in the initial argument, and that there were passages which needed further buttressing (especially in relation to Communion in one kind, and the doctrine of the Mass). But what is striking is that Murner's theme of 'the lies of Martin Luther' has become a ground bass, the explicit theme of the opening chapters and one to which he again and again returns. For Fisher, the voice of authority was final and paramount. What the Church taught is to be received without question, especially by laymen.[44] There is a long section on the judgment of the people, beginning with classical authorities, which, if it comes nearer than he knew to Luther's repudiation of *Herr Omnes*, displays the élitism and clericalism of the age of Gerson, and may have some root in the Dionysian hierarchical view. At any rate he did not think that serious doctrinal questions should be discussed, as he witheringly told the young Cambridge Reformers, 'before the Butchers of Cambridge':

Fisher wrote much polemic: in particular, a defence of the priesthood against Luther, and two immense volumes, learned and meticulous, in reply to the eucharistic treatises of Oecolampadius. One sighs for a modern critical analysis of these volumes. It is said that, at the end, Fisher regretted spending so much energy in polemic when he would have been better occupied saying his prayers.

41 E. L. Surtz, *The Works and Days of J. Fisher* (Cambridge, Mass., 1967); cf. J. Rouschausse, *La vie et l'oeuvre de J. Fisher* (Nieuwkoop, 1972).
42 J. Fisher, *Opera Omnia* (reprinted 1967); cf. *Assertionis Lutheranae confutatio*, cols 272–745.
43 *Assertionum Regis Angliae de fide Catholica adv. Lutheri Babylonicam Captivitatem Defensio* (1525).
44 Cf. *De judicio plebis*, pp. 232ff.

Luther could have agreed with this, for the two men, in their devotional writings, come closer than they could have known.

For Fisher, the authority of the Church is above question. There is an unwritten tradition, handed down from the apostles, out of which the Church interprets the meaning of Scripture; and though the Fathers might err, they could not have been seriously mistaken. There is, moreover, always at hand the Holy Spirit, to become what scientists complain of as 'the God of the gaps' which plugs the holes in demonstration. He cannot make admissions and admit criticisms of the Church. Such were made, not by Wycliffe and Luther, but by Colet and Erasmus, not to mention John Henry Newman and the Second Vatican Council's exposition of the apostolate of the laity. Perhaps John Fisher, Chancellor of the University of Cambridge, choking with tears outside Great St Mary's as he excommunicated those who had torn down a papal bull and refused to own up, may have begun to realize the tide was turning against him. There was certainly a discernible difference between his two sermons at St Paul's – the last preached before young Cambridge divines who would not accept his contemptuous dismissal of Luther.

He who has threaded his way through the labyrinthine argument of this theological controversy, the repetition and hackneyed quotations from Luther, Catherinus, Henry VIII, 'Rosseus' and Fisher, is unlikely to say with Mr Valiant-for-Truth, '. . . though with great difficulty I have got hither, yet I do not repent me of all the trouble I have been at to arrive where I am'. The absence of Christian manners is wearisome, like the constant attribution of the basest motives and the refusal to admit any single truth on the other side – both of them in the hallowed and ancient tradition of polemical writing. There is also the incessant scolding ('Liar', 'Fox', 'Wolf', 'Mad Dog' or 'insane fool') appearing every few lines to make Fisher little better than Murner. In marked contrast, too, there is the curious deference shown to the 'Christian King' (who, if he were not himself a liar, was certainly a lecher and probably an adulterer!) – a kind of metaphorical doffing of the square at every mention of Henry and his virtues, so that the royal script is treated as if it had descended from heaven. The result is certainly an unintended aura of sanctimonious humbug on all sides, with upturned faces and rolling eyes at every mention of the 'godly Prince', all of it in marked contrast to those curling lips and contemptuous sneers for Martin Luther.

Now what, by 1525, did all this comprise? A glance at the list of books proscribed in England in the next years shows that, while the Wittenberg theologians are still well represented, their writings are now outnumbered by those of others (Zwingli, Pellicanus, Bibliander, Vadianus, Lambert of Avignon, Capito, Bucer); and from a hundred presses in scores of cities, an immense flood of quite unstoppable ideas was on the move. In 1525 it did not really matter any more whether in fact Luther was inconsistent, whether he contradicted himself, whether indeed he were an unconscionable liar, whether an argument was fallacious or a citation inaccurate. Intricate polemic of this kind, notably by Eck and Cochlaeus, was to follow Luther all his days. But such writings could do nothing to halt the Reformation. In five years, where would be the Queen, 'Defendress of the Faith'? Five years after that, on Tower Hill, the question would be existentially and poignantly raised by John Fisher and Thomas More: and who shall defend the defenders of the 'Defender of the Faith'?

II

The Real Thomas More?

❧

G. R. ELTON

How well do we really know Thomas More? Directed to one of the most familiar figures of the sixteenth century, the question must appear absurd. Even without the aid of stage and screen, surely everyone has a clear idea of England's leading humanist, great wit, friend of Erasmus and other Continental humanists, author of *Utopia*, family man, man of convictions, ultimately martyr. The familiar Holbein portrait seems to sum it all up, as does at greater length the much admired biography of R. W. Chambers. Chambers, in fact, completed the picture when, to his own satisfaction and that of others, he disposed of 'inconsistencies' discerned by earlier observers between the cheerful reformer and 'liberal' of 1516 on the one hand, and the fierce opponent of Lutheran reform and savage polemicist of 1528–33 on the other. No man's personality in that age, not even King Henry's, seems more fully explored and more generally agreed than More's.

If nevertheless I cannot accept that we yet can be sure of knowing Thomas More it is in part because of the way in which his portrait has been created. All modern assessments start axiomatically from an image constructed out of two sorts of evidence and brought to perfection in those famous last scenes – imprisonment, trial and death. More's life has in effect become a preliminary to his end and is written with that end in view. The evidence mentioned consist of Roper's *Life* and the descriptions left by More's friends, good sources indeed but like even the best sources in need of critical inspection. Roper's book – which permeates all the early lives and indeed still dominates in tone and structure even Chambers's book – was written with two motives in mind: filial affection, and a desire to prove his great father-in-law worthy of canonization. The words of Erasmus or Vives, all of them incidentally about the early More, the More of the Erasmian heyday, tell us why they were More's good friends and assuredly present a truth about the man, but again they do not form dispassionate or rounded appraisals. And even when the other massive evidence is employed – the evidence especially of More's own writings and deeds – it is always, no doubt unconsciously, adjusted to the figure first created out of Roper and those letters. Chambers in particular, while seeming to weigh judiciously the difficulties posed by some of More's books, really works hard at bringing them within the limits defined by the stereotype of the great and good Sir Thomas. Of course, I acknowledge that More so appeared to many who knew him, though even among his acquaintance other opinions could at times be found, and I know that the traditional More existed; but is he the whole, the real, More?

My difficulty in accepting that he might be can be stated simply. I do not find More inconsistent, or hard to understand on given occasions, or improbably described by those who knew him. I find him consistently ambiguous: at all sorts of points, his mind, his views, his actions, his person seem to me to tend in more than one direction, withdrawing from observation into consecutive layers of indeterminacy. Like any adept user of the ironical front, he hides his self behind vaguely transparent curtains; as the light flickers over him, so his face changes, subtly and strangely. His wit, which so enchanted his friends, nearly always had a sharp edge to it: he often, and knowingly, wounded his targets. We are told that his temper was exceptionally equable and his manner ever courteous; yet through nearly all his life he displayed restlessly combative moods and in his controversies lost his temper, dealing ruthless and often unfair blows. His famous merry tales pose some manifest psychological problems. Is it not strange that when this man, who created such a happy family life, wished to amuse he constantly resorted to strikingly antifeminist tales? I can recall no single story that shows a woman in a favourable light; that world of parables is peopled by shrews and much-oppressed males – almost the world of James Thurber's cartoons, and certainly the world of one well-established medieval tradition, but also a world presented by More with manifest enjoyment. His attitude to his second wife, Dame Alice, leaves me bewildered. He is supposed to have treated her with affection; yet the conviction that she was foolish and tiresome rests in great part on the sly allusions to female deficiencies scattered through his works which, as family tradition knew, were directed at her. More in office – flexible, diplomatic, at times accommodating – differs visibly from More the scholar and More at home. Some of his public attitudes can be called lawyer-like, in the pejorative sense of that term. The persecutor of heretics cannot really be buried in the sophistical arguments deployed by Chambers: he did in practice deny those forms of toleration which he had incorporated in *Utopia*. His part in the parliamentary opposition to Henry VIII's proceedings and his contacts with the Imperial ambassador's intrigues were not straightforward; his refusal to accept a friendly letter from Charles V, on the grounds that without it he could be of better use to their common cause, must be called ambiguous. And what did he really think of the papacy? He never properly explained his position, and the hints tend more than one way; I can well understand why Rome hesitated for four hundred years before bestowing the saint's halo.

I once spent half an hour before that splendid fireplace in the Frick Museum in New York above which Thomas Cromwell and Thomas More for ever stare past one another, with St Jerome in the middle keeping the peace. In the end I thought that I understood the plain, solid, straightforward man on the right, but the other man, with that subtle Machiavellian smile, whose looks and look kept altering before one's eyes, left a sense of unplumbable ambiguity. And I then did not even know what an X-ray investigation has since discovered: that the famous portrait is painted over an earlier attempt which reveals a much less refined, less humanist, Thomas More. Why, even the man's year of birth is uncertain because his father in recording it contrived to puzzle posterity: the year date first put down was rendered dubious by the addition of a weekday which does not fit the year. Ambiguity, wherever one touches him, in matters weighty and indifferent.

In one sense, of course, the ambiguity of Thomas More does not matter; his ability to present a kaleidoscope of aspects even helps to make him more interesting and attractive, especially as those variations quite clearly inhere in the man and are not merely reflections of the observer. They are of his essence and of his choosing. Yet anyone concerned to understand the early sixteenth century, the age of the Reformation, and the character of a powerful intellectual movement with far-reaching influences upon later generations, needs to come to terms with Thomas More. Once one ceases to be satisfied with the plaster saint created by the worshippers, one is cast loose upon an uncharted ocean where there lurk too many rocks and whirlpools to permit complacency. If More was not simply the finest, kindest, wisest of men foully done to death by wicked enemies who could not bear his saintliness, many things about that age need reconsidering. If he was not really that steadfast figure of tradition, we would want to know what exactly he died for – though that is a question I shall not pursue here. His ambiguity, if he was ambiguous, also makes his own actions harder to understand: why, for instance, did this man, who all his life had avoided the simplicities of a total and unmistakable public commitment, suddenly harden his conscience on an issue which on the face of it was itself ambiguous enough? I feel convinced that we need to understand Thomas More, or at least to make every effort to do so, even though in the end he may well escape us. Especially for someone who sees him so characterized by ambiguity as I do, the ambition to penetrate to his inner core may well be foolish, but it is worth the attempt. Where is the real Thomas More?

The best way to go about this search would seem to lie in ignoring what others said about him and in trying to grasp More's relation to mankind from what he himself said to those among whom he lived, from his books. I propose to look at three of his works which at first sight seem to have little enough in common, in order to see whether they can nonetheless reveal that common element which must be there if there is a real Thomas More to be fetched forth from the veils in which he hid himself. *Utopia*, not without reason always his most famous work, appears as an exciting intellectual exercise, a critique of the world of his day, a dream of better things, lively and sunny in manner, the product of true wit. *The Confutation of Tyndale's Answer*, endless, nearly always tedious, passionate, devoid of humour and markedly obsessive, was, of course, written in very different circumstances and for a very different purpose, but it was still written by the same man. *The Dialogue of Comfort*, too, in which passion is left behind and serenity deals sovereignly with some of the most frightful of human problems, breathes an air which is quite different again – but air from the same pair of lungs. Who is this Thomas More who held three such diverse manifestoes together in one single mind, however capacious?

The essence of *Utopia* is nowadays usually sought in More's condemnatory analysis of the political and social structure which he wished to reform, but that seems to me the wrong approach. Surely the ideal commonwealth of his devising can tell us more about him. His description is detailed enough to give us a very vivid sense of life in the island of Nowhere – ordered and orderly, hierarchically structured through a system of interlocked authorities, permanent and apparently not only incapable of change but not interested in any. Life in *Utopia* was comfortable and worthy enough, so long as no one resented its lack of diversity, lack of colour, indeed lack of anything dynamic. This is, as no one has ever doubted, a very restrictive commonwealth, subduing the individual to the common purpose and setting each man's life in predetermined, unalterable grooves. Whether More really thought such a commonwealth to be feasible, or whether he was perhaps hinting that the only good polity was also one unattainable on earth, is not the issue here, though the likelihood that the second alternative more correctly defines his intent bears on the object of our search. The fundamental question is this: why did More think it necessary to erect so rigid and oppressive a system for the sake of preserving his supreme good – peace and justice? And the answer lies in his identification of the wrong at the heart of all existing human communities. This wrong is the nature of man, fallen man, whom he regarded as incurably tainted with the sin of covetousness. Greed, he argued, underlay everything that troubled mankind. Wealth, and the search for it, ruined the human existence and all possibility of human contentment; the only cure that could work must remove all opportunity of acquiring wealth by prohibiting all private property and allowing to each man his sufficient subsistence at the hands of an all-wise, and despotic, ruling order. To judge from *Utopia*, that 'sunny' book written by a man in the fullness of his powers and before his world collapsed in a welter of contending ideologies, More from the first held a deeply pessimistic view of mankind whose natural instincts were, he maintained, totally selfish, anarchic and sinful.

By the time he came to do battle with Tyndale he had, of course, reason to think that the sinfulness of man had found a new and vastly more dangerous area of operations. The *Confutation* is really a distressing book to read – an interminable, high-pitched scream of rage and disgust which at times borders on hysteria. Even allowing for the conventions of sixteenth-century polemics, it is hard to feel that More had retained any sort of balance when confronted with the consequences of Luther's rebellion. Even among the opponents of Lutheran heresy More stands out for the violence of his explosion, as Erasmus was to note in his last remarks on his old friend, by then dead. The helpless fury of the *Confutation* is not convention; it is the very personal reaction of a very specific man. Yet this is the man who had always impressed his circle by the evenness of his temper, the man of whom William Roper alleged that in fourteen years of close acquaintance he had never known him to be in a fume.

Why did More lose all sense of proportion when faced with the new heresies, to the point of making his book vastly less effective than it might have been? The very passion of his involvement diminished the success of his assault. Surely we are once again in the presence of More's fundamental conviction about human nature. If man was by his nature so incapable of living the good life, it followed that only the outward restraints imposed by organized and institutional structures saved his world from falling into chaos; only obedience to the order decreed by God preserved the chance of salvation. If the Utopians, with all their advantages, could maintain their orderly commonwealth only by submitting to exceptional restraints, how much more necessary was it for real people, ever driven on by the pressures of sinful desires, to adhere to the established order? Because he thought that he understood the dark heart of man, More, it would seem, was exceptionally conscious of the thinness of the crust upon which civilization rests, a conclusion which our age has no cause to doubt. In consequence he held that in attacking the Church the Lutheran heretics had pierced that crust. There is no need to suppose that he wished to withdraw any of the criticisms of the Church that he had so freely uttered in earlier days; even when, in the *Dialogue of Comfort*, he regretted that he and Erasmus had in their time published critical views of what now stood in mortal danger, he wished only that they had not made those views public, not that they had never held them. More's defence of the Church arose not from a change of mind but from the same ultimate convictions which had earlier led him to attack it. It, too, was a human institution and therefore inexorably tainted with original sin, but it was also the instrument chosen by God to restrain and guide men towards their only hope, salvation through faith in Christ. Just because the Protestants made that hope the centre of their message, while destroying and denouncing the chosen instrument, More had to defend the Church with such immoderate commitment, such furious rage.

Thus whether he was planning the good commonwealth of humanist devising, or fighting off the threat to the divine order on earth in his war with the Lutherans, More rested all his argument on an inexorably pessimistic view of fallen man. In the extent of his Augustinianism he seems to me to have had only one equal among the major figures of the day – Martin Luther himself – however different the conclusions were that these two prophets drew from their identical premiss. More (unlike Luther) was evidently of an essentially conservative temperament, concerned to preserve existing institutions because – man being what he is – all change is at the very least risky, while such revolutionary change as he discerned in the heretics' demands must certainly lead to the dissolution of all good order. Man simply could not be trusted to command his own fate, and a beneficent deity had recognized this fact when he provided institutional means for channelling the anarchic instinct into the restraints of enforced obedience. And those institutional instruments must therefore be allowed to preserve themselves at all costs, which meant enforcing the law with prison and the stake. The alternative was certain chaos here and now, and all hope gone for salvation in the hereafter. Sitting as he was on an eggshell beneath which raged the fires of hell, man could be permitted to dream and talk about how nice it would be to paint that shell in splendid colours, so long as he kept his feet still. But when he started dancing upon his fragile earthly habitation he must at once be stopped by the most drastic means available. The danger was simply too overwhelming to be tolerated.

If it is objected that the More I am describing – the deep pessimist about man and his nature – cannot be reconciled with the More we have heard so much about (a man full of human kindness and friendship), I reply that on the contrary this supposed contradiction supports my interpretation. Anyone so deeply conscious of the unhappy state of mankind in the mass is always likely to do what he can for particular specimens of it. Believing that man has cast away grace does not necessarily make the believer into a misanthrope; and in his courteous and considerate behaviour towards all and sundry More was only testifying to the compassion of his conservative instincts. Genuine conservatives despair of humanity but cherish individuals, even as true radicals, believing in man's capacity to better himself unaided, love mankind and express that love in hatred of particular individuals. To avoid any rash inferences touching the author of these remarks, I had better add that most of us oscillate between those extremes most of the time. More was more consistent.

The *Dialogue of Comfort* does not breathe quite so pervasive an air of despair about the human condition, for the interesting reason (in part at least) that it confronted genuine and real tribulations instead of the intellectual challenge of *Utopia* or the wild apprehensions of the *Confutation*. This is not the place to discuss it at length, though it matters that its chief purpose was not, I should assert, to discover a way in which man can overcome the miseries of his life, but rather to offer instructed guidance to this end. More was not seeking comfort but giving it, having himself long since found it in his meditations on the Passion. In consequence, the keynote of the work is a kind of hortatory and pedagogic serenity – that address to the individual human being who must be cherished, rather than to the whole of fallen mankind who must be despaired of, which was so noticeably absent from the other two works considered. However, the *Dialogue* also provides one specific clue helpful in the present search. Concerned with imminent death, More needs to attend to the problem of hell and does so several times, in the process making his views very plain. Hell to him was a physical place – 'the very pit and dungeon of the devil of hell' sited at 'the centre of the earth' – where the souls of sinners suffered 'torment world without end'. Not for More those modern evasions. Hell was to him not other people, or eternal ice, or eternal loneliness, or a state of mind, or any of the devices for expressing merely human despair. It was yet another of the creator's chosen instruments for the control of his creation, with a real location, where real devils inflicted real pain on real souls. Hell was there to take care of the consequences of the Fall for those who refused to admit those consequences and thus despised the means of redemption. Even more, perhaps, than his vision of the blessed in heaven, More's matter-of-fact description of hell defines him as a man of his day: the world he saw here and beyond was the medieval world in every physical detail, ascribed to the purposeful creation of God.

Of course, there was nothing original in More's 'medieval' world-view, in his pessimism about mankind. Conventional Christianity in his day (and after) entirely agreed with it, indeed demanded it. The last thing More would wish to display was originality in religion. Only those who have tried to make him an improbable saint all his life, or (perhaps worse) some sort of a star in the liberal firmament (between, as it were, Socrates and John Stuart Mill), can be put out by discovering that More believed in hell and damnation. Nevertheless, a question arises. More's faith in the conventional doctrine of his day does seem to have been particularly complete and passionate, much more so than was found in the men with whom he shared his life, his thought and his death. I do not know that Erasmus spoke of hell in More's terms, any more than that he opposed the manifestations of covetous sin with More's horrified intensity. There is here a strong hint that More's acceptance of conventional teaching on the Fall was exceptionally personal. He does seem to have been exceptionally conscious of sin, with the result that not humanism but antihumanism – the relentlessly unoptimistic conception of human nature – stood at the heart of all his serious writing. Such a powerful consciousness of sin argues a personal experience of it: envisaging sin in a very special, very personal way, More talks like a man who has found and fought sin in himself.

At this point we begin to tread on dangerous ground. Entering into a dead man's mind and private experiences (especially one so concerned to hide himself) is at best a speculative enterprise, and the line I shall take will in addition cause displeasure. However, I mean to do no more than follow the signposts which More himself has left behind. Let me list some of them. For four years in his youth More tried to find out whether he had a vocation for the monastic life, and he did so in the strictest order of the day, the Charterhouse. Even after he decided that he could not abandon the world, he wore a hairshirt. There are strong echoes of the monastic principle in the organization of Utopia, though the Utopians knew nothing of that heart of the monastic existence, the vow of chastity. In fact, they are unmistakably concerned with sex and pro-creation, their attitudes including both the rule that engaged couples shall see each other naked before they have taken the irrevocable decision to marry, and

an off-hand likening of the carnal act to an easing of an itch, or of the bowels –
both common sense and a mild distaste. In his private existence, too, More
notoriously worked hard at combining some of the monastic practices with a
transformation of the sexual instinct into a family life pleasing to God. At the
same time his merry tales evince a notable strain of distrust of women, at times
rising to positive dislike. One main thread in the *Confutation* is provided by
Luther's special vileness in breaking his vow of chastity, a theme that is treated
with obsessional frequency, nor is Luther the only heretic whose special heinous-
ness lies in this particular sin. In the *Dialogue of Comfort*, so generally compas-
sionate, the kindness of God is illustrated with a very odd parable about a
beautiful young woman who is saved from adultery by a heaven-sent fever which
destroys her beauty – 'beautifieth her fair fell with the colour of the kite's claw' –
and so entirely destroys her lust that the close presence of her lover would make
her vomit at the very thought of desire. It is a strangely disgusted, and rather
disgusting, passage; and it is really not possible to deny that More, attentive to
humanity, was more frequently than most preoccupied with the problems of
sexuality, with what he would have called 'the flesh'.

Such a preoccupation was bound to come to one so deeply concerned about
the human condition, about the future of mankind, the injunctions of religion
and the life eternal, but once again one feels that in More the preoccupation was
sharpened by personal experience. His youthful attraction to the life religious,
and the manner in which echoes of that life resound throughout his later years,
argue powerfully that here lay his true ambition. In that case he was bound to
regard celibacy as the only condition really acceptable to God, and of celibacy
he had proved incapable. More, after all, throughout his life proved himself to
be a passionate man – passionate in his beliefs, passionate in his friendships,
passionate in his reactions to insults and contumely, passionate in his attacks
upon heresy. It would have been strange if he had not also known the passions
of the flesh: and what were hairshirts for except for the mortifying of it? But
his inmost convictions about the true claims of God and religion made his
inability to renounce the world and live celibate into a sin, into his personal
experience of the Fall of man. Being a man of sense and wisdom, he had for all
practical purposes come to terms with his failure in the face of the monastic
challenge: the least he could do, and the most, if he could not live in a cloistered
chastity, was to beautify the consequences of his carnal nature by building a
family life which transcended the original impulse of mere desire, and for the
rest to come as close as possible in life and in thought to his monastic ideal.
But none of these compensations can have altered a conviction that he had failed
to live up to what he (that very medieval man) regarded as God's ultimate
demand on man, and had thus found in himself a plain case of original sin.
What indeed was the Fall all about, and what had been the fruit of the tree of
knowledge? He knew about the Fall with that special intensity that came from

30

experience and self-knowledge. He must have held that he had seen the right way and had proved incapable of it: for a man of his integrity and conscience, that knowledge could never cease to torment. If this passionate man was really never seen 'in a fume', his powers of self-control were indeed formidable: and all his life, especially his last three years, show how formidable they were. But it is to do him almost an injustice to suppose him always serene and equable, effortlessly kind and considerate, a man of ever-undisturbed balance. Such qualities had to be worked for, and outbursts had to be guarded against. The guard did slip at times – in the argument with Germain de Brie, in his often cutting remarks at the expense of inferior beings, most of all in the reckless and often untruthful vituperation of his polemics. More, I suggest, knew demons – demons whom he could subdue and tame but never exorcise. Grounds enough for withdrawing into privacy and ambiguity.

More, then, understood the problems of man's unregenerate nature because he shared them, and his deep consciousness of the implications at times overrode his sympathy. So long as he lived an active and public life he remained determined to apply coercion and judgement to dangerous sinners rather than compassion and comprehension. But we can now understand why he appeared to change so notably after he resigned the chancellorship, and especially after he began his imprisonment. The Thomas More of the 'Tower works', and of those last letters to Margaret Roper is, on the face of it, a very different person from the persecutor of Protestants, and the hammer of poor Christopher St German – even from the More who translated Lucian with Erasmus and dreamed up the island of Nowhere. No more aggression or combativeness; no more sarcasm, no more savagery; even the censoriousness of the loving father, who was also a judge, had gone. But he was, of course, not really a different man. He had displayed those qualities of calm good sense and gentle kindness often enough throughout his life, as he was to display them so remarkably at the end. Before this, however, they had cost him self-control and discipline; now, they came easily. He had found peace; the demons were gone at last. In the most splendid passage of the *Dialogue of Comfort*, perhaps the most splendid passage he ever wrote, More asked why men should so much dread imprisonment and the prospect of death. The life to which man's disobedience to God had condemned him was itself a prison, with death at the end its only certainty. What could others do to a man to aggravate that inescapable fate? 'There is no more difference between your grace and me but that I shall die today and you to-morrow.' He spoke these words to Norfolk on the eve of his imprisonment, and before the end of 1534 he knew that he meant them exactly. The Tower liberated him, because here, at last, he had reached his only possible cloister, out of the world. What others thought of as a good man's prison was to him his monk's cell. He had found the tonsure in the Tower.[1]

[1] I have not burdened this essay with footnotes; the evidence used is all familiar enough.

III

Lay Response to the Protestant Reformation in Germany, 1520 – 1528

❧

MIRIAM USHER CHRISMAN

The Protestant Reformation was the creation of the clergy. It endured because it aroused the support of ordinary laymen. They listened to the sermons, were opened to the message of the gospels, changed their beliefs and their modes of worship. Much attention has been paid to the writings of the reformers, yet there has been little attempt to make a systematic examination of the lay treatises which proliferated in the first, excited years of the Reform.[1] This essay is an attempt to introduce a subject which deserves broader study.

Lay writing on theological issues was a new phenomenon. There had been popular songs on religious themes, poetry and stories which dealt with clerical abuses,[2] but the Roman Church provided little opportunity for laymen to bring together prayers and hymns to make a prayer book or a hymnal,[3] nor did the Roman clergy permit the laity to write on doctrine. The latter was the exclusive prerogative of the Church, written and published only in Latin.[4] The Reformation brought an immediate change. By 1522 numerous laymen had addressed the issues of the new doctrine in treatises characterized by careful reference to

1 For the purposes of this essay I have defined a lay man or woman as a person without any clerical appointment or experience. With the exception of one student, I have selected persons without university education. The pamphlets are drawn from those found in my study of all books published in Strasbourg between 1480 and 1599, and from the collection of the Simmler Sammlung in Zurich. The major printed collections of *Flugschriften* must be used very selectively. Most of the pamphlets in Otto Clemen's four-volume *Flugschriften aus den ersten Jahren der Reformation* (Halle, 1906–10) are by clergy or by anonymous authors. The latter cannot always be clearly identified as the work of laymen. In the Clemen collection, in addition to those I have cited below, there is a pamphlet by one Hans Schwalb (1521), who states that he is a layman (vol. i, pp. 339–61); and another by Nikolaus Hermann. Hermann was a church singer and thus close to the clergy (vol. ii, pp. 245–76). The collection also includes a pamphlet by the printer Pamphilius Gegenbach (vol. iii, pp. 185–219). Arnold E. Berger's *Die Sturmtruppen der Reformation* (Leipzig, 1931) includes the same treatises by Stanberger and Hermann, another by Hans Sachs. Currently lay pamphlets are being collected and collated by a research team of the *Historische Seminar* at Tübingen. Their work will make a substantial number of pamphlets available for further study.

2 Lay devotional songs in the vernacular went back to the Middle Ages. See Karl Goedeke, *Grundriss zur Geschichte der Deutschen Dichtung* (Dresden, 1884), vol. i, pp. 254–9. In the century before the Reformation there were hymns to Mary in German, but many of these were composed by clergy. A favourite subject of the period were songs on the Passion. See Goedeke, vol. i, pp. 228–38. Boccacio's *Decameron*, a major source of anticlerical stories, was translated into German and republished every decade. The British Library Catalogue lists four German editions between 1473 and 1519 (vol. xxii, col. 232).

3 In my forthcoming book, *Lay Culture and the Culture of the Learned: Books, Men and Ideas in Strasbourg, 1480–1599* (London, 1980) there are no German hymnals published in the Catholic period. There was a popular prayer book, *Hortulus Animae*, published sometimes in Latin, sometimes in German, which contained prayers and meditations used by clergy and laymen alike. Johann Geiler von Kayserberg published a *Beichtspiegel* for the laity, and a manual to be used in preparation for death. Both of these were published in German.

4 Seventy-four Catholic doctrinal works were published in Strasbourg from 1480 to 1523. All were in Latin.

Scripture. Although their scriptural knowledge may have been acquired after 1519, it probably had deeper roots in the past. As early as 1506, for example, Johann Knobloch, a Strasbourg printer, published a folio edition of the Passion of Christ in German, using the texts from all four gospels. He commissioned the Swiss artist, Urs Graf, to do the handsome illustrations.[5] It was assumed that readers would be interested in differences in the accounts of the four apostles. The popularity of the book was reflected in four re-editions.[6] Translations of the Bible had been undertaken in the 1480s; indeed the German Bible was relatively easily available in the Vulgate version before Luther's translation.[7] When Luther wrote of the priesthood of all believers, the right of the laity to interpret Biblical texts, he touched a note which led to an immediate response. Laymen were by no means as ignorant and coarse as the clergy and humanists had tended to assume.[8] Many of them were already well acquainted with the Bible. They had been aroused by the preaching of the evangelical ministers and they were anxious to share their views with other laymen.

In the earliest years of the Reformation lay writers rose to the defence of Luther and other reformers, usually against the actions taken by the pope or the Roman curia. The pamphlets were, in essence, anticlerical, but it was a new kind of anticlericalism. The laity were no longer concerned about the immorality of the clergy, the sexual mores of the monks, the wealth and luxury of the monastic or chapter clergy. Rather, the lay writers felt that the clergy had cheated, deceived and misled the people. In short, they had been gulled. It was

5 *Der text des passion oder lidens christi usz der vier evangelisten zusammen ... bracht* (Strasbourg, J. Knobloch, 1506). Texts of the Harmonic Gospels were printed in Germany in the vernacular as early as 1482 (Augsburg). See British Library Catalogue, vol. xviii, col. 1558 Knobloch asked Geiler von Kaysberg to provide the Latin text for his 1506 edition, then had it translated into German by Matthias Ringman. (Léon Dacheux, *Un Réformateur catholique, Jean de Kayserberg* (Paris, 1876), p. 564.) Initiative for the editions came from Knobloch.
6 Knobloch published new editions in 1507 and 1509. Johann Grüninger published an edition in 1509, Matthias Hupfuff another in 1513.
7 *The Short Title Catalogue of Books Printed in the German Speaking Countries now in the British Museum* (London, 1962) lists 14 German Bibles between 1466 and 1518. Geoffrey Dickens has pointed to the continuing availability of the Wycliffite Bible in English.
8 The attitude of the humanists toward the laity is reflected rather unconsciously in the letters of Erasmus. In 1501, for example, he wrote that the people of Holland 'are mean and uncultivated. Humane studies are most actively despised. There is no money to be made in scholarship'. (*The Correspondence of Erasmus*, Collected Works of Erasmus (Toronto, 1974–), vol. ii, p. 45.) He refused the magistrates of Louvain when they offered him a lectureship because 'I am so close to these Dutch tongues ... [which] have never learnt to be helpful to anyone.' (*Correspondence*, vol. ii, p. 59.) Girolamo Aleandro wrote to Erasmus from Paris: 'The vast majority of the uneducated, whose name is legion, understand the [ignorant lecturers] and esteem them more highly than the scholars ... mule scratches mule.' (*Correspondence*, vol. ii, p. 222.) The examples are recurrent. The humanists were not interested in disseminating knowledge beyond their own circle. The learned also believed that the common people were incapable of understanding the deeper truths of religion. Thus Johann Ulrich Surgant, a priest and canon of Basel, told the readers of his curate's manual that most of their audience would be rude and uneducated and they should preach accordingly (Ulrich Surgant, *Manuale Curatorum* (Strasbourg, J. Schott, 1516), fol. 50).

no longer merely a matter of money or the misuse of clerical power. It was a question of doctrine. The clergy had preached the horrors of hell fire and damnation. No one, the preachers had claimed, could be saved from the tortures of the damned unless masses were said for his soul. Men had paid out their money for these masses and for the clergy's prayers but, in fact, both were worthless. Only Christ could save men from damnation; and that was a matter of the individual's faith in Christ. The laity understood the doctrinal issues and felt competent to write about them. More than that, they believed that salvation was too important to be left to the Catholic clergy.

One of the earliest lay pamphlets was written by a student, Lux Gemigger von Heinfelt. Bluntly, at the beginning, he stated his purpose: 'If anyone wants to know the name of the person who wrote this, it was done by a free student because they burned Luther's books.'[9] The pamphlet bore no date, and neither the name of the printer nor the place of publication. Since the burning of the books occurred in 1520, however, the pamphlet probably appeared within that year or, at the latest, at the beginning of the next. On the last of the ten pages Gemigger gave his own name in a closing sentence which ended: 'I have tried, no matter what happens. Next time I will do better.'[10]

Gemigger was nothing if not courageous, a small David against the Goliath of the Church. Luther, he stated, was hated by the pope, the priests and monks, who wished to kill him. The word of God was not pleasing to the clergy and they would not tolerate anyone who brought it to light. Thus the pope and the curia issued bulls and decrees in an attempt to stifle good teaching. They had falsified the Bible to make it conform to their own doctrines. This, Gemigger continued, was the greatest evil perpetrated by the clergy because their dishonesty harmed men in body and in soul.[11] The second evil wrought by the clergy was that they fleeced men of their money. They took silver and gold, especially from the Germans, under instructions from the devil.[12] Gemigger's solution was simple and direct. Christians should arise to reform the clergy, if necessary with cold steel. Their property should be taken away from them, their fine cloaks and tunics stripped away. Then they would be poor as monks and priests ought to be.[13] For the truth did not reside with the clergy or within the Church, but in Christ. Christ had called all men holy, not just the clergy.[14]

Anticlericalism and antipapalism had taken on new dimensions. The traditional complaints of wealth, immorality and laziness appeared as minor themes

9 Lux Gemigger, *Zu lob dem Luther und eeren der gantzen Christenheit* (Strasbourg, J. Pruss II, 1520). Another pamphlet by a student is included in Otto Clemen, vol. i, pp. 9–18: *Ein Sendbrieff von einem jungen Studenten zu Wittenberg an seine Eltern in Schwabenland von wegen die Lutherischen Lehre zugeschreiben* (1523).
10 Gemigger, *Zu lob dem Luther*, sig. avi.
11 Ibid., sigs aii^v–aiii.
12 Ibid., sigs aiii^v–aiiii.
13 Ibid., sig. aiiii.
14 Ibid., sig. avi.

among these German writers; the graver charge was the conscious teaching of false doctrine. In a dialogue written in Strasbourg, clerical deception was the major argument used by the son to win his father over to the new teaching. The dialogue appeared over the signature of Steffan von Büllheym, who remains unidentified.[15] By 1523 several preachers had been dismissed by the bishop of Strasbourg for Lutheran preaching, but Matthias Zell, the priest of the St Lawrence chapel in the cathedral, had begun to preach from the gospels, beginning with the Epistle to the Romans. People pressed into the cathedral to hear him. The bishop and the cathedral chapter were locked in a jurisdictional dispute over his dismissal.[16] Büllheym rose to warn Master Matthias that he was in danger. At the same time he wished to explain the truth of the new teaching to his father.

In the opening stanzas of the dialogue, written in verse, the son urged his father to accept the evangelical belief and abandon his old ways. He should believe very little of what the old clergy said and, above all, he should not give them any money because the clergy had led the laity astray, bombarding them with indulgences, carrying relics around claiming that the one was the stone thrown at St Stephen, the other a bone of St Claus, when in reality it was a sheep's bone.[17] The father was reluctant to follow his son. In the past, he said, the clergy had never made such errors. Every morning he, himself, had always offered a penny on the altar to save a soul from hell. What was wrong with that? The son laughed. That was a pretty powerful penny, was it not? Powerful enough to release a soul from hell? The mint-master was indeed a very holy man to be able to make such fine pennies.[18] But the father refused to be moved; he wanted the old Church and the old ways. He certainly did not want to read Luther's books. However, he was willing to agree that Master Matthias in the cathedral was a fine preacher, and was sorry he had been attacked by the benefice eaters and the hangers-on around the cathedral and in the bishop's administrative staff. What, he asked, did Dr Peter Wickram think about it all, for there was a man who was a real preacher?[19] That was just the point, the son replied. Doctor Peter had not helped at all. He did not agree with Master Matthias and he shrieked from the pulpit that Matthias was murdering the Church.[20]

---

15 Steffan von Büllheym, *Ein Brüderliche warnung am meister Mathis Pfarrherren zu Sanct Lorentzen im Münster zu Strassburg* (n.p., 1523 or 1524). This pamphlet will be printed, with scholarly notes, by Professor Marc Lienhard in an article entitled 'Mentalité populaire, gens d'église et mouvement évangelique à Strasbourg en 1523,' which will appear in *Horizons européens de la Réforme en Alsace, Mélanges Jean Rott*, forthcoming from E. J. Brill, Leiden. Another father and son dialogue is included in Clemen, i, pp. 25–47, *Ein Dialogus . . . zwischen einem Vater and sohn die Lehre Martin Luthers belangend* (1523).

16 Miriam Usher Chrisman, *Strasbourg and the Reform* (New Haven, 1967), pp. 100–1.

17 Büllheym, *Ein brüderliche warnung*, sig. aii[v].

18 Ibid., sig. aiii.   19 Ibid., sig. B.

20 Ibid., sig. B[v].

When he recognized the depth of the opposition to Zell, the father's attitude changed. He feared for the preacher's life because of recent actions taken against heretics. Son, he said, you had better warn Master Matthias right away that he should not preach tomorrow. The secular authorities at Bern had charged the Dominican monks there with heresy, and the spiritual authorities had condemned the monks. If Master Matthias should fall into the hands of the spiritual authorities they would surely take action against him. The biggest flies, said the father, rarely got caught. It is the little ones that are eaten by the spider. For example, Peter Stoffelus, who had preached Lutheran doctrine at Alt St Peter, was only a little gnat, but the ecclesiastical authorities had expelled him. Master Matthias was too learned for them, and they would certainly not ignore him.[21] The basic mistrust of the clergy was manifested in this speech by the father. The burning of heretics was repugnant to the laity, and they were convinced that there was little justice in the ecclesiastical courts.

The injustice within the Church was further developed by the son, particularly with regard to the priests' concubines. He spoke of them sympathetically, naming several Strasbourg *pfarrherrinnen*, including Frau Beatrix of St Claus with the fat legs. He pitied these women. They willingly submitted to hatred and abuse because they loved their consorts. They knew that priests needed wives, like other men, and they accepted ostracism from the rest of the society.[22]

Here, again, was a change in attitude. Büllheym held the Church culpable for concubinage, not the priests nor their women. The old cry had been to get the women out of the priests' houses. The new solution was to favour the marriage of the clergy.

At the end of the dialogue the father agreed that the clergy had turned everything upside down. He could no longer believe them. Instead, he would believe in 'the Evangelical teaching and the truth of God's word.'[23] A swift conversion. The Büllheym pamphlet, however, revealed the deep distrust within the lay community. There was genuine fear that Zell would be taken by force, similar to Gemigger's fear that Luther would be seized and subjected to bodily harm. Once a man was in the hands of the clerical authorities, the laymen believed there was no hope of justice. Fear and mistrust of the ecclesiastical arm helped to shape the lay response to the Reform. Their eagerness to dissolve the ecclesiastical courts or to curb their jurisdiction stemmed, in part, from the fact that they saw them as arbitrary, capricious and repressive, a threat to the peace of the community.

The deceptiveness of the clergy was even more bluntly described in a play

21 Ibid., sig. Bii.
22 Ibid., sigs Biiiᵛ–Biv.
23 Ibid., sig. Bv.

written by Niklaus Manuel, an artist and playwright in the city of Bern. In 1522, six years before the Reformation was established in that city, Manuel wrote a Shrovetide play which was presented in a square near the Ratshaus by the sons of the *burgherschaft*. The play went through six editions between 1523 and 1529, and there were more reprints which bore no date.[24] Clearly it achieved popularity in other cities and towns besides Bern.

The play opened with the pope seated in splendour among his courtiers, the ecclesiastical hierarchy and his military officers. St Peter and St Paul stood at the back, bewildered by the pomp. On either side of the pope were noblemen, burghers, beggars and others. A corpse prepared for burial was carried to the stage on a beam. Each member of the clergy then spoke, describing his powers and revealing his attitude towards death and towards the common man. The pope was particularly callous and brazen. Death was a good thing, he said. It brought profits to the Church and kept his men occupied. Because of death, the Church had been able to establish its control over the laity. Churchmen were now lords of the whole world, for all the gold, money and interest flowed into their coffers from the poor Swiss who, in their ignorance, believed the pope was the all-powerful God whose commandments had to be obeyed. The Church's income was assured because men could always be scared into doing penance by sermons on hell fire, a subject which could be relied on to terrorize the common people.[25] The bishop then described the benefits which flowed to him through the power of the pope. Although he was meant to serve his people as a shepherd, in fact he could function both as the shepherd and the wolf. He could fleece his flock by selling indulgences, by threatening them with the ban if they did not pay up. He made another two thousand *gulden* a year from taxes priests were required to pay for keeping concubines. He thus favoured clerical celibacy. Priests should not marry, as long as there was no rule obliging them to be chaste.[26] A scholar with the mellifluous name of Policarpus Schabgnaw stepped forward to eulogize the pope. The pope provided many things for money which were otherwise unavailable: heaven, hell, sin, virtue. Money was power. This had been dramatically shown by Christ and St Peter. Both poor, neither of them had been able to accomplish a thing. They had died in ignominy.[27]

Remedies for this ecclesiastical greed and callousness were not strongly stated until the very end of the play. The lay characters lamented the state of affairs but offered no solutions. The nobleman complained that his family had long supported the Church through donations and benefices, yet the clergy had deceived his father by promising him that heaven was in their gift.[28] A knight,

24 *Niklaus Manuel*, hrsg. von Dr Jakob Baechthold (Frauenfeld, 1878), pp. cxli–cl. The play is reprinted in this volume by Baechthold. My notes refer to this reprinted edition.
25 Ibid., pp. 33–4.
26 Ibid., pp. 36–7.
27 Ibid., pp. 63–4.
28 Ibid., p. 59.

a peasant and an official made similar criticisms.[29] In the concluding lines of the play, however, Manuel set forth an unequivocal Protestant doctrine. Christ, and Christ alone, was the Saviour and Creator. Men should follow Christ rather than man-made commandments and the false ways taught by the Church. Men were born in sin and were eternally lost; but Christ, by his death on the cross, had acquired the mercy of God for all men for eternity. All this was clear in the gospels, yet the Church had ignored these truths and had relied on other sources. The priests had lied from the pulpits. Theologians praised Aristotle instead of preaching the words of Christ.[30]

In 1522 these were strong words. Yet the burghers of Bern permitted their sons to say the lines and to represent the Catholic clergy as dishonest, untrustworthy and false. Niklaus Manuel spoke not only for himself: he reflected the common opinion of his fellow citizens, which had a major influence on the development of the Reformation. No matter how strongly the Church of Rome might state its case, it had already lost its credibility. A large number of ordinary citizens no longer believed what the clergy said.

Rejection of monasticism was another facet of lay criticism. In several cases this seems to have stemmed from familial concern for daughters placed in convents. Matthias Wurm von Geydertheym, an Alsatian nobleman and burgher of Strasbourg, dedicated his one-hundred-page treatise *Trost Closter-gefangner* to his friend and fellow nobleman, Eckhard zum Treubel. Matthias and his brother had placed one of their sisters in the convent of St Nikolaus-in-Undis. Wurm was aware that two of Eckhard's daughters were in convents. As guardians for the women, the men needed to reconsider their decisions and determine whether conventual life was a viable way to achieve eternal life.[31]

Wurm did not analyze the strengths and weaknesses of monastic life. He presented arguments against entering the cloister. He echoed Luther's teaching about oaths. The oath of chastity was against God's law. The oath of poverty was not kept. The oath of obedience conflicted with men's obedience to God. God created men in his own image and women to be the help-meet of men.[32] It was sinful for an individual of either sex to take an oath of chastity because it went against the will of God, who had ordered men and women to mate and to be fruitful.[33] The monastic order of obedience placed the rules of the order before the commandments of God. Monks and nuns might claim that they swear obedience to God first, and then to the patron of their order, St Dominic,

---

29 Ibid., pp. 70, 73, 77–8.
30 Ibid., pp. 100–1.
31 Matthias Wurm von Geydertheym, *Trost Clostergefangner Grund und ursach darumb mengklich sein Kind, geschwister oder freund uss den clostern nemen* (1923), sigs aii–aiii. For biographical information on Wurm, see Timotheus W. Röhrich, *Mittheilungen aus der Geschichte der Evangelische Kirche des Elsasses* (Strasbourg, 1855), 3rd edn, pp. 6–18.
32 Ibid., sig. i.
33 Ibid., sig. iv.

St Francis or St Clare; in fact, they placed their patron saint next to God and created their own religious practices and ceremonies.[34] To Wurm this was blasphemous, a point which he developed at length, moving back and forth from the Old to the New Testament in support of his argument.[35] He did not, like some laymen, merely cite the Biblical passage. The Biblical examples were woven into his argument. Wurm concluded that the foundation of monastic life was unsound.[36] Thus he decided to remove his sister from the convent so that she could devote herself to truly Christian works. He urged Eckhard zum Treubel to do the same for his daughters. He should suffer no scruples nor pangs of conscience, nor should he fear the criticism of the world. Obedience to God's commandments would free him from fear.[37]

Another pamphlet took the form of a letter from a married woman to her sister, who was a nun.[38] The latter, together with her mother superior, was fearful that her sister and brother-in-law had become Lutherans. The married woman wrote to defend herself and her husband. Apologizing that, as an un-learned person, she should undertake to write on religious matters, she stated that she merely wished to relieve the anxiety of her sister, the mother superior, and the rest of the convent.[39] The question, she said, was how to lead a Christian life. Christ taught, 'I am the door through which you must go to the Father.'[40] The monastic orders, instead of following this simple path provided by God, had created a special religious life involving tonsures, special clothing, and regulations about food.[41] Furthermore, despite Paul's admonitions against breaking up into sects, they had split into competing groups. How much holier was one order than another? Franciscans, lesser brothers, greater brothers, some in wooden shoes, others in leather shoes, others on stilts. One wears black, another grey. One does not handle money, another does not touch the plough in the field. The conventuals had set up their own rules, forgetting the unity of the spirit, the bond of peace which Christ had preached.[42] By their different costumes and customs they had separated themselves from other Christians.[43] The married woman went on to beseech her sister to read the

34 Ibid., sig. ix^v.
35 Ibid., sigs. xi–xvi^v.
36 Ibid., sig. xx^v.
37 Ibid., sig. lxvii^v.
38 *Ayn bezwungene antwort uber eynen Sendtbrieff eyner Closter nunnen an ir schwester im Eeliche standt zugeschickt* (n.p., 1524). Internal evidence leads me to attribute this pamphlet to a lay woman. The letter was written in reply to a letter announcing the birth of a new baby. The writer refers to the infant in several places, as well as to her husband. The most compelling detail is that the nun refused to call the baby by name. Her sister is grieved by the nun's indifference. These passages seem to authenticate the pamphlet as the work of a woman.
39 Ibid., sig. aii^v.
40 Ibid., sig. aiiii^v.
41 Ibid., sig. Bi^v.
42 Ibid., sig. Bii.
43 Ibid., sig. Cii.

Scriptures, to learn from them to love God with all her heart, soul and might.[44] That was the only commandment of God. How much, the married sister asked, do you and your cloistered sisters understand of your Latin songs and chants? Probably not much more than the miller's donkey. Where was their knowledge, their understanding and the source of their truth?[45] The Scriptures should be their only guide, not rules which had been drawn up by another human. The married sister closed by saying that she would pray to God to forgive her sister, the mother superior and the other sisters in the convent.[46]

It was hardly a letter designed to comfort or console, but the married sister was genuinely convinced that her sister's soul was in danger. Both pamphlets show that lay men and women did not simply repeat, parrot fashion, the arguments of the theologians. The theological points, the blasphemy of the monastic services developed by Wurm, the sectarianism described by the married woman, had been stated by Luther, Zwingli and other reformers; but in each case the lay person constructed his own argument, reflecting his own particular grasp of the problem. The married woman's characterization of the different monastic orders was witty as well as penetrating.

Laymen also felt free to discuss doctrinal questions, to define for themselves the meaning of the Eucharist, the nature of Grace or salvation. When these writings have been analyzed by theologians or historians, emphasis has been laid on whether the particular individual was Lutheran, Zwinglian, Spiritualist or an Anabaptist. In fact, their theology defies orderly classification. Few of the lay writers were formally educated. They read widely, particularly in their Bibles, but not necessarily analytically. Their ideas tended to come out of their own experience. They did not fit into the established theological categories. Their religious writing surged forth spontaneously, incorporating some of the ideas of the leading theologians of the period, but each individual expressed these in his own way. Zorn von Plobsheim, an Alsatian nobleman, provides an excellent example of the lay attitude towards theology. In 1530 Plobsheim wanted to read the Bible. Luther's translation was not complete so he put together his own version. He bought the books which Luther had completed in German: the Pentateuch, the historical and poetical books and the Gospels. He found a German translation of the prophets prepared by the Anabaptists Hans Denck and Ludwig Hetzer, and a translation of the Apocrypha, written by the Zwinglian, Leo Jud. He had all his separate pieces bound together, oblivious of the theological differences of the translators.[47]

That the laity were unencumbered by the complex rules which governed the theologians is also apparent from their doctrinal writings. Hans Greiffenberger

44 Ibid., sigs Ciii–Ciii[v].
45 Ibid., sig. Ci[v].
46 Ibid., sig. Civ.
47 Jane Abray, 'The Long Reformation, Magistrates, Clergy and People in Strasbourg, 1520–1599' (unpublished Ph.D. dissertation, Yale University, 1978), p. 271.

was a Nuremberg painter. Early drawn to the Reformation, he wrote and published seven pamphlets between 1523–4.[48] He tangled with the city authorities
and with the Nuremberg reformer, Andreas Osiander, because of his beliefs on
the Eucharist. Drinking the communion wine or eating the bread meant nothing,
he said, unless the individual approached the sacrament as a means of reaffirming
his faith. The supper was a commemorative service, the body of Christ was not
literally broken.[49] Believing that any man of faith could celebrate the Eucharist,
Greiffenberger gave communion to his wife.[50]

Greffenberger's eucharistic beliefs were based on the understanding of the
nature of the spirit of God. The spirit was all-powerful. Salvation would be
granted to those who followed the spirit rather than the flesh. Men must reject
their own selfish desires, nature and fancies to direct their lives by God's words
and commandments. Men were enabled to do this through the action of God's
spirit. The laws of the spirit, made manifest in Jesus, freed men from the laws
of sin and death. Fortified by Christ's sacrifice, men should turn from the flesh
to live according to the spirit.[51] It was the old battle between the spiritual side
of man's nature and the desires of the flesh. Instead of calling for penance,
however, Greiffenberger believed that any creature born of God could overcome
the world and his material nature. Faith was the outward sign that the world
had been defeated, the battle won.[52]

In another pamphlet Greiffenberger addressed himself to what it meant to
be a true Christian.[53] Like the lay woman writing to her sister, he believed that
no man could make himself a Christian by becoming a monk. In particular, no
one could lead a sinful life and then compensate for it by donning a monastic
robe and accepting monastic discipline.[54] Greiffenberger then went further.
His belief in the inner working of God's spirit led him to a strong belief in
divine election. No human being had the power to forgive sin; indeed, God had
clearly warned mankind against such people. No one could know God's truth
except those to whom it was specially sent. It could not be attained through

---

48 The pamphlets are listed by Thurman E. Philoon in his article 'Hans Greiffenberger and
the Reformation in Nuernberg,' in *The Mennonite Quarterly Review*, vol. xxxvi (1962), pp.
61–75: (1) *Die welt sagt sy sehe kain besserung von denn sie sy Lutherisch nennet*, 1523; (2) *Diess
biechlin zaigt an was uns lerner und gelernet haben unsern Maister der geschrifft*, 1523; (3) *Ein
Kurtzer begrif von guten werken*, 1524; (4) *Ein Christenliche Antwort denen, die da sprechen, das
Evangelio sein krafft von Kirchen*, 1524; (5) *Ein Warnung vor dem Teuffel*, 1524; (6) *Ein trastliche
ermanung den angefochten in gewissen*, 1524; (7) *Disz biechlin zaigt an die Falschen Propheten*, n.d.
49 Philoon, 'Hans Greiffenberger', p. 62.
50 Ibid., p. 66.
51 Hans Greiffenberger, *Ein trostliche ermanung den Angefochten in gewissen von wegen Gethaner
sundt* (n.p., 1524), unpaginated (modern pp. 4–5).
52 Ibid., sig. Bᵛ.
53 Hans Greiffenberger, *Die welt sagt sy sehe Kain besserung von den die sy Lutherisch nennen*
(n.p., 1524).
54 Ibid., sig. aiii.

man's own exertions, his own will or his reason. It flowed from the spirit of God.[55] This did not mean that a man was forced to wait passively for God's spirit. He could carry out the commandments of God and read the Scriptures. Greiffenberger defended the latter in particular. Some learned men might say that the common man should not read the Scriptures because it was not appropriate for a shoemaker to read the gospels, or to wear feathers and bright colours instead of sturdy leather and black clothing. Only people weak in their faith and sinful in their ways would raise such arguments.[56]

Since the power of God rested in the spirit, the Church was not important to the Christian life. In a short, five-page treatise, he asked how the first Christian had been converted, before the Church was in existence. St Augustine, he pointed out, had asked the same question. Greiffenberger's answer was that the Christian Church had grown out of the teachings of Christ and his Gospel. The Church developed from the gospels and thus was secondary to them.[57] This belief in the primacy of the gospels undoubtedly freed Greiffenberger from feeling responsible to clerical authority and emboldened him to give communion to his wife. He saw the Church, whether Catholic or Reformed, as a rather poor intermediary. The teachers and the clergy had neither faith nor understanding. That was why Christ had chosen his disciples from the poor and the uneducated. They could understand what the learned could not.[58] In the time of Christ the Pharisees argued over fine points of the law, claiming that the common people were ignorant. There were still Pharisees who behaved the same way. If a layman talked about Christ, he was branded as a Lutheran heretic. No one should be deceived by the learned, or dependent on them. All men should read the Scriptures. If a man could not read, he should find someone to read to him.[59] Greiffenberger knew that ordinary men, cowed by threats, feared the clergy. He wished to comfort the people, to give them self-confidence. His teaching of the power of the Holy Spirit counteracted the doctrine of penance. It wrested salvation from the control of the clergy and placed it in the hands of God and his Son.

Some of the most sophisticated theological doctrines developed by a layman were the work of Clement Ziegler, a Strasbourg gardener. During a flood of 1524 Christ had revealed himself to Ziegler in a vision. Awakened by this experience, Ziegler became a self-appointed preacher to his fellow gardeners, arousing the ire of both the Protestant clergy and the magistrates since he was neither educated or ordained. He wrote several treatises which were published; several

---

55 Ibid.
56 Ibid., sig. aiiii.
57 Hans Greiffenberger, *Ein Christenliche Antwordt denen die da sprechen das Evangelio hab sein kraft von der Kirchen* (n.p., 1524), sig. aii.
58 Hans Greiffenberger, *Diss biechlin zaygt an was uns lernen und gelernt haben unsere maister der geschrifft* (n.p., 1523), sig. Diiiᵛ.
59 Ibid., sig. Diiii.

more were suppressed by censorship of the Magistracy.[60] Ziegler's Spiritualist doctrines were well-developed before Schwenckfeld had published, and certainly before Schwenckfeld arrived in Strasbourg.[61] Ziegler's earliest tract dealt with the dual nature of Christ: his theology was logically constructed from his understanding of the spiritual essence of Christ. He did not deny Christ's corporeal materialization in his birth through Mary, but Ziegler regarded the bodily Christ as a momentary phase. Christ was born of the Father, present in the Trinity from the very beginning of time.[62] This concept of the nature of Christ led Ziegler to reject doctrines of transubstantiation and Real Presence and to develop his own teaching on the Eucharist. He realized, he wrote, that he was a simple and uneducated person, but the errors emanating from the lack of understanding of the nature of the body of Christ forced him to write.[63] The word Sacrament was, in itself, a great abuse. It was never used in the Scriptures. Christ took the bread and called it his body, He took the wine and called it the New Testament. Thus, the Eucharist should be referred to as the body of Christ and his testament, or as Christ's Supper, but never as a sacrament.[64] The breaking of the bread was a wonderful example of Christ's use of symbolism. To understand it any other way would lead to idolatry. Men would worship the wine or the bread, not Christ.

Now pious Christians listen well, for the opposing party has taught us that the bread or the body of Christ is not bread but flesh. Oh, God in heaven that we should understand so little! For Jesus Christ himself made it very clear, for he said, 'The spirit is the effective power, the body is of no use. And the words which I say are spirit and life.' And Christ himself explained that when he spoke of flesh and blood this should be understood in a spiritual way. . . . Thus the papal teachings which say that the bread is flesh and is no longer bread are thrown to the ground. It is all in error and a great lie. Furthermore the opposition tells the people they must believe that even when the wafer is broken into a hundred pieces, still the body of Christ remains in every piece, just as though it still hung on the cross. . . . That is not true at all.[65]

It was an error to place emphasis on whether or how the substance of the

---

60 The published treatises include: (1) *Ain Kurtz Register und ausszug der Bibel in welchem man findet was Abgöterey sey* (Strasbourg, 1524); (2) *Von der Vermählung Mariä und Josephs* (Strasbourg, 1524); (3) *Von der waren nyessung beyd leibs und bluts Christi . . . und von der Tauff . . .* (Strasbourg, J. Schott, 1524); (4) *Eine fast schöne Auslegung der Vater Unser* (1525); (5) *Buchlein claren verstandt von dem leib und blut Christi* (Strasbourg, J. Schwan, 1525). As late as 1550 Ziegler was still writing and trying to have his work printed. In February 1550 he gave the Ammeister a book to be passed by the censors. He was told to stick to his *handtwerck*. When he asked that the MS be returned in June, the *Rat* refused to give it back, again telling him to stick to his work. A.M.S. Ratsprotocol, 12 February 1550, fol. 73ᵛ; 4 June 1550, fol. 257ᵛ.
61 George H. Williams, *The Radical Reformation* (London, 1962), p. 337.
62 Ibid., p. 328.
63 Clement Ziegler, *Von der waren nyessung beid leibs und bluts Christi* (Strasbourg, 1524), fol. aiii.
64 Ibid., sig. aiiii.
65 Ibid., sigs. B–Bii.

bread and the wine changed. Defining the material elements of the Supper had nothing to do with understanding the nature of God and of Christ. The theologians spent their time arguing about the wrong things. God was spirit, living and everlasting. Matter did not have to exist in a bodily sense in order to life. This had first been shown by God who appeared to Moses in a cloud, yet spoke to him with the voice of a man.[66] In the same way Christ never said his body was in the bread. He did not think of the material flesh of his body. He spoke of life. Ziegler concluded that only the words of Christ should be used in the communion service, precisely as they appeared in the Scriptures. There was no need for any other words of consecration, nor was it necessary to limit communion to given times and places, especially for the sick. Christ had eaten the Last Supper not in a church but in a house, and he had not restricted the commemoration of the event to a special time.[67]

Ziegler stated his beliefs with clarity and vigour. He did not hesitate to read the gospels and to interpret them. He assumed they were open to be understood by all men. He did not confine himself to a literal interpretation of Scripture. His beliefs were based on a comprehensive theological framework, rooted in his own understanding of the spiritual nature of the Godhead. At no time in his tracts did he refer to Luther or Zwingli. He considered himself capable of developing his own doctrines, without recourse to the learned.

Moral and ethical standards were another concern of the laity, exemplified in the work of Eckhard zum Treubel. Treubel was a patrician and a nobleman. The family held several villages near Strasbourg, including Hindisheim, Innenheim and Ergersheim. Various relatives had served at the upper levels of the magistracy.[68] Eckhard himself had no university education but had followed a military career, returning to live in Strasbourg.[69] Two of his daughters had entered convents. Dissatisfied with the life they led there, Treubel was early open to the influence of the Reformation. He read the Scriptures and discussed theological questions with like-minded friends, including Matthias Wurm von Geydertheim.[70] As early as 1521 Treubel published a short tract deploring the customs which led the Roman Church to sell masses, indulgences and prayers for the dead.[71] In 1524 he wrote in support of the Magistrat's edict abolishing begging and creating a new welfare system, hoping that similar reforms would be carried out among the peasants.[72] Later in the same year he exhorted the

---

66 Ibid., sig. B^v.   67 Ibid., sig. Biii, sig. Ci.
68 Thomas Brady, *Ruling Class, Regime and Reformation at Strasbourg, 1520–1555* (Leiden, 1977), pp. 202–3, n. 361, 385, 392.
69 Timotheus W. Röhrich, *Mittheilungen aus der Geschichte der Evangelischen Kirche* (Strasbourg, 1855), vol. iii, pp. 21–3.
70 Ibid., p. 22.
71 Eckhard zum Treubel, *Ein dermütige ermanung an ein gantze gemeine Christenheit . . . Man soll in der Kirchen nit mit gelt umbgen* (Strasbourg, R. Beck, *c.* 1522).
72 Eckhard zum Treubel, *Christelich lob und vermanung an die hochberumpte Christeliche statt Straszburg* (Strasbourg, M. Flach II, 1524).

laity to stand fast by the Gospel in the crisis of the Peasants' War.[73] A longer work, published in 1528, summarized for his children the main tenets of his faith, incorporating a good deal of fatherly advice. In a final tract he censured Luther, Zwingli and the Anabaptists for doctrinal wrangling which had led to sectarianism.[74] Each sect, he wrote, had its own tenets and its outward emblem to which its members vowed allegiance. The Baptists had their water, the Zwinglians the bread of the Eucharist, and the Lutherans the bread of the Lord. Out of these differences three sects had arisen. Treubel would leave each to its own opinion. He would base his beliefs on the true Word of Christ.[75] Like several other laymen he solved the problem of the nature of the Eucharist by adopting a Spiritualist view. He believed that he truly received the body and blood of Christ in communion as spiritual food for his soul, but as spirit only, as all actions concerning Christ should be comprehended. It did not matter whether Christ's body was in the bread, or whether the bread was in Christ's body. What mattered was man's faith in God's Word, which was not based on visual or material things.[76]

Treubel's *Ein vetterliche, gedruge, gute zucht, lere und bericht* provides an excellent example of the layman's eagerness to apply the teaching of the gospels directly to his own life. Frustrated by the corruption of the Roman Church and its unwillingness to address itself to moral issues, laymen searched for ethical standards which could be applied to the realities of everyday life. Treubel made no differentiation between faith and action: the latter was an expression of the former. Faith was meaningless if it did not lead to a good Christian life. He began his treatise by arguing that as part of his responsibility as a father, he would provide his children with Christian rules for their souls, bodies and property. His first concern, obviously, was for the salvation of their souls, the holiness of conscience. His rules were simple and direct. They must place the love of God above and beyond all other things, and they must love their neighbours as themselves.[77] They must act as responsible members of the Church, accepting its outward customs while preserving their own inner freedom:

Hold yourself true to the corporate body of the Christian church and to your chief parish church. Wherever it is, attend it. For the great St Peter's cathedral in Rome, with all its court and court followers, is not the Christian church, nor the great church chapter in Strasbourg, nor one of those meetings where all prelates come together like the *Reichstag* or the councils. The church is not in cowls nor in cloisters. But where

---

73 Eckhard zum Treubel, *Ein christlich bryederlich, treuwlich warnung vor auffrur und trostlich bestendig bey dem Evangelio zu beharren* (1524).
74 Eckhard zum Treubel, *Da gloriam Deo – Von dem eynigen Gott . . . Von denen so Luterisch und Evangelisch genannt sein wöllen . . . Von den Wiederteuffern* (Strasbourg, 1534). Major sections of this pamphlet are included in Röhrich's *Mittheilungen*, iii, pp. 40–53.
75 Röhrich, *Mittheilungen*, iii, p. 45.
76 Ibid.
77 Eckhart zum Treubel, *Ein Vetterliche, gedruge, gute zucht, lere und bericht Christlich zu leben und sterben an meine Kynder und alle frummen Christen* (Strasbourg, 1528), sig. aii.

pious, believing Christians come together, whether it be in wild woods or in the fields, that is the true Christian church. It does not consist in wood, in stone sculpture. It consists in faith and in the love of God and one's neighbour. But your rightful parish, dear son, is in the cathedral of Strasbourg and you should support what it does and what it teaches. You should not be ashamed of doing these things if they are in the sacraments and according to the Christian ordinances. And I will do the same things.[78]

Treubel's concept of an individual's spiritual duty was clearly influenced by Luther and the teachings of the Strasbourg reformers. At the same time he seems to counsel a Schwenckfeldian form of action. Carry out the observed practices but keep your inner self free. As far as the sacraments were concerned, he recognized only baptism and communion. God had commanded us to believe and to be baptized, but he had said nothing about ordination or confirmation. Neither God nor his apostles had commanded such practices. Therefore it would be sufficient if his children saw to the baptism of their own children, and taught them to believe in, and love, God and their neighbour.[79] The threat of purgatory and the practice of auricular confession, he believed, had done irreparable harm to Christianity. These practices had made the Church rich, the people poor. Nevertheless, Treubel believed that some form of confession was useful, and that the Christian should recognize his guilt before God; but it should be a matter between God and himself. He thus included in his treatise a form which he believed would be appropriate for confession, and the words to be used by a priest or confessor in granting absolution:[80]

The following is the proper way in which confession should be administered. The priest of confession shall say: 'Brother, you believe that Christ has obtained the remission of all sins, yours and those of all the world, by his own merits and death. Do you also believe that God has forgiven your sins and will remit them at your petition and request?' Then, as the sinner says, 'Yes. I believe that from my heart,' the confessor says, 'Act according to your belief. Go out and sin no more.'

Absolution, whether granted by a priest or a confessor, should sound like this:

'Our Lord Jesus Christ, through his Holy suffering, death and sufficient merit, be gracious and merciful to you, pardon and forgive your sins. May he grant you a Christlike faith and kindle in you his Christlike love. . . . I, through his Godly command and instruction (for He said what has been bound or unbound to you on earth, shall be bound or unbound by Me in heaven) absolve you. God himself pardons and forgives all your sins. In the name of the Father, the Son and the Holy Ghost. Amen.'[81]

These paragraphs defined the practices which Treubel believed should be followed. Since the treatise was written for his own family, it is doubtful that he envisaged his words being incorporated into the liturgy of the new Church.

78 Ibid., sig. aii^v.
79 Ibid., sig. aiii.
80 Ibid.
81 Ibid., sigs aiiii^v–av.

Indeed, he had just finished counselling his sons and daughters to follow along in what was taught and practised at the cathedral. Were these instructions intended for use within the family? Did members of the family confess to one another, accepting Luther's early statement that every Christian had the power of absolution?

In the second part of his treatise Treubel turned to everyday life to discuss the attitude Christians should take towards money, towards property, towards life in the world. It was an ethic which emphasized simplicity of life. First, he said, his children should refrain from all unnecessary spending, such as an elaborate household, pomp and ostentatious entertaining. They should save honourably what they could, taking and receiving that which belonged to them from God or by other right. But they should use their money for Christian purposes, not for ostentation or display. If they had a surplus and were inclined to use it for luxury, they should give it to the poor.[82] His fatherly advice continued:

Hold back from all legal disputes, for every lawyer is a wolf. Also where there is peace, there is God and holiness, happiness, honour and good. Do not go in for building a new house, because it will be too expensive. It is better to fix up the old one you already have. . . . For I find my food and drink tastes just as good and I sleep just as well in my old house as I would in a new one. And night and day come just the same way as if I were in a great palace. But if you call in the builder to look at your old house, he will tell you you need to tear it down and build a new one. But the carpenters, the masons, the woodworkers and the painter work together, like the doctors and apothecaries, and when they say that the work will cost fifty *gulden*, it will certainly be closer to a hundred. For what they can stretch out to two days, they never accomplish in one. . . . Guard yourself especially against the burghers, for they create discord, ridicule, error and ruin.[83] . . . And guard against putting on airs and against all courtly life, especially with regard to clothes. For I have seen many fools in silk clothes and golden shoes and gloves. There is nothing in feathers except for the birds. High court life is the height of folly for, dear children, to live simply is to live well.[84]

These admonitions provide valuable social insight. However Christian he was, and Treubel was clearly sincere, the gap between noble and burgher remained. Although the Treubel family had lived in the city for at least two hundred years, craftsmen, artisans, and ordinary burghers were to be regarded with the same degree of suspicion as lawyers, doctors and apothecaries. The requirement to love one's neighbour did not require that you must also trust him.

In his closing paragraphs Treubel justified himself for writing the treatise. Criticism might be made that only those anointed and ordained should preach in this way. Treubel disagreed. He and every other Christian had the power to

82 Ibid., sigs Bii–Bii[v].
83 Ibid., sigs Bii[v]–Biii.
84 Ibid., sig. C.

write, sing, advise, speak, teach and instruct. For Christ said, wherever two or three are gathered together in my name, I am there in the midst of them. He did not specify whether these people were priests or laymen, nor did He speak of a church or a chancel. Indeed, he preached in the fields, on a ship, in private houses, in schools, in synagogues, in a garden and, at last, from the cross. And the apostles preached in chains, from dungeons and from prisons. Thus, every Christian had not only the right, but also the obligation, to preach the Word of God in all lands and places.[85]

A student; two artists; a housewife; Büllheym, who was probably an artisan or craftsman; a gardener and two noble patricians. The pamphlet writers represented the full spectrum of sixteenth-century urban society. The pamphlets themselves bear witness to the fact that men and women at all levels of society read the Bible, followed current theological debates, formulated their own ideas, wrote them down and found publishers willing to print them. This type of activity forces scholars to re-examine their assumptions with regard to lay literacy and the level of lay learning on the eve of the Reformation, a pursuit ably pioneered by Professor A. G. Dickens. Since these men and women were able to contribute so quickly, it must mean that even before the Reform laymen had the capability to read and to express themselves in writing. The Roman Church, however, did not permit them to use these powers. The earliest years of the Reformation gave them new opportunities which they were quick to exploit. In their earliest tracts, written in 1520 and 1523, the laymen attacked the Roman clergy and defended the reformers, in one case Luther, in the other Matthias Zell. By 1523 the monastic orders had become an important issue. After 1524 the lay writers were less interested in the abuses and errors of the old Church. They turned away from the past to consider the present, to formulate doctrines based on the Scriptures. The burst of lay writing ended abruptly. In Strasbourg only one lay writer, Eckhard zum Treubel, published after 1525. Between 1520 and 1525 twenty-eight treatises by laymen were printed in Strasbourg. After 1526 there were only eleven, nine of them written by Swiss. The Peasants' War frightened the clergy and the magistrates. While the former had welcomed the lay polemicists in the early days of the Reform, when it became necessary to define new doctrines they did not wish to be encumbered or embarrassed by the theological opinions of the laity.

Doctrine was important to all the lay writers. Three of those examined here, Greiffenberger, Ziegler and Treubel, held essentially Spiritualist views. They criticized the Protestant clergy for attempting to define the exact nature of the Eucharist. They understood it spiritually, and were angered by the Lutheran and Zwinglian arguments over the material elements of the bread and wine. They wanted simple doctrines, based directly on Scripture, and free from rigid theological definition. They wanted to be freed from the restraints of penitential

85 Ibid., sig. Diii–Diii^v

doctrine and from clerical domination.[86] They were ready to create their own theology, their own formulations of belief. In Germany, however, this lay activity was restricted after 1525. The new territorial and urban churches demanded acceptance of the *Confession of Augsburg* or other articles of faith, and conformity to the established *Kirchenordnung*. But how conformist was the conformity of the laity? Did they go to church, as Eckhard zum Treubel counselled them to do, and believe differently in their hearts? The treatises examined would indicate that in the brief period from 1520 to 1525 a tradition of lay independence of mind was created which would continue to nurture nonconformity in the Protestant Churches, despite the efforts of the theologians to establish orthodoxy.

86 Steven E. Ozment, *The Reformation in the Cities* (New Haven, 1975), pp. 118–19.

IV

Politics and Expediency
in the Augsburg Reformation

❧

PHILIP BROADHEAD

In 1533 the City Council of Augsburg was forced to consider the introduction of religious reform, but, unable to decide on the best course, commissioned its leading lawyers and advisers to compile a series of memoranda.[1] They were to discuss all the advantages and problems which a reformation would create and to assess the strength of forces acting for and against religious reform. The Council was aware of taking a momentous decision which would have permanent effects, and refused to act without giving due consideration to all the problems. Fortunately most of these memoranda survive in the Augsburg *Stadtarchiv* and provide invaluable insights into the process of sixteenth-century decision-making.

Augsburg was placed in a critical dilemma by the Reformation since most of the populace and Councillors supported religious reform, although the city itself was hemmed in by powerful Catholic rulers who controlled the food supply and trade routes.[2] The most lucrative trading by city merchants was with the Emperor or in the Habsburg territories. If the city thus accepted religious reform it could expect serious economic and political repercussions. Consequently the Council prevaricated and Lutheran and Zwinglian pastors were encouraged to work in Augsburg. They took wives, from 1525 they gave Communion in both kinds, and they had their books printed in the city without interference from the authorities. At the same time the Council would permit neither action against the Catholic clergy nor iconoclasm and it scrupulously published the Imperial Mandates on religion although making no real attempt to enforce them.[3] The Council was deliberately following a middle course in an attempt to avoid offence to either party by allowing an unofficial religious dualism to develop. This policy was demonstrated at the 1530 *Reichstag* in Augsburg when the city not only refused to accept the Catholic policies contained in the final speech (*Reichstagsabschied*) composed by the Emperor, but also refused to join the 'protesting' powers. Instead the Council promised Charles V that, although it could not accept his policies, it would not interfere with the Catholic Church in Augsburg.

If the Council was satisfied with this solution, the dangerously tempestuous population of the city, amongst whom the Zwinglians had overwhelming support, forced the authorities to expel rival Lutheran preachers. These were replaced by men from Strasbourg who, once established, abandoned the conciliatory theology of Bucer and, to popular approbation, began attacking both

1 I wish to express my gratitude to the Anglo-German Group of Historians for providing me with a grant to undertake research in Augsburg.
2 The rulers were the Dukes of Bavaria, the bishop of Augsburg and the Emperor.
3 For the early history of the Reformation in Augsburg see F. Roth, *Augsburgs Reformationsgeschichte* 2nd edn, vol. i (Munich, 1901).

Lutherans and Catholics in their sermons. The situation was further complicated for the Council when, on 21 January 1533, it was presented with a petition, signed by all the preachers, demanding that immediate action be taken against the Catholic Church in Augsburg.[4] The petition attacked the Councillors for refusing to accept their responsibilities by taking an active part in religious reform. The preachers maintained that the Council had been appointed by God to govern Augsburg and that it had a duty to protect the true Christian faith, and prevent its subjects being misled by false doctrines. The preachers said that for two years they had been preaching against the iniquities of the Church of Rome, and had many times spoken of the undeniable authority and duty which the Council possessed to rid the city of falsehood and superstition. Since the Council had appointed them, they had always believed they had its support. Yet no action had been forthcoming. When Catholicism was eradicated in Augsburg, however, the preachers promised love, peace, loyalty and the willing obedience of the citizens: 'in sum, all happiness, well-being, honour and glory before God and all Godly men.' Indeed, with cooperation between Godly magistrates (*gotseligen magistrat*) and 'true preachers', they promised that Augsburg would be as the kingdom of God on earth, '. . . *das reich Christi bey euch in euer stat*.'[5]

The petition was accompanied by firm words from Doctor Sebastian Maier, who, delivering it on behalf of his colleagues, urged the Councillors not to shirk their duty as servants of God but to unite with the preachers. He acknowledged that the Council had promised Charles V that it would not move against the Roman Church, but despite this their duty to obey God exceeded their obedience to the Emperor. In Maier's words, '. . . We are all messengers and ambassadors of the great emperor, the lord of all emperors – our God in heaven.'[6] It is clear from this petition that the pastors envisaged a kind of theocracy developing in Augsburg controlled by the Council and themselves. This could hardly have been a tempting prospect for the secular authorities, although it is perhaps significant that this was by no means a private discussion, as the pastors claimed to have preached on this subject many times. Indeed, they had prepared their ground by a propaganda campaign from the pulpit, and must have been confident of support in the city before they made such sweeping demands to the Council. The responsibility for enacting religious reform had been placed with the Council, which could no longer justify inactivity by the excuse of waiting for the long promised General Council of the Church. As far as the pastors and their supporters were concerned, if the Council wanted to act, it was fully entitled to do so.

The situation was intolerable for the authorities, but the preachers could not

4 This document is printed in full by K. Wohlfart, *Die Augsburger Reformation in den Jahren 1533–34* (Leipzig, 1901), pp. 127ff.
5 Ibid., p. 128.
6 Maier's comments to the Council are printed in full by F. Roth, *Augsburgs Reformationsgeschichte*, vol. ii (Munich, 1904), pp. 135ff.

be silenced for fear of arousing their supporters and the mob. Consequently, the Council's Committee for Religion, formed in 1530, asked for memoranda on a civic reformation to be prepared. An 'Instruction' was drawn up in secret by the Committee which decided on the topics of relevance and controversy upon which it required guidance, assigning one topic to each of the men consulted according to their acknowledged expertise. In order to preserve secrecy, all were sworn to silence and each man was given only his own question and not told of other memoranda in preparation. In this way, it was hoped to prevent the enemies of the city gaining knowledge of the scheme. Each lawyer was asked to discuss the general question 'Whether the town Council of Augsburg, as a temporal power, has the authority to institute changes and new ordinances in religious matters or not.'[7] The emphasis placed on the question was significant, for the Council was not seeking advice on disputed doctrines. Instead, it wanted guidance from the lawyers on legal aspects of reform, questioning both the extent of its jurisdiction and the degree to which it was bound by earlier undertakings given to the Catholic Church.

Of the supplementary questions, the most important asked how religious and social disunity in the city could best be healed, and whether religious reform would have this effect. This was assigned to the civic secretary *Stadtschreiber* Konrad Peutinger, architect of the religious *via media* policies of the Council and a man well known for his concern to foster civic unity. The Committee also wished to know the extent to which the doctrinal differences could be judged from the Bible, and the best way of phasing out errors or restricting the worship of the Roman Church. This question presupposes the answer in favour of change which would certainly be given by the court secretary, *Gerichtschreiber* Franz Kötzler, who was known to be a firm supporter of the Zwinglians. Another lawyer employed by the Council, Hans Hagk, also a Zwinglian supporter, was asked to discuss how Catholic worship could be restricted in the city, while another lawyer, Doctor Balthasar Langnauer, was required to find out how the authorities should deal with Church property in the event of a civic reformation. The matter could prove a delicate one if the Council were to proceed, and guidance was sought on the ownership of monastic and Church buildings, the property and the moveable assets of the clergy, not to mention income and endowment given to the Church. The lawyer Konrad Hel was likewise requested to advise the Council on changes in matrimonial legislation which would occur if canon law lost its force. For example, should the Council act to prevent unlawful marriages which might produce children in need of support at civic expense? Hel was also instructed to elaborate on the political dangers which would arise from religious reform; whilst two further questions concerning diplomatic repercussions and the necessity to safeguard the property of citizens were either destroyed or never commissioned.

7 Ibid., Beilage 2, pp. 137ff.

When the Committee received these memoranda it stated that it would consider all the views they represented before recommending the best course of action to the Council. Yet should the authors think the Council did not have the authority to institute religious reforms, they might not on that score proceed to answer their subsidiary questions. Nevertheless, there was a clear disparity in the memoranda as they were eventually completed. Those of Peutinger, Hel and Rehlinger were long (sixty folios in Peutinger's case), and the arguments were carefully presented with copious examples as proof. The memoranda of Kötzler, Langnauer and Hagk were short. They were obviously written in haste and gave only the major points of their arguments. Langnauer, for example, argued in his introduction that he had only recently been asked to state his views (*in kurtzverschiner zeit*).[8] It would certainly seem from this that the first three lawyers, the most distinguished of the group, were given longer to prepare their memoranda, the others being commissioned only at the last minute.

Konrad Peutinger had been civic secretary since 1498, and was to hold the post until 1535. He came from an established Augsburg merchant family, had served as adviser to the Emperors Maximilian and Charles V, and had a considerable reputation as a humanist and scholar, being a correspondent of Erasmus. Peutinger had little interest in theology, but he was a noted lawyer and played a crucial role in framing the politics of the city. He was frequently asked for his views during meetings of the important Council of Thirteen, and his advice was generally accepted, although his strongly imperialist views probably brought about a gradual decline in his influence over the Council during the 1530s. His memorandum contained a vigorous attack on the idea that religious doctrine could be changed whenever dissent arose, and maintained that only a General Council of the Church was empowered to alter matters of doctrine.[9] Peutinger warned that if any prince, duke or city could follow whatever doctrines they wished, it would not be long before all would demand the same freedom. The result would be the kind of anarchy and insurrection which had occurred in the Peasants' War, when the Anabaptists and the lower orders had attacked the established social framework with the excuse that they were following their religious beliefs.

. . . Should every minor, separate authority such as a duke or city be tolerated to decide upon and proceed with changes in religion or belief, then it would follow that not only market towns and villages but even separate groups in towns and villages would develop differences and awaken division against each other and seek to force events so that nothing but animosity, rebellion and sedition would flourish, just as with the loud and clear examples of the peasants in 1525 and the 'Swiss' rebellions, which took place under the guise of the Holy Gospel.[10]

8 Stadtarchiv Augsburg (hereafter St A) Literalien 1534, Nachtrag 1, Nr. 22, fol. 1.
9 St A Literalien 1534, Nachtrag 1, Nr. 15.
10 Ibid., fol. 31f.

In addition to these objections, Peutinger saw practical considerations which made a Protestant Reformation impossible. Most important amongst these were the undertakings the city had given at the meetings of the *Reichstag* at Speyer in 1529 to uphold the Catholic faith. At the Augsburg *Reichstag* of 1530, the Council had decided to follow and maintain a middle and mild path, '. . . and had promised to do nothing which would affect the Catholic Church before the religious controversy was settled by a Council of the Church'.[11] Augsburg was also bound by the religious truce (*Stillstand*), and general peace (*Landfriede*) declared by the Emperor at the Regensburg *Reichstag* of 1532. Peutinger believed that any religious changes would result in the city being declared a destroyer of the peace, so that inevitable economic and political retribution would follow from the *Reichskammergericht*. The city would be outlawed, its goods declared forfeit, its trade halted and eventually ruined to the detriment of rich and poor alike. He also forecast that the Dukes of Bavaria would use the opportunity to attack the city and sever its food supplies. The result would be hardship and revolution amongst lower orders already suffering the ill-effects of 'these costly years'.[12]

Implicit in Peutinger's warning, of course, was the belief that Augsburg was bound to obey the Emperor as the supreme authority in the land. For Peutinger believed that the existence of a strong Emperor was vital to the maintenance of peace, order and trade. In short, if Charles was to be disobeyed, the Empire and Augsburg would suffer. '. . . the Holy Roman Empire of the German nation is a body on which the Almighty has bestowed grace and blessings and in particular on this city [Augsburg] as a member. But in such a body, wherever possible, no disagreement should appear.'[13] In Peutinger's view, everyone had a duty to obey the authorities set over them by God and, in the case of the City Council, that was the Emperor. Accordingly, he urged the Council not to act against the wishes of Charles V: '. . . in my judgement in these difficult times the best course to follow is the middle and mild way.' If the Council associated itself with any policies which damaged 'good Christian order', it would bring on rich and poor alike, 'trouble, travail, confusion, opposition, animosity and in many other ways injury and damage.'[14]

There was no indication in this memorandum that Peutinger was influenced by religious convictions, and although he remained bitterly anticlerical all his life, his natural conservatism and fear of any religious division that could weaken the Empire prompted him to stay loyal to the Papal cause. He saw the problems as both a merchant and a politician; and he knew how important it was to secure the support of the Emperor for the protection of trade routes and the grant of

11 Ibid., fol. 47.
12 Ibid., fol. 59.
13 Ibid., fol. 54.
14 Ibid., fol. 58.

trading privileges and monopolies.[15] By nature an aristocrat, he rejected any participation of the lower orders in government, fearing a repeat of the events of 1525. If the Council disobeyed the Emperor, Peutinger believed this would set a dangerous precedent and cause all authority to be brought into question, even that of the City Council over its citizens. In short, this significant lawyer and principal adviser to the Council strenuously argued that Augsburg should not proceed with reform but beware the disaster which might follow such precipitate action. Accordingly, Peutinger counselled a careful preservation of the *status quo*.

The Council also turned for advice to the rich lawyer and patrician, Johann Rehlinger. The son of a mayor, Rehlinger had held his post with distinction since 1511, and although he was to remain loyal to the Roman faith, he retained his post in Augsburg until his death in 1538, perhaps inspired by an annual salary of 300 *gulden*.[16] Rehlinger produced a cogent and spirited defence of the old religion and demonstrated a clear understanding of the complex issues at stake. Like Peutinger, he maintained that no authority but a General Council of the Church had the right to dictate changes in religious observance; and he stressed the division which had always existed between secular and spiritual jurisdictions, implying that, as a secular authority, the City Council had no power to interfere in the Church.[17] In order to dissuade the Council from staging a public disputation as a means of justifying reformation, Rehlinger attacked theological disputations as being inconclusive, blasphemous and one-sided, being well aware that theologians could argue indefinitely on a proposition without reaching any conclusions. As Councillors were neither theologians nor Biblical scholars, they would need advice. Yet merely to consult their Zwinglian preachers must expose them as biassed, with the result that the Council was strongly urged to seek counsel from as many sources as possible. That the debate should be made open to all religious opinions, and the Council seek advice from all sects, was probably the most favourable treatment the Catholic cause could reasonably expect; and Rehlinger hoped that bitter feuds among the Protestants would weaken the claim of each group to speak with divine authority. In short, he believed it to be a mistaken concept that every preacher had the right to expound his own views on religion. Such an assumption had caused the current disputes; and it was his clear conviction that the Zwinglians were largely responsible for such divisions. If the Council therefore adopted a Zwinglian-style Reformation, Rehlinger believed that, far from curing civic disunity, it would only increase it. Disunity he held to be endemic to Zwinglianism, for

15 See the defence of monopolies written by Peutinger in C. Bauer, 'Gutachten zur Monopol-frage', in *AR*, xlv (1954), pp. 16ff.
16 W. Hans, *Gutachten und Streitschriften über das jus reformandi des Rates vor und während der Einführung der offiziellen Kirchenreform in Augsburg, 1534–37* (Augsburg, 1901), p. 15.
17 St A Literalien 1534, Nachtrag 1, Nr. 21 fol. 2.

even their own pastors could not agree on what they believed: '. . . all Zwinglian preachers . . . in justification of their false and misleading doctrines cannot agree but have indeed five or six opposing and incompatible views, the one inclined to [believe] this the other that.'[18] If the Council allowed the Zwinglians to force it into making reforms, Rehlinger was clear that it must then face opposition from all Catholics and Lutherans in the city, with the result that disunity would deepen.

There were also practical considerations which made religious reform appear unwise to Rehlinger. For example, if the city took measures against its religious houses, the rights of their patrons and protectors would be so infringed that they would inevitably make reprisals. This would involve Augsburg in disputes with the Dukes of Bavaria (who were patrons of the monastery of St Ulrich), the Emperor (as patron of the convent of St Katherina), and the Bishop (as patron of St Georg, St Moritz, Hl Kreuz and St Peter).[19] Rehlinger reminded the Council that religious reform must be viewed by the Catholic powers as an attack on the Church of Rome and contrary to the terms of the general peace (*Landfriede*) and promises made to the Swabian League. These were not idle threats, for Rehlinger still believed the League to be a potent force despite talk of its demise; and many of the cathedral clergy had friends and relatives amongst the local nobility who could themselves cause difficulties for the city.

In short, Rehlinger recommended that the Council should not go back on the agreements it had made with the Emperor concerning religion. He acknowledged that there were abuses in the religious life of the city, but that these were the responsibility of a General Council of the Church. Rehlinger clearly had little faith that the old religion would be restored in Augsburg, and he ended his memorandum with a plea, unusual from the Catholic side, for religious freedom. This clearly demonstrated the weakness of the Catholic cause in the city, and Rehlinger's belief that Zwinglian religious reform was imminent. He demanded not the full restoration of the Church of Rome, but that those Catholics who chose to remain in Augsburg should not be forced to accept the Zwinglian doctrines as this could lead to violence, foreign intervention and disorder.[20]

The third memorandum was the work of the Augsburg lawyer Konrad Hel. From a patrician family, he had been employed by the Council since 1531, and had previously served on delegations negotiating for the city with the Swabian League, the Bishop of Augsburg and the Regensburg *Reichstag* of 1532. Hel was known to be a critic of the clergy and papacy, and a supporter of Luther. Nevertheless, he warned the Council that it had no authority to interfere in the affairs of the Church: 'The noble Council as the secular authority of this city of Augsburg has in no way . . . the right to act in matters concerning religion,

18 Ibid., fol. 7.
19 Ibid., fol. 10.
20 Ibid., fol. 20.

still less to plan, establish and uphold changes and new ordinances.'[21] He also reminded the Councillors that, at the meetings of the *Reichstag* in Worms, Speyer and Augsburg, they had promised not to proceed with religious reform. Although the people of Augsburg were therefore clearly exasperated with the failings of their clergy, the City Council should wait for a General Council of the Church to be held and by no means break faith with the Emperor.

Hel then proceeded, just as Peutinger and Rehlinger had done, to catalogue the disasters which must befall Augsburg if it pursued religious change. The city would be outlawed, the property of the citizenry seized and its trade routes and food supplies severed. This was the excuse which Hel believed Augsburg's jealous neighbours had long desired, for it would give them an excuse to cripple the power of the city, to plunder its merchandise and wealth, ruin the citizenry and renounce considerable debts to Augsburg financiers. He said it was no use the Council looking at the example of other cities which had adopted religious reform. For, unlike most of them, Augsburg was both a conspicuous and a tempting prize, owing not only to its wealth and size, but also to its sheer vulnerability to blockade and siege. Hel described how he believed Charles V would soon be in a position to make peace with his Turkish, French and Bavarian foes: when this was achieved, the Emperor would surely turn his attention to Augsburg which, once having lost Imperial protection and investments in Habsburg lands, would also lose all commercial prestige.[22]

For Hel, religious reform was not the means of curing divisions in civic society, as disenchanted groups of Catholics would then be forced to oppose the Council. A final comment on the reform which he had suggested, left his reader in no doubt of Hel's views:

I can give my thoughts no other interpretation but that with new ordinances and changes in our faith and religion nothing but disaster, error and every misfortune and adversity would follow for the entire city. And finally, I fear that through these events the renowned glory and honour of this city and its people would be ruined and die: devastated, cast aside and overthrown.[23]

Peutinger, Rehlinger and Hel were the three leading lawyers in Augsburg, and amongst the most respected advisers to the Council. All had unequivocally opposed any measures of reform; and Hel was a Protestant, while Peutinger hated the clergy. They were united in the belief that the Council had no legal or traditional right to interfere in religious affairs, especially where doctrinal issues were at stake, as these were the responsibility of a General Council of the Church. They were also agreed that religious reform must have dire consequences for Augsburg, forcibly explaining that economic blockade, seizure of goods, repudiation of debts, and loss of trade in Habsburg lands, would

21 St A Literalien 1534, Nachtrag 1, Nr. 18, fol. 22.
22 Ibid., fol. 34.
23 Ibid., fol. 35.

result, while the city itself would be victim to starvation and the kind of unemployment that would bring insurrection and bloodshed. In short, these lawyers maintained that Augsburg was bound by promises made to Charles V, and that to break such promises would bring the city into conflict with the Emperor.

Anyone reading these documents is left in no doubt that religious reform must place Augsburg in profound danger. It seems, however, that the Committee for Religion was caught unawares by the strength of opposition to reforming proposals, and that they were disappointed by the work of the lawyers. The memoranda were to be presented to a meeting of the small Council, probably held in early April 1533,[24] and apparently, at the last moment, the Committee asked lawyers known to be favourable to the Reformation to produce memoranda as well. For the first time, the Committee was forced to reveal the true motivation behind its actions, for it was not seeking objective advice but rather a justification for action already considered to be both desirable and inevitable.

Of the memoranda hastily commissioned by the Committee for Religion, only a small fragment of that written by Hans Hagk has survived. Hagk was a lawyer and secretary in the civic chancellory. He was to succeed Peutinger as civic secretary in 1535. Known to be a Zwinglian, in the opening paragraphs of his memorandum Hagk declared that the Emperor had no power to enforce religious practices against the commands of the Bible, and that the Council had a duty to protect religion and goodness, thus safeguarding the body and souls of its citizens.[25]

Fortunately, the memorandum by Doctor Balthasar Langnauer has survived in full, although he included an apology for the brevity of his contribution.[26] Another lawyer known to have Zwinglian views, Langnauer's memorandum adopted a religious rather than a legalistic approach to the question. He agreed that only a Council of the Church was entitled to legislate for matters of religion, and also that the debates about the Christian faith were forbidden. Nevertheless, he introduced several religious considerations which he believed outweighed legal objections. For Langnauer, the practices of the Church of Rome were contrary to what he read in Holy Scripture, and he believed that the City Council had therefore a clear duty to reform:

When one looks in the Holy Writ one finds that authority was ordained and established by God, that it should be a tool of God to remove everything contrary to His Word. As authority is named as the servant of God in the Scriptures, it wields the sword, not in vain, but as a judge to punish the wicked . . . [and], since the practices of popery are contrary to God and His Holy Word, they [the authorities] are bound to eradicate them and root them out.[27]

24 The minutes of this meeting have unfortunately not survived.
25 St A Literalien 1534, Nachtrag 1.
26 St A Literalien 1534, Nachtrag 1, Nr. 22, fol. 1.   27 Ibid., fol. 3.

Langnauer thus advocated a doctrine which held that, although the City Council had no legal right to reform the Church, it had a religious duty to reform, a duty that exceeded both loyalty to the Emperor and all legal obligations. He strongly opposed Peutinger's view that, as subjects of the Emperor, Councillors were bound to obey him; for Langnauer maintained that the Council was directly responsible to God, to whom every Councillor would ultimately have to defend his actions.[28] According to Langnauer, the Council should not rule by the laws made by men, but rather follow those ordained by God. By such measures, Langnauer was proposing that the authority of the City Council be extended beyond previously accepted limits, for his argument asserted that the Council was subject to the Emperor only in temporal matters, and that it was not bound to obey him, or any other earthly authority, if such commands conflicted with the will of God. The first loyalty of the Council should always be to God, and this gave it both the responsibility of interpreting the divine will and also the freedom to govern all its own actions without interference from any other temporal authority. 'The Almighty God bestows to your gracious worthy [Council] His Godly favour to rule to His praise and wishes.'[29] This rejected the belief that the Council had originally gained authority by the *Stadtrecht* of 1276, or that it was subject to the Emperor as the *obere oberkait*. It was a novel doctrine, for the Council had always acknowledged the Imperial allegiance. Extremist both in its treatment of religion and politics, the doctrine reflected the abnormal conditions in Augsburg and it was surprising that Langnauer escaped condemnation as being seditious, for his theories attacked the very basis of Imperial power in Germany. Such theorizing certainly removed from every lesser authority in the Empire the duty of obedience to the Emperor. For, by objecting to his laws on religious grounds, and offering virtual independence to every authority, the doctrine would inevitably lead to the erosion of Imperial power and the fragmentation of the Empire.

Langnauer also ascribed to the City Council a new and powerful role for godly magistrates who were answerable only to God, and who would base all their policies and actions on the divine will. Langnauer evidently envisaged a new organization of political life in which the Council, freed from its ties to the Emperor and the Swabian League, would expect preachers, men recruited largely in Strasbourg, to make clear to Councillors the will of God. With the spiritual welfare of the city uppermost in their mind, the Council would then legislate. It was a vision of society which showed a remarkable similarity to that later envisaged by Calvin, and which, to a considerable degree, the Swiss Reformer established in Geneva – a reflection perhaps of the importance of Calvin's Strasbourg period.

28 Ibid., fol. 4. *In handlungen des glauben Christenlich eindrungen furzunemen, des si sich gegen Gott zuthuon schuldig waist, und si getraut vor dem strengen Richter Rechnung zugeben.*
29 Ibid.

When the Council met in April 1533 to hear the various recommendations, it decided to reject the advice of Peutinger, Hel and Rehlinger, urging them not to act in favour of reform. This was an extraordinary decision. It had been proved that the Council had no authority to reform, and that its three leading advisers had produced considerable evidence to demonstrate the disastrous consequences which must inevitably befall an Augsburg committed to the Reformation. In the face of such arguments, the Council preferred to accept Langnauer's argument that it must above all fulfil its duty to God.

The Council was clear that it would prove difficult to justify religious reform; but, on the basis of memoranda from Peutinger, Hel and Rehlinger, the Councillors were at least conversant with the main arguments against the proposed changes. These were compiled into a twenty-two point document, which was then given to prominent lawyers favourable to reform and to the pastor, Wolfgang Musculus.[30] The questions fell into three categories, of which the first concerned the impact of reform on the life of the city. In this case, the Council sought answers to a number of objections, in particular the fact that if reform could silence Zwinglian sympathizers, it would simultaneously arouse the hostility of Catholic and Lutheran citizens. Likewise, there was the belief that disunity in Augsburg did not result from religious differences, so that the Council would be wise to tackle other pressing but uncontentious subjects. It had been alleged that religious changes would cause those wealthy merchants who feared reprisals from the Emperor to leave the city, and therefore result in loss of taxation; and the Council was also concerned about the vulnerability of the city's trade to an economic blockade. The Councillors wanted further views on the contentions that religious reform would promote a lack of respect for authority as well as leaving Zwinglian clergy free to mount an attack on them. Secondly, objections were raised concerning legal rights of the clergy in Augsburg, which might hinder reform and cause losses in alms and charity bound to afflict the city once the clergy were expelled. Finally, the Council wanted advice on any possibility of intervention from the Emperor, the Swabian League or Dukes Wilhelm and Ludwig of Bavaria, should reformation take place. Such a lengthy compilation by the City Council of all the arguments against reform made it clear that the Augsburg authorities by no means planned to act in haste or blindness, but rather in full knowledge of the consequences which might be the inevitable corollary of implementing religious reform.

The most important answer to the twenty-two articles came from the court secretary, *Gerichtschreiber* Franz Kötzler, a Zwinglian, who had been in the service of the city since 1507. He made it clear that he thought the issue of religious reform to be a spiritual and not a secular matter. The Council must therefore be guided in all its deliberations by Scriptural and not by worldly

30 The copy sent to Musculus has survived and is printed in full by F. Roth, loc. cit., vol. ii, pp. 140ff.

considerations: 'This affair is not a worldly one but concerns our holy faith and is a spiritual matter. You must keep before your eyes and in your heart the Holy Scriptures which are the clear Word of God which remain eternally, unaffected by worldly wisdom and cunning.'[31]

Kötzler dismissed the arguments about the expulsion of clergy as mere arguments of the flesh (*fleischlichen Argumenten*). To suggest that this would bring an end to the distribution of alms in the city and to the clergy selling corn from their estates in Augsburg was to expose the weakness of those traditionalists who could find only base motives for defending the clergy and no word of Scripture. He also questioned the importance of clerical alms-giving, claiming that priests kept most of the money for themselves in any case. It was well-known that they lived in plenty, while in recent years the poor of the city would have starved to death if the Council had not passed the Poor Law of 1522 and distributed bread in time of need.[32] Kötzler clearly rated municipal charity more highly than clerical charity, and he also urged the Council to trust in God. If the Councillors governed according to His will, then God would protect the city of Augsburg and there would be no need to worry either about food supplies or threats from Catholic rulers.[33]

To Kötzler, the clergy were a group of sinners and blasphemers: 'Now these people (the so-called clergy) should be denounced and punished by the Council through a Christian reformation, which the authorities have a Christian duty to enact.'[34] Far from harming the city, Kötzler believed that in the long term the expulsion of the clergy would be for the common good, just as, he argued, had been the case with the Jews at an earlier date. The clergy had no function in the life of the city, and Kötzler was clear that citizens would be far better off under the leadership of pious, learned and godfearing pastors.

The diplomatic power of the Roman Church also failed to impress Kötzler. He was convinced that the city need fear neither Emperor, nor *Reichstag* nor Swabian League if it only carried out godly reforms. For Augsburg would be protected by God, and he pointed to the Turkish threat to the Habsburg lands as being a measure of divine punishment for Charles, because of the Emperor's support of false religious beliefs. Kötzler also found the promises made by the Council at Speyer and Augsburg not to enact religious reform to be no barrier to reformation in the city as promises which were contrary to the Word of God and against His will could not be considered binding.[35] Himself a lawyer, Kötzler was offering the Council Scriptural justification for breaking what

31 St A Literalien 1534, Nachtrag 2, Nr. 29, fol. 2 *'Das ain E Rat gewalt hab von gott, alle auswendige Egernusse under der Germain gottes hinweg zu thun.'*
32 See Sender, 'Der Chronik von Clemens Sender', in *Die Chroniken der deutschen Städte*, vol. xxiii (Leipzig, 1894), pp. 164 and 332ff.
33 St A Literalien 1534, Nachtrag 2, Nr. 29, fol. 5.
34 Ibid., fol. 4.
35 Ibid., fol. 10

Peutinger, Hel and Rehlinger agreed to be legally binding promises. If this doctrine, like that proposed by Langnauer, was applied to all aspects of Imperial and canon law, it would give the Council the freedom to decide which laws to obey and which to disregard, always bearing in mind the subjective manner in which Scripture could be interpreted. As further justification, Kötzler found that the undertaking made by the Council in 1530 had been given under duress with the purpose of preventing Councillors from performing their religious duties. It was therefore in no way to be considered as binding.

In order to calm fears of retribution from the Emperor in the wake of any religious reform, Kötzler cited examples from other cities which had altered their religions without being punished as disturbers of the peace. This was a somewhat specious illustration since Kötzler cited examples which had occurred before the recent *Landfriede* was declared in 1532, and he wilfully misinterpreted the spirit of the peace, claiming that it would not be broken by a reform of the Church and expulsion of the clergy unless violence was used.[36] He urged the Council to proceed, claiming it had more to fear from the wrath of God than that of the Emperor. But on the issue of how to silence the clergy and what should happen to the wealth and property of the Roman Church, Kötzler remained silent.

Kötzler acknowledged the disunity in Augsburg, but held that this was only because the Council allowed false doctrines to be preached. If the Council turned to the Gospel, it would find there a source of unity. There was even an admonitory section in the memorandum, clearly marked in the margin.[37] It was specially aimed at the consciences of Councillors, for had they not appointed Protestant preachers in 1531 because they agreed with their doctrines? They must therefore have attended numerous sermons and been urged to expel the Roman religion from the city. Why then had they taken no action, even though Councillors themselves upheld such criticisms and acknowledged the evils of Catholicism? The Council, Kötzler urged, could no longer pretend to support the Protestants without taking action. If it knew the truth about Catholicism, but refused to act against it, the whole Council would stand guilty at the Day of Judgement. Such a double standard in religious affairs could no longer be justified; if the Council believed its own preachers, it had a duty to support them and correct religious abuses.

Kötzler was an ardent Zwinglian, and aimed to convince the Council to act at once. The mainstay of his argument was a Biblicism which he believed outweighed any other authority and provided ample justification for the Council to reform even despite its earlier promises not to take action. He believed that the Council, owing its authority to God, was answerable directly to God as the guardian and protector of souls in the city. His political thought certainly owed

36 Ibid., fol. 19.
37 Ibid., fol. 12.

more to the Swiss tradition, where each city could determine its own policies, than to the tradition of the free Imperial cities which, although self-governing, were subject to the Emperor. For the very real concern over the city's food supply and trade routes, Kötzler had no answer, and this was the weak point of his case. Augsburg had to rely on the cooperation of its neighbours for its very survival, and Kötzler's recommendation to trust in God was but small comfort to a city facing starvation and economic ruin.

Apart from its own lawyers, the Council also invited Doctor Franciscus Frosch, the eminent Strasbourg lawyer, for his views. Frosch agreed with Kötzler that the Council was justified in breaking any laws and promises if these were contrary to the will of God; but he elaborated by describing how the Emperor had passed legislation concerning religion and gave it as his opinion that the Council should follow the example of the Emperor and pass any legislation it thought necessary to protect the souls of citizens God had entrusted to its care.[38] Frosch claimed that every government had the power and duty to regulate religion within its own territories, as long as such legislation was based on the Bible. He also provided two reasons that effectively released the Council of its promises to the Emperor, the first being, '. . . that it is held by all scholars of the law that one is bound to keep one's oath when the soul is not damaged by so doing. When the soul would be damaged the oath is not binding.' And secondly, Frosch held that, as the Emperor had not kept his promise (given at the Augsburg *Reichstag* in 1530) to call a General Council of the Church within six months, he could not expect to hold the Council to its undertaking.

The Council also requested the views of the most influential pastor in Augsburg, Wolfgang Musculus, and his answers to fifteen of the points have survived.[39] It is of interest that the answers to the last seven sections (which dealt with the city's relationship with the Emperor) have been torn away, either by a friend attempting at a later date to protect Musculus, or by an enemy eager for evidence of his disloyalty. In the majority of his answers, Musculus echoed opinions in the other memoranda presented to the Council, which Musculus indicated he had read. In his answer to the proposition that, once the Catholic clergy were expelled, the pastors would turn their attacks against the Council, Musculus offered an important concession and asserted that the Council had no cause to fear, for once Augsburg was Protestant, the authorities could regulate the pastors. Protestant ministers could, in short, be placed under a contract which exactly specified their rights and duties. '[*Die*] *Prädikanten kann man durch eine Bestallung und genaue Festsetzung ihrer Rechte und Pflichten hintanhalten.*'[40] This must have weighed heavily with the Council then desperately trying to win back control of the religious life in the city which it had lost to the

---

38 St A Literalien 1534 (dated 1533).
39 This document is printed in full in F. Roth, loc. cit., vol. ii, pp. 140ff.
40 Ibid., p. 141.

pastors and their supporters. These pastors, which the Council had originally appointed in 1531 in an effort to placate the populace of the city, had adopted an increasingly independent role and were using widespread popular support to force the Council to adopt religious reforms. Their enemies claimed, with some justification, that the pastors deliberately inflamed the populace with anti-Catholic sermons to the point where, if the Council would not agree to their demands, disorder was unavoidable.[41] Fearing the reaction of the populace, the Council was unable to silence the pastors. Yet the situation where policies originated from the pulpit rather than from the Council-chamber was seriously damaging authority in the city, and the Councillors were anxious to remove the powerful role the Pastorate had assumed. With this experience in mind, the Council was likely to obstruct any trend towards theocracy; yet Musculus apparently offered a compromise, for if the Council agreed to the demands of the preachers to establish the 'new religion' as the sole Church in Augsburg, they in return would accept the restraints and obligations of a formal contract with the authorities.

The decision to proceed with religious reform had been taken by the Council in mid-1533, but, with the warnings of Peutinger, Hel and Rehlinger resounding in their ears, the authorities procrastinated in the hope of finding some propitious moment to act. The disbanding of the Swabian League in February 1534 removed some of the dangers for the Councillors, but they continued to hesitate until July 1534, when an urgent letter was sent to the mayor, Hieronymus Imhof, absent in Nuremberg, ordering him to return to the city, as public order could not be maintained unless there was an immediate response to the demand for religious reform.[42] At last, in July, the Council passed a measure containing a number of reforms: many Catholic churches were closed for worship, all preaching of the 'old religion' was to cease, and the property of parish churches and monasteries was placed in the control of lay administrators (*Zechpfleger*). In the few Catholic churches which remained open, celebration of the Roman Mass was permitted.

Such reforms had never been desired by the Council which, until 1533, had been committed to its policy of pursuing a middle course in religion. Yet because of continual threats by both pastors and people, it was seen that reform must come to the city. In short, fearful that protests might at any time develop into violent insurrection, foreign troops were brought into the city in the summer of 1533 by a Council attempting to preserve law and order. This could only be a temporary expedient, and when demands for reform showed no signs of diminishing, the authorities acknowledged that they must be met if permanent civic peace were to be ensured.

The Council had, however, no intention of being rushed into change, as the

41 W. Germann, *D. Johann Forster der hennebergische Reformator* (1894), pp. 79ff.
42 St A Literalien 7 July 1534.

commissioning of the various memoranda demonstrated. In fact, the instructions for those documents clearly indicate what the Council considered to be its major problems and it was on these topics that discussion and comment was invited. The instructions reveal that the main concerns of the Council were not with the doctrinal, but with the legal aspects of reform – not to mention the political and economic results of breaking faith with the Emperor and the Catholic Church. The memoranda themselves provided copious evidence of the consequences of religious reform for Augsburg, and they prove that the Council did not proceed with reform blindly, but only after considerable consultation and deliberation, and with some foreknowledge of what the social, political and economic consequences were likely to be. The Council identified and assessed the forces for both change and conservatism which were dividing civic society, and after much discussion it decided that it had no choice but to accede to the demand for change.

This was a remarkable choice, for the arguments against reform were powerful, and the undeniable truths which they contained made the Council hesitate until July 1534 before taking any real action. Reform amounted to economic and political suicide, a threat which became tragic reality for the citizens of Augsburg in 1548. Yet the Council agreed to such a policy, with only the promise of winning God's favour for the city against the barrage of retaliation it expected from its neighbours. In the event, Councillors were forced to act against their better judgement, and to reject the advice they had solicited from most trusted servants in order to pass legislation restricting Catholic worship in the city. They did so, not because their Council was dedicated to the Protestant cause, nor yet because they believed religious reform would best serve the long-term interests of Augsburg. They went ahead solely to maintain their authority as a Council and prevent the popular rebellion of their own citizenry.

V

Protestant Monastery?
A Reformation Hospital in Hesse

H. C. ERIK MIDELFORT

Historians often seem to assume that the Protestant Reformation hit Europe like a mind-altering drug, transforming old attitudes and practices beyond recognition. Only a few scholars have followed the example of E. W. Zeeden in looking for lingering remnants of Catholicism behind a Protestant façade.[1] Thus, even in the creation of institutions as thoroughly medieval as hospitals, the usual emphasis is on what was new, progressive and Protestant about the actions of the Lutheran princes of sixteenth-century Germany. In this essay for Professor A. G. Dickens, I propose to look at the Protestant territory of Hesse, which became famous for its newly 'Protestant' social-welfare system and especially for its hospitals, which thrived and were slowly converted into infirmaries almost exclusively for the mentally deficient and mentally ill.[2] In the hospital established at Haina, for example, the historian can observe with unusual precision the process by which an important Cistercian monastery was converted into a major Protestant hospital.

The hereditary ruler of the landgraviate of Hesse was Philipp, son of William II and Anna of Mecklenburg. Born in 1504, he lost his father in 1509 and grew up under the influence of a greedy, ruthless, energetic mother.[3] At the age of fourteen, Philipp was declared old enough to rule Hesse without a regent. No one suspected in 1518 that the young ruler of this territory, which stretched from Kassel in the north to Darmstadt south of Frankfurt, would become the single most zealous and effective secular proponent of Reformation, a prince without whom the Reformation is scarcely conceivable.[4] As a youth, his religious concerns, to the extent that they are at all discernible, were thoroughly superficial and conventional. In 1521 Philipp met Luther at the Diet of Worms, but failed to take sides on the issue then beginning to divide Europe. In 1522 an

1 E. W. Zeeden, *Katholische Überlieferungen in den lutherischen Kirchenordnungen des 16. Jahrhunderts* (Münster, 1959).
2 On the welfare system in Hesse, see William J. Wright, 'Reformation Contributions to the Development of Public Welfare Policy in Hesse', *Journal of Modern History*, 49 (1977), D1145. In general, see David B. Miller, 'The Dissolution of the Religious Houses of Hesse during the Reformation' (unpublished Ph.D. dissertation, Yale University, 1971); and John C. Stalnaker, 'The Emergence of the Protestant Clergy in Central Germany: The Case of Hesse' (unpublished Ph.D. dissertation, University of California at Berkeley, 1970). See also Paul Holthausen, *Das Landeshospital Haina in Hessen, eine Stiftung Landgraf Philipps des Grossmütigen, von 1527–1907* (Frankenberg i. H., 1907), p. 15.
3 Gustav Freiherr Schenk zu Schweinsberg, 'Aus der Jugendzeit Landgraf Philipps des Grossmütigen', in *Philipp der Grossmütige. Beiträge zur Geschichte seines Lebens und seiner Zeit*, ed. by the Historischer Verein für das Grossherzogtum Hessen (Marburg, 1904), pp. 73–143; H. Stutte, 'Landgraf Philipp der Grossmütige von Hessen aus medizinischer Sicht', *Hessisches Ärzteblatt*, 30 (1969), pp. 1085–97.
4 Hans J. Hillerbrand, *Landgrave Philipp of Hesse, 1504–1567: Religion and Politics in the Reformation* (Reformation Essays and Studies, no. 1; St Louis, 1967), p. 37. Hillerbrand's short essay is the only general study of Philipp available in English.

observer reported that Philipp 'wants to remain in the faith in which he was born and raised until his papal holiness, his Roman imperial majesty, together with the Christian kings, spiritual and secular electors and princes, and the estates of holy Christendom decide on another or a better one.'[5] Until 1524 Philipp was content to let others decide, but in the summer of that year a meeting with Melanchthon brought about his conversion to the Lutheran cause. In 1523, it was therefore as a conventional Catholic prince, concerned for the welfare of his Catholic territory, that Philipp attempted to reform the Cistercian monastery at Haina.

Monks had lived in Haina, about 25 km north of Marburg, since the early thirteenth century, erecting there one of the most significant early Gothic churches in Germany. A venerable Protestant tradition has it that the monasteries, though well-run and orderly at first, fell progressively deeper and deeper into corruption, reaching a nadir in the late Middle Ages. This picture is almost always overdrawn, and when he reads in the first Protestant history of Haina that by the beginning of the sixteenth century the monks were godless, lazy, drunken voluptuaries, dedicated to *impietas, luxuria, superbia, discordia*, the modern reader may be forgiven for diagnosing an overdose of Protestant bias.[6] With accusations such as these it is usually difficult to separate fact from bias, but in the case of Haina there are fairly good records dealing with the monastery before the Reformation. These records enable scholars to see that, even if the Protestant charges of corruption were one-sided and biassed, there were nevertheless staunch Catholics who agreed that Haina fell far short of the monastic ideal. In 1508, for example, an ecclesiastical visitation report complained that there was too much drinking at Haina, too much mixing with the laity, too many violations of the ideal of cloistered isolation, and a generally too relaxed attitude towards the seriousness of divine services.[7] On 22 March 1523 Philipp of Hesse certainly confirmed it as his duty to protect the monastery of Haina on the specific condition that it return to a 'spiritual, reformed life'.[8] In September of that same year Philipp complained to the abbot and monks of Haina that he still heard reports of many visitors and guests in the monastery whose meetings disturbed divine services. Giving refuge to a few lone travellers was appropriate, he concluded, but Haina must stop being a hotel.[9]

After Philipp turned to the Gospel as expounded in Wittenberg, his desire

5 Cited Ibid., pp. 3–4.
6 Johann Letzener, *Historische, kurtze, einfaltige und ordentliche Beschreibung des Closters und Hospitals zu Haina in Hessen gelegen. Auffs newe übersehen und verbessert* (Mühlhausen, 1588), Sig. G2r.
7 Eckhart G. Franz (ed.), *Kloster Haina. Regesten und Urkunden*, vol. ii (1300–1560), erste Hälfte: Regesten [Veröffentlichungen der Historischen Kommission für Hessen und Waldeck. 9: Klosterarchive; vol. vi] (Marburg, 1970), pp. 515–16.
8 Ibid., p. 556.
9 Ibid., p. 557.

to see the monastery at Haina reformed merged with the more general questions of the secular control of morals and of Church property.[10] Already in 1524 Philipp had promulgated a Hessian *Polizeiordnung* for the control of immorality, and especially drunkenness. In 1526, taking advantage of the decree of the Diet of Speyer, which granted territories the responsibility for religion, Philipp held an assembly of secular and ecclesiastical officials at Homberg. This 'synod' recommended sweeping legal changes, including the abolition of monasticism in Hesse, the confiscation of monastic property, and the use of monastic buildings and revenues for such public purposes as schools.[11] Spurned by Luther as a 'pile of laws', the ordinances of the Homberg synod were never put into effect, but reflected an early inclination to put monastic property to common use.[12] In February 1527 Philipp ordered an inventory of all Hessian monasteries (about fifty in all) with a view to sequestering them. By mid-December the inventory and sequestration were formally complete, but some monasteries clung resolutely to the hope that Imperial courts might reverse what seemed to them to be a gross invasion of their rights. Probably the single most dramatic instance of resistance was the long and ultimately futile suit of the abbots of Haina in the *Reichskammergericht*.[13] As the process of secularization went forward, therefore, Philipp was under steady pressure to find grounds that might justify such novel measures.

Curiously enough, Philipp and his government took refuge in a monastic ethic in order to defeat the monasteries. He accused the regular religious orders of selfishness, and claimed that his Reformation would foster a true Christian communalism. As the territorial estates concluded in October 1527, monastic property 'should serve the common weal'[14] The only immorality was selfishness (*Eigennutz*). Philipp appointed reformers who continued to emphasize the kinds of public tasks to which the selfish monasteries could be put. As a result, most of the secularized Church property did in fact go for charitable or educational purposes, including the founding of Marburg's university in 1527. One recent estimate concludes that about 60% of secularized monastic revenues went for charitable purposes, while 40% found its way to the court and the central administration.[15]

10 See Miller, 'The Dissolution' (above, note 2), and Walter Sohm, *Territorium und Reformation in der hessischen Geschichte* (Marburg, 1957), pp. 19–20. [Günther Franz (ed.), *Urkundliche Quellen zur hessischen Reformationsgeschichte* vol. i].
11 Karl August Credner (ed.), *Philipps des Grossmütigen Hessische Kirchenreformations-Ordnung* (Giessen, 1852), pp. 46–7, 108–10.
12 Sohm, *Terriutorium und Reformation*, p. 28. Electoral Saxony began to sequester its monasteries only in 1531. For the legal questions, see Hans Lehnert, *Kirchengut und Reformation. Eine Kirchenrechtliche Studie* [Erlanger Abhandlungen zur mittleren und neueren Geschichte vol. xx] (Erlangen, 1935).
13 For the documents in this long case see Eckhart G. Franz, *Kloster Haina* (above, note 7).
14 Sohm, *Territorium und Reformation*, p. 40.
15 Karl E. Demandt, *Geschichte des Landes Hessen*, 2nd edn (Kassel, 1972), pp. 226–7.

To give the impression that he was merely applying a monastic (Christian communal) ethic to the monasteries, Philipp had to be careful to avoid the appearance of force. Thus, as early as October 1525, Philipp advised the margraves of Brandenburg to allow monks to return to monasteries abandoned during the Peasants' War a few months earlier, and to let them live out their lives there unless some other purpose were found for the monasteries.[16] In Hesse, Philipp and his agents proceeded as if they were merely reforming the monasteries, returning them to their original purposes.[17] Officials arrived at each monastery and tried to persuade the monks (or nuns) that Luther's interpretation of the Gospel was correct, that the Roman mass was a form of idolatry, and that monasticism, as currently practised, was a selfish form of arrogance. Usually the officials then ordered the abolition of the mass and offered settlements to those monks or nuns who wished to renounce their vocation. Those who wished to stay on in the monastery were usually allowed to do so if they willingly conformed to the new dispensation. Abbot Dithmar von Wetter of Haina complained in 1530 that such procedures amounted to force; but Philipp responded blandly that 'on the basis of evangelical preaching the greater part of Haina's monks asked for settlements', which, of course, he could by no means refuse. It was true, he said, that the abbot and three or four brothers had left without his knowledge; but Philipp insisted that he had forced no one.[18] Of the thirty-six monks and lay brothers at Haina in 1527, thirty-two accepted settlements.[19] Four years passed before Philipp took advantage of the abandoned monastery. During March 1531 Philipp began to speak regularly of his plans to convert the monastery at Haina, together with the Augustinian canonry at Merxhausen, into hospitals for the rural poor.[20] On 26 August 1533 he founded these two hospitals.[21] It is not clear how long he had harboured such plans, but there were a number of compelling reasons for creating hospitals. First, in purely emotional terms, may well have been Philipp's sense that he stood in a long tradition of princes who had tried to aid the poor, stretching back to his most famous ancestor, St Elisabeth, a woman who had worn herself out in acts of charity three hundred years earlier, and whose pilgrimage church in Marburg constituted the first fully Gothic church on German soil.[22] Even more compelling

16 Günther Franz, *Urkundliche Quellen zur hessischen Reformationsgeschichte*, vol. ii: 1525–47 (Marburg, 1954), p. 12, doc. 11.
17 F. W. Schäfer, 'Adam Krafft, der Reformator Hessens', *Archiv für hessische Geschichte und Altertumskunde*, N. F. 8 (1912), pp. 1–46, 67–110, at p. 85.
18 Eckhart G. Franz, *Kloster Haina* (above, note 7), vol. ii, p. 620.   19 Ibid., pp. 575–8.
20 Ibid., pp. 621–2. It is not clear what basis Holthausen had for claiming that Haina became a hospital in 1527 or 1528: *Landeshospital Haina* (above, note 2), pp. 6–7.
21 The act of foundation is printed in Günther Franz, *Urkundliche Quellen* (above, note 16), vol. ii, p. 183.
22 Wilhelm Maurer, 'Die heilige Elisabeth und ihr Marburger Hospital', in *Kirche und Geschichte. Gesammelte Aufsätze*, vol. ii: E. W. Kohls and G. Muller (eds), *Beiträge zu Grundsatzfragen und zur Frömmigkeitsgeschichte* (Göttingen, 1970), pp. 284–319. See also 'Zum Verständnis der heiligen Elisabeth von Thüringen', Ibid., pp. 231–83.

may have been his awareness of the needs of the rural folk of Hesse. Princes did not live so far from the smells of the village or the cries of country people that they could easily remain oblivious to the needs of the elderly poor. There are cases from the later sixteenth century of the landgrave himself examining the needs of a poor man when stopped on the road. And what was plain enough to any prince who would learn was that, although most towns had hospitals to serve as nursing homes for their elderly poor, the countryside had none.[23] Finally, Philipp was naturally aware that his claims to Haina, and to the other secularized monasteries, would be strengthened if he could create from some of them institutions that were so clearly Christian that monks wishing to recapture them for the Catholic faith would be placed in an impossible moral position.

This last motive seems to relate to a favourite pious legend concerned with the founding of Haina hospital. When the outraged abbot of Haina took his case to court, he is said to have received not only the support of the archbishop of Mainz, but that of the Pope as well. These powerful men secured a hearing before the Emperor Charles V, who is said to have decided to send a team of investigators to Haina. The earliest Protestant history of Haina (1588) praised Charles's caution in this matter, and noted that Philipp moved swiftly to convert Haina into a hospital, and to fill it with 'poor people, and the blind, lame, dumb, deaf, foolish, lunatic, mad, possessed, deformed, leprous, and similar sorts of afflicted people.'[24] When the investigators arrived in Haina, the superintendent of the hospital, Heinz von Lüder, is said to have lined up all the unfortunate patients of the new hospital, and to have asked whether the imperial officials intended to expel them and to bring back proud, gluttonous, useless monks. The demonstration apparently had the desired effect.[25]

I have found no mention of such an Imperial visitation to Haina in the contemporary local records, but this is not to state that the pious story is completely false. During the late 1540s, after Charles V had crushed the Schmalkaldic League in battle, fears ran through the Hessian administration that its defeat would mean the restoration of the monasteries to Catholic control. On 7 October 1548, for example, the hospital superintendent and military captain, Heinz von Lüder, wrote to Lieutenant Rudolf Schenck zu Schweinsberg in Kassel, that Haina had two hundred 'poor propertyless men from Hesse', of whom over thirty were 'born fools and blind men', and ten were 'mad men kept under lock and key'. In fact, it took fifty persons to care for these unfortunates.

Now before we bend to the claims of three complaining monks and destroy this

23 Helmut Siefert, 'Kloster und Hospital Haina. Eine medizinhistorische Skizze', *Hessisches Ärzteblatt*, 32 (1971), pp. 963–83.
24 Letzner, *Historische . . . Beschreibung* (above, note 6), fol. G3ᵛ. The careful sketch by Siefert assumes too easily the reliability of this story.
25 Ibid., fols G4ʳ–H1ʳ.

Christian work, so useful to our land, we ought to receive those three into the hospital and up to twenty more and let them live as monks if they will help with caring for the poor and not insist on governing, especially since some eight former monks are already living there.[26]

So, the threat of Catholic takeover seemed real enough. Later in the same month von Lüder warned repeatedly that if the abbot of Haina were to appear in Haina with an Imperial mandate, there would be no way of refusing him entry. The professors and rector of the new university were similarly threatened by attempts to restore the abbot. In fact, early in 1549 Charles did go so far as to order the return of Haina to its rightful abbot.[27] In the long, drawn-out negotiations that followed, Hessian officials insisted that since Haina was not being used for private purposes, Charles should leave the hospital and university alone. The Emperor remained unconvinced, but Hesse succeeded in stalling until 1552, when Charles's political defeat turned the tables. Actually, the abbots of Haina pursued their hopeless case in imperial courts until 1558.[28] In all of these proceedings there is no mention of Heinz von Lüder's mustering of the patients before the Imperial investigators, but there is no question that the Hessian officials spent years lining them up before Charles's mental eye. To that extent, the pious legend has preserved an important fact. A basic reason for the survival of the hospital was that it was able plausibly to fulfil certain Christian (or monastic?) functions more perfectly than the Cistercians who had lived there until 1527. The abbot might have grumbled that Philipp's actions were 'an open affront to natural, divine, and written law, even if they are "perfumed with the appearance of God's Word" '.[29] But that was only to be expected of a man in his position.

Legally, therefore, Philipp had won the right to establish hospitals. Eventually he created four territorial hospitals for destitute country people, at Haina and Gronau for men, and at Merxhausen and Hofheim for women, places well distributed throughout his lands.[30] For a better understanding of these hospitals the historian must examine the regulations which governed them, and determine, if possible, the actual daily conditions there. The hospital founded at Haina has remarkable records that permit careful scrutiny of both questions.

In the first ordinance for the hospital at Haina, the unknown author laid down basic guidelines that were to govern life there for the next couple of centuries. The hospital was to take in up to a hundred poor men from the countryside;

26 Eckhart G. Franz, *Kloster Haina* (above, note 7), p. 657.
27 Ibid., p. 658.
28 Ibid., pp. 658–72.
29 Ibid., p. 641.
30 Haina was in Oberhessen (near Marburg), Merxhausen in Niederhessen (near Kassel), Hofheim in the Obergrafschaft Katzenelnbogen (near Darmstadt), and Gronau in the Niedergrafschaft Katzenelnbogen (near Rheinfels).

town dwellers were explicitly excluded, and there was no provision for married couples. Patients were to be admitted solely on grounds of poverty and need, and not in return for money, favours or friendship. A 'brother' was also supposed to be at least sixty years of age 'unless he is so feeble that he is useless and could not otherwise work to earn his bread.'[31] These were the admission requirements for a nursing home, rather than a hospital. The former monastery was also to continue to display a strictly Christian character, accepting only those of good Christian character and maintaining a holy style of life appropriate to the Christian alms which supported the foundation. It is sometimes thought that the Protestant Reformation broke with the ethic of alms-giving, establishing community chests instead. While much of this may be true in general, the Hessian hospital regulations refer repeatedly to alms as the moral basis of the hospitals, a basis which demanded a high level throughout the institution.

The ordinance proceeded to prescribe a semi-monastic life of celibacy and regular prayer, work and instruction for the hospital's inhabitants. Those 'brethren' who could still move about were to awaken together at the sound of a bell, and spend half an hour washing, combing their hair, and dressing 'so that they do not live like pigs in a pen'. Nor should they remain in bed once awake, 'for then the devil is not far, and he tempts the flesh. He scratches and rubs, and by much touching of the limbs of the body brings a man to luxury and to horrible sins, which occur as Paul says "in chambering and wantonness" [Romans 13:13].'[32] After half an hour, at the sound of the bell, the brethren were to gather for prayers in the church, at 5 a.m. during the summer, or in the large heated day rooms at 7 a.m. during the winter. There they were to be taught to thank the God who had watched over them in the night. The preacher was to follow with a short lesson from the *Catechism*, and prayers for the peace and welfare of the prince, the governor of the hospital, and the needs of Christendom. Taking the poor memory of old men into account, the pastor was never to let this divine service exceed half an hour.

Having first sought the kingdom of God, the residents were then ready to turn to various sorts of light work. The point was not to extract profit from the aged, but 'to avoid laziness' by making baskets or brooms, tidying up, working in the garden, splitting wood, watering the meadow, 'not for the great usefulness of such work but so as not through idleness to give the devil room'.[33] Those residents who were too ill to attend morning prayers could expect a visit from the pastor, who would repeat his lessons 'in order that these people too as they leave this world may be prepared and sent to their Father. And it would be good if every day the sick could hear some words of comfort, if short and full of

---

31 Günther Franz, *Urkundliche Quellen* (above, note 16), vol. ii, p. 190. Franz prints most of the ordinance, which he dates after 29 April 1534, on pp. 189–97.
32 Ibid., p. 190.
33 Ibid., p. 191.

consolation, so that they might be cheerful and undismayed by death and eager for eternal life.'[34]

While the able-bodied were working and the sick were praying, the first meal of the day was being prepared, the tables set with bread and drink: 'For these two things are almost the most important in the hospital: (1) that one supervise the kitchen to assure that everything is clean, useful, well cooked, and faithfully given to the poor [brethren], and (2) that the poor are visited daily that they do not remain unconsoled.'[35] Even hardened sceptics of the twentieth century may be struck by the quiet humanity of such ideals.

About 9 a.m., when they came together to eat, the brethren were to wash, sit down and pray. During the morning meal someone was to read aloud from the New Testament (but not from the Book of the Revelation). At the evening meal the reading was always to be taken from Luther's *Catechism*, for newcomers had need of formal instruction. The ordinance suggested that hospital officials eat at some other time so that they could supervise meals and ensure that everyone was well served. Meat, fish and cheese were to be available in bowls large enough for four men to use; and cooks had thus to cut such foods into four so that the men would 'have no cause of discord, since some of them have learned no table manners.'[36] After the meal and a prayer of thanks, the men were to have about an hour free to make their beds, tidy up, or rest. It was then back to work until 1 p.m. when there was a lunch of beer, bread and cheese. After this break there was more work for each according to his ability, until the evening meal at about 4 or 5 p.m. After supper the men might rest before going to bed at a set hour.

After prescribing a diet with adequate meat, fish and vegetables, the ordinances went on to forbid the brethren access to the nearby village without good reason, for otherwise trouble and rumours could spread.

The Lord's Supper was to be observed monthly, preferably on one of the holidays of the Church's year. Brethren who felt unworthy to receive the body and blood of Christ were to be excused, and those who felt a special need for the sacrament between these regular celebrations should be accommodated. Before anyone was permitted to take the Lord's Supper, however, he had to go before the hospital pastor to give an account of his faith, life, sins and conscience, and to repeat parts of the *Catechism*. The pastor might spend the evenings of an entire week examining members of his congregation in this way, for 'Whoever does not know his ten commandments, creed, Lord's prayer, etc., should not be admitted to the sacrament until he learns them, for they are established for Christians. And if he doesn't know about Christ, how can he be called a Christian or be one?'[37] Those with weak consciences might be strengthened with

34 Ibid.   35 Ibid.
36 Ibid., p. 192.
37 Ibid., p. 193.

absolution; and the hard-hearted had to be braced with God's law. Thus, brought to a knowledge of their sins, they would become capable of receiving the Gospel. Those brethren who could sing were to be taught psalms and prayers from the Wittenberg Order, which they might sing in church and before the evening meal. 'But be sure to take enough time in this task, for old people learn slowly.'[38]

To keep this religious community well-ordered, the ordinance emphasized the importance of finding an upright, godfearing man as governor (*Spitals-meister*). This man, who was regularly described in religious language as *Pater*, could be married or single; but if married, he must have no children. He must agree to spend the rest of his days in the hospital with a privileged provision that he could himself retire there. At his death, any estate was to go to the hospital. After describing his daily duties, the ordinance laid stress on maintaining Christian unity and order. Hospital servants too were to avoid all argument and discord, for 'a kingdom divided against itself cannot stand.' And, of course, harmony depended on constant prayer to God, 'for where man is, there is the devil also, the enemy of all men.'[39]

The hospital made no provision for medical care, for men assumed that sickness was the last stop before death. It is not surprising, therefore, that the hospital ordinance placed its heaviest stress on religion, and on the importance of finding a full-time pastor 'who will preach at least one sermon a day, will visit the poor in their sicknesses, comforting them with the Holy Scriptures; at table, if there is no other reader present, he should read to the men something edifying from the Bible and also teach the people Christian behaviour and what they need to know as Christians'.[40] Clearly, as a kind of Protestant monastery, the hospital offered mainly spiritual medicines mixed with proper food and work.[41] Superintendent Reinhard Schenck repeated this ideal in his revised ordinance of 1573, when he recommended that 'those smitten with illness should not be left alone but should be brought to the common rooms, visited by the pastor, comforted with God's Word, and refreshed with special drinks and light foods.'[42]

A lengthy section of the ordinance regulated the jurisdiction, buildings, forests, agriculture and financial affairs of the hospital, for the revenues to support the new establishments continued to be the seigneurial dues, tithes and rents collected from the former monastic lands. As in the period before 1527, a pious gatekeeper was deemed necessary, a man who would open the hospital

38 Ibid., p. 194.
39 Ibid., p. 194-5.
40 Ibid., p. 195.
41 See the perceptive remarks of Johann Jürgen Rohde, *Soziologie des Krankenhauses. Zur Einführung in die Soziologie der Medizin* (Stuttgart, 1962), pp. 65-9.
42 Staatsarchiv Marburg 40a XXIV generalia 2; Reinhard Schenk zu Schweinsberg, 'Ordnung wie sich ein jeder Ampts Diener im Hospitall Heina in seinem Ampt verhalten soll (1573)'. This archive will hereafter be referred to as StAM.

to the outside world at 4 a.m. in the summer (6 a.m. in the winter) and close up at 8 p.m. in the summer (7 p.m. in winter). It was his constant duty to control those who came and went.[43] One of the gatekeeper's tasks reflects clearly the monastic framework of its origins. A clause near the end of the ordinance considers pilgrims, strangers and other poor wayfarers and ruled that, if they asked in the name of God for refuge, they should not be denied food, drink and a room in the guest house by the gate; but, no doubt with an eye on monastic abuse, the regulations limited such hospitality to 'one night and no longer'. If poor servants, widows and orphans living in the nearby villages came to beg for alms, they too should be given grain or other food, but only after it was clear that they were truly needy and worthy.[44] Here again the monastic ethic evidently lived on in the heart of a 'Protestant' institution.

This then was the original ideal outline of life at Haina. The three other territorial hospitals founded by Philipp followed this model, making changes only where necessary. At Merxhausen, for example, because the residents were mostly women, the jobs at which they worked were sewing, knitting, crocheting, and other sorts of 'women's work'. Interestingly, the Merxhausen regulations omitted all reference to the dangers of luxuriously lingering in bed, but they went on in much more detail about the evils of arguing, cursing, envying, grousing, and gossiping. The women at Merxhausen were likewise explicitly told to sit at table in orderly fashion without clambering over one another, and during prayers they were strictly warned to remain silent.[45]

The rules determining conduct in the hospital spotlight the ideals at Haina, but what was life there really like? One source of help to the historian in this matter is the laudatory Protestant history by the Lutheran pastor of Leuthorst, Johann Letzener. Published in 1588, this was dedicated to the 'Christian Brethren of Poor Lazarus at Haina in Hesse'. Letzener takes his reader on a tour of Haina, examining first the buildings that survived from the monastery. He includes the ambulatory with its many refectory rooms and chapter house; the dormitory with its easy access to the choir of the church; the infirmary; the guest house; the wash house; the kitchen house with piped water; the granary with its mill and bakery where thirty-two Malters (366 bushels or 133 hectolitres) of grain were ground and baked weekly; the saw mill; the brewery with huge stone vats larger than those found in towns or princely palaces; the dairy, stalls, barns, hoghouse, sheep-house, implements shed; and the buildings that housed the various craftsmen who served both the old and new foundation. He mentions the shoemaker, tailor, linen weaver, cloth maker, *Lober*, smith, cabinet-workers,

43 Since Günther Franz did not reprint this section of the ordinance, one must still consult the MS, 'Hainaer Hospitals-Ordnung', in StAM 40a XXIV generalia 2 (Hess. Kammer), 11 fols, at fol. 8ʳ.
44 Günther Franz, *Urkundliche Quellen* (above, note 16), vol. ii, p. 196.
45 'Hospitals-Fundation', StAM 40a XXIV generalia 2, 10 fols, at fols 2ʳ and 4ʳ.

latheman, carpenter, wagoners; and the houses of various hospital officials like the pastor, schoolmaster, treasurer, governor, chief of the kitchen, chief of clothing distribution; and even a house built by the landgrave for his own occasional visits. By far the most conspicuous building, visible for miles in the rolling Kellerwald valley of the Wohra, was of course the early Gothic church, built with a Cistercian simplicity and lacking even the modest steeple it has today. Letzener praised it as the finest monastic church he had ever seen.[46]

Most of these outbuildings served the hospital just as they had served the monastery. The largest rooms (*Brüderstube*) of the old monastery itself were used by those brethren who could still walk and do various kinds of work. Another room was reserved for helpless old men and for the blind and epileptic. Unlike the able-bodied, who sat down four men to a bowl, each man in the second room received his own bowl of food. A third room included the bedridden and diseased and was called the infirmary (*Krankenstube*). Here the men were fed by two servants. In a fourth room, known as the 'vault', were to be found 'several mad and lunatic persons, lying in chains; and also several dumb, deaf, and clumsy (*ungeschickt* – retarded?) poor people, for whom special caretakers are appointed.'[47]

A fifth room contained 'eighteen massively strong cells under which flows a stream which removes all waste and excrement. And they have three iron ovens placed next to each other so that the poor raving people who lie locked in these boxes may be kept warm.'[48] Special custodians were also appointed for this department. Their job was to care for dangerously mad people day and night. Situated above these five rooms was a laundry where eight women daily washed shirts, linen and bedding for hospital residents. In addition to the five 'wards' here described, Letzener also mentions a sixth, a *leprosarium* for eighteen men, who lived separately, ate separately, and had their own place in church, their own path to church, and their own laundry with three women assigned to it.

From Letzener's detailed account it appears that the hospital had found it necessary to add at least a couple of new buildings since 1534.[49] The 'vault' may be the new 'block house' mentioned in some sixteenth-century records. In Karl Wilhelm Justi's account of 1803 this building had a stone-ground floor with living quarters for the custodian and small rooms only five feet high and eight feet long. In his day the upper floors were made of wood and held 'the more reasonable, sometimes only melancholy patients'.[50] It is not clear if the

46 Letzener, *Historische . . . Beschreibung* (above, note 6), chapters 4 and 5.
47 Ibid., fol. J3ʳ.
48 Ibid.
49 Holthausen, *Landeshospital Haina* (above, note 2), pp. 12, 21–32. Carl Wickel, *Gründung und Beschreibung des Zisterzienser-Klosters Haina in Hessen, sowie einiges aus der Geschichte des Klosters und der Anstalt.* 2nd edn (Frankenberg, 1929), has a useful survey of former buildings at Haina.
50 Karl Wilhelm Justi, *Das Hospital zu Haina. Versuch einer Darstellung seiner ehemaligen und gegenwärtigen Beschaffenheit* (Marburg, 1803), p. 20.

eighteen cages were in this building, nor is it known exactly where the *leprosarium* stood or when it was built. It may have been a monastic structure.[51]

In Letzener's day the pastor, Johannes Pinactus, preached twice on Sundays, once on Wednesday, and also on Friday. On the other days of the week he held only morning and evening prayers. Letzener considered him a worthy servant of the Lord, struggling valiantly against the grossest vices. He employed a sexton to ring the bell, that regular punctuation of daily routine. As can be seen from Letzener's list of chief officers, by the 1580s a schoolmaster was employed to teach young orphaned boys their *Catechism* and the rudiments of reading, writing and singing. The ordinance of 1534, of course, made no mention of orphans or other young boys at Haina; but the ordinance of 1577, intended for the general superintendent of the four Hessian territorial hospitals, declared that rich persons were not to leave their children at Haina for schooling, 'for it ought to be a hospital and not a school, especially since these children always eat the best food, which the poor, needy residents observe and endure with great bitterness.'[52] It was a different matter for the foundlings and 'similar poor fatherless children who have been transferred here.' They should be taught to pray, to read and write, and also to work diligently, so that when they were twelve years old, they could be sent out as servants or apprentices and thus not loaf around the hospital like 'lazy gallows birds'.

Letzener's description provides scholars with one source for understanding how the original ordinance of 1534 was put into practice. Other sources shed indirect light on the same question. From revisions of and additions to the hospital ordinances, for example, an impression may be gained of real life in constrast to the theoretical ideal. There are hints in the 1577 ordinance that Haina was so attractive that even substantial families were tempted to leave their children there for schooling. Similarly, the ordinances of 1573, 1574 and 1577 all emphasized that the hospital was intended exclusively for subjects of Hesse living in the country but unable to earn a living.[53] The implication seems to be that these hospitals proved so attractive that persons from Hessian towns, or from outside Hesse altogether, were attempting to gain admission. As a hospital survey of 1575 noted, officials were to check to see if any unauthorized young, strong, able-bodied persons had crept into the hospitals.[54] The ordinance of 1577 also clarified the admissions criteria when it went beyond the original requirement of disability and poverty to insist that applicants also lack support among relatives and friends. In short, Philipp of Hesse only intended these

---

51 When the monastery was secularized, one resident was a leper. Eckhart G. Franz, *Kloster Haina* (above, note 7), p. 552.
52 StAM 40a XXIV generalia 2: 'Obervorsteher Ordnung 1577', 6 fols.
53 StAM 40a XXIV generalia 2: 'Obervorsteher Ordnung 1577'; Reinhard Schenck, 'Haina Amts Diener Ordnung 1573'; 'Ordnung für Hermann Pauli, 1574'.
54 StAM S60 A: 'Salbuch Hessische Hospitäler 1575', Instruction by Landgraf Ludwig, 16 July 1575.

hospitals for those poor persons who had no means of subsistence whatsoever. This document also took up the (rather unexpected) chance that the sick or disabled might actually improve while in the hospital. Such were to leave and find honest work.[55]

Documents of this kind prompt suspicion of regular infractions of or departure from the original rules of admission. In addition to the orphaned children already mentioned, the 1575 survey of Haina and Merxhausen revealed that a number of married couples had been granted entry.[56] Indeed this exception to the original rules became so common that a commission of inquiry in 1627 reported complaints that the married now numbered '40, 50, 100, and even sometimes more than that.' To make matters worse, such couples insisted on eating before the poor brethren and on other special privileges. These persons had apparently succeeded in buying places for themselves in the Haina hospital, another practice forbidden by all the sixteenth-century ordinances and considered harmful to general morale.[57]

Other well-to-do persons found their way into Haina under special circumstances, as in the case of a mentally ill nobleman (Merx von Ramrodt) who was in custody there in 1575, and accompanied by two maidservants.[58] Uncontrollable mad persons from the towns were often granted admission if it could be shown that there was no other secure place for them.[59] The largest deviation from the original model was the rapid growth of the hospital from the hundred patients originally planned for, to two hundred residents and fifty staff in 1548, and to something approaching three hundred residents and about seventy staff in 1591.[60]

In 1591 the Hessian central administration was concerned by the rising tide of poor and disabled, and ordered a survey of the four territorial hospitals. The list they drew up covered the years 1550 to 1591 and revealed that total hospital population had more than doubled in forty years. The poor brethren comprised about 80–85% of the figures given here.

55 StAM 40a XXIV generalia 2: 'Obervorsteher Ordnung 1577'.

56 StAM S60 G: 'Verzeichnis der personen so zur zeitt im Spittal Haina sint, 16 July 1575'.

57 StAM 40a XXIV generalia 2: '1627 Bericht der zur Samt-Visitation der Hohen Hospitalien', dated 26 September 1627.

58 'Verzeichnis der personen' (above, note 56).

59 The admission of urban lunatics remained an exceptional practice until 1728, when an ordinance allowed for their regular transfer to Haina 'if they have a crazed mind and are so wild that they could not be kept in the town hospitals without great danger; and if they have enough wealth not only to pay for their keep but to leave something to the hospitals': Holthausen, *Landeshospital Haina* (above, note 3), p. 13. Only in 1881 were the mentally ill from Hessian towns sent to Haina as a matter of course.

60 Günther Franz, *Urkundliche Quellen* (above, note 16), vol. iii, p. 84; Siefert, 'Kloster und Hospital Haina' (above, note 23); StAM 40a XXIV generalia 2: 'Summarischer Extract was vom Jahr 50 ahn bis uff das 91sten Jahr in den vier hohen Hospitalien in Hessen . . . underhalten worden'.

TABLE I

Total hospital residents (poor brethren, servants and officials)
1550–91 in five-year averages.[61]

	HAINA	MERX-HAUSEN	GRONAU	HOFHEIM	MEN H & G	WOMEN M & HO	AVERAGE TOTAL
1550–1555	196	114	66	59	262	173	435
(6 years)	(45%)	(26%)	(15%)	(14%)	(60.2%)	(39.8%)	(100%)
1556–1560	197	157	91	71	288	228	516
	(38%)	(30%)	(18%)	(14%)	(55.8%)	(44.2%)	(100%)
1561–1565	284	213	100	83	384	296	680
	(42%)	(31%)	(15%)	(12%)	(56.5%)	(43.5%)	(100%)
1566–1570	338	273	116	100	454	373	827
	(41%)	(33%)	(14%)	(12%)	(54.9%)	(45.1%)	(100%)
1571–1575	345	313	120	115	465	428	893
	(39%)	(35%)	(13%)	(13%)	(52.1%)	(47.9%)	(100%)
1576–1580	317	354	102	122	419	476	895
	(35%)	(40%)	(11%)	(14%)	(46.8%)	(53.2%)	(100%)
1581–1585	395	396	114	158	509	554	1063
	(37%)	(37%)	(11%)	(15%)	(47.9%)	(52.1%)	(100%)
1586–1591	391	369	123	173	514	542	1056
(6 years)	(37%)	(35%)	(12%)	(16%)	(48.7%)	(51.3%)	(100%)

H & G = Haina & Gronau   M & Ho = Merxhausen & Hofheim

It is noteworthy that the numbers of residents increased in all four territorial hospitals, but almost as remarkable was the rise of Merxhausen and Hofheim, both dedicated to disabled and aged women. In the forty-one years between 1550 and 1591 the hospitals for men almost doubled (up 96.2%) in size, while in the same period the women's hospitals more than tripled their size (up 213.3%) to house more residents than the men's hospitals. Haina had begun with a clear preponderance, but was gradually overtaken by Merxhausen until both were of roughly equal size. The particular reasons for this development are obscure, but the general cause of such rapid growth is not. Repeatedly the landgraves of Hesse urged the hospital superintendent and the hospital governors to admit more poor people. As expressed in the 1574 ordinance of the new superintendent Hermann Pauli, 'at all times, but especially in these times of spiralling inflation, you shall keep as many poor persons as the income of the hospital can possibly stand, for the estate of the hospitals ought not to grow by

61 'Summarischer Extract', cited in note 60. In 1575 the poor at Haina comprised at least 294 of the 346 residents (85.0%); in 1598 they made up 264 of the 323 residents (81.7%). StAM S60 G: 'Verzeichnis der personen so zur zeit im Spittal Heine sint, 16 July 1575'; StAM 40a XXIV generalia 2: Landgraf Ludwig der Elter to Landgraf Moritz, 13 December 1598. In 1575 the poor at Merxhausen numbered 270 women and 33 men out of 356 (85.1%), not counting the nine persons on leave to visit friends, of whom six were poor. Including them would bring the percentage of poor down to 84.6. StAM S60 H: 'Verzeichnis der personen zu Merxhausen, 15 July 1575'.

admitting few people; but instead whatever God Almighty grants at any time ought to be shared to the advantage of the poor.'[62]

By the 1590s the hospitals at Haina and Merxhausen were packed to the doors. Yet many more poor and disabled continued to clamour for relief. In 1592, for example, landgrave Moritz ordered superintendent Johann Clauer to admit to Haina a lame boy who had lost the use of his hands and feet, even though 'the territorial hospital is already overflowing with disabled persons'. In order to find room for the boy, the authorities were to examine all who were there already and expel someone who might perhaps be able to earn a living outside the hospital.[63] In a similar case from 1592, landgrave Wilhelm told Clauer that he was sure that there were at Haina some able-bodied men capable of earning their own bread, and that one of them should be expelled to make room for a truly needy lame man.[64] There are records of similar orders in 1575, 1592 again, 1598, 1609 and 1616; and even these are far from complete.[65] The hospitals had clearly admitted too many poor persons and overstrained their resources. On 31 May 1602 landgrave Ludwig the Elder wrote to his brother landgrave Moritz that Haina was now losing 2,000 *fl.* per annum and must be helped out if they hoped to avoid 'turning the wretched out and ruthlessly letting those who qualify for alms (according to the ordinances) loose upon the countryside to wander and decay in poverty, hunger and misery.'[66] The hospitals should be pruned back from the current 407 and 380 (Haina and Merxhausen respectively) to 300 and 250, and only the most needy should be admitted.

How long did the average resident remain in the hospital? Some, who arrived as children, might look forward to forty or fifty years there. Others who arrived aged sixty or seventy years probably spent only five or at most ten years there. There are no records that would permit a direct answer. In 1575, however, the landgraves conducted a thorough enquiry into the affairs of the hospital and had drawn up a list of those who died or left the hospital in that year. To assume that 1575 was a normal or average year would be to conclude that generally 13.9% of the brethren left each year and 25% of the servants or officials. It is, perhaps, surprising that only 8.5% of the brethren died in 1575, a very low figure considering they were predominantly aged and completely

62 StAM 40a XXIV generalia 2: 'Ordnung für Hermann Pauli 1574'; repeated verbatim in the 1577 Obervorsteher Ordnung.
63 Haina Hospitalsarchiv: 'Receptions-Rescripte von den Jahren 1500', Landgraf Moritz to Johann Clauer, n.d. The boy was ordered by Clauer to be admitted on 2 November 1592. This archive will hereafter be referred to as HHA: the Receptions-Rescripte will be referred to as RR.
64 HHA RR, Landgraf Wilhelm to Johann Clauer, 22 June 1592.
65 HHA 'Receptions Rescripte von den Jahren 1500', and also from the cellar room (*Klammer*) 'Ganz alte Receptions Rescripte von den Jahren 1500 u. 1600'.
66 StAM S60 A: Salbuch Hessische Hospitäler 1575 (instruction of 16 July 1575). StAM 40a XXIV generalia 2.

TABLE 2

Departures from Haina (1575)

	BRETHREN n = 294	% OF TOTAL BRETHREN	STAFF n = 52	% OF TOTAL STAFF
Died	25	8.5	5	9.6
Left voluntarily	7	2.4	8	15.4
Expelled	9	3.1	0	0
Total	41	13.9	13	25

disabled. These figures in turn would imply that the average term was 7.2 years for the average poor brother and four years for the average staff member if the hospital had reached a steady state of equal entries and departures.[67]

Records from Merxhausen in 1585 and 1597 indicate departure rates of 24.6% and 20.0%, which would indicate shorter average stays in Merxhausen than in Haina (about four and five years respectively). But a note in the same record indicates that fifty-six out of the sixty-seven who died in 1597 had died of *Pestilenz*, which might mean that both 1585 and 1597 were years of extraordinarily high mortality.[68] Of course, these are only averages which provide little real information about actual conditions. In any event it is noteworthy that the country people of Hesse obviously valued the free room and board of the hospitals. Unlike the later hospitals elsewhere which sometimes functioned as prisons, the worst punishment for many in Hesse was expulsion from the hospital. And the landgraves were probably correct in thinking that some able-bodied peasants succeeded in slipping away from the world of family and work to gain the comfort of a Christian community.

The food consumed at Haina and Merxhausen guaranteed a higher standard of living than many working families enjoyed. This fact tended to make hospital officials touchy or even defensive when it came to explaining the existence of the hospital. The obligation to be (and to seem to be) a worthy charitable foundation put residents of the hospitals under a code of behaviour much stricter than that imposed on persons living normal lives.

Yet before the scholar can even attempt an assessment of the extent to which the hospital was expected to meet a higher moral and religious standard than that imposed on the 'world', he would have to know by what standard the world lived. Fortunately, the Haina hospital archive has preserved an ordinance issued by landgrave Philipp for the common inhabitants of Haina and the surrounding

---

67 It can be shown that in a steady state the average number of years in the hospital for the average person was approximately the inverse of the fraction leaving each year. If the hospital was still growing, as it was in 1575, then the average number of years per person is somewhat less than the inverse of the fraction leaving each year.

68 StAM 229 BIIIa Landeshospital Merxhausen, lit. H, Nr. 2, 'Acta generalia die Aufnahme der Hospitalitinnen in das Landeshospital Merxhausen betreffend'.

lands subject to the jurisdiction of the hospital. The very first point suggests that religious rules played a large part in the outside world as well as in the hospital:

First, God's Word and teaching should be held up before everyone's eyes . . . and all those who are of another faith and doctrine than that taught in the principality of Hesse are not to be tolerated; instead they are to be notorious like those involved in magic, witchcraft, and other works of the devil; and after being publicly rebuked, they may be punished according to the seriousness of their offense.[69]

The people living near Haina were warned that they must not swear by God's wounds, his mother or the sacraments; the penalties could be severe even for those who tolerated such swearing. Those caught working on a Sunday or holiday might have to pay up to two *gulden* as penalty. During church services each householder was to see to it that his servants and family attended the service and did not stay at home 'practising knavery and villainy'. Infractions were punished at a rate of five shillings for the householder, while servants were to be imprisoned. Those notorious for adultery or other immorality were to pay up to ten *gulden*. Whoring and common fornication were offences leading to a ten *gulden* fine against the householder who tolerated such vices, a two *gulden* fine against the male servant and a one *gulden* fine against the maid-servant. Far more serious was fraudulent contract with the hospital. Anyone cheating the hospital could be fined up to twenty *gulden*. Abusing the standards of measurement could lead to a fine of fifty *gulden* and corporal punishment. Petty offences against a man's neighbour or against the hospital generally cost from six *alber* to five *gulden*. No man or woman, for example, could slander another 'with immoral, gross words or with any kind of libel or insult' without paying a fine of one *gulden*. In the event of fire, all must help to fight it, or pay a fine of ten *gulden*. Failure to attend a village court or assembly meeting might cost one *gulden*. Dances of certain sorts were forbidden: 'Sunday dancing and other suspect evening dances are herewith completely forbidden; and if this is disobeyed, the men shall pay a fine of one *gulden* and the woman a fine of thirteen *alber*.'[70] Such ordinances obviously attempted to set a general standard of Christian conduct and communal responsibility; but it is noteworthy that the punishments for false measures, adultery and fornication were far less severe than those imposed by the Imperial criminal code, the *Carolina*.[71]

Although this set of village regulations tried to establish Christian community as an ideal, there can be no doubt that the hospital, with its regular daily religious observances, strained to maintain a higher moral order. A prayer used at Merxhausen asked God for help in obeying the hospital officials, 'and let us

69 HHA: 'Des Hohen Hospitals Policey Ordnung', in a volume of 'Hospitals-Ordnungen und Vergleiche', a book of 139 pp. in an eighteenth-century hand, pp. 57–93.
70 Ibid., articles 1, 2, 3, 4, 5, 6, 7, 12, 38, 40, 45, 46.
71 Gustav Radbruch (ed.), *Die peinliche Gerichtsordnung Kaiser Karls V. von 1532 (Carolina)* (Stuttgart, 1962), articles 113, 120–3.

not misuse these alms in laziness, lechery or in other scandalous vices resulting in our eternal damnation.'[72] In the words of the original ordinance of 1534: 'And because alms should be given mainly to Christians in need, it is Christian, reasonable, and necessary that the poor who are to be cared for in the hospital shall live in Christian order and maintain a fine and honourable way of life.'[73] Many applicants to the hospital emphasized their religious character and their readiness to live 'as befits Christian brethren'.[74] The preacher at Haina was to urge the poor to hear God's Word not only at the regular services but at special services as well, and to inculcate an attitude of constant (*ohn unterlass*) prayer and thankfulness.[75] The hospital may even have moved to institute a regular half-hour evening prayer service to balance the one in the morning. The original ordinance of the hospital (1534) required only one sermon a day and stated simply that 'after supper and the prayer of thanks, let them rest and have them go to bed at a set time.'[76] Already in the undated 'Hospitals-Fundation' this thanksgiving is explicitly described as a church service set for 6 p.m. in the summer, and directly after supper in the large common room during the winter. The prayers were to include special thanks to the territorial prince for his benevolence; and in 1573 Schenck's ordinance described this evening service as a half-hour service with Bible reading and preaching as well as prayers of thanks.[77] Perhaps this is merely a case of ordinary practice becoming more and more explicit in the records; but it could also indicate an intensified religious life for residents of the hospital, with two services on normal weekdays in addition to special holiday services, the two Sunday sermons, and the extra services on Wednesday and Friday mentioned by Letzener in 1588.

Such a privileged life of semi-monasticism certainly demanded a higher standard of social behaviour. This is why residents of the hospital were not allowed to leave the institution to visit the nearby villages. The rule was apparently as hard to enforce as it had been in the days of the monastery. In 1573 the superintendent Reinhard Schenck zu Schweinsberg observed that some of the brethren at Haina 'are involved in all kinds of crafts, commerce, and trading, even on Sundays; and they go out weekly to the villages and attend church fairs and weddings, where they obtain wine and beer and pass the time in drunkenness, immorality [fornication], and wantonness; all of which mightily enrages

---

72 StAM 40a XXIV Generalia 2: 'Hospitals Fundation' (an undated document of 10 fols intended primarily for Merxhausen), 'Ein Gebet', fols 5^v–7^r.
73 Günther Franz, *Urkundliche Quellen* (above, note 16), vol. ii, p. 190.
74 HHA RR, see, e.g., the cases of Ciriax Fischer (19 March 1564), Valtin Niphudt (8 November 1587), Henn Cleinhens (n.d.), Hans Schneider (Wednesday after *Invocavit*, 1562), Klaus Fischer (30 August 1581).
75 StAM 40a XXIV Generalia 2: Schenck, 'Haina Amts-Diener Ordnung, 1573'.
76 Günther Franz, *Urkundliche Quellen* (above, note 16), vol. ii, pp. 195, 192.
77 StAM 40a XXIV Generalia 2: 'Hospitals Fundation'; Schenck, 'Haina Amts-Diener Ordnung, 1573'. Letzener confirms the existence of a regular evening service in the late sixteenth century (*Historische . . . Beschreibung*, chapter 16).

God at the misuse of alms and gives the fine institution a bad name.'[78] To correct this dangerous breach of the rules, the men must be threatened with sharp punishments (including prison), and the gatekeeper was not to allow any brother to go out without a special pass, or he could find himself imprisoned as well.

Perhaps the discrepancy between the good life at Haina and the hard times in the countryside, together with the observed failure of hospital residents to live up to the high spiritual standards set for them, produced resentment. One result may have been the surprising degree of defensiveness about the value of charity observed among pastors and hospital officials in the late sixteenth century. Schenck's 1573 ordinance concluded with the thought that the poor were Christ's representatives on earth. To neglect them was to neglect one's own salvation. It is surprising that he found it necessary to state as much. Johann Letzener, too, spent the eighteenth chapter of his description of Haina defending the virtue of charity, and attacking those who ridiculed the care of the poor or did not take such responsibilities seriously. After rehearsing the history of Christian views of charity from Biblical writers to St Elisabeth, with Socrates thrown in for good measure, Letzener expounded St Basil's fifth sermon on the fourteenth Psalm: 'Everything given to the poor is received as an interest-bearing loan by God. And who would not gladly have God as one's debtor?' And taking a cue from Chrysostom's third sermon on Genesis 1, Letzener repeated this idea: 'Whoever receives the poor sets up a loan to God. One party takes the money and uses it. But Another, namely God, stands as surety and pays a high interest rate, and has moreover promised to repay the principal one hundred-fold.'[79]

These sentiments stand in a venerable Christian tradition of mercy, and doubtless provided an elegant reason for charitable giving. They nevertheless sound very odd in the mouth of a Lutheran pastor committed, in theory at least, to the wholesale rejection of works righteousness. It may be that, by retaining a monastic institution, the Lutherans of Hesse also retained a basically Catholic and monastic attitude toward charity and alms. It may have been natural, therefore, that the hospitals inherited the anticlericalism that had once focussed on privileged, leisured monks.[80]

To cope with disorderly and troublesome residents, the hospital officials learned to rely on more than the increasingly frequent exhortations of the pastor. In the years after their founding, the hospitals developed a list of moral regulations with a sliding scale of punishments. The earliest version of such a list of infractions is in the undated, but undoubtedly early, hospital ordinances for

78 Schenck, 'Haina Amts-Diener Ordnung, 1573'.
79 Letzener, *Historische . . . Beschreibung*, fols L4v–N1r.
80 See especially the excellent analysis of Stalnaker, 'The Emergence of the Protestant Clergy' (above, note 2).

Haina and Merxhausen, entitled 'Hospitals-Fundation'.[81] Here are to be found frequent mention of punishments for refusal to work; for arguing; for fighting; for those carrying bread or beer back to their rooms; for those who cooked their own food; for making unauthorized things and for selling them; for disobeying an official; for failure to care properly for the sick; for going out walking without permission; for unauthorized loitering or trespassing in the kitchen, cellars, brewery, bakery, laundry, weaving house, etc.; and for failure to attend funerals and other special meetings. The women at Merxhausen were especially warned to 'maintain modesty and chastity and to avoid all evil society with men both in words and deeds; and anyone discovered in immorality shall be removed from the hospital.' As a general rule the punishments ranged from missing a meal to being locked in gaol or in the 'hole' (*loch*) with only beer and bread to eat. The incorrigible, and those who incited others to break the rules, were to be expelled from the hospital.[82] Most of these infractions were construed as breaches of fellowship and community. Failure to accept the religious ground-rules of the hospital could also lead to punishment. Those who missed the morning prayers and sermons, for example, were obliged to miss a meal. To refuse to learn the *Catechism* likewise led to a spell in gaol. Stubborn refusal to learn could lead to expulsion, but officials were told to give newcomers time off from work so that they could learn what was expected of them. Anyone arriving for a meal after prayers was to miss the meal unless he had a good excuse. During mealtime, when the Bible or *Catechism* was being read, residents were to be silent. Those who 'carried on with their gossip' could be sent away from the table. Blasphemy was to be punished with whipping for the first offence, and expulsion for the second.

It seems clear that this list of infractions was not drawn up *a priori*, but rather from close experience with the sometimes disorderly old peasants who resided in the hospitals. It should not be surprising, therefore, that these rules and regulations underwent little modification during the rest of the sixteenth century. Schenck's 1573 ordinance made only a few additions, urging for example a sympathetic understanding of the problems experienced by elderly and feeble-minded persons obliged to learn the *Catechism*. The hospital treasurer was told to punish the rebellious and to allow no drunkenness or noisy carousing. The wine steward could help by controlling the pouring of wine and thus prevent the men from having drunken parties in their rooms. It was Schenck who called special attention to the failure of some residents to curb their commercial instincts or their public thirst. His ordinance also dealt with the problem the hospitals continued to have with guests. In contrast to the earlier ordinances, Schenck declared that these institutions were not hotels but hospitals for the

---

81 StAM 40a XXIV Generalia 2: 'Hospitals Fundation' (n.d., but clearly composed before 1567).
82 Ibid., fols 4^r-5^r, 7^v-9^r.

poor. Strangers passing by, therefore, were not to be received by the hospital except on the order of princely councillors or officials, and then only for one meal.[83] By the late sixteenth century, Letzener reported that a sign had been placed at the gate stating that the hospital was no longer a monastery offering lodging.[84] Thus it took over forty years for the monastic reputation for hospitality to disappear as an ideal of the Hessian hospitals. The basic reason for that disappearance, moreover, was its conflict with an equally venerable monastic and hospital concept of intense Christian community, separate from the world, and dedicated to *ora et labora*.

The Lutheran Reformation evidently did not transform all institutions or habits of thought beyond recognition, and many features of medieval Christendom survived for decades. When the Protestant Churches recruited most of their early clergy from among the ranks of Catholic clergy, it was hardly surprising that the Lutheran reformers continued to hold services in churches that looked Catholic in most details. It took almost a century of discussion and argument before Protestants and Catholics concluded that they should disagree on almost every issue. The Reformation hospitals of Hesse stand as a reminder of this long period of continuity. Although offering no heavenly rewards for entering, they did claim to lead a religious life dependent on the alms of pious Hessians. In a real sense these 'Protestant monasteries' reformulated an ethic of poverty, obedience and chastity; and when, after a century, they fell on evil days, they too resembled the corrupt monasteries from which they had sprung.

83 Schenck, 'Amts-Diener Ordnung, 1573' (above, note 77).
84 Letzener, *Historische . . . Beschreibung*, chapter 17.

VI

Practice and Principle in the German Towns: Preachers and People

❦

R. W. SCRIBNER

In 1524 the parish of St Michael in Worms deposed its parish priest, Johann Leininger, and appointed in his place a former monk who had taken a wife. Leininger complained to the Dean of the Cathedral, who raised the matter with the Town Council. They in turn asked the parish to explain its action. The reply of the churchwardens and parishioners of St Michael's provides a rare view of the relations between pastors and people at the grass roots.[1] The parish had often complained, it stated, of the scandalous life of its parish priest. He lived in sin with a woman by whom he had begotten a child; and, not content with this, the woman had for some time occupied the post of parish sexton. This had made the whole parish an object of derision and had given rise to the saying 'The parson of St Michael's sleeps with his sexton.' The woman herself was a shrew, and had once said that she would sell all her clothes to buy rope with which to hang all who went to hear heretical sermons.

They accused Leininger of misusing parish funds. A costly green cloth had been purchased to make Mass vestments, but he had made a coat for his bastard from it instead. A rent of ten *Gulden* belonging to the church he had appropriated to his own use; and he had handed the parish register over to the Dean of the Cathedral, although it was rightly under the control of the churchwardens. Worst of all, when a woman of the parish lay gravely ill, he was asked to administer the Sacrament to her. He said that he would come only after he had been paid his Mass-penny, so that the woman had laid unattended until the following morning when the penny could be brought to him.

Complaints of Leininger's behaviour to the proper authorities had achieved nothing. For the past two years, however, the preacher at St Magnus had taught that every Christian community had the power, indeed the responsibility, to elect its own pastor; and they had thus decided, without force or disturbance, to send Leininger on his way. He had been found, according to the divine Word, to be unreliable and unfit for office: just as he had received his appointment from them or their fathers, he now received his dismissal. In his place, they had elected a good and loyal pastor, a servant of the parish, an honourable man who lived in the married state and did not keep house with immoral persons in the manner of the priests. He would see to the needs of their souls, and they, to the best of their ability, would see to his worldly needs.

Professor A. G. Dickens has argued persuasively that the Reformation was less a matter of doctrine than of working practical belief,[2] and nowhere can such

---

1 *Stadtarchiv Worms, Reichsstadt Worms 1947: des Rats Antwort auf gemeiner Pfaffheit clag* (no. 2), Article 14. There is some suspicion that the Town Council had a hand in evoking this reply, but none that it actually influenced its contents.
2 A. G. Dickens, *The German Nation and Martin Luther* (London, 1974), pp. 132–4, 224–5.

judgement receive more direct illustration than in this document. First, the parish was primarily concerned to find someone to minister to their needs according to Scripture. Secondly, that man should be a godly person of good moral standing. Thirdly, his ministry should be freely performed, in return for which the community would see to his upkeep. Fourthly, there is a sense of communal pride and concern for moral probity inherent in the parish's image of itself. And fifthly, there is the sense of a considered collective decision, firmly taken and justified by the yardstick of Scripture.

These points put simply and undogmatically the essential link between practice and principle in the German Reformation. What made the Reformation a movement rather than a collection of abstract theological ideas was the attempt of ordinary people to put their belief into action. The most important step was to obtain a godly preacher who would proclaim the Word and share in the building of some kind of revivified Christian community. For this reason, the efforts of little communities like St Michael's to find and keep a godly preacher are central to the understanding of Reformation. This article will examine some important aspects of this search for a godly preacher, and how the relations between preacher and people were shaped in the process.

In order to discuss the relationship between preacher and people, it is essential to know something about the Reformation preacher himself. Strangely, almost nothing exists to afford a general picture of such a man. Much has been written about the leading Reformers, largely in terms of their individual genius, but there is no biography of the average preacher, the man who stood at the centre of the religious struggle in the many parishes like St Michael's.[3] A discussion of practice and principle without this ordinary figure would be like Hamlet without the prince. What was his status, his social origin, his age, his education? Where and how was he active, how did he come by his position, how did he get on in the job? It is scarcely possible to answer any of these questions adequately in the scope of this essay, but it may be possible to provide a preliminary sketch. To this purpose I have assembled some basic biographical data about 176 preachers active in Germany during the years between *c.* 1520 and *c.* 1550. It is

3 The sketch in P. Drews, *Der evangelische Geistliche in der deutschen Vergangenheit* (Jena, 1905), pp. 7–48, probably based on Saxon visitation records, is one of the few general studies. However, there have been some very good local studies: M. Brecht, 'Herkunft und Ausbildung der protestantischen Geistlichen des Herzogtums Württemberg im 16. Jahrhundert', *Zeitschrift für Kirchengeschichte*, vol. lxxx (1969), pp. 163–75; O. Haug, 'Die evangelische Pfarrerschaft der Reichsstadt Hall in Stadt und Land', *Württembergisch Franken*, vol. lviii (1974), pp. 359–75; B. Klaus, 'Soziale Herkunft und theologische Bildung lutherischer Pfarrer der reformatorischen Neuzeit', *Zeitschtift fur Kirchengeschichte*, vol. lxxx (1969), pp. 22–49 (on Franconia). These are slightly different in emphasis from the investigation here, concentrating on the Protestant clergy, rather than the preachers of the formative, uninstitutionalized stages of the Reformation. They thus include many clergy who became Protestant through expediency, or passively through a territorial Reformation. Nonetheless, there are striking similarities between some of the findings of Brecht and Klaus and those which emerge in this study.

difficult to ascertain details about the lives of minor figures of the sixteenth century, and the analysis is inevitably biassed towards the better-known, those for whom data was more readily available.[4] However, the group includes all the major German Reformers, many second-rank figures and many men of little significance for the broader sweep of Reformation. 80% of the group began their preaching before 1530 (see Table 2), and the remainder provide a useful check on the patterns which would be revealed by analysis only of those active in this seminal period. The group is a sufficiently large and random sample to hazard some generalizations, hedged about with necessary qualifications. From this it should prove possible to gain, if not a clear profile of the average preacher, at least a plausible silhouette.

The assiduous reader of Reformation pamphlets may well expect the average Reformation preacher to be the articulate layman, the figure popularised by Karsthans and embodied in real life by the Peasant of Woehrd.[5] As with the Peasant of Woehrd, it proves to be an illusion fostered by skilful propaganda. The clerical or lay status of this group of preachers before they commenced their evangelical activity can be traced for all but a handful (Table 1).

Three-quarters of them were clerics, either priests or members of monastic orders. Laymen account for only a fragment of the group. Slightly larger is the number of those who were teachers, but this scarcely strengthens the lay element.[6] They occupied a position as close to the clergy as to the laity, many teachers were also priests and it was common for them to have at least minor orders. If the German Reformation was a revolt against clerical domination of religion,[7] it was also a revolt led from within.

4 These facts have been compiled from the following lexica: *Allgemeine Deutsche Biographie* (56 vols, Leipzig, 1875–1912) [hereafter, *ADB*]; *Neue Deutsche Biographie* (vols i–xi A–K, Berlin, 1953–77) [*NDB*]; *Realencyclopädie für protestantische Theologie und Kirche*, 3rd edn (24 vols, Leipzig, 1896–1913); *Die Religion in Geschichte und Gegenwart*, 3rd edn (7 vols, Tübingen, 1957–65) [*RGG*]; F. W. Bautz, *Biographisch-Bibliographisches Kirchenlexikon* (parts i–xiv A–Hee, Hamm/Westf., 1975–7). Use has also been made of the regionally-organized series of biographies *Lebensbilder*, which will be referred to more precisely in the footnotes below. The modern biographical lexica are incomplete, and the *ADB* is dated and inaccurate on many details. All lexica were often imprecise or uninformative on several categories of data sought, and frequent recourse was made to specialized literature on individual preachers, using standard Reformation bibliographies. The evidence has been gathered as extensively and precisely as the present state of Reformation research permits, although a more thorough investigation would be possible, using a larger sample and electronic data processing, by careful scrutinizing of original-source materials. The expense of such a task, however, would only be justifiable within the framework of a wider quantitative investigation.

5 P. Böckmann, 'Der gemeine Mann in den Flugschriften der Reformation', *Deutsche Vierteljahrschrift für Litteraturwissenschaft und Geistesgeschichte*, vol. xxii (1944), pp. 186–230; O. Clemen, *Beiträge zur Reformationsgeschichte*, Heft ii (Berlin, 1902), pp. 85–97.

6 In fact, the number of teachers is considerably higher since 13 priests who were also teachers are included in the former category. This shows how close was the overlap between teachers and the clergy.

7 Drews, *Der evangelische Geistliche*, p. 7, and more recently S. E. Ozment, *The Reformation in the Cities* (New Haven, 1975), pp. 84–5.

TABLE I
Clerical/lay status

Layman	14	7.9%
Teacher	21	11.9
Priest	74	42.1
Religious		
Augustinian	18	10.2
Franciscan	13	7.4
Benedictine	6	3.4
Dominican	4	2.3
Other orders	16	9.1
(total monks – 54)		(32.4)
No data	10	5.7
	176	100.0

Other orders: inspecified 4, Premonstratensian 3, Cistercian 3, Carthusian 2, Carmelite 2, Celestiner 1, Hermit of St Anthony 1.

The Lutheran Reformation thus had a clerical stamp on it from the beginning, shown by the importance that ordination continued to have for the new movement. In 1525 one of the earliest pastors lacking episcopal ordination, Ambrosius Moibanus, was called by the Town Council to be parson of St Elisabeth in Breslau. Although the bishop of Breslau insisted that he take orders, Moibanus did not do so and was attacked for usurping the cure of souls. Johannes Cochlaeus was one of the leading critics in this case, but this was not just Catholic cavilling, for Lutheran pastors felt just as uneasy about unordained preachers. In Nuremberg the first non-ordained cleric, Veit Dietrich, Luther's former amanuensis, was not appointed until 1535, yet the leading preacher in Nuremberg, Andreas Osiander, was greatly disturbed by the fact and opposed Dietrich assuming the post without orders. The supporters of the new faith also expected their preachers to be ordained. Johann Isenmann, a mere sub-deacon, was called in 1524 to be city parson of Schwäbisch Hall. He did not proceed to higher orders, and was strongly criticized for this within the community. Even Luther was uneasy on the question, and when an unordained man, Georg Rörer, was called to be deacon of the City Church of Wittenberg in 1525, Luther felt obliged to ordain him himself. As late as 1550 a major dispute was provoked in the Lutheran church over the non-ordination of a pastor in Rostock, Johann Freder.[8] Ordination became a major point of reproach against Lutheranism by the Anabaptists, who saw it as abandonment of the priesthood of all believers. The Lutheran tradition, however, continued to stress the need for the *minister rite vocatus*, and held as suspect anyone who operated outside the traditional framework. Thus, in Wittenberg in 1537 a

8 *ADB*, vol. xxii, p. 81 (Moibanus); B. Klaus, 'Veit Dietrich', *Frankische Lebensbilder*, vol. ii (1969), p. 147; G. Wünder, 'Johann Isenmann', *Lebensbilder aus Schwaben und Franken*, vol. xii (1972), p. 60; B. Klaus, 'Soziale Herkunft', p. 41 (Rörer); *NDB*, vol. v, p. 378 (Freder).

young Magister whose religious enthusiasm led him to preach irregularly from the pulpit of the Castle Church was arrested on suspicion of Anabaptism.[9]

The impression that new preacher was but old priest renamed is strengthened by the fact that there are many more in this sample group from the secular clergy than from monastic orders. Given the liberation that the Reformation message brought to the regular clergy, it is surprising not to find a greater proportion of monks turning to active proclamation of the new belief. There are two possible explanations. First, this sample may be untypical in so far as it does not show a wide variety of former monks who turned to irregular preaching. Many of these are unknown by name, and appear in historical records only in the form in which Wilhelm Rem noted the brief appearance of a preaching monk in Augsburg in 1522: 'In April a Franciscan monk from Ulm left town. He preached well and spoke constantly of the Gospel and Holy Scripture. The common folk heard him with pleasure, but others heard him with little pleasure, so he had to leave.'[10] Secondly, it is also possible that many of those monks who abandoned the cloister had little taste for the religious life, and were so relieved to be freed from it that they had no wish to return to a similar kind of activity. This explanation is supported by the example of several ex-monks who turned to preaching only reluctantly, of whom the most notable was Ambrosius Blaurer.[11]

The distribution of such former monks among the various orders provides no surprises. Luther's order predominates, followed by the Franciscans and at some distance the Benedictines. The Dominicans, energetic opponents of the Reformation, supplied only four preachers in this group; while the remaining monks are scattered across five different orders. Here, however, bald figures may be deceptive, shown by the remarkable example of the Premonstratensian Abbey of Belbuck, near Treptow in Pomerania. This provided six preachers from the ranks of its former inmates and pupils, although the decisive influence was Johann Bugenhagen's activity in the school at Treptow and later in the Abbey school.[12]

A glance at the laymen in the group confirms the impression of its over-whelmingly clerical nature. Half of these laymen commenced their preaching activity after 1530, when the Reformation was well on the way to becoming

---

9 G. J. Neumann, 'Predigt und Predigerstand in den Täuferdiskussionen der Reformations-zeit', *Zeitschrift für Religions und Geistesgeschichte*, vol. x (1958), p. 217; *RGG*, vol. v, p. 522 (*minister rite vocatus*); on the 1537 incident, 'Georg Karg', *ADB*, vol. xv, p. 119.
10 *Chroniken der deutschen Städte*, vol. xxv (Leipzig, 1896), p. 171.
11 T. Pressel, *Ambrosius Blaurer* (Elberfeld, 1861), pp. 32, 39. Similar cases were those of Christian Ketelhodt in Stralsund and Jakob Strauss in Hall/Tyrol, discussed below.
12 The six were the abbot Bodewan, the monks Christian Ketelhodt and Johann Kureke, Georg Kempe and Heinrich Sichermann, both probably pupils at the school, and Bugenhagen's assistant teacher, Andreas Knopken: *ADB*, vol. xv, p. 666. Bodewan, Kempe and Sichermann were probably active as irregular and temporary preachers, and are not included in our sample group because of absence of significant biographical data.

institutionalized. It was clear by then that a new Church was being created, with its own distinctive clergy. The lure of the priesthood must have weakened considerably with this development. Five of these post-1530 laymen-preachers were younger than thirty years old, and so spent the most formative years of their adult life with the antipriestly polemic of the early Reformation ringing in their ears. They can be contrasted with some of the enthusiastic young preachers of the early 1520s, who took the final step into the priesthood on discovering their evangelical calling. Johannes Brenz, for example, took his priestly orders only after being called to the preacher's position in Schwäbisch Hall. An exception which proves the general rule was the one preacher commencing his activity in the early 1520s whose lay status is clearly traceable to deep personal conviction. Erasmus Alberus was the son of a priest, something which had a strong emotional influence on him. He was determined not to become a 'whoring priest' (*Hurenpfaff*), and later expressed sincere gratitude for the religious alteration: 'Now the child of a pious evangelical priest is not called a whore's child, but an honourable child. For this good deed alone we can never thank God enough.'[13]

This marked continuity with the old priestly caste raises an intriguing question about the relations of preachers and people. Insofar as these men were called to their office by the communities in which they operated, they demonstrate how slight a hold the notion of the 'priesthood of all believers' had achieved in practice. In seeking a man to provide for its spiritual needs, the community sought him among the ranks of that group professionally inured to the task. Although they came with new ideas, new vigour and renewed spiritual purpose, the preachers' reflexes were those of the old clerical estate. This background may well explain much of the social and ecclesiastical conservatism of the Lutheran Reformation.

Conservatism, however, can be as much influenced by age as by background. Were the evangelical preachers perhaps a new breed of fiery young priests, whose youthful temperament led them to break impatiently with the old church? The idea is contradicted by the age distribution of this sample group (Table 2).

Two-thirds of the group began preaching before 1525, in the most stormy and controversial years of the Reformation. Yet few could be called really young, since roughly but one in four were younger than thirty on commencing preaching. Well over half were older than thirty, and by far the largest section fell into the age band 31-40, the age of mature adulthood in the sixteenth century. The preachers of the early years of the Reformation were not spurred by the brashness of youth, but were experienced men at the peak of their intellectual powers. This picture is only slightly altered by considering the entire group,

13 Cited in E. Körner, *Erasmus Alber* (Leipzig, 1910), p. 3.

TABLE 2
Age and date of commencing preaching

AGE OF 1ST PREACHMENT	DATE OF FIRST PREACHMENT					
	BEFORE 1525	1526–30	1531–40	AFTER 1540	TOTALS	%
Under 25	9	7.5%	1	1	–	11	6.3
25–30	23	19.2	9	10	1	43	24.4
31–40	52	43.3	5	7	1	65	36.9
over 40	12	10.0	1	4	1	18	10.2
No data	24	20.0	5	8	2	39	22.2
TOTALS	120		21	30	5	176	
%	68.2		11.9	17.1	2.8		100.0

where the under-30s now make up almost a third. As the new belief became established, it clearly began to produce its own younger generation of preachers. Significantly, these came from the ranks of mature youth, the age band 25–30, a reflection of the conviction that education and training were necessary for the aspiring preacher.

The educational background of the 176 preachers proved difficult to trace precisely, although it can be ascertained in some form for 81% of the group (Table 3). Three-quarters of the entire group had attended university – a surprisingly high number given the substantial proportion of those for whom no educational-background information could be obtained. Five others were described by contemporaries as 'learned'. One of these claimed to be a doctor, presumably of theology, although his literary style and range of knowledge did not betray such academic excellence. Three of the 'learned' preachers had probably studied in the *studium generale* of their monastic order, achieving the

TABLE 3
Education

D. Theol.	27	15.3%
Theology	25	14.2
M.A.	40	22.3
University	33	18.8
Law	7	4.0
Medicine	1	0.6
later D. Theol.	2	1.1
(total university studies – 135)		(76.7)
'Learned'	5	2.8
School education	1	0.6
No education	2	1.1
No data	33	18.8
	176	100.0

equivalent of a basic university education in liberal arts.[14] Only two explicitly had no education, and one was educated to school level alone. But these preachers were not just educated men – they were also well-educated, for over half commenced or completed a higher degree, taking an M.A. or studying in the three higher faculties of Medicine, Law or Theology. The low number who trained for a secular profession (law or medicine) is surprising, but in keeping with the clerical stamp of the group as a whole. A third had studied theology, and it was fairly common for aspiring priests to take a Master's degree.

These figures highlight some important facts about Reformation preachers. First, they were a very unrepresentative section of the population. Only a tiny number of the male population aspired to university education; fewer still took a higher degree; and those who went on to study theology formed a minute educational élite. Their uniqueness can be best illustrated by two men from either end of the preachers' educational spectrum. At one extreme, Wolfgang Capito studied Arts, Law, Medicine and Theology, taking doctorates in Medicine and Theology and becoming one of the leading Hebrew scholars of his day. At the other end there is Antonius Corvinus, who was educated in the Dominican school of his home town, studied briefly in the *studium generale* of his order, the Cistercians, and then became an autodidact before finally taking an M.A. at the late age of 35.[15] Secondly, a substantial part of them took religion seriously enough from the start to wish to specialize in its formal study. The priesthood might well be seen as the formal prerequisite for a job entered as much for secular as for religious considerations, but the student of theology was displaying an earnestness about religious belief which placed him in a select minority.

A further point worthy of mention is that 37.5% of the group studied at the University of Wittenberg. This seems to be powerful testimony of its extraordinary attraction as a centre of evangelical ideas. The fact must be qualified, however, by the fact that 15.9% had attended there either before discovering their evangelical commitment or before commencing preaching. This reveals another reason why Wittenberg became the powerhouse of the German evangelical movement. As a newer and largely successful university foundation, especially one offering a shorter doctorate than the older universities, it had an established popularity before the Reformation. This laid the foundation for its role in the first generation of the new belief. It was natural that former students

14 On the alleged doctor, Johann Amandus, see P. Tschackert, *Urkundenbuch zur Reformationsgeschichte des Herzogtums Preussen* (Leipzig, 1890), pp. 48–9. The three 'learned' preachers who probably studied in their order were men of note: the Franciscans Friedrich Myconius and Heinrich von Kettenbach, and the Cistercian Antonius Corvinus.
15 On university attendance, see F. Eulenburg, *Die Frequenz der deutschen Universitäten von ihrer Gründung bis zur Gegenwart* (Leipzig, 1904), p. 51, who mentions a peak figure for the early sixteenth century of 4,200 matriculants per year from a population of around 17 million. Only around 30% of matriculated students took a B.A., and between 4% and 14% an M.A.; see F. W. Oediger, *Über die Bildung der Geistlichen im späten Mittelalter* (Cologne, 1953), p. 67. On Capito, *ADB*, vol. iii, p. 772; on Corvinus, ibid., vol. iv, p. 508.

would turn for advice and guidance to their old university, the more so when it stood at the centre of public interest.[16]

This sketch of the background of evangelical preachers can be rounded off with some information on their social origins. This proved to be the most difficult to trace, and father's status or occupation could be ascertained for only half of the group (Table 4).

TABLE 4
Father's status or occupation

Town councillor/patrician	22	24.4%
Merchant/wealthy	9	10.0
Official	8	8.9
Artisans	23	25.6
Bürgerlich	8	8.9
Poor	8	8.9
Rural	10	11.1
Priest	2	2.2
	90	100.0
No data	86	
	176	

Officials: City syndic 1, city judge 1, city secretary 1, *Amtmann* 1, bailiff 1, notary 1, customs officer 1.
Rural: Peasant 4, vintner 1, urban cultivator 1, large farmer 1, property-owner 1, 'Junker' 1, unspecified 1.

This is a disappointingly small proportion, but nevertheless reveals some interesting trends. A quarter of those traceable came from the families of town councillors or patricians. Even if this were expressed as a percentage of the total group, it would still be far in excess of the proportion of the population belonging to this social category.[17] If men whose fathers were identified as wealthy, merchants or officials (most of whom were of high status) are included with these, then two from every five preachers whose social background can be identified came from the upper stratum of society. Such people are always easier to trace than the poor and unknown, but even if it is assumed that none

16 Wittenberg's popularity before the Reformation is reflected in its five-yearly averages of matriculants for the period 1501–20, where it was the third most popular university 1501–5, the fifth 1506–10 and 1511–15, and the second most popular 1516–20; see Eulenburg, *Die Frequenz der deutschen Universitäten*, p. 55. On the advantages of Wittenberg's shorter doctorate over other universities such as Erfurt, see E. Kleineidam, *Universitas Studii Erffordiensis*, vol. ii (Leipzig, 1969), p. 168.
17 The calculation of the political and economic upper stratum in sixteenth-century German towns is extremely complex; see for example P. Eitel, *Die oberschwäbischen Reichsstädte im Zeitalter der Zunftherrschaft. Untersuchungen zu ihrer politischen und sozialen Struktur* (Stuttgart, 1970). The results of recent research have not yet been brought together into any adequate general overview; however, the politically and economically dominant elite in any town would scarcely exceed 5%.

of the unidentified belonged to this upper-class group, it would still seem that one preacher in five did so.[18]

Numerically, the next strongest group are those from artisan backgrounds, although they are well under-represented in terms of the artisan share of the urban population. The handful designated as *bürgerlich* were probably urban families of modest means, close to the artisans at one end and to the poor at the other. Those identified as poor were probably urban poor, and it is striking how overwhelmingly urban the preachers' social background was. Only ten came from explicitly rural backgrounds, to which must be added one or two of the officials. Participation by the nobility was low, with only Nicolaus von Amsdorf, whose father was a Saxon official, coming from the lower nobility.[19] About half of those with rural backgrounds came from high-status families, so that the peasant preacher was almost as fictitious a creature as Karsthans himself. Only one man could be discovered who even approximated to the type – Bartholomeus Rieseberg, born in 1492 as the son of a peasant in Brandenburg. Until he was seventeen he was engaged in agricultural work. Then he decided to study and was taught to read by a priest in nearby Gardelegen. He attended several schools in Brandenburg and the University of Wittenberg in 1518, returning to Gardelegen, still a layman, as a teacher. He was attacked as a Lutheran heretic and forced to flee, taking up preaching in 1522. He led an insecure existence until 1526, when he found a permanent position as a preacher near Halle, returning to Gardelegen as pastor after the Reformation was introduced in 1539. His passing similarity to Karsthans is heightened by the fact that he produced no written works because he was uninterested in them, believing that the Bible and Luther's works were enough for any Christian.[20]

The four indices examined so far – clerical status, age, education and family background – establish some salient social features of this sample group. They were well-educated clergy from urban backgrounds, and mature enough in years to be firmly established in their chosen profession. Although most social groups were represented in their ranks, a powerful leaven from the upper strata gave an upper-class flavour to the group. Age, education and social status thus place these men among the establishment of their day, and it is hard to envisage them as rebels advocating radical change in either Church or society. Indeed, they seem little qualified to lead any popular movement, or to address the mass

18 This may account in part for the high level of education among the preachers. Taking a higher degree was a costly business, possible only for those from prominent families or with wealthy benefices, in the acquisition of which family connections also played an important part; see Oediger, *Über die Bildung der Geistichen*, p. 64.

19 There were, however, few traces of his noble background in Amsdorf's outlook, according to R. Kolb, *Nikolaus von Amsdorf (1483-1565). Popular Polemics in the Preservation of Luther's Legacy* (Nieuwkoop, 1978), p. 16.

20 *ADB*, vol. xxix, p. 757.

of the people in their own terms. As highly-trained men of religion, it can be seen that they would emerge as advocates of Reformation principle. How did they exercise such decisive influence in terms of evangelical practice?

One answer to this question is that they were responding to a demand from the people, to the desire of the community for a godly preacher. Two examples illustrate the strength of such a desire. In 1521 the Dominican Jakob Strauss came to Hall in Tyrol, where he gave readings from St Matthew's Gospel in Latin to local priests. He gained such a reputation by this that the Town Council asked him to preach, and he proved to be so popular that it was arranged with the parish priest that he should preach in St Nicholas. When the bishop of Brixen attempted to expel him, the Town Council lobbied the Habsburg government in Innsbruck and prevented the bishop from publishing placards condemning Strauss with the argument that these would cause popular disturbance. In Hall itself a number of citizens, sometimes as many as forty at a time, appointed themselves an informal bodyguard to forestall any direct episcopal action. Two priests, who attempted to serve an episcopal citation on Strauss as he returned home after preaching, found themselves pursued by an angry crowd, which was about to storm the house where they sought refuge when the mayor arrived to cool inflamed tempers.[21]

In the north, the ex-monk Christian Ketelhodt arrived in Stralsund in 1523, intending to learn a trade. Identified as a follower of Luther, he was asked to preach and became so popular that a parish church was arranged for his use, this time with the passive agreement of the Town Council. Complaints from the Catholic clergy that Ketelhodt was arousing disturbance led to orders from the Dukes of Pomerania to expel him, commands which the city ignored for almost two years. In June 1524 an attempt by a Catholic mayor and the arch-deacon to force Ketelhodt to quit the city by sunrise provoked a deputation of a hundred citizens, supported by several evangelical town councillors, who proclaimed that they were willing to give their lives to keep the preacher in the city. The balance was tipped by the return from the *Reichstag* of Nuremberg that same day of the second mayor, who threw his seniority behind the preacher.[22]

These examples are interesting, because in both cases the men concerned were approached by the community and asked to preach. Neither held any particular ecclesiastical office in the towns, showing that the desire for godly preaching led the community to go outside the regular structures of the Church to satisfy its religious needs. In some cases, this involved literally preaching outside the church. There are numerous cases during the early years of the Reformation of open-air preaching, because the preachers did not have the right

21 D. Schönherr, *Franz Schweygers Chronik der Stadt Hall 1303–1572* (Innsbrück, 1867), pp. 80–2.
22 M. Wehrmann, 'Christian Ketelhut', *Pommersche Jahrbücher*, vol. xxviii (1934), p. 40.

to use a parish church. This was the case when Ketelhodt was originally asked to preach in Stralsund, and for the first two weeks preached under a lime tree in St George's churchyard. In August his friend Johann Kureke also preached in the same churchyard, and in the cloister of St Catherine's, until a church could be found for him. Paulus von Rode had to preach in the open air in Stettin in 1523 because he had no official position, and Caspar Güttel similarly preached seven sermons in the market square of Arnstadt in 1522.[23]

In some cases open-air preaching was merely the result of the great numbers who wished to hear a sermon, but it often arose from opposition to the new ideas which denied preachers the use of churches. Jurgen Aportanus was forbidden to use the churches in Emden in 1524 and preached in the open air until popular pressure enabled him to return. In Leipzig, Sebastian Fröschel's followers set up a pulpit in the churchyard when the doors of St John's were locked against him in October 1523. Sylvester Tegetmeyer was preaching during the *Landtag* at Wolmar in July 1525 when he was interrupted by a disturbance created by a Dominican and other Catholic opponents. He promptly led the congregation outside and finished his sermon 'in the open field'. During the early days of the Reformation in Danzig, a crowd gathered on a hill outside the town to hear an expelled preacher, and in Husum in 1522 Hermann Tast first preached in a private chapel and then in a churchyard. Here he was surrounded by a circle of armed men, a foreshadowing of the style of hedgepreaching to be adopted in the Netherlands in the 1560s.[24]

This suggests that other influences may have been of more immediate importance than the conservative background of these preachers. First, demands for preaching often paid little attention to the niceties of Church legality or regular forms of procedure. Insofar as preachers responded to such demands, they were likely to find themselves in the role of dissenters, however contrary this was to their natural inclinations. Secondly, they were forced into a dissenting position by the reaction of Catholic secular and ecclesiastical authorities. This can be clearly seen from the sample group, where one in five had to flee from his post because of evangelical activity (39 cases or 22.2%). Yet impermanence cannot be said to be a unique characteristic of the group. This can be seen from an analysis of the first position held by each of the group as evangelical preachers (Table 5).

Four out of five held some kind of regular position during their first activity as evangelical preachers, even if only in the minor posts of vicar, chaplain or

---

23 *ADB*, vol. xv, p. 566 (Kureke); vol. xxix, p. 7 (von Rode); G. Kawerau, 'Caspar Güttel', *Zeitschrift des Harz-Vereins für Geschichte und Altertumskunde*, vol. xiv (1881), p. 73.
24 *NDB*, vol. i, p. 328 (Aportanus); K. Beier and A. Dobritzsch, *Tausend Jahre deutsche Vergangenheit in Quellen heimatlicher Geschichte*, vol. i (Leipzig, 1911), p. 212 (Fröschel); F. Bienemann, 'Sylvester Tegetmeyers Tagebuch', *Mitteilungen aus dem Gebiet der Geschichte Liv-, Est-und Kurlands*, vol. xii (1875), p. 505; H. Barge, *Jakob Strauss* (Leipzig, 1937), p. 9 (Danzig); *ADB*, vol. xxxvii, p. 413 (Tast).

TABLE 5

Nature of first position as evangelical preacher

Parish priest	50	28.4%
Canon/provost	3	1.7
Court preacher	1	0.6
Preacher (regular)	74	42.1
Preacher (irregular)	31	17.6
Vicar, chaplain, etc.	16	9.1
Unspecified	1	0.6
	176	100.0

mass-priest. The kind of irregular preaching activity shown in cases of open-air preaching was therefore atypical. Why it was atypical is informative.

Irregular preachers had one advantage for the infant evangelical movement: they stood outside the formal structures of the church and so had more latitude for dissenting activity. This gave the same advantages of flexibility and ease of innovation enjoyed by the mendicant orders when they had founded a religious revival based on preaching which also took root primarily in towns. However the position of an irregular preacher without institutional support was correspondingly weak. He could be accused of usurping Church offices and of breaches in legality, and so required the protective hand of a sympathetic secular authority. Besides, an irregular preacher could be more easily removed, and was always likely to seek more secure employment. The progress of the evangelical movement in many towns was thus checked by the loss of a temporary preacher.[25] Not many communities had the courage of the parish of St Michael in Worms, who simply appropriated a permanent post for the man of their choice.

One solution was for the community to support a preacher at their own expense alongside the regular parish clergy. This solution, of course, had its attendant problems, particularly those created by divisive preaching. That it was at all possible was the result of the upsurge of funded preacherships before the Reformation. This was largely an urban phenomenon, but one which extended even to tiny communities that were doubtless villages in all but name. It is thus no surprise that nearly 60% of the sample group held posts as preachers, and that 42% held them as regular posts.[26] The fairly high proportion of parish priests in Table 5 shows another aspect of the employment prospects of evangelical preachers. The position of parish pastor (*Pfarrer*) was usually higher in

25 In Lübeck, for example, the departure of Johann Fritze checked the progress of the Reformation there: *NDB*, vol. v, p. 634.
26 On divisive preaching, see R. W. Scribner, 'Sozialkontrolle und die Möglichkeit einer städtischen Reformation', in B. Moeller (ed.), *Stadt und Kirche im 16. Jahrhundert* (Gutersloh, 1978), pp. 60–1; on funded preacherships, see for example P. Mai, 'Predigtstiftungen des späten Mittelalters in Bistum Regensburg', *Beiträge zur Geschichte des Bistums Regensburg*, vol. ii (1968), pp. 7–33.

status, and it was clearly held to be preferable that the evangelical preacher occupy the higher position where possible. This was the case where the community could elect its own parish priest or where the secular authority, usually the Town Council, held this right. Its importance is shown by the frequency with which it was demanded during the social unrest of the mid-1520s.[27] Least satisfactory of all was the situation in which the man desired by the evangelical community was temporary, or held the minor position of vicar, chaplain, mass-priest or something similar. The post was likely to be poorly paid, and the likelihood that the preacher would move elsewhere was thus increased.

All these factors acted against the irregular preachers becoming at all typical of the Reformation movement. Indeed, the fact that preachers were drawn from the ranks of the old clergy inclined both the communities and the preachers themselves to fit them into the established career structure. This can be demonstrated by an analysis of job mobility of preachers between their first and second posts (Table 6).

TABLE 6
Mobility of preachers

	CHAPLAIN	FIRST POST			No.	%
		PREACHER IRREGULAR	PREACHER REGULAR	PFARRER		
	17 (9.7)	31 (17.6)	74 (42.1)	54 (30.7)	176 (100)	
SECOND POST						
Chaplain etc.	2	3	3	–	8	6.7
Preacher (irregular)	–	9	6	3	18	15.0
Preacher (regular)	7	9	22	5	43	35.8
Pfarrer etc.	4	7	22	18	51	42.5
					120	100.0
Second post not mentioned	4	3	21	28	56	

Here the categories from Table 5 have been regrouped into an ascending scale of status and permanence. Thus chaplain, vicar or mass-priest is regarded as of lower status, in evangelical terms, than an irregular preacher. Parish pastor (*Pfarrer*) has been grouped with canon or provost as posts higher in status than that of regular preacher. The cases where a second post is not mentioned includes both those where the information was not available and those where

27 This demand appeared in one third of peasant grievances during the Peasants' War: H. J. Hillerbrand, 'The German Reformation and the Peasants' War', in L. P. Buck and J. W. Zophy (eds), *The Social History of the Reformation* (Columbus, Ohio, 1972), p. 33.

the preacher held only one post. The correspondingly reduced numbers still show a clear trend, a movement into posts higher in status and permanence.

That such job mobility was possible compounded the problems of the evangelical community. To the difficulty of obtaining an evangelical preacher was added that of keeping him. Many towns jealously refused to release a valued preacher to others desirous of a spur to their evangelical fervour, or else they sent the preacher on short-term secondment, with the express condition that he was to return as soon as possible. This may have played its part, alongside local patriotism, in the frequent desire to have a preacher who was a son of the town. In fact, one in five of this sample group was active in his home town (36 cases or 20.5%). Yet given their high level of education, it might be expected that few preachers, except in the more prominent towns, would be content with the limited horizon of a single city. Indeed, even preachers offered appointments in their home towns proved unwilling to limit their activity to these alone. Less than half of those involved in their home towns were only active there (16 cases or 9.1%). Overall, job mobility was matched by geographical mobility (Table 7).

TABLE 7

Area of activity

Locally only	49	27.8%
Regionally	59	33.5
Super-regionally	59	33.5
Peripatetic	9	5.1

Well over 70% of preachers were active beyond the confines of one locality. Naturally enough, this gave them a wider horizon of experience, and a third knew the religious situation beyond regional boundaries. On the other hand, few were restless and transient enough in their posts to be classed as genuinely peripatetic. The classic example of this type of preacher, who accounts for only one case in twenty, is Johann Freysleben, the first evangelical preacher in the Upper Palatinate, whose preaching activity spanned the years 1520–57. During these thirty-seven years he held no less than twelve positions, an average of three years per post, within an area bounded by Bavaria, Hessen and Thuringia whose furthest points were up to 250 km apart. Such preachers, who included colourful and enigmatic figures like Johann Rot-Locher or Hans Maurer, called Zundauf, both of whom identified themselves with Karsthans, are extremely difficult to trace.[28] Yet it seems a reasonable generalization, in terms of the

28 M. Simon, 'Der Lebensgang des ersten evangelischen Predigers in der Oberpfalz, Johann Freysleben', *Zeitschrift für bayerische Kirchengeschichte*, vol. xxix (1960), pp. 25–32; on Locher K. Schottenloher, *Der Munchner Buchdrucker Hans Schobser 1500–1530* (Munich, 1925), pp. 111–42; on Maurer, *NDB*, vol. xi, p. 308.

patterns shown by this sample group, that the wandering preacher, no more than the articulate lay preacher, was not the typical figure of the Reformation.

The search for a godly preacher was perhaps most complicated by questions of politics. The relations of any given city with the surrounding powers is a well-documented factor in its ability to appoint an evangelical preacher and introduce the Reformation. It is unnecessary to press the point further here, except to mention that for such reasons the parish coup in St Michael's was short-lived. In 1526 the parish was forced, in the context of wider negotiations between Worms and its bishop over clerical rights, to remove the new preacher and restore the original incumbent.[29] No less decisive was the balance of internal politics, where two different kinds of relationship became entangled – that between preachers and people, and that between rulers and ruled.

Three matters stood at the heart of the evangelical community's commitment to its new preacher. The first was a dislike of the old clergy and awareness of their failure. The grounds for this anticlericalism have been acutely summed up by Prof. Heiko Oberman. The 'old religion', and that meant the old clergy as its embodiment, had deceived the people, repressed them and treated them as dumb.[30] The appeal of the new preacher was that he spoke the truth, plainly and without reservation, and proclaimed the liberation of the Christian believer. The second matter was the religious enthusiasm aroused by the new preaching. It included a pragmatic and down-to-earth understanding of evangelical belief, the placid assurance expressed in the Worms document that a man's spiritual needs would be catered for in and through the Bible. It also included the arousal of eschatological hopes and emotions, which led, among other things, to the demand for the preaching solely of 'right' belief and the eradication of the old.[31] The third matter, not unrelated to the other two, was a demand for the application of Gospel principles to the problems of daily life, the search for a new ethics. On each of these three matters, preachers and people could find themselves in conflict with authority.

Anticlericalism was the most sensitive of issues during the Reformation. Secular authority wished to assert its dominance over the clergy, whatever the religious allegiance on either side. Town Councils thus wished to play some part in the appointment or dismissal of the preacher, and to ensure that he conformed to their notion of a 'suitable' man. Their view is bluntly expressed in a memorandum prepared for the Town Council of Speyer in 1538, when it was con-

29 *Stadtarchiv Worms, Reichsstadt Worms* 1947: Ratsenschluss von Freitag nach Leonhardi, 9 November 1526.
30 H. A. Oberman, *Werden und Wertung der Reformation. Vom Wegestreit zum Glaubenskampf* (Tubingen, 1977), p. 238.
31 The importance of eschatology is a much-neglected theme in Reformation studies, although Oberman has suggested its importance for understanding differing responses to Luther (*Werden und Wertung der Reformation*, p. 373).

sidering the open appointment of a Lutheran preacher. The new preachers, it wrote, are to be as little trusted as the old, since most have been shown to seek only their own interests. They demand high wages and teach their followers only innovation and refractoriness. No less than the papists, moreover, they seek to encroach on secular rights. They draw the common folk to them and, when they are too strong for the authorities, reveal their effrontery and defend it with the Word. One may not rule other than by their version of the Gospel, which has little to do with that of Christ, who taught that his kingdom was not of this world. Through such men, many towns have suffered disturbance.[32]

The kind of situation the magistrates of Speyer were concerned about was familiar enough in the early years of the Reformation, and is illustrated by the manner in which the first evangelical pastor was appointed in Hamburg. In January 1526 the four Hamburg parishes decided that in future no parish priest should be chosen without the approval of the parish concerned. The Town Council was asked to respect this decision and not to hinder its implementation, for the citizenry were determined to uphold it with life and limb. In April the Town Council tried to prohibit Johann Zegenhagen from preaching in St Katherine's on the grounds that he had caused disturbance in Magdeburg, whence he had recently come to Hamburg. On 14 April a deputation was sent from the citizenry to the Town Council to protest against this, and seemed to obtain its objective, that Zegenhagen be allowed to continue preaching. However at the beginning of May the Council ordered him to leave town within three days. Further representations were made to the Council on 6 May and 7 May, that on the latter date consisting of forty citizens chosen from an assembly of four thousand. The preacher was again accused of fomenting disturbance, but the citizens, with such a mass display of strength, had their way and Zegenhagen remained. In September there was another confrontation, when the Council refused to accept Zegenhagen's election as parish priest of St Nicolaus. After pressure from the citizenry through assemblies and deputations the Council was forced to yield.[33]

No urban government of the sixteenth century was happy about such challenges to its authority. Faced with a preacher it considered undesirable, it wished to be able to remove him. Yet the commitment of the community to the man of its choice could lead to stubborn confrontations such as those in Hamburg, which had unpleasant implications about where the fount of political sovereignty lay. *In extremis*, such confrontations led to open rebellion which released the floodgates of social grievance. This occurred in the Zwickau weavers' revolt of April 1521, protesting about Müntzer's dismissal as preacher,

32 *Stadtarchiv Speyer* I A 450/4. I have published this important document as 'Memorandum on the Appointment of a Preacher in Speyer, 1538', *Bulletin of the Institute of Historical Research*, vol. xlviii (1975), pp. 248–55.

33 K. Koppmann, 'Die erste Wahl eines Lutherischen Pastors in Hamburg', *Mitteilungen des Vereins für Hamburgische Geschichte*, vol. vi (1883), pp. 137–44.

and the Johann Schilling revolt in Augsburg in 1524. For such reasons urban magistrates preferred a preacher who was as much their choice as the community's, exemplified in Ulm by Conrad Sam, who was designated as 'the Council's preacher'.[34]

In one way, the civic authorities were simply applying their deep-rooted anticlericalism to the preachers as a kind of conditioned reflex, understandable given their origins in the traditional clergy. On the other hand, the attitude of evangelical preachers towards secular authority often seemed to justify this. One consequence of the eschatological moment of the Reformation was the desire to achieve a holy community, living as far as possible in a state of Christian perfection. Here no allowance was often made for the magistrate, who was regarded as another Christian to be admonished and reproved, chastised and corrected by those who proclaimed God's Word. The kind of clash between preacher and authority this occasioned can be seen in the person of Johann Amandus.

From 1523 until his death in 1530, Amandus was constantly in trouble with secular authority. He was expelled as preacher in Koenigsberg in 1524 after a year of tangling with the Town Council. He went to Danzig, where he was immediately expelled: doubtless acting on information supplied by the Koenigsberg authorities, he was given a summary hearing by the Town Council and put straight back on the wagon from which he had stepped only a few hours earlier. He was imprisoned in Saxony on suspicion of fomenting sedition, probably during 1525–26. In 1529 he was called to lead the newly-reformed church in Goslar, and again fell out with the civic authorities. In Koenigsberg, Danzig, Goslar, and in 1525–26 in Saxony, Amandus faced similar charges, of fomenting sedition by criticism of authority. Yet he was no persistent troublemaker. He spent a period as preacher in Stettin and Stolpe, to the satisfaction of Council and community in both instances. His defence of himself in Goslar more than adequately refuted the charge that he stirred up disunity between Council and commune. What seems to have been at stake was his insistence on a serious implementation of the Gospel which extended to ruling élites. In Koenigsberg and Goslar it was his criticism of magistrates' indifference to the new belief which created conflict. His moral earnestness led him to combat the kind of outward conformity which was not matched in inward improvement. He desired a purified religion which was taken seriously by all citizens, a characteristic he shared with Calvin. Like Calvin, he believed in the use of the ban to enforce it. All this led him to be accused, unjustly, of being a fanatic and Anabaptist (*Schwärmer*). Allied to his popularity with the people at large, which

---

34 P. Wappler, *Thomas Müntzer in Zwickau und die 'Zwickauer Propheten'* (Gutersloh, 1966), pp. 40–3; W. Vogt, 'Johann Schilling der Barfüsser-Mönch und der Aufstand in Augsburg im Jahr 1524', *Zeitschrift des historischen Vereins für Schwaben und Neuburg*, vol. vi (1879), pp. 1–32; Stadtarchiv Ulm, Ratsprotokolle 8, fols 135, 264, 276, for designation of Sam as *des rats prediger*.

is attested for all the towns in which he was active, this made him an embarrassment and a political danger.[35]

Amandus's case is striking, but not exceptional. In Augsburg, for example, Michael Cellarius was disliked both for his popularity with the commons and his zeal for fuller implementation of reform. His sermons were held to arouse iconoclastic passions, and Cellarius himself was involved in an image-breaking incident. The political danger of his popularity was such that satirical verses attacked him as 'the idol in the Franciscans' (the church in which he preached), and he was accused of exerting influence on civic elections.[36] This political danger was the more evident in the third area of conflict, the ethical interpretation of the Gospel. It was concern with questions of social ethics and justice which formed much of Luther's public image before the Peasants' War, and which accounts for the widespread popularity of a writer like Eberlin von Günzburg. The figure who most clearly demonstrates the implications of these questions, however, is Jakob Strauss.

As preacher in Eisenach from 1523 to 1525, Strauss sparked off a major controversy over usury. In sermons and pamphlets he condemned usury as unchristian, a position in which he stood not far from Luther. However, he also extended the condemnation to all forms of interest, including annuities, a not uncommon form of financing income for ecclesiastical foundations, cities and princes. He hinted obliquely that even to give interest involved the debtor in the same sin as the usurer; and although he did not advocate direct refusal of interest or annuity payments, this conclusion was drawn by many debtors in Eisenach. His stand created consternation with secular authorities in Saxony, especially the Ernestine princes, who seem to have been genuinely concerned about the question of sin involved. The upshot was a limitation of interest in Saxony to 5%, but Strauss was branded as a troublemaker and identified with Karlstadt and Müntzer. Doctrinally there was little in this charge, but it was sufficiently incriminating for him to be accused of sedition during the Peasants' War. His stand was understandably popular with the common people, and his name appeared alongside those of Luther and Melanchthon in the *Memminger Bundesordnung* as that of a godly preacher acceptable as a mediator in the peasants' dispute with their lords. Strauss's chief concern was to formulate a social ethic consonant with evangelical belief. This took seriously the implementation of the Gospel in social life and condemned self-interest, even if it came from authority

35 P. Tschackert, *Urkundenbuch . . . Preussen*, nos 141, 192–3, 246, 295, 305, 331, 473a, 624a; F. A. Meckelberg, *Die Königsberger Chroniken aus der Zeit des Herzogs Albrecht* (Königsberg, 1865), p. 164 on Amandus' criticism of the Council for going to council sittings instead of sermons; *Acta Borussica ecclesiastica, civilia, literaria* (Leipzig, 1731), vol. ii, pp. 426–30, for a jaundiced, pro-Council view by the *Stadtschreiber* Caspar Platner; U. Hölscher, *Die Geschichte der Reformation in Goslar* (Hannover, 1902), pp. 54–5, 64–75, especially pp. 66–75, for Amandus's letter of justification of 10 July 1529.
36 W. Zorn, 'Michael Keller', *Lebensbilder aus Schwaben und Franken*, vol. vii (1960), pp. 165, 177.

and those in power. He was thus accused of wishing to set himself above authority and of belittling it in the eyes of its subjects.[37]

The question of social justice was one of the most important to emerge during the early years of the Reformation, and one on which views among adherents of the new belief were to diverge radically. A preacher like Strauss who was too outspoken on such matters could find himself disliked by those in power, however popular he was with the people. Such problems did not end with the Peasants' War. In Ulm, where the Town Council insisted on tight control of ecclesiastical affairs, there were two significant encounters between preachers and secular authority over social ethics in 1533. In the first, the leading preachers in Ulm, Conrad Sam and Martin Frecht, both Council appointees, presented the Council with a list of ten articles which they deemed to be contrary to the Gospel and love of neighbour. These included matters which might be considered rightly the concern of the clergy – the holding of a church synod, the provision of books for rural parsons and the continued existence of the town brothel. However they also touched grievances within the guilds, the right of masters to lend at interest to their journeymen and the level of interest on grain rentes.[38] On the 'secular' issues the Town Council replied firmly that it did not see many of them as contrary to the Gospel, and in effect told the preachers to mind their own business on guild matters.[39]

The second incident was more serious in its implications. Several rural parsons held an informal synod to discuss the justification according to the Gospel of serfdom and of the great and small tithe. They were clearly troubled in conscience about these questions, as they were about how far they were obliged to obey unconditionally secular authority, which must surely stand as other men under the Word of God. They were little inclined to do anything other than voice their disquiet to one another, accepting that the Council had a number of skilled and learned preachers who would doubtless protest if it acted against the Word. However they had little confidence in secular authority itself. One complained that the Gospel was now as oppressed as it had been under the papacy, another that authority would not allow them to do as they desired, and that to oppose it would only lead to its coming down on them with force.[40] The resignation of these country parsons speaks volumes. The creation of an erastian territorial church was as much the work of city governments as it

37 H. Barge, *Jakob Strauss*, especially p. 62 on similarity of his views to Luther's; R. Jauernig, 'D. Jakob Strauss, Eisenachs erster evangelischer Geistliche und der Zinswucherstreit in Eisenach', *Mitteilungen des Eisenacher Geschichtsvereins*, vol. iv (1928), pp. 30–48; J. Rogge, *Der Beitrag des Predigers Jakob Strauss zur frühen Reformationsgeschichte* (Berlin, 1957), especially pp. 90–103 on Strauss in the Peasant War and pp. 109–111 on Strauss's social ethics.
38 *Stadtarchiv Ulm* XV, 9000, fols 23–4. Frecht and Sam had mixed views on the last matters: they seemed to favour masters lending to their journeymen on the grounds that this helped the latter to obtain loans; the level of interest on grain rentes, however, they regarded as too high.
39 Ibid., fols 21–2.
40 Ibid., fols 28–36.

was of princes. In the long run, citizens had as little say in the choice of their preacher as subjects.

The ethical questions raised by the Reformation movements indicate that there are two different concepts concealed beneath the term 'the popular preacher'. There is the preacher demanded by the people because he is expected to bring a revival of communal religious life. This kind of popular demand often had little to do with the personal qualities of the preacher himself. This is nowhere more apparent than in the example of Johann Fritze, the first evangelical preacher in Lübeck. For two years (1524–5) Fritze hovered between proclaiming the new belief and faintheartedly giving in to the Town Council's demands that he mend his unorthodox ways. He condemned the Mass as the devil's work and tried to dissuade others from saying it, although continuing to celebrate it himself. After his first clash with authority, in December 1524, he intended to leave Lübeck, but was asked to remain by the mayor, who believed that his departure would provoke disturbance because his preaching was so popular.[41]

A second kind of popularity was that of the preacher who spoke of the social needs of the people, and gave loyal support to attempts to deal with them. This accounts for much of Luther's early popularity among simple folk who could have understood little of the sophistication of his theology – not to mention figures as disparate as Eberlin von Günzburg, Jakob Strauss and Thomas Müntzer. Here the Gospel was popular because it was also 'the Gospel of social unrest'. Both kinds of popularity explain the viewpoint from which the people, burdened with spiritual and social pressures, viewed what historians term the Reformation.[42] In fact, the people did not always get the preachers they desired, nor indeed the preachers they deserved. If few can be found who seemed qualified to address the mass of the people in their own terms, the few who made the attempt were frustrated by the interventions of rulers and of politics. The preachers who were found acceptable were those whose conformity of background was matched by conformity of views. In this way, the new preachers became the new clergy of the territorial church.

This seems a long way from the stunningly simple aspirations of the parishioners of St Michael's in Worms, but the contrast sums up, perhaps, the relation between practice and principle in the German Reformation. Truly, in the words used by Professor A. G. Dickens about the outcome of the Reformation in Erfurt, 'providence used the children of the world to confound the godly.'[43]

41 W. Janatsch, *Reformationsgeschichte Lübecks* (Lübeck, 1958), pp. 121, 126, 130–1, 135–6, 145, 153–4.
42 See H. A. Oberman, 'The Gospel of Social Unrest' in B. Scribner and G. Benecke (eds), *The German Peasant War of 1525. New Viewpoints* (London, 1978), pp. 39–51. The theme of spiritual and social pressure runs throughout Dickens, *German Nation*.
43 Dickens, *German Nation*, p. 176.

VII

The Principle and Practice of Primitive Protestantism in Tudor England: Cranmer, Parker and Grindal as Chief Pastors

1535 - 1577

❧

PETER NEWMAN BROOKS

Writing from Otford on 12 May 1535 a cautious Cranmer afforded Thomas Cromwell his detailed reaction to the opinion of the bishop of Winchester, the King's Principal Secretary having recently informed him that, in Gardiner's considered view, the archiepiscopal style stood in 'derogation and prejudice of the King's high power and authority, [Henry] being supreme head of the church.'[1] In terms of 'king's authority' it was, to be sure, something of an *embarras de richesse* and prompted the scrupulous primate to 'pray to God never [to] be merciful to me at the general judgement, if I perceive in my heart that I set more by any title, name, or style that I write, than I do by the paring of an apple, farther than it shall be to the setting forth of God's word and will.' For Cranmer was clear that he, and those who were genuinely his brother bishops, should 'leave all our styles . . . calling ourselves *apostolos Jesu Christi.*'

The observation provides an early illustration of acute pastoral sensitivity in the English Church of the Reformation, a dimension that increasingly revealed itself as the movement advanced. For what Thomas Cranmer desired for the dioceses of his native land was both simple and straightforward, namely that 'neither paper, parchment, lead, nor wax, but the very christian conversation of the people might be the letters and seals of our offices, as the Corinthians were unto Paul . . .'[2]

Although historians have objected to the concept of Cranmer as a kind of Protestant patriarch, such a notion nevertheless has much to commend it in logical argument. Pursued through the primacy of sober primitives like Parker and Grindal indeed, the idea usefully clarifies a number of principles motivating these leaders of the English Reformation. The historiography of this vexed period thus usefully focuses the dilemma facing those seeking to revise partisan portraits of a primate who, for political reasons, was rarely able to know his own mind. With the advance of the Oxford Movement in the nineteenth century, however, the negative 'Low Church' attitudes of eighteenth-century ease in Sion were gradually repudiated. For as long as polemic was able to masquerade as genuine historical study, Cranmer proved the perfect scapegoat, clergy hostile to the Reformation being at pains to manufacture an exaggerated 'doubting Thomas' image calculated to discredit. The cause of respectability and party strife certainly prompted many churchmen to abandon those formative stages of the English Reformation as

> . . . old, unhappy, far-off things,
> And battles long ago.

1 J. E. Cox (ed.), *Miscellaneous Writings and Letters of Thomas Cranmer* (edited for the Parker Society; 2 vols, Cambridge, 1846). Vol. II, p. 305. Hereafter referred to as PS *Cranmer II*.
2 PS *Cranmer II*, p. 305.

Yet far different are the facts that support the remarkable dedication of Henry's 'new Archbishop', the Cranmer shrewdly assessed in the pages of Professor A. G. Dickens's masterpiece as a churchman who 'had strong sympathies with the Lutherans.'[3] For Cranmer's role as Chief Pastor, firmly founded in a genuine regard for scriptural and patristic scholarship, was rapidly adopted and forwarded by those who succeeded him in the see of Canterbury. Thus whether consciously or unconsciously, much that Matthew Parker and Edmund Grindal strove to implement, Thomas Cranmer had first set in motion himself to leave a fascinating legacy.

By the standards of a contemporary patronage that valued legal training as the *sine qua non* of such promotion, Cranmer, Parker and Grindal were singularly unsuited to high office in the Church. All three were manifestly scholars in a new tradition. They unquestionably made their names in the congenial atmosphere of a Cambridge where 'the New Divinity' was the reigning intellectual fashion, so that only cruel accidents of fate brought the royal favour that ultimately lodged them at Lambeth. With Cranmer it was the plague, a chance meeting with Gardiner and Fox, and some eccentric views about 'the King's great matter' that placed him beneath Tudor scrutiny. With Parker and Grindal it was a brilliant academic career, Parker gaining the Mastership of Bene't College and the University Vice-Chancellorship, and Grindal the Cambridge Proctorship and a Presidency at Pembroke Hall.

Matthew Parker's learning certainly brought him to the notice of those in high places, for but rarely had the Fellows of a Cambridge college received such a communication:

HENRY R

Trusty and well-beloved, we greet you well. And whereas it is come to our understanding that your master and governor either lieth now at the extreme point of death, or is already departed out of this transitory life, by occasion whereof ye be, or shortly are like to be, destitute of a good head and governor: we, therefore, for the zeal and love we bear to the advancement of good letters . . . commend unto you our well-beloved chaplain, doctor Parker . . .[4]

If the Crown was prepared to jump the gun, so to state, for once the Fellows by no means doubted reference to the candidate's 'approved learning, wisdom and honesty', not to mention his 'singular grace and industry in bringing up youth in virtue and learning.'[5]

Twice Vice-Chancellor, Parker unquestionably showed the University that he knew how to handle youth on the one hand and the old-maidish prying of Chancellor Stephen Gardiner on the other. In 1545 the undergraduates of

---

3 A. G. Dickens, *The English Reformation* (London, 1964), p. 328.
4 J. Bruce (ed.), *Correspondence of Matthew Parker* (Cambridge, 1853), pp. 16–17. Hereafter referred to as PS *Park. Cor.*
5 Ibid., p. 17.

Christ's College performed a play – in Gardiner's phrase, a tragedy brimful of 'pestiferous' potential – and complaints duly reached the highest authority. The Chancellor at once demanded an inquiry, urging with over-fussy vigilance that youth must learn the 'truth of obedience'. With consummate tact, Parker set about cooling the situation, and drew Council's attention to the fact that only a single Fellow had opposed the play.[6] He, a Senior named Scot, deemed the work as 'throughout poison', and steadfastly refused to heed the democratic counsel of colleagues prepared to use the censor's blue pencil and thereby recognize at least some degree of dramatic potential.

When, some twenty years later, Cecil sought Parker's advice about two troublesome fellows of Gonville Hall, the Primate's assurance that 'My old experience . . . hath taught me to spy daylight at a small hole'[7] expressed volumes about his Cambridge know-how. For it was Parker who had helped none other than Martin Bucer to plan his lectures, after Cranmer gained the Regius Chair of Divinity for that Strasbourg exile; Parker who had given one hundred costly and rare volumes to the University Library (Cranmer's personal library was far larger than that of the Old Schools in his day); Parker who at his own expense had paved and walled a road to the Schools; and supremely, of course, Parker who had benefited his 'old nurse', Bene't College.[8]

The parallel with Cranmer is pronounced. For if Cranmer's meteoric rise early removed him from Cambridge, yet his love and understanding of his old College prompted him when primate to send the Master of Jesus 'a buck to be bestowed amonges your company . . . And forasmuch as you have more store of money, and also less need than I at this time, therefore I bequeath a noble of your purse towards the baking and seasoning of him.'[9] It is a comparison that likewise relates to Parker's own successor, Edmund Grindal. For it was, after all, he who left Pembroke, Cambridge, so enmeshed in a kind of old-boy net that he became chaplain to bishop Nicholas Ridley, the Hall's former Master, and, in August 1551, Prebendary of St Paul's cathedral.

In every case to be sure, destiny seemed to lend a hand – despite reasoned *noli episcopare* from those who fought the very prospect of being placed in the ultimate office. Such proved of no avail, and as if determined to serve regardless of the summons they deplored, first Cranmer, and then Parker and Grindal busied themselves with pastoral concerns that evidently became the mainspring and motivating force of principled ministry. From the newly-realized eminence of Canterbury, a profound and perceptive vision was thus shown and handed on in a number of significant respects.

First, from the abundant witness of Cranmer's *Commonplaces*, from Parker's

6 The tragedy *Pammachius*. Cf. PS *Park. Cor.*, pp. 21–30.
7 PS *Park. Cor.*, p. 249. The fellows in question were Clarke and Dethick.
8 Ibid., p. 438.
9 PS *Cranmer II*, p. 247.

passion for patristics (the study Cranmer himself had pioneered in England at the outset of Reformation), and indeed from Grindal's determined attempt to raise the standard of preaching among the clergy, it is manifestly the case that these three men in their respective periods made bold to mould a ministry both reformed and scholarly.

In a letter to the deprived archbishop of York, Nicholas Heath, for example, Parker's reasoned rationale of the Reformation position spotlights a man conscious of the mantle of the martyred Cranmer: 'What was it occasioned the Romish writers to write against the Bishop of Rome? What was it caused Luther, Calvin, and other orthodox clergymen to renounce Rome and her church for this thing called the bishop of Rome's tribunal?'[10] For Parker was concerned to retrieve the *Commonplaces*, and secured those 'noble written books of my predecessor' from the clutches of Nevinson by authority of the Council. That he also gained Bale's *Antiquities* for hard cash (being well-placed to do so as Bale's executor), and devoted much time compiling the *De Antiquitate Britannicae Ecclesiae*, underlines his care as a Reformer of scholarly pretensions. By tracing the history of the faith 'from Augustine until the days of King Henry VIIIth, when religion began to grow better and more agreeable to the Gospel . . .,'[11] Parker thus satisfied himself that, just as the ancient British Church had existed apart from Rome, so too his own reformed communion of the faithful could continue to justify its independent role in Christendom. He had, in fact, arrived at precisely Cranmer's position – Cranmer who, having gleaned the good grain of patristic study from Oecolampadius, the learned Reformer of Basel, first showed his own grasp of the situation to effect in the significant argument of the *Defence* (1550). Such a careful exposition of eucharistic theology inexorably exposed the papal claims with material rooted out from the Fathers. Likewise, in the celebrated discussion on the Sacrament in the House of Lords (December 1548), as well as in the *Defence*, Cranmer's sense of scholarship applied primitive historical argument with such skill that, in terms of Reformation pamphlet warfare, he had chosen to commandeer the secret weapon of patristics, so effectively used on the Continent, for service in the English arena. In countering debating points made by Day and Bonner, the archbishop thus replied: 'But answere to Ireneus that auncyente wryter, the disciple of Policarpus which was John's disciple.'[12]

These were early days when the cause of Reformation must stand or fall according to the depth and dedication of its scholarship. When pundits thus point to the achievement of Jewel's celebrated *Apology* for the English Church, they frequently forget the foundations laid by men of the calibre of Cranmer and Parker. Independence from Rome meant lonely and vulnerable isolation.

10 PS *Park. Cor.*, p. 112.
11 Quoted in V. K. J. Brook, *A Life of Archbishop Parker*, p. 323.
12 Cf. Peter Brooks, *Thomas Cranmer's Doctrine of the Eucharist* (London, 1965), p. 50, note 3.

It was a most difficult existence unless justified in terms of that quest for sound scholarship which was to provide the Reformed Church of England with its timeless, and sadly unfulfilled, aspiration – 'a learned man in every parish.' The point is admirably expounded in a letter of Parker to Edmund Grindal who, when it was written (August 1560), was already bishop of London:

Whereas, occasioned by the great want of ministers, we . . . have hitherto admitted . . . sundry artificers and others, not traded and brought up in learning . . . now by experience it is seen that such manner of men, partly by reason of their former profane arts, partly by their light behaviour . . . are very offensive unto the people, yea, and to the wise of this realm are thought to do great deal more hurt than good, the Gospel there sustaining slander; . . . hereafter . . . be very circumspect in admitting any to the ministry, and only to allow such as, having good testimony of their honest conversation, have been traded and exercised in learning . . .[13]

In a vital sense of course, the dimension is superficial. For in the final analysis, the whole point of patristic scholarship concerned its relationship to Biblical study. The Fathers furnished the Reformers with an invaluable second front against the ravages of Rome. What significant Continental divines like Melanchthon, Oecolampadius and Calvin had thus forwarded to effect, Cranmer eagerly used to the advantage of the English Church. Scripture was the sheet-anchor of ultimate argument against tiresome and threatening opposition; and in the polished language of the *fifth Article of Religion* set forth in 1553, its role was clearly focussed:

Holy Scripture containeth all things necessary to Salvation: so that whatsoever is neither read therein, nor may be proved thereby, although it be sometime received of the faithful as godly, and profitable for an order, and comeliness; yet no man ought to be constrained to believe it as an article of faith, or repute it to the necessity of Salvation.[14]

It was, needless to state, an article Parker himself strengthened as *Article VI* in 1563; and there is little need to emphasize Grindal's stand for the supremacy of Scripture and its consequences for his career at Canterbury.

Matthew Parker spent much of his primacy superintending the production of the *Bishops' Bible*. If in one sense he intended this as a work to beat the Puritans at their own game by reducing the circulation of the remarkably successful *Geneva Bible* with its decidedly 'presbyterian' understanding of ministry, in another it was a masterly attempt by the primate to keep his brother bishops up to scratch in Biblical scholarship. Published in 1568, the Bible has been sadly underrated by historians. Parker's part in the enterprise certainly merits recognition. The original 'Nosey Parker' only in the sense that he invariably had his head in a book, the archbishop was editor and contributor on a grand scale,

13 PS *Park. Cor.*, pp. 120–1.
14 J. Ketley, *The Two Liturgies . . . set forth . . . in the Reign of King Edward VI* (Cambridge, 1844), p. 527.

particularly in view of his wider responsibilities. Thus not only did he contribute various prefaces and translate Genesis and Exodus, Matthew and Mark, but, with the exception of Romans and 1 Corinthians, all the letters of Paul to the Early Church, and the Letter to the Hebrews for good measure. As editor, Parker's pastoral sense proved paramount, the primate attaching great importance to the use of direct day-to-day language that could readily communicate the Christian Gospel. 'I would wish that such usual words that we English people be acquainted with might still remain in their form and sound, so far forth as the Hebrew will bear. Inkhorn terms to be avoided.'[15] It was a singular achievement for the man Cranmer once recommended to preach at Paul's Cross, naming the young Parker at that time (1548) as one who 'could purely and sincerely set out the holy scriptures, so as God's glory may be advanced, and the people with wholesome doctrine edified.'[16]

Secondly, the logic of their pastoral commitment indicated to these responsible primates that they concern themselves with education at every level. In early days, Thomas Cranmer had done his level best to educate a king. His surviving *Notes on Henry VIII's Corrections* of the *Institution of a Christian Man*[17] are certainly reminiscent of the role of a conscientious Cambridge supervisor confronted by casual composition from one who was after all the prototype Trinity man. Commenting on the phrase 'only by his suffrance' in the royal usage, Cranmer thus penned a most donnish, grammatical gloss: 'This word "suffrance" diminisheth the goodness of God, and agreeth not with the three verbs to whom it is referred . . .'[18]

Likewise, writing to Edward VI at the outset of his sad little reign, Cranmer was clear that, just as Paul had stressed 'that Timothy was brought up even from a child in holy Scriptures', so the young King might aid the youth of his realm 'to know God' if he adopted the archbishop's translation of the Lutheran *Catechism of Justas Jonas* for their use. Very much the 'young Josiah', indeed, Edward followed Cranmer's counsel and not merely urged this 'short and plain order of Cathechism' on 'all schoolmasters and teachers of youth', but by an *Injunction* of 1553 commanded them that they 'truly and diligently teach' his own royal *Catechismus Brevis* published that same year. At the time of the Dissolution of the Chantries, moreover, Cranmer, who openly voted against the Second Act, did what he could to conserve Chantry assets for Edward to use for godly purposes once he came of age. It could well be that the Primate proved as important as the bishop of London in persuading Edward to found his sixteen Grammar Schools, although Ridley has customarily received the credit. A similar concern undoubtedly recurred in metropolitical visitations, and

15 PS *Park. Cor.*, p. 282.
16 Ibid., p. 39.
17 The so-called *King's Book* of 1538.
18 PS *Cranmer II*, p. 84.

Grindal, for example, made due inquiry in his seventh article of 1536: '*Item*, Whether your grammar-school be well ordered . . .'[19]

In his turn, Parker not only patronized learning at both his *alma mater* and Oxford University, but also cared for the King's School, Canterbury, founded a Grammar School in Lancashire, and did much to encourage the establishment of Sir Roger Manwood's School at Sandwich. A recent biographer described Matthew Parker as 'incredibly trivial' for spending time licensing schoolmasters and in one case a midwife, but such conscientious activity can equally well illustrate the meticulous stewardship of the primate as a committed educational-ist and pastor who made the most of every opportunity to know his own men.[20]

A loyal Englishman, Parker certainly related a sound Reformation education to prizing the safety of the Protestant Realm, and argued that those fully committed to 'the new religion' could not for a moment relax their vigilance in ways that might give advantage to the emissaries of Rome. With the exag-gerated public spirit of a Captain Mainwaring, Parker proved himself a Homeguard vigilante when, in order to warn a visiting French embassy that Englishmen faced with invasion could rapidly achieve mobilization, he made ostentatious display of a personal suit of armour at the Primate's Bekesbourne property:

. . . because they much noted the tract of this country in the fair plains and downs so nigh the sea, and to mark the strength we were of, in a little vain brag (unpriestly ye may say) I thought good to have a piece of mine armoury in a lower chamber, nigh to my court, subject to their eyes; whereby they did see that some preparation we had against their invasion, if it had been so purposed. And so some of them expressed, that if a bishop hath regard of such provision, belike other had a more care thereabout.[21]

Thirdly, in a truly apostolic sense, the pastoral concern of these primates can be well appreciated from the fact that all three were very much 'given to hospitality.'[22] Once again, Cranmer set the standard, and cared for significant strangers like Martin Bucer and Peter Martyr far above the accepted norm. Bucer thus not only gained the Regius Chair of Divinity at Cambridge, but also the personal gift of a stove to heat the dank Fenland air that infiltrated the Keeping Room of the distinguished Strasbourg exile. To cite another example, John Laski the Pole could well have embarrassed the cause of Reformation in England. A known hothead, Laski wished to go beyond the *Act of Uniformity* and use his own service book for the worship of the Austin Friars community. As bishop of London, Nicholas Ridley was clear that such acts would abuse archiepiscopal authority (Cranmer had generously made over the Church of the Austin Friars to Laski and his congregation of exiles), and his addiction to

19 William Nicholson (ed.), *The Remains of Edmund Grindal, DD* (Cambridge, 1843), p. 180. Hereafter referred to as PS *Grindal*.
20 V. K. J. Brook, *Archbishop Parker*, p. 236.
21 PS *Park. Cor.*, p. 216.
22 Cf. Romans 12:13 and 1 Peter 4:9.

a narrow law-and-order theology prompted him to oppose the extension of any such latitude to the strangers. It was a tricky moment, but Ridley achieved little, archbishop Cranmer's deep sense of charitable hospitality firmly overruling his suffragan.

Most generous to his household, and indeed to all comers, Matthew Parker lived up to the height of his income. Yet he was also shrewdly aware of hardship whenever it came to his notice. He thus not only postponed the visitation of his diocese until such time as his clergy could reasonably afford to meet the demands a new regime inevitably made on parochial expenditure, but also took up the cause of the married clergy whose wives were effectively outlawed from cathedral and college precincts by the Queen's Order of August, 1561. His representation to Cecil in the matter showed Parker to be well capable of spirited defence: 'Horsekeepers' wives, porters', pantlers', and butlers' wives may have their cradles going, and honest learned men expulsed with open note, who only keep the hospitality, who only be unfeigned orators, in open prayers, for the Queen's Majesty's prosperity and continuance; where others say their back *pater-nosters* for her in corners.'[23]

The matter suggests an early clash at court, for despite his faithful allegiance to the Crown, Parker was decidedly ill-used of Elizabeth I, being subjected on occasions to those towering Tudor rages so effectively dramatized of late by actress Glenda Jackson. When his manors were thus exchanged, and his parks purloined under the *Act relating to bishops' lands* (1559), the archbishop recalled with evident nostalgia the good old days when Anne Boleyn had sent her chaplain a buck or two. But as Cecil was reminded, times had changed: 'Marry I doubt in these days whether bishops or ministers may be thought worthy to eat venison, I will hold me to my beef.'[24] Good humour in adversity may charm posterity with an endearing quality, but in context such incidents as these symbolized the way Tudor legalism was able to blight the careers of even the State's most promising pastors. For in the final analysis, of course, Cranmer, Parker and Grindal were bound to come to terms with the reality of royal supremacy.

As a kind of English Protestant patriarch, Cranmer once again set the stage. With the repudiation of Papal authority, he was clear that there was Scriptural warrant for the Godly Prince as Head of the Church, and there is no doubting the special relationship he enjoyed with Henry VIII. Under Edward too, Reformation advanced considerably because the royal favour for Protestantism happened to suit the ambition of those enjoying real political power, the Regents Somerset and Northumberland. Happily for the young King and the reforming party in the English Church, it also impinged on many of the spiritual designs of the archbishop. With Mary I, however, the crisis came when Cranmer

23 PS *Park. Cor.*, p. 158.
24 Ibid., p. 178.

proved personally unable to withstand Edward's dying request that his archbishop sign the instrument for the accession of Jane Grey. That Lady's nine-day
wonder over, Cranmer soon faced deprivation, and a cruel dilemma in terms of
the obedience he still felt obliged in conscience to show an heretic, Romish
Queen. Urged on by Spanish advisers, Mary resolved for her part to overturn
the whole work of Reformation. Yet in the Scriptural understanding he had
come to cherish, she lawfully remained Cranmer's Godly Prince. This basic
realization not only explains the tedious rigmarole of recantation; it also stresses
the complex legacy that, after the Elizabethan Church Settlement, descended
on Parker and Grindal.

Matthew Parker's principal task as Primate in the Tudor manner was the
unenviable drudgery of enforcing the state ecclesiastical in the service of the
Queen. It was difficult enough to find men who would preach a Scriptural
Gospel in their ministry without the distraction of dissent in Church order; and
however patiently he tried, the archbishop utterly failed to make the point with
Cecil and the Queen. Granted the availability of suitable men and due support
from the Council, uniformity had everything to recommend it. But the circumstances that faced Parker, Grindal and their suffragans were far removed from
such an ideal. The Primate well knew 'what the Queen's Majesty expecteth',
and to a degree was prepared to show his loyalty in deference. Yet his was
hardly the Gilbertian 'Defer, defer, to the Lord High Executioner', if only
because he had emphasized to Council that such insistence on dull conformity
must discourage 'some good protestants.'[25] Clearly, if once he became entram-
melled in such legalism, Parker was fully aware that his reputation as Chief
Pastor must suffer. Accordingly, he duly informed Cecil that '. . . if I draw
forward, and others draw backwards, what shall it avail, but raise exclamations
and privy mutterings against your honour and against me, by whom they think
these matters be stirred.'[26] In any case, a Council genuinely desirous of uniformity ought surely to have acted when 'some of your preachers preached before
the Queen's Majesty without tippet, and had nothing said to them for it.'[27]

The whole matter was largely a repeat performance of the crisis of 1565 when
the Primate had advised Cecil in the plainest language that Elizabeth must afford
her express authority in such matters. For as he wrote to the Principal Secretary
at the time: 'If this ball shall be tossed unto us and then have no authority by the
Queen's hand, we will set still.'[28] If the superficial judgements of some historians have tended to damn Parker out of hand as a compliant establishment
figure, the detailed evidence of his correspondence cannot be used to sustain
the charge. As year followed year, indeed, the archbishop's letters testified to

25 Ibid., p. 263.
26 Ibid.
27 Ibid.
28 Ibid., p. 235.

his new-found conviction that Gospel, not legal, affairs constituted his properly primatial concern. What, for example, was the point of Parker ordering the Puritans Humphrey and Sampson 'to wear the cap appointed by Injunction, to wear no hats in their long gowns, to wear a surplice with a non-regent hood in their quires at their Colleges, according to the ancient manner there, to communicate kneeling in wafer-bread'; what was the point when Dr Turner, Dean of Wells (as the archbishop informed Cecil obliquely in a postscript), 'yesterday . . . enjoined a common adulterer to do his open penance in a square priest's cap.'[29] What, to be sure, was the point when some London church-wardens effectively sabotaged a Eucharist by their refusal to supply either surplice or 'singing cakes' (wafer bread) as enjoined by the *Injunctions*? In the face of such pointless legalism, and an implicit refusal to allow some compromise embodying the spirit as distinct from the letter of the Royal *Injunctions*, Parker felt he could 'do no more, nor . . . promise any more; my age will not suffer me to peruse all the parishes.'[30] Written on Good Friday 1566, no less, the words suggest a new sadness in so sensitive a man. After all, had not the Primate warned the authorities of the immense uphill task ahead if thorough-going, unqualified uniformity was ever to be achieved? And it certainly took him ill with 'shame to be so vilely reported.'[31]

Parker's loyalty need not for one moment be questioned; but he shrank increasingly from what became for him an irrelevant establishment role that failed to recognize an archbishop's properly pastoral commitment. 'I am not weary to bear, to do service to God and to my prince; but an ox can draw no more than he can.'[32] Despite such scruples, he bravely continued to haul his load for almost another decade, perhaps steadfast in the hope that the Supreme Governor would give the longed-for lead at the last. At the same time, however, it was as if an iron rigidity seized his very soul. Correspondence discloses a burden he found intolerable. When Cecil lay ill in December 1573, Parker admittedly wrote words of comfort to an old friend and pleaded that he believe with St Paul that 'to live is Christ' and so make good his recovery. But when the archbishop's own end came in view, it was a Parker broken with care for conformity and tired of the tyranny of the trivial who spoke out with concern and courage: 'Does your lordship think that I care either for cap, tippet, surplice, or wafer-bread, or any such? But for the laws so established I esteem them, and not more for exercise of contempt against law and authority, which I see will be the end of it . . .'[33] By now Parker was so convinced of the vanity of 'dancing in a net' that he questioned the extent of the royal prerogative: 'Whatever the

29 Ibid., p. 241.
30 Ibid., p. 278.
31 Ibid., p. 279.
32 Ibid.
33 Ibid., pp. 478–9.

ecclesiastical prerogative is, I fear it is not so great as your pen hath given it her . . . and her governance is of more prerogative than the head papists would grant . . .'[34] Significant language from such a sensitive scholar, these words clearly indicate the trials and tribulations Parker endured in his high sphere of service.

Against such a backcloth, the tragedy of Edmund Grindal was played. In perspective, it is best viewed as the climax of a development that began with Cranmer. As archbishop, Grindal early resolved to continue his policy of enhancing clerical education by urging his clergy, many of them decidedly 'puritan', to attend the exercises known as 'prophesyings'. The editor of the Parker Society volume quaintly entitled *The Remains of Edmund Grindal* was shrewdly aware of the design, and noted that 'the archbishop looked with a favourable eye upon the exercises . . . considering that they might, notwithstanding certain incidental inconveniences, be made, in the main, subservient to the cause of true religion.'[35] Later, quoting Collier's *Ecclesiastical History*, he posed the problem in succinct terms:

But the queen was of a different sentiment. She thought these meetings gave encouragement to novelty, made people ramble in their fancy, and neglect their affairs. That their curiosity was too much indulged, and their heads overcharged with notions by these discourses; and that by raising disputes, and forming parties, things might possibly grow up to a public disturbance. She told the archbishop the kingdom was overfurnished with instructions of this nature: that she would have the exercise of prophesying suppressed, the preachers reduced to a smaller number, and homilies read instead of sermons. She conceived three or four preachers in a county might be sufficient, and that therefore licenses for the pulpit should be granted with more reserve. The queen delivered herself upon this subject with something of vehemence and disgust; and gave her pleasure in charge to the archbishop.[36]

It was as if Elizabeth had lanced a tender part of Grindal's conscience, for the Primate at once stressed that the reading of homilies set forth by public authority was 'nothing comparable to the office of preaching'.[37] As Chief Pastor he felt obliged to give a lead to the ministry, and rallied to defend a key Reformation principle against encroachment from the Crown. On 20 December 1576 he thus wrote a considered rejoinder: 'Alas Madam! Is the Scripture more plain in any one thing, than that the Gospel of Christ should be plentifully preached; and that plenty of labourers should be sent into the Lord's harvest; which, being great and large, standeth in need, not of a few, but many workmen?'[38]

Whereas archbishop Parker had shared his concern about the state of play

34 Ibid., p. 479.
35 PS *Grindal*, p. xi.
36 Ibid., pp. xi–xii. Cf. Jeremy Collier, *An Ecclesiastical History of Great Britain, chiefly of England, from the first planting of Christianity, to the end of the Reign of King Charles the Second*, ed. F. Barham (9 vols, London, 1840), vol. vi, pp. 566–7.
37 PS *Grindal*, p. 382.
38 Ibid., p. 378.

in a confidential letter to Cecil, Edmund Grindal seemed immediately to sense not merely that a point of no return had been reached, but that matters had in fact now gone too far. He accordingly proceeded to take the Queen openly to task. As had been the case with Cranmer, an archbishop had boldly determined to uphold what he held to be a basic principle of the Reformed faith in defiance of opposition from a Tudor queen. The parallel is dramatic, and the immediate outcome – namely the defeat of the Primate – very similar. If Cranmer was burnt at the stake, Grindal was made to resign (at one stage Elizabeth actually sought his deprivation[39]). The Tudors would not be thwarted and, to a woman, interpreted the headship of the Church as an instrument that gave them the last word in religious matters.

Yet just as Cranmer's martyrdom was branded on to the memory of Englishmen, so in its turn Grindal's stand also proved of great significance. For it surely prompted the faithful to think again about the meaning of Reformation in terms of the role of both bishops and princes. Grindal used bold but courteous language to the Queen: 'Bear with me, I beseech you, Madam, if I choose rather to offend your earthly majesty, than to offend the heavenly majesty of God . . .'[40] And there followed the celebrated 'Remember, Madam, that you are a mortal creature . . .' But his subsequent patristic allusion to advice given by Ambrose to Theodosius, coupled as it was with counsel that Elizabeth gaze not upon the purple too much, amounted to a calculated and gratuitous insult, and went far beyond the deference of Cranmer's dealings with Henry and Mary, or even Parker and the Queen.[41] Nevertheless, Cranmer, Parker and Grindal all believed that God had called them to the office of bishop. As 'apostles of Jesus Christ', moreover, they had no illusions of grandeur, being clear that bishops were no separate *ordo* in the Reformed or 'new religion'. Equally, they acknowledged that, under God, the Prince had every Scriptural warrant to uphold the sceptre and rule. Yet that rule had its limitations, and just as they kept strictly within the jurisdictional authority assigned to them as officers of the Tudor State, so too they expected the authorities to recognize the freedom of the bishop to be what Richard Hooker later defined as a 'principal ecclesiastical overseer' with responsibility for the spiritual affairs of the Church.[42] Infringement of such a principle was held to be the usurpation of popes; and it was no coincidence that, in his letter to Elizabeth I, Edmund Grindal rebuked his Queen for her resolute and peremptory pronouncements in the matter of the preachers: 'It is the antichristian voice of the pope, *Sic volo, sic jubeo; stet pro ratione voluntas.*'[43]

39 Cf. Claire Cross, *The Royal Supremacy in the Elizabethan Church* (London, 1969), p. 63.
40 PS *Grindal*, p. 387.
41 Ibid., p. 389.
42 Richard Hooker, *Laws*, Book VII, cap. ii, 2 (in the Keble edition of the *Works*, vol. iii, p. 147).
43 PS *Grindal*, p. 389.

Truly, if Thomas Cranmer left a legacy followed by Parker and perfected by Grindal – an apostolic legacy of sound Biblical scholarship and pastoral concern – the Tudors also made bequests to their successors dating from the time when Henry VIII decided to become his own pope.

VIII

Salvation by Coercion: the Controversy Surrounding the 'Inquisition' in the Low Countries on the Eve of the Revolt

❧

ALASTAIR DUKE

A version of this article was read by invitation of Professor A. G. Dickens to the Anglo-American Conference of Historians in July 1977.

When the Protestant gentry behind the Compromise devised their programme late in 1565, they knew it had to appeal to their predominantly Catholic compeers. So instead of brusque demands for religious freedom, which would have met with a bleak response, they called for the abolition of the inquisition 'in whatever shape, open or covert, under whatever disguise or mask it may assume'.[1] Fear and hatred of the inquisition evidently provided the best hope of uniting the political malcontents and religious dissidents, whose paths had been converging since the Peace of Cateau-Cambrésis. In the event the common policy still proved too brittle to withstand the emotional shock of the imagebreaking. But an initially favourable response showed that the authors of the Compromise had gauged accurately the mood of anxiety. Nor was concern about the inquisition confined to the four hundred or so signatories of the Compromise. The representative estates of Brabant and Flanders had registered quite separate protests in the spring of 1566, and the States of Holland followed in July with a remonstrance that, in its original form, bore an embarrassing resemblance to the Request presented by Hendrik van Brederode in April. That the inquisition was hated 'like the plague' in the Low Countries is certain; it is less obvious why the suppression of heresy should have aroused so much resentment in a society still overwhelmingly Catholic, the more so since very few of those convicted of heresy were tried by the inquisition proper.

Elsewhere in Europe north of the Alps the eradication of religious dissidence, be it by Catholics of Protestants or by Protestants of Anabaptists, excited no such outcry, except of course from the victims. Everywhere the severity of the repression was tempered by the inertia, incompetence or connivance of those responsible for enforcing the law and complicated by protracted wrangles between rival courts; but in the Low Countries the measures taken against the heretics gravely strained the loyalty of the aristocracy, lawyers and town magistrates to the prince. This was not the first time the inquisition had helped foment a political storm in the Habsburg lands. In 1563 the Milanese had rioted when Philip II wanted to introduce the Spanish Inquisition and the nobles and burghers of the city of Naples had banded together when similarly threatened in 1547. On both occasions the King had yielded to these demands for the withdrawal of the Spanish Inquisition.[2] This turn of events did not go unnoticed in the Netherlands, and in the Compromise the example of Naples was expressly commended. In these Italian territories the fear had been that the

1 *Texts concerning the Revolt of the Netherlands*, ed. E. H. Kossmann and A. F. Mellink (Cambridge, 1975), p. 60.
2 H. G. Koenigsberger, *The Habsburgs and Europe, 1516–1660* (Ithaca and London, 1971), pp. 52–3 and 103; also *Correspondance de Marguerite d'Autriche . . . avec Philippe II*, ed. L. P. Gachard, vol. ii (Brussels, 1870), p. 95.

inquisition would encroach on existing rights of ecclesiastical jurisdiction. The envy of established courts certainly contributed to the resentment against the inquisition in the Low Countries, though here the spread of the Reformation, especially in the maritime provinces, made the opposition more obstinate.

On 28 September 1520 Charles V signed an edict at Antwerp ordering the destruction of Luther's books in his hereditary lands in obedience to the Bull *Exsurge domine*.[3] This was the first in a long series of placards of increasing complexity and severity, culminating in the notorious 'placard of blood' in 1550. To combat heresy Charles also instituted, probably on the advice of Alonso Manrique de Lara, his Spanish chaplain, a shortlived extraordinary tribunal in 1522 whose subordination to the prince was as complete as the royal-controlled inquisition he had lately come to know in Spain.[4] As Holy Roman Emperor, Charles V might on occasion be driven to reach an accommodation with the evangelical estates, but in the Habsburg Netherlands he took his oath to maintain the Catholic faith in deadly earnest. Addressing the States General in 1531 the emperor declared that were any member of his own family to become infected with the Lutheran sect he would consider him 'his enemy'.[5] Indeed, Charles honoured Erasmus by making him a councillor – though as the Rotter-dammer complained his salary was often in arrears – but in religion he aligned himself with the conservative theologians of Louvain and the mendicant opponents of Luther. The decision to prosecute 'heresy' so rigorously was momentous, for it estranged many among the governing classes who, though in no sense formal heretics, did not share their prince's starkly simple world-picture of religion to accept that all varieties of heresy necessarily threatened traditional values or undermined political stability.

After 1530 the edicts almost invariably denounced the negligence of the police and the lenience of the judges to suspects. In a memorandum from Philip II to his stadholders and provincial councils in August 1559, just before he sailed for Spain, the King blamed the continued advance of heresy on the indifference, even malevolence, of those charged with the enforcement of anti-heresy legislation.[6] These were sentiments echoed by all concerned about the

---

3 L. E. Halkin, 'L'édit de Worms et la répression du lutheranisme dans la principauté de Liège' in *Miscellanea Historica in honorem Alberti de Meyer* (Louvain and Brussels, 1946), vol. ii, pp. 791–800.

4 J. Scheerder, 'De werking van de inquisitie' in *Opstand en Pacificatie in de Lage Landen* (Ghent, 1976), pp. 155–8; F. Walser, 'Alonso Manrique und Karl V. Ein Vorschlag für Einführung Spanischer Inquisitionsgerichte in den Niederlanden, 1520–1521', *AR*, xxx (1933), pp. 112–18. See also letter of Charles V of 29 May 1558 where he refers to the inquisition created in 1522, cited by R. C. Bakhuizen van den Brink in, *Studiën en schetsen over vaderlandsche geschiedenis en letteren* (The Hague, 1913), vol. v, pp. 348–9.

5 *Resolutiën van de Staten van Holland*, 1531, p. 171 (7 October); cf. J. G. de Hoop Scheffer, *Geschiedenis der kerkhervorming in Nederland van haar ontstaan tot 1531* (Amsterdam, 1873), p. 610.

6 L. P. Gachard, *Collection de documens*[sic] *inédits concernant l'histoire de la Belgique*, (Brussels 1833), vol. i, pp. 332–9.

maintenance of Catholicism in these provinces. Lindanus who had served as ecclesiastical commissary to the provincial court of Friesland and later as inquisitor in Holland, thus declared in 1578: 'There is no doubt at all that Holland and Zeeland lapsed from the Catholic faith and rebelled against the King chiefly because the magistrates failed to do their duty. Everywhere they were either lax or corrupt in the administration of justice or sympathetic to the new doctrines or downright indifferent to religion . . . Consequently the salvation of the Low Countries [*salus Belgicarum*] requires that the magistracy be thoroughly renewed.'[7]

In Flanders, inquisitor Pieter Titelmans energetically opposed the tide of heresy for more than twenty years with all the resources at his disposal, but by 1560 he was close to despair. Apart from threats made on his life by heretics, he suffered the anguish of knowing that the magistrates of the towns (even the Council of Flanders, which should have given him every help in his sacred mission) had often obstructed his work.[8] In February 1534, the two *commissarissen der luteriaensche secte* on the Court of Holland asked that their burdensome and unpopular task should be shared by the other councillors: it was unfair that they should have been singled out 'to watch the misery of poor wretches under interrogation and torture and to preside in public while judgement was passed on them'.[9] This same college also rallied to the defence of the town corporations when these were reproached by Lindanus for being soft on heresy, and in Friesland the provincial court virtually sabotaged the repressive policy after 1557.[10] The reluctance of these *hoven van justicie* to execute the religious policy of the prince is especially remarkable because the central government traditionally relied on these bodies of jurists to implement its policies in the provinces.

Though fervent Catholics certainly sat in these provincial councils, many of the jurists professed an undogmatic Catholicism. Perhaps as lawyers and judges they were more than usually aware how precariously order was maintained in society. 'Une foi, une loi, un roi' might remain the political ideal, but, after the Reformation, though the theologians continued to insist on doctrinal unity, even when this threatened to provoke civil disorder, the lawyers were temperamentally disposed to look for pragmatic solutions.[11]

7 Cited by P. T. van Beuningen, *Wilhelmus Lindanus als inquisiteur en bisschop* (Assen, 1966), p. 190.
8 J. Decavele, *De dageraad van de reformatie in Vlaanderen, 1520–1565* (Brussels, 1975), vol. i, pp. 26–31.
9 J. S. Theissen, *De regeering van Karel V in de noordelijke Nederlanden* (Amsterdam, 1912), p. 274; cf. F. H. Waterbolk, 'Humanisme en de tolerantie-gedachte' in *Opstand en Pacificatie*, p. 310. Jan Benninck, a member of the Court of Holland, was alleged to have refused to vote in favour of the death sentence for heretics. Cf. A. F. Mellink, *Amsterdam en de Wederdopers* (Nijmegen, 1978), pp. 21–2.
10 J. J. Woltjer, *Friesland in hervormingstijd* (Leiden, 1962), pp. 116–22.
11 See W. J. Bouwsma, 'Lawyers and early modern culture', *American Historical Review*,

The familiar antagonism between the 'gens de robe longue' and 'de robe courte' has perhaps obscured the tension that often existed between the clergy and secular lawyers. In 1520 the mendicant Glapion reviled those judges prepared to hang some unfortunate wretch for stealing a few pence; yet nothing was done about blasphemers, 'qui seront cause de la perdition d'ung peuple tout entier.'[12] Precisely the same charge was brought in 1533 by some conservatives, enraged by the indulgence shown towards alleged Lutherans in cosmopolitan Antwerp. The magistrates were accused of letting notorious heretics, who dishonoured God and the holy sacraments, go freely abroad, though they were prompt to bring any petty thief to trial.[13] The sympathy shown by the legal profession for Erasmus has received comment before. When Erasmus was uprooted by the Reformation in Basel in 1529, a Flemish Carthusian, Livinius Ammonius, invited him to settle at Ghent, where he was sure of congenial company because 'the whole Council of Flanders is devoted to you'. His testimony was corroborated by the president of the Council, who opposed the edict of 1529 against the 'Lutherans', declaring that he would rather be dismissed than enforce its savage provisions.[14] Significantly the Dominicans in the Low Countries forbade the reading of Erasmus's works in 1531, and the Crutched Friars in 1534; yet the provincial Council of Brabant was critical when, in 1557, the theologians at Louvain decided to ban his books.[15] Only a few years before Erasmus was put on the *Index*, Charles de Croy, *évêque-fainéant* of Tournai, had sharply attacked the younger set of jurists attached to the provincial courts for soliciting popular favour by mocking Church ceremonies and insulting the clergy, bad habits the bishop ascribed to the 'colloques d'Erasme et autres livres plains de dérisions'.[16] This blend of anticlericalism and modish intellectual curiosity helps to explain why, in 1566, six of the lawyers belonging to the *Grand Conseil* at Mechelen and a dozen or so lawyers from the Council of Flanders openly patronised the Calvinist preachings.[17]

lxxviii (1973), pp. 303–27; J. Dewald, 'The "Perfect Magistrate": Parlementaires and crimes in sixteenth-century Rouen', *AR*, lxvii (1976), pp. 284–6.

12 A. Godin, 'La société au XVIe siècle, vue par J. Glapion (1460?–1522), frère mineur, confesseur de Charles-Quint', *Revue du Nord*, xlvi (1964), p. 363.

13 R. van Roosbroeck, 'Een nieuw dokument over de beginperiode van het lutheranisme te Antwerpen', *De gulden passer*, v (1927), p. 279.

14 Decavele, *op. cit.*, vol. i, pp. 76–7. For the Court of Holland's sympathy towards Erasmus in 1519, see J. Trapman, *De summa der godliker scrifturen 1523* (Leiden, 1978), pp. 112–13.

15 *Acta capitulorum provinciae germaniae inferioris ordinis fratrum praedicatorum ab anno MDXV usque ad annum MDLIX*, ed. S. P. Wolfs (The Hague. 1964), p. 112; P. van den Bosch, 'De bibliotheken van de kruisherenkloosters in de Nederlanden vóór 1550', *Archief-en bibliotheek-wezen in België*, Extranummer xi, *Studies over boekenbezit en boekengebruik in de Nederlanden vóór 1600* (Brussels, 1974), p. 579; J. Tenret, 'La police des livres dans les Pays-Bas espagnols au XVIe siècle' (University of Brussels licence, 1957–8), pp. 37–8.

16 G. Moreau, *Histoire du protestantisme à Tournai jusqu'à la veille de la révolution des Pays-Bas* (Paris, 1962), p. 134, n. 1.

17 E. van Autenboer, 'Het wonderjaar te Mechelen, 1566–1567' (University of Louvain doctoral thesis, 1952), pp. 235–6; Decavele, op. cit., vol. i, p. 105.

By 1500 humanist education had begun to modify the curriculum in the grammar schools. Alexander's *Doctrinale* was ousted by 1536,[18] and greater attention was being paid to Latinity, helped by the models of Cornelius Crocus of Amsterdam and, above all, Despauterius and Erasmus. In 1518 the *Collegium Trilingue* opened its doors at Louvain; that year also saw Greek being taught at Bruges, and in 1533 the corporation of Amsterdam sponsored a *Hebreeuwsche meester*. Publishing may be considered a rough guide to a society's intellectual and religious appetites. Between 1500 and 1540 approximately four thousand books poured from presses in the Low Countries, of which more than half were printed in Antwerp. About 40% of the books printed in this city had a religious character, including a significant scattering of heterodox works; 30% concerned literature and pedagogy; and another 18% treated historical, geographical, scientific and medical subjects. Slightly more than half were printed in Latin.[19] Even if the governing classes and great merchants did not fully appreciate humanist scholarship, they were willing to patronize the authors and buy their books.

Religious observance among the burghers remained staunchly Catholic until the middle of the sixteenth century. But the patterns of spirituality had been changing well before the Reformation. By 1450 the spate of enthusiasm for monastic foundations was spent and few new religious houses were established in the next fifty years. Instead, the laity lavished gifts on parish churches, many of which were extensively rebuilt and embellished: indeed the majority of the great Gothic churches in the northern provinces received their final shape at the close of the Middle Ages. The laity also poured money into chantries and obits, endowed the singing of the divine office in the parish churches in the towns and created charitable foundations, the governors of which were responsible to the magistrates. This process of laicization ought not to be interpreted as an expression of mistrust in the clergy, but in Flanders, when the haphazard provision for poor relief was channelled into a *bursa communis*, the mendicants at Bruges denounced the reform as 'heretical'. The enlightened Catholicism characteristic of the leading families in the great towns of the Low Countries was regarded with suspicion by conservatives, apt to confound the religious stance of Erasmus or Cassander with the theology of Wittenberg. Nor were they entirely mistaken: certain magistrates and intellectuals in Tournai, Ghent, Bruges, Amsterdam and Antwerp did indulge in a sort of 'salon Protestantism',[20] which could lead on to wholehearted commitment. In the 1550s a supple Reformed minister like Adriaan van Haemstede in Antwerp, prepared to go

18 R. R. Psot, *Scholen en onderwijs in Nederland gedurende de middeleeuwen* (Utrecht and Antwerp, 1954), p. 146.
19 J. G. C. A. Briels, *Zuidnederlandse boekdrukkers en boekverkopers in de Republiek der Verenigde Nederlanden* (Nieuwkoop, 1974), pp. 4–5; L. Voet, *Antwerp in the Golden Age. The Rise and Glory of the Metropolis in the Sixteenth Century* (Antwerp, 1975), p. 395.
20 Decavele, op. cit., vol. i, p. 322.

discretely to the houses of rich even though these were not yet ready to enter the 'church under the cross', could thus exert a great appeal.[21] Alternatively, such people might dispense with dogmas and, while continuing to conform outwardly, cultivate the religion of the spirit that came to characterize the circle around the Antwerp printer Christopher Plantin. But whatever their own religious inclinations the town magistrates in the Low Countries had the delicate, sometimes disagreeable, task of accommodating their 'open' Catholicism with the rigid orthodoxy preached by the mendicants and prescribed by the placards.

The prevailing climate at Antwerp in the early 1530s is illumined by the lament of certain conservatives that plain heresy masqueraded there as 'good and evangelical'; in their despairing view, nothing short of a full-blooded Spanish-style inquisition could turn the tide.[22] The Amsterdam town authorities had been reprimanded in the late 1520s for their lenience towards convicted heretics. Moreover some of the chaplains and schoolmasters appointed by the town had shown marked evangelical sympathies. The mood among the regents there is revealed in a comment made by one of the burgomasters in 1534. After some Anabaptists from Amsterdam had been executed in The Hague, he was overheard to say that the burgomasters would 'no longer deliver them to the butcher's block'. In the ensuing investigations, the *schout* was dismissed; he later fled rather than stand trial on heresy charges, and in 1538 the moderates among the magistrates were ousted.[23]

No feature of the antiheresy legislation touched the 'gens de lettres et de justice' more closely than the prohibition laid on the reading of certain books. Since 1529 the mere possession of forbidden literature – a category which by 1550 had been stretched to include many books an educated man would have in his library – had been made a capital offence. No wonder the Council of Holland complained in 1531 that such a penalty was 'exorbitant', a view reiterated by the States of Friesland in 1554.[24] Even the *Conseil Privé* advised the Council of Flanders in 1549 that the penalty for reading forbidden books ought not to be imposed automatically. But with Charles V and Philip II insisting that the edicts be enforced literally, the position of the judges' discretionary powers was very uncertain.[25] When a Protestant pamphleteer, Gilles

21 A. J. Jelsma, *Adriaan van Haemstede en zijn martelaarsboek* (The Hague, 1970), pp. 49–53.
22 Van Roesbroeck, op. cit., p. 282.
23 A. F. Mellink, *De wederdopers in de noordelijke Nederlanden, 1531–1544* (Groningen and Djakarta, 1953), p. 105; G. Grosheide, *Bijdrage tot de geschiedenis der anabaptisten in Amsterdam* (Hilversum, 1938), pp. 87–94.
24 De Hoop Scheffer, op. cit., p. 475, n. 3; J. S. Theissen, *Centraal gezag en Friesche vrijheid. Friesland onder Karel V* (Groningen, 1907), pp. 493–4.
25 Decavele, op. cit., vol. i, p. 35, n. 120. For discussion about discretionary powers of judges in the sixteenth century, see E. Poullet, 'Histoire du droit pénal dans le duché de Brabant depuis l'avènement de Charles-Quint jusqu'à la réunion de la Belgique à la France, à la fin du XVIIIe siècle', *Mémoires couronnés et mémoires des savants étrangers publiés par l'academie royale ... de Belgique*, vol. xxxv (1870), pp. 40–2; Gachard, *Collection*, vol. i, p. 336.

le Clercq, wanted in May 1566 to expose the grotesque and arbitrary cruelty of the placards, he pointed out that someone could be put to death in the Netherlands for having in his house a book which, though forbidden by the Louvain doctors, might have escaped the censure of the Sorbonne.[26]

Gilles le Clercq was probably thinking of the inconsistent rulings given by civil and ecclesiastical authorities about the standing of Erasmus and vernacular translations of the Bible. In effect he was calling attention to the problem of determining the boundary between 'orthodoxy' and 'heresy'. One reason for the antipathy felt towards the edicts on religion was the discrepancy between the religious conservatism of Charles V and the latitudinarianism of many gentry, lawyers and regents. But it is important not to exaggerate the indulgence of the judges. Iconoclasts, Münsterites and Batenburgers received short shrift from the courts; indeed, the Anabaptists as a whole had little cause to extol the humanity and clemency of their judges. Dissidents among the *kleine luyden* felt the law more severely than the rich and well-connected, and, as Guicciardini noted, strangers to a town would be dealt with more harshly because they lacked the privileged protection enjoyed by the burghers.[27]

If antiheresy legislation offended the tolerant susceptibilities of the high nobility and the practical good sense of the jurists, it also caused disquiet to the town corporations and representative estates because it threatened their privileges. Above all, the legal principles invoked by the edicts and the methods used to convict heretics were widely considered to infringe traditional notions of criminal justice.

Before a burgher 'de bon nom et de bonne renommée' were arrested, the *schout* had first to investigate the credentials of the witnesses. Then, having satisfied himself that a *prima facie* case had been established, he would seek the consent of the burgomasters to make an arrest. This preliminary enquiry, known as the *informatie precedente*, gave protection against arrests arising from frivolous or spiteful allegations, a clear risk where law enforcement often depended on informers for intelligence. Moreover, once capital charges had been laid the guilt of the accused was presumed: the object of the trial was to extract the confession of guilt from the accused, without which the death sentence could not be passed. By that confession made in open court the accused effectively signed his own death warrant, there being no appeal against a capital

26 See his 'Remonstrance ofte vertoogh . . . op de Requeste by den edelen', in *Historie van het verbond en de smeekschriften der nederlandsche edelen*, ed. J. W. te Water (Middelburg, 1796), vol. iv, pp. 110–11. This commentary on the Request was printed in May 1566; see Moreau, op. cit., p. 165, n. 4, and P. A. M. Guerts, *De nederlandse opstand in de pamfletten, 1566–1584* (Nijmegen, 1956), p. 17.

27 On discrimination, see G. Moreau, 'La corrélation entre le milieu social et professionnel et le choix de religion à Tournai', in *Bibliothèque de la revue d'histoire ecclésiastique*, vol. xlvii: *Bronnen voor de religieuze geschiedenis van België* (Louvain, 1968), pp. 294–5; on Guicciardini, see E. Poullet, op. cit., pp. 37–9.

sentence for a self-confessed crime! In criminal law, only the prosecution had the right to seek revision of sentence.

For those whose chief concern was the preservation of the Catholic faith, the preliminary enquiry constituted a tiresome obstacle, for word of the investigation often came to the suspect's ear, and he then took refuge in flight. Ways were therefore devised to circumvent this procedure. When in 1534 the magistrates of the town of Limburg had jurisdiction in heresy cases restored to them, they were warned that privileges that postponed the arrest of suspects until after the *informatie precedente* should be set aside; in matters touching God and the Faith such privileges were null.[28] Despite such endeavours to curtail the trial the preliminary enquiry remained an intrinsic part of the judicial process. In 1546 the government therefore tried another tack. Under a new instruction the inquisitors were empowered to examine anyone. If they suspected that a layman had transgressed the placards on religion, they were to invoke the police to make the arrest, but – and this qualification is crucial – they were not obliged to disclose the grounds of their suspicion. When in 1557 an inquisitor duly called on the law officers of Delft to arrest a suspect without further ado, the States of Holland were promptly alerted because of the implied threat to their privileges. In the view of the estates the inquisitors should only concern themselves with the canonical offence of heresy and leave the enforcement of the edicts to the civil authorities. Failure to distinguish between these two quite separate categories of offence made them very uneasy; ironically their disquiet was shared by some scrupulous inquisitors who now found themselves obliged to denounce to the civil courts suspects for crimes carrying the death penalty. But when the States of Holland tried to persuade the other patrimonial provinces to join with them in making a collective protest, they failed to win their support.[29] Yet in both Flanders and Brabant the same anxiety was expressed. In 1562 Antwerp drew the attention of Brussels to article XV of the *Joyeuse Entrée* of Brabant: this stated that no one of good repute should be arrested 'sans précédente planière information'.[30] To the chagrin of 'honest fanatics' like Villavicencio and Titelmans, the magistrates of Bruges insisted the inquisitor should submit his evidence to them before making any arrests, a demand which was repeated in the remonstrance of the Four Members of Flanders in April 1566.[31] Gilles le Clercq returned to the issue in his *Remonstrance ofte vertoogh*, when he protested against arrests based on 'dubious rumours or the delation of a single person'.[32] Behind such grievances lay more than a concern for simple justice. The burgomasters, as guardians of municipal privileges, had a duty to

28 *Recueil des ordonnances des Pays-Bas*, ser. 2, ed. M. J. Lameere (Brussels, 1902), vol. iii, pp. 453–4.
29 See below, note 64.
30 *Correspondance de Marguerite d'Autriche*, vol. ii, p. 118.
31 Decavele, op. cit., vol. i, pp. 178–90.
32 'Remonstrance ofte vertoogh', p. 103.

defend the burghers against improper proceedings by ecclesiastical as well as lay officers.[33] Were they to accede to the demands of the inquisitors, they would weaken their standing in the local community. Though they would continue to regard themselves as sincere Catholics, they did not necessarily accept that the removal of judicial safeguards was a justifiable price to pay for the suppression of 'heresy'.

Heresy was often hard to prove, even by the far from exacting rules of evidence applied by sixteenth-century courts. Above all, evidence against suspects 'de qualité' was hard to obtain. In 1553 an erstwhile Anabaptist, who had already informed for profit on her co-religionists, told a zealous, priest that Willem Bardes, the worldly-wise *schout* of Amsterdam, had been rebaptized many years before. This sensational news confirmed the suspicions of the priest, long irked by the *schout*'s nonchalance towards the heretics. Eventually, after a most thorough investigation, Willem Bardes was cleared and his menial accuser was burnt for giving false testimony. As for the priest, he was arrested in 1558, accused of having suborned witnesses, and was finally banished from Amsterdam in 1562. Though later rewarded with a plum benefice in Brussels, his treatment by the civil courts was seen by Lindanus as further proof of how the fastidiousness of the judges had frustrated the campaign against heresy.[34] About this time, the magistrates of Gouda, Hoorn and Leiden also found themselves the targets of unfounded heresy charges. After such disillusioning experiences the government in Brussels was inclined to discount information of this kind, so that when a renegade Anabaptist listed several hundred heretics in Middelburg, Margaret of Parma refused to order their arrest unless more substantial evidence could be obtained.[35] But the low esteem the inquisitors had of the officers' and judges' zeal for the Faith naturally disposed them to take such reports seriously – and not without some cause. In 1566 Protestantism burst forth in localities alleged only a year or so before by their magistrates to be innocent of heresy. Probably the inquisitors had been right to suppose the authorities often connived at the activities of the dissidents.

The detection of heresy proper remained in the sixteenth century, as it had been in the Middle Ages, a matter for the ecclesiastical judge. As the Flemish *jurisconsult* Philips Wielant put it, 'heresy is punished by burning, with the ecclesiastical judge conducting the trial and the secular judge carrying out the sentence'. Yet the vast majority of so-called heretics were tried by the civil courts in the Low Countries. By the Edict of Worms cognizance had been expressly granted to the provincial and municipal courts in the Habsburg Netherlands, and the imperial mandate of 1529, concerning the prosecution of

33 *Resolutiën van de Staten van Holland*, 1565, p. 20 (12 July).
34 J. J. Woltjer, 'Het conflict tussen Willem Bardes en Hendrick Dirckszoon', *Bijdragen en mededelingen betreffende de geschiedenis der Nederlanden*, lxxxvi (1971), pp. 178–99.
35 *Correspondance de Marguerite d'Autriche*, ed. R. C. Bakhuizen van den Brink and J. S. Theissen, vol. iv (Utrecht, 1925), p. 34.

Anabaptists, made no mention of the ecclesiastical judge. For several reasons the government of Charles V had no wish to allow Church courts a prominent part in the campaign against the religious dissidents. This may be attributable to the longstanding antagonism between the civil and ecclesiastical jurisdictions, but more to the point was the anxiety that, if prosecution was left to the ecclesiastical inquisitors and episcopal officials, the process would be unduly protracted by the desire to bring the miscreant to abjure his false opinions. Dissent on the large scale encountered in the Netherlands required summary trials and sharp punishments.

The crime established by the Caroline edicts was hybrid. According to these edicts it was a capital offence to possess forbidden books, to give lodging to heretics, to debate points of scripture with laymen and to neglect to denounce heretics to the police. Strictly these acts did not in themselves constitute heresy proper; they only gave rise to vehement suspicion of heresy. Thus far, the edicts may be held to have short-circuited the ecclesiastical inquisition, offenders being prosecuted in the civil courts. But in several respects the penal code recapitulated, sometimes verbatim, the medieval canon law on heresy.[36] The foremost notion of canon law to be incorporated into the Caroline edicts was that of heresy as a species of divine lese-majesty. This concept had gained acceptance in the late twelfth century and been introduced into imperial law by Frederick II between 1220 and 1239. In defence of the assimilation of heresy as treason, Aquinas had argued that the perversion of faith endangered men's souls, so that such an offence was more heinous than the counterfeiting of coin, a crime held under Roman law to be treasonable and punishable by death. *A fortiori* justice demanded that the stubborn heretic be put to death.[37] But whereas the Church courts would commute the death sentence of misbelievers, prepared to renounce their false doctrines, to the penance of lifelong imprisonment, the civil judges in the Netherlands were denied any such latitude. Abjuration thus merely changed the mode of execution from the stake to the scaffold. In this respect offences against the edicts were treated as though they were crimes against the state. Accordingly there is a close parallel between the machinery Frederick II used against heresy in the Kingdom of Sicily, and the means employed in the Habsburg Netherlands. In Sicily, too, heresy had been accounted high treason and prosecuted without resort to the ecclesiastical courts.[38]

---

36 For example, the judicial procedure laid down in Frans vander Hulst's instruction in 1522 echoed the decretal of 3 March 1298; the notion that forfeiture occurred as soon as heresy was committed recurs in the Edict of 22 September 1540.
37 J. Lecler, *Toleration and the Reformation* (London, 1960), vol. i, p. 85.
38 On the legal notions informing the edicts of Frederick II, see E. Kantorowicz, *Kaiser Friedrich der Zweite* (Dusseldorf and Munich, 1963), vol. i, pp. 238–48 and vol. ii, *Ergänzungsband*, pp. 109–12. I am indebted to Dr E. O. Blake of the University of Southampton for drawing this parallel to my attention.

No wonder the civil courts in the Low Countries were bewildered. In 1527 the president of the *Grand Conseil* had to explain to puzzled deputies from Amsterdam that, though they should punish those who broke the edicts, they were not responsible for prosecuting those 'who *thought* ill of the doctrine and sacraments of the Church'.[39] But as the scope of the edicts widened, and the inquisitors became associated with the enforcement of those edicts, the mental crime of heresy proper became increasingly difficult to distinguish from offences against the placards of Charles V.

In imitation of the Roman law of treason the medieval inquisition held that an heretic's estate passed to the prince's treasury the moment he broke with the Catholic Church. This notion duly appeared in the Edict of Worms, and more explicitly in the comprehensive edict of 1529. No part of the antiheresy legislation aroused more anxiety than the insistence that those who broke the placards should forfeit their property, as well as their lives. At first sight the indignation seems puzzling: after all, confiscation had been recognized in most provinces as a fitting punishment for treason long before 1500, and Wielant already considered heresy as a form of *crimen laesae maiestatis divinae*.[40] But heresy had been comparatively rare in the Low Countries during the fifteenth century, so that a legal theory, familiar to canonists and civilians, could still strike the town magistrates in the sixteenth century as newfangled.

Moreover, though the maxim 'qui confisque le corps confisque les biens' was widely known in the Low Countries and applied to certain crimes, the consequences for the legal heirs had been mitigated by local privileges, which fixed the maximum sum liable to forfeiture, at least for crimes other than treason, and exempted the dowries of Catholic widows. In the provinces more strongly affected by the *Sachsenspiegel* – namely Utrecht, Overijssel and Groningen – the estate of the executed criminal invariably passed to his heirs, and not to the prince. Willem van der Tanerijen, a Brabanter jurist of the late fifteenth century, also insisted that the sins of the heretical father should not be visited upon his orthodox children, who ought to succeed to his estate.[41] Clearly the placards on religion were deeply resented because the penalty of confiscation curtailed immemorial custom and authentic charters, and because it threatened the property of both 'gens de petite estoffe' and 'gens de qualité'.

At first the edicts respected the local privileges limiting confiscation, but by the mid-1530s the towns in Holland and Zeeland had already been forced to recognize that breaches of these edicts amounted to acts of divine lese-majesty.

---

39 *Corpus documentorum inquisitionis haereticae pravitatis Neerlandicae*, ed. P. Fredericq (Ghent and The Hague, 1906), vol. v, p. 207. In 1527 the magistrates of Lille consulted colleagues in nearby towns to discover how they should proceed against persons accused of 'ayant seme parolles Luteriennes'; M. P. Willems-Closset, 'Le protestantisme à Lille jusqu'à la veille de la révolution des Pays-Bas', *Revue du Nord*, lii (1970), p. 199, n. 5.
40 W. van Iterson, *Geschiedenis der confiscatie in Nederland* (Utrecht, 1957), p. 113.
41 *Corpus documentorum*, vol. ii, p. 285.

Where the sentences of the local courts limited confiscation in keeping with the privileges, the attorney-general succeeded in having these revised on appeal so that the entire estate of the executed Anabaptists passed to the fisc.[42] In French Flanders the towns and castellanies claimed they had always been exempt from confiscation, even for *crimen laesae maiestatis divinae*, and cited the sentence of certain heretics, condemned to death in 1429, when the magistrates of Lille had prevented confiscation.[43] But when this privilege was scrutinized again in 1545 the *Grand Conseil* declared bluntly that heresy was an offence touching 'la puyssance plainière et absolute selon laquelle icelle Sa Majesté . . . peut tollir previlèges', including those of non-confiscation.[44] More ominous still was an ordinance of 1549, for this stated that confiscation for the crimes of lese-majesty 'divine et humaine' should be enforced 'nonobstant coustumes, privileges et usances pretendues au contraire per aulcunes villes ou pays'.[45] Valenciennes fought doggedly until 1564 to sustain this privilege, and several Flemish towns gained a respite until the arrival of Alva, while the States of Overijssel were still defending their 'old and immemorial freedom' from confiscation in 1571.[46]

Confiscation for heresy was enforced more strictly in the Habsburg Netherlands than elsewhere in the Empire. In Liège, where the antiheresy legislation closely resembled that in force in the Netherlands, the prince-bishop was forced to abandon the penalty of confiscation in 1545 because of the resolute opposition of the third estate.[47] In the free city of Cologne the property of convicted Anabaptists was not sequestered, and in the duchies of Jülich and Mark the children of Anabaptists succeeded to their parents' estate.[48] Anabap-

42 See Algemeen Rijksarchief 's-Gravenhage: Hof van Holland, 5654, fols l^v–3 21^v–23. But in 1542 the provincial court upheld a local privilege of limited confiscation, when the attorney-general demanded total confiscation of a convicted murderer's estate; see fols 97–98^v and also Grosheide, op. cit., pp. 259–72.
43 *Corpus documentorum*, vol. iii, pp. 76–80, 121–2; also Van Iterson, op. cit., p. 95.
44 J. Verteneuil, 'Contribution à l'étude de la législation de Charles-Quint contre les hérétiques dans les Pays-Bas' (University of Liège licence, 1958–9), pp. 145–7. I am indebted to Professor G. Moreau for arranging for me to consult this and other unpublished theses of the University of Liège.
45 *Recueil des ordonnances*, vol. v, p. 577. Similar *non-obstante* clauses had been used against the privileges of non-confiscation claimed by Arras in 1460: *Corpus documentorum*, vol. i, p. 460. For the opinion of jurists about these clauses, see J. H. Franklin, *Jean Bodin and the Rise of Absolutist Theory* (Cambridge, 1973), pp. 13–14. According to 'Remonstrance ofte vertoogh', p. 122, the *Conseil Privé* had confirmed the privileges of non-confiscation on 13 September 1549.
46 On Valenciennes, C. Paillard, *Histoire des troubles religieux de Valenciennes, 1560–1567* (Brussels, 1876), vol. iv, pp. 42–69; on Flanders, Decavele, op. cit., vol. i, pp. 44–8; on Overijssel, Van Iterson, op. cit., pp. 312–14, 403–4.
47 P. Harsin, 'De l'édit de Worms à la paix d'Augsbourg, 1521–1555. Étude critique de la législation liègeoise en matière d'hérésie', *Bulletin de la commission royale des anciennes lois et ordonnances de Belgique*, xx (1959–60), p. 47.
48 H. T. T. Stiasny, *Die strafrechtliche Verfolgungen der Täufer in der freien Reichsstadt Köln 1529 bis 1618* (Münster, 1962), pp. 154–5.

tists expelled from Hesse were even allowed to take their property with them, for as the landgrave said, he wanted 'weder irer leibe noch guts'.[49]

Because breaches of placards on religion were treated as treason, they were classified as 'cas privilégiés': consequently the provincial courts were entitled to act as courts of first instance, like the French *parlements*.[50] By the end of the Middle Ages, most local jurisdictions enjoyed privileges of *de non evocando* so that local inhabitants could not be cited before ecclesiastical or civil courts outside their place of residence, except for crimes infringing the *hoogheydt ende heerlijckheyt* of the prince. Such offences had been few, but prosecutions for heresy were, if not exactly two-a-penny, nevertheless fairly common. Naturally the towns and provinces strongly resisted this threat to their jurisdictional autonomy.

Holland, which had possessed a privilege of *de non evocando* since 1452, was compelled to defend that privilege in the first years of the Reformation. In 1523 the lay commissary with special responsibilities for heresy had a suspect conveyed outside the province, but the estates protested so vigorously that Brussels henceforth respected the provincial privilege and instructed inquisitors at work in Holland on no account to try suspects outside the county.[51] This still left unresolved the status of the local courts in the matter of heresy.

As a rule the autonomy of the courts in the towns and bailiwicks and those seigneurial courts with criminal jurisdiction was secured by privileges of *de non evocando*. Judgements in these courts could only be overturned if the prosecution could prove that this sentence infringed the law, for, as already noted, the accused had no right of appeal once he had freely confessed to a capital crime. In practice, the provincial courts acted as a sort of judicial long-stop, intervening if the local forces of law were unequal to the occasion. But the criminal cognizance of the provincial courts was chiefly concerned with matters reserved to the jurisdiction of the prince.

Already in the 1520s jurisdiction in heresy cases in Holland was proving contentious. The States of Holland protested hotly at what they considered to be the meddling of the provincial court, and during the summer of 1528 the estates heard fighting words about the need to defend their privileges at any price.[52] But the storm did not break at this time because in 1529 the sole competence in heresy cases was vested in special 'commissaires sur le fait des luthériens', and when the jurisdiction of the local courts in Holland was restored

49 H. W. Schraepler, *Die rechtliche Behandlung der Täufer in der deutschen Schweiz, Sudwestdeutschland und Hessen, 1525–1618* (Tübingen, 1957), pp. 72–6.

50 For discussion of heresy as a 'cas privilégié' in France, see R. J. Knecht, 'Francis I, "Defender of the Faith"?', in *Wealth and Power in Tudor England. Essays presented to S. T. Bindoff*, ed. F. W. Ives, R. J. Knecht and J. J. Scarisbrick (London, 1978), p. 110.

51 De Hoop Scheffer, op. cit., pp. 155–61, 174–99; for an inquisitor's commission, see Algemeen Rijksarchief 's-Gravenhage: Hof van Holland, 37, fols 37^v–40^v.

52 *Corpus documentorum*, vol. v, p. 344.

in 1534, the Anabaptist menace pushed the juridical argument into the background. By 1544, however, that threat was at an end, and the earlier controversy was revived when the attorney-general had an heretic removed from Amsterdam to stand trial in The Hague. The towns reacted by demanding from the Governess, Mary of Hungary, an unequivocal confirmation of their privileges of *de non evocando*. To their dismay the Queen replied that, though it had never been intended to diminish the jurisdiction of the local courts, the alleged offence of heresy was akin to lese-majesty, and therefore properly belonged to the provincial court.[53] For all their indignant bluster the estates could adduce no solid counter argument. Though the local courts continued to try most cases of heresy until the Council of Troubles was set up in 1567, they did so only on the sufferance of the government.

This reverse continued to worry the estates. In 1548 they claimed that, if the privileges of *de non evocando* could be subverted, then 'all the other privileges might easily be called into question, and the province stripped of these'.[54] For that reason they began to study their privileges more carefully and to gather precedents. At that time the government was not planning any general assault on privileges, but the experience of the estates in the affair had been thoroughly frustrating, and served to remind them how limited was the protection given by such privileges, and how impotent they were to defend those privileges. By, as it were, rewriting the rules of the game, the government had notionally withdrawn a whole range of offences from the purview of the local courts. All the States of Holland could do, as the guardians of those privileges, was to remind the provincial council of its duty to ensure that edicts published in the county did not violate the privileges.

In the other patrimonial provinces this particular privilege does not seem to have stirred the same passions. In Flanders, for example, the sheer volume of business created for the courts by the antiheresy legislation required the continued use of the magistrates. When jurisdiction in heresy cases was transferred in 1529 to the special commissions, the States of Flanders protested and the jurisdiction of the local courts was promptly restored.[55] Indeed after the *schepenen* of Ghent had been forbidden to try heretics in 1540, it was the provincial court that urged the restoration of the municipal court's jurisdiction in 1545. But instead of welcoming this, the magistrates of Ghent would have been content to leave the whole burdensome and disagreeable business to the jurists of the provincial court, the 'gens lettrez et scavans en droist divin et humain'.[56] Under a privilege granted in 1290 the burghers of Valenciennes claimed exemp-

53 Grosheide, op. cit., pp. 276–81.
54 *Resolutiën van de Staten van Holland*, 1548, p. 12 (27 February).
55 Decavele, op. cit., vol. i, p. 33.
56 Ibid., pp. 37–8; Verteneuil, op. cit., pp. 142–4. The local courts in Franche Comté were also reluctant to exercise their jurisdiction in cases of heresy; see L. Febvre, *Notes et documents sur la réforme et l'inquisition en Franche-Comté* (Paris, 1912), pp. 42–5.

tion from examination under torture; but this was disputed by Brussels in 1562, on the by now familiar grounds that such a privilege did not cover the 'crime de lèse Majesté divine et humaine'. Eventually the town conceded the substance and agreed to 'desbourgeoiser' prisoners accused of heresy.[57]

In Gelderland and Groningen the debate about the antiheresy measures took place in a quite different political and constitutional setting. Together they composed what Margaret of Parma could still describe in 1560 as the 'pays . . . de nouvelle conqueste' to indicate their untried loyalty to the Habsburg dynasty, and their aloofness from the hereditary provinces.[58] For that reason Brussels treated them with special delicacy. These provinces also differed in two other respects. First, they were not subject to the antiheresy legislation in force elsewhere in the Netherlands, offences carrying the death penalty in the patrimonial lands being punished by a scale of fines in Groningen and Gelderland.[59] And secondly, the growth of confessional consciousness was markedly slower here than in the provinces to the south and west. Gelderland, especially, had been affected by the eirenicism fashionable in the duchy of Cleves and the evangelical reforms inspired by Herman von Wied. In Gelderland the provincial court, set up after the duchy had been incorporated into the Netherlands in 1543, rather than the heresy edicts themselves, stood at the heart of the controversy. Nevertheless, the estates displayed an allergic sensitivity, particularly when the provincial court claimed the right to gather information on suspected heretics in the towns. They saw in such commissions an inquisition in another guise.[60] In Groningen, too, 'inquisition' was used in this way. In 1556 the stadholder warned the burgomasters of the provincial capital that, unless effective steps were taken against the sectaries, he would fetch a special commission and 'even conduct an *inquisitie*'.[61] Similar inquisitorial commissions were sent to Tournai and Valenciennes in 1554 and again in 1561 to sit alongside the local judges, when it seemed that they were no longer willing or able to enforce the edicts against heretics.[62]

57 Paillard, op. cit., vol. iv, pp. 35–42.
58 *Correspondance de Marguerite d'Autriche*, vol. i, p. 540; see also *Historie van Groningen. Stad en Land*, ed. W. J. Formsma *et al.* (Groningen, 1976), p. 216.
59 See C. H. Ris Lambers, *De kerkhervorming op de Veluwe, 1523–1578* (Barneveld, 1890), pp. x–xiii; *Documenta Anabaptistica Neerlandica I: Friesland en Groningen, 1530–1550*, ed. A. F. Mellink (Leiden, 1975), pp. 139–41, 163–5.
60 Ris Lambers, op. cit., pp. lxviii–lxix; A. Zijp, *De strijd tusschen de Staten van Gelderland en het Hof, 1543–1566* (Arnhem, 1913), p. 144.
61 *Diarium van Egbert Alting, 1553–1594*, ed. W. J. Formsma and R. van Roijen (The Hague, 1964), p. 63. For parallel usage in Cleves, see I. G. Sardemann, 'Der Landtag zu Essen und die Inquisition', *Zeitschrift des bergischen Geschichts verein*, i (1863), pp. 201–14.
62 Moreau, *Histoire du protestantisme à Tournai*, pp. 176–82, 230–9; C. Muller, 'La réforme à Valenciennes pendant la révolution des Pays-Bay, 1565–1573' (University of Liège licence, 1973–4), pp. 1–2, 19–20. In 1561 the Council of Flanders proposed 'une inquisition générale par forme de grandz jours', but this was rejected because such extraordinary commissions were unknown in the Low Countries; Decavele, op. cit., vol. i, pp. 39–40.

When in 1560 Groningen refused to issue an edict against heretics, it argued that since the towns and provinces enjoyed different privileges, the new edicts could not be implemented uniformly. Instead, these should be tailored to the local constitutions.[63] But these disparities between and within the provinces hampered cooperation in the defence of the privileges. When at the States General of 1557–8 Holland tried to persuade the other provinces to combine in order to reduce the powers of the inquisitors to conform to canon law, their proposal was rejected by certain provinces. Brabant objected on the grounds that the duchy knew nothing of any ecclesiastical inquisition, and Hainault demurred lest recognition of a canonical inquisition should prejudice the provincial privilege of non-confiscation. At the same assembly Tournai proposed that a bargain be struck with the King who, in return for a subsidy, would grant all the patrimonial provinces exemption from confiscation. But this too came to nothing, because some provinces saw no point in paying for a privilege already enjoyed.[64] Moreover the States General could not speak for the newly-incorporated provinces, who neither were nor wished to be represented at these meetings.

But after 1559 common fears helped to draw the aggrieved groups in the provinces closer together. With the wars ended, Philip was more than ever eager to enforce the rigid religious policy inherited from his father. But this repressive policy coincided with the introduction of Protestant church orders in Sedan, Scotland and, above all, England. In France, too, the Huguenot star was in the ascendant, as was shown by the Colloquy of Poissy and the Edict of January (1562). To the King these alarming alterations only seemed to underline the necessity to root out heresy in the Low Countries. In vain, Margaret of Parma tried to deflect royal policy from a procrustean orthodoxy, suitable for Spain 'fermez de mer et de montagnes', but plainly impractical for a small trading country like the Netherlands, hemmed in on all sides by heretical neighbours.[65] Many of the gentry, magistrates and jurists had, for example, never wholeheartedly endorsed a policy of indiscriminate repression. Their disquiet led to the severity of the edicts unofficially being moderated, first in Holland and Friesland, but after Granvelle's departure in 1564 also in the southern provinces. Proposals for a drastic reform of diocesan organization provoked an outcry from politically influential chapters and abbeys, whose privileges were thereby curtailed. The increased number of bishops intensified apprehension about the inquisition, henceforth mistakenly, but damningly, confounded with its Spanish namesake. Like the controversial decision to publish the Tridentine

63 J. A. Feith, 'Eene mislukte poging tot invoering der inquisitie in Groningen', *Historische avonden*, i (1896), p. 173.
64 'Notulen en generaal advies van de Staten Generaal van 1557–1558', ed. P. A. Meilink *Bijdragen en mededeelingen van het historisch genootschap*, lv (1934), pp. 276 and 311; G. Griffiths, *Representative Government in Western Europe* (Oxford, 1968), pp. 359–60.
65 *Correspondance de Marguerite d'Autriche*, vol. iii, pp. 462 and 542.

decrees in July 1565, the scheme for the new dioceses showed how little protection the privileges gave when the King had made up his mind. Nevertheless, the moderates could console themselves with the hope that Granvelle's recall, and the return of the high nobility to the *Conseil d'État* in 1564, heralded a change of policy. Such optimism was shown to be without foundation in December 1565, when the King made it plain that on the matter of religion he stood where he had always stood, foursquare behind his inquisitors. For the small Protestant lobby behind the Compromise this reminder of royal intransigence could not have been more timely.

In order to prevent damaging disputes about the privileges, such as had taken place at the States General some years earlier, the Compromise refrained from making precise demands. Signatories bound themselves to prevent the introduction of 'this inquisition in whatever shape . . . whether bearing the name of inquisition, visitation, edicts or otherwise'. Such a protean inquisition could be taken in Flanders and Holland to refer to the ecclesiastical inquisition headed by Titelmans and Lindanus, and in the Walloon towns and Gelderland to mean the government commissions that had overriden local jurisdictions in the pursuit of suspected heretics. Again the inquisition was, as Granvelle's correspondent Morillon complained in February 1566, equated by some with the placards of Charles V;[66] and in its Spanish guise it conjured up, especially in Antwerp, the nightmare of paid informers, anonymous delations and secret trials.

In an essay on the causes of the Revolt the nineteenth-century man of letters Bakhuizen van den Brink remarked, somewhat disparagingly, on the 'heady power' the word privileges then possessed. Clearly the publicists of the Revolt exaggerated when they pretended the *Joyeuse Entrée* of Brabant justified taking up arms against their lawful prince. But the antiheresy legislation had created a tension between the prince, who bore 'le soing principale de garder et de faire observer ladicte religion catholique',[67] and his subjects, who thought their judicial and property rights had been secured by privileges. Usually comprehensive edicts were sent to the provincial courts for registration and allowance was made for custom, usage and the privileges. To some degree this continued to be the practice until 1567, even with the placards on religion. But Charles V had intended that much of the criminal legislation should be enforced uniformly, at least in the patrimonial provinces, hence the controversial *non obstante* clauses inserted in certain edicts. Provided the governing class accepted the necessity for such measures all was reasonably well; but with the edicts against heresy this consensus was often conspicuously lacking. Furthermore, these edicts created an offence that exposed the upper reaches of society

66 *Archives ou correspondance de la maison d'Orange-Nassau*, ed. G. Groen van Prinsterer (Leiden, 1841), vol. i, p. 439.
67 *Recueil des ordonnances*, vol. v, p. 576.

to prosecution. The magistrates found themselves not only passing capital sentences on 'gens de basse sorte', the staple diet of the courts, but also on skilled craftsmen, schoolmasters, merchants, lawyers and even gentry. And because a breach of these edicts was treated as heresy and classified as a 'délit du cas privilégié', an accused could not invoke privileges which otherwise would have spared him examination under torture and permitted his estate to descend to his lawful heirs.

In a *Ständestaat* like the 'seventeen Netherlands' it was difficult to reconcile the privileges with the legislative initiative of the prince. Groningen was uniquely well-placed to defend its constitution, for edicts detrimental to the privileges were not published and the provincial estates could meet freely. Though the representative bodies of Gelderland and Utrecht also claimed the right to convoke themselves, in practice the consent of the stadholder was required. In 1565 the States of Holland tried to argue that privilege and 'good usage' entitled the *landsadvokaat* or the towns to summon the estates. At that time William of Orange, who was stadholder, rejected this claim; but ironically it was this assertion that gave a semblance of legality to the meeting at Dordrecht in July 1572, at which William was recognized as the legitimate stadholder of Holland and Zeeland.[68] Although the estates were moreover guardians of the privileges, they could only defend these indirectly, by withholding consent for subsidies and calling on the provincial councils to ensure the edicts were in keeping with the privileges. In 1554 the States of Friesland denied that the prince could make law as he pleased, irrespective of their treaties and privileges; but Charles V resisted their demand to be allowed to examine the edicts before these were published. The right to issue placards belonged to the prince alone. Rather than push the constitutional argument too far, the estates backed down, preferring to seek remedies for specific grievances.[69] Relations between the prince and the estates were often strained by demands for subsidies; but sooner or later a balance of sorts would be struck between the need for supply and redress of grievances. The edicts against heresy did not provide the same scope for compromise, especially because Charles V and Philip II took their supreme obligation to uphold the Catholic faith seriously, and interpreted 'orthodoxy' so narrowly. In 1562 the States of Brabant protested that the incorporation of certain abbeys to endow the new bishoprics overrode 'ancient customs, usages and immemorial rights'. In his reply the King explained that even well-founded privileges ought not to obstruct measures taken for the good of the Church. In support he cited two tags: *cum summa sit ratio quae pro religione facit et salus populi suprema lex sit*. The first, which made the benefit of religion the highest concern, may be medieval in origin; the second maxim derives from Cicero's *De Legibus*, and had become a commonplace in the Middle Ages, when *salus*

68 See *Resolutiën der Staten van Holland* between 14 September 1565 and 27 January 1566.
69 Woltjer, *Friesland*, p. 36; Theissen, *Centraal gezag*, p. 406.

often embraced the notion of 'salvation' as well as 'preservation'.[70] What precisely Philip II had in mind is uncertain, but he certainly felt a heavy responsibility for the souls of his people.

In 1566 two separate, though related, solutions to the constitutional problem were being advanced. Gilles le Clercq concluded his *Remonstrance ofte vertoogh* by advocating freedom of conscience, which implies that the prince relinquishes his role as defender of the faith. Another way out of the impasse was also proposed by a Protestant who was closely involved with the Compromise. Thus Nicholas de Hames asserted in February 1566 that the evils in the common-wealth could be remedied by the States General, for they were empowered to take the initiative and convoke themselves.[71] Both the Request of April 1566 and the remonstrance of the States of Holland, before it was diluted to spare embarrassment, wanted a new religious policy to be framed with the 'advice and *consent*' of the States General. In 1566 the notion of the prince as legislator was still intact, though the great majority of the edicts were devised in answer to petitions from towns, guilds, provincial courts and the estates. But the anti-heresy legislation had been directly inspired by the prince, though the States General had been consulted on one previous occasion in 1531.[72] Probably the petitioners of 1566 sought to extend the principle of consultation so that it covered edicts on religion.

But Philip II utterly rejected collaboration with the States General on this matter, and the constitutional debate petered out once the government regained the upper hand in 1567. However, the defection of the towns in Holland and Zeeland to William of Orange in 1572 pitched those provinces into an unforeseen constitutional predicament. Willy-nilly – and the 'rebels' began by trying hard to conceal the fact from themselves – sovereignty had passed to those towns with votes in the provincial estates. In their turn, the town corporations claimed to represent the *corpus* of the community.[73]

Paradoxically the Revolt, justified on the basis of the privileges of *de non evocando* and non-confiscation, and partly undertaken in their defence, gave birth to a state where such privileges lost much of their *raison d'être*, at least for those with political power. But the anomalous character of the new constitu-tion was too perplexing for this to be grasped at first. Indeed, after the eloquent defences of privileges in general, the new state could scarcely abandon its faith

70 *Correspondance de Marguerite d'Autriche*, vol. ii, p. 143.
71 Griffiths, op. cit., pp. 406–7. The claim was probably based on the *Grand Privilège* of 1477, but this had been repudiated by Philip the Fair in 1493.
72 J. Gilissen, 'Les Etats Généraux des pays de par deçà, 1464–1632', in *Assemblées d'Etats* (Louvain and Paris, 1965), pp. 309–10.
73 P. Geyl, 'An Interpretation of Vrancken's *Deduction* of 1587 on the Nature of the States of Holland's Power', in *From the Renaissance to the Counter-Reformation. Essays in Honour of Garrett Mattingly*, ed. C. H. Carter (London, 1966), pp. 230–46. Even before the Revolt, the burgomasters of Gouda described themselves in official documents as 'representerende 't corpus vande stadt'; see Oud-Archief Gouda, 175 (Letter dated 19 December 1571).

in their necessity, especially as long as there was a possibility of the King resuming some sort of loose suzerainty over the rebellious provinces. Moreover the urban privileges, which entitled towns to freedom from tolls, right of staple and all the other privileges characterized by Huizinga as the 'I may do what you may not do' variety, retained their local significance.[74] Eventually the exigencies of war prompted a muted criticism of these local privileges in the 1580s: too rigid an adherence to 'pretended privileges' could damage the common weal. Whereas the preamble of the Act of Abjuration asserted that 'the prince is created for the subjects', six years later a convinced Calvinist and strong supporter of Leicester warned that 'the privileges are there for the sake of the people, the people do not exist for the sake of the privileges'.[75]

But, if the constitutional privileges ceased to fulfil the same need in the United Provinces as they had performed before princely authority had been forsworn in 1581, the religious disposition of the ruling classes did not change fundamentally as a consequence of the Revolt. Of course many town regents and gentry now attended sermons delivered by the *predikanten* in churches whose austerity was relieved by their hatchments and imposing box-pews: but, as a body, the *heren* showed no eagerness to become professed members of the Reformed Church. Indeed they remained distinctly wary, lest the discipline of this Church should give rise to a 'new monkery'. Those who had once feared that they would become 'miserable and everlasting slaves of the inquisition' had no intention of exchanging 'l'inquisition d'Espaigne' for 'de Geneefsche inquisitie'. For that reason the Union of Utrecht laid down the principle that each individual should enjoy freedom of religion.

74 J. J. Woltjer, 'Dutch Privileges, Real and Imaginary', in *Britain and the Netherlands*, vol. v (*Some Political Mythologies*), ed. J. S. Bromley and E. H. Kossmann (The Hague, 1975), pp. 19–35.
75 *Texts concerning the Revolt*, p. 272.

IX

The Mental World of
a Saxon Pastor

❧

GERALD STRAUSS

Of the many pressing tasks facing the territorial Reformation in Germany in the first half of the sixteenth century, the improvement of pastoral services seemed the most urgent. Ignorance of the faith and corruption of morals were deep-seated and widespread among all classes and in all parts of the land: parish visitations revealed the full measure of this fatal deviation from Christian belief and practice. Reformers and politicians postulated that a meaningful, lasting amelioration of the religious behaviour of fallen men and women could come only from an inner change expressing a spiritual renewal effected by preaching and teaching – the two chief roles assigned to the Protestant clergy. Given the largely dismal states of body and mind in which ministers were forced to carry on their duties (these, too, became shockingly evident during the visitations of the late 1520s, 1530s and 1540s) the task of raising the level of pastoral performance loomed as a Herculean undertaking. But Church and State considered themselves equal to it. Pooling their ideological and material resources, consistory and chancellery set about reformation where it was most needed: in church, school, and parsonage.[1]

Results were spotty and slow in coming.[2] But by the third quarter of the century, the procedures devised for the refinement of the clergy – seminaries to give professional training to aspiring ministers prepared in refurbished Latin schools, careful selection of candidates, rigorous examination of incumbents by means of frequent visitations – were beginning to show some qualitative changes for the better. Wealthier cities had always attracted competent clergymen; but from the 1560s and 1570s able ministers could also be found in some lesser parishes. The bitter doctrinal controversies shaking the Lutheran establishment in the second half of the century lent special point to the indoctrination and surveillance of clerics. Every village pastor was a potential disseminator of heresy unless schooled and controlled as a guardian of orthodox belief. Strenuous attempts were made, therefore, by nearly all German governments, to gather information on incumbents in order to be able to intervene promptly where corrective action was indicated. Visitors on their yearly rounds interrogated pastors on their comprehension of the Faith and their grasp of the frequent

1 For arguments sustaining this synopsis, and literature, see my *Luther's House of Learning. Indoctrinating the Young in the German Reformation* (Baltimore, Maryland, 1979), chapters 1, 12, 13.
2 The best evidence for this is contained in the voluminous *Visitationsprotokolle* taken down in the German territories in the mid- and late sixteenth century. For references see ibid., chapters 12 and 13. Also: Bernhard Klaus, 'Soziale Herkunft und theologische Bildung lutherischer Pfarrer der reformatorischen Frühzeit,' *Zeitschrift für Kirchengeschichte*, 80:1 (1960), 22–49. On the preparation of Calvinist clergymen in the Palatinate, see Bernard Vogler, *Le clergé protestant rhénan au siècle de la réforme (1555–1619)* (Paris, 1976), especially chapter 1.

doctrinal shifts redefining it. Requirements were set for private study and reading so as to avert perfunctory and routine preaching. Wherever possible, inept preachers were replaced by informed and fluent speakers. Parishioners were encouraged to testify to their pastors' performance and come forward with criticisms. The information collected in this way is still available in the voluminous protocols of territorial visitations – a fabulously rich source for the condition of the Lutheran (as well as the Catholic) Church in the centuries following the Reformation.[3]

A single instance may illustrate the occasional success gained by the Lutheran state Church in Germany in its endeavour to lift the professional level of its priests and assign dedicated ministers to humble parishes. I take the case from the visitation documents of Saxony, which constitute a wonderfully detailed record of ecclesiastical and religious life in the electorate and its attached territories. In Saxony, as elsewhere in the Holy Roman Empire, parishes were 'visited' – that is, inspected and their officials and church members questioned – at least once a year. In addition to gathering data on the financial conditions and administrative operations of rural and urban churches, the authorities wished to discover how securely evangelical faith was being planted in people's minds and what impact, if any, its spiritual message was making on the conduct of their lives. As Duke Johann Friedrich put it in his visitation instructions of 1554 for Saxony and Thuringia:

In order to note and record the names of those pastors who have improved their parishioners and succeeded in teaching them the catechism, our visitors are to call together and interrogate [*verhören*] these same parishioners in every place; for it matters little whether or not a pastor be a learned and accomplished man if he does not apply himself diligently and with devotion to the work of instructing his parishioners in the essentials of Christian knowledge.[4]

With the aid of a lengthy questionnaire furnished by the duke, visitors subjected every pastor to systematic questioning on his conduct in office, the manner in which he prepared himself for his preaching and teaching duties, and what kind of response his efforts were evoking.[5] On this last point the pastor normally submitted a written document detailing his observations of public behaviour, and summarizing his complaints of shortcomings in his parishioners' Christian knowledge and walk of life. Most of these memoranda make dismal reading, an impression reinforced by the visitors' own investigations of public morality. All sources portray a population scarcely touched by Christian doctrine and for

---

3 For a partial guide to the printed and manuscript visitation literature, see Ernst Walter Zeeden and Hansgeorg Molitor (eds), *Die Visitation im Dienst der kirchlichen Reform* (Münster, 1967). For a discussion of visitation materials as evidence, see chapter 12 of my *Luther's House of Learning*.
4 Staatsarchiv Weimar Reg. I, No. 23, fol. 8[r,v]. Printed in Emil Sehling, *Die evangelischen Kirchenordnungen des XVI. Jahrhunderts* (Leipzig, 1902), I, i, p. 224.
5 The questionnaire is given in Staatsarchiv Weimar Reg. I, No. 42[I], fols 23[r]ff.

the most part uninterested in its religious content.[6] Here and there the documents record exceptions to this rule, and an occasional clergyman was able to
report a measure of success. In general, however, ministerial efforts seem to
have bred mainly indifference, if not opposition, in the populace – and this at a
time when pastors were becoming better trained, and willing to devote themselves to their vocation as shepherds of a wild flock.

One such man was Johann Langepeter, an otherwise unknown pastor in the
insignificant village of Kapellendorf (near Apolda, not far from Weimar) in
northern Thuringia. In 1570 he submitted to ducal visitors an impressively long
catalogue of books which, he stated, he used in the preparation of his sermons
and for nourishing his own mind and soul for the performance of his obligations. Library lists are common among visitation documents. Pastors were
obliged to supply them from time to time to enable ecclesiastical and state
authorities to gauge the advancement of learning among their ministers and –
more immediately important – ensure the reign of orthodoxy by locating and
removing suspect material. Most such rosters are meagre: a Bible, a book of
Psalms, a *Postille*, a pamphlet by Luther, the church agenda, and a book of
hymns. Langepeter's catalogue is unusual (though not unique) in the number
and range of titles in his possession. Assuming that a man tends to acquire and
keep books in response to his needs and preferences, Langepeter's library sheds
at least some light on the working life of a small-time Protestant minister in the
age of Reformation.

This conclusion gains strength when it is recalled that books were expensive
in the early modern period, and that a village pastor's income was nearly always
inadequate and painstakingly – often humiliatingly – procured.[7] In fact, pastor
Langepeter's professional dedication, as suggested by his books, is all the more
impressive when viewed in the context of his material preoccupations as these
emerge from clerical pleas and grievances peppering all visitation documents.
An outsider living among a clannish, suspicious population, miserably provided
with material goods – often barely able to house and feed his family – regi-
mented and often browbeaten by his superiors in the hierarchy, working long
hours in a thankless attempt to instil a little religion in his stubborn flock but
often scarcely able to gather an audience, the conscientious pastor could not
have found in the external circumstances of his life much of an incentive to
deepen his learning and broaden his vision. Where, as in the case of Langepeter,
the sources give evidence of studious reading, the impulse must have come from
within the man: a symptom of a commitment to the pastoral calling still rare
in the generation after Luther's death.

6 For evidence relating to Lutheran Germany in general, see my *Luther's House of Learning*,
chapter 13.
7 On this point, too, visitation documents for all Germany give abundant information. For some
accessible evidence see Karl Pallas (ed.), *Die Registraturen der Kirchenvisitationen im ehemals
sächsischen Kurkreise. Geschichtsquellen der Provinz Sachsen* (Halle, 1906–14), vols 41–41[5] passim.

Langepeter's list includes seventy-seven items and is headed 'Register of the Books Owned by me, Johann Langepeter, Currently Pastor in Kapellendorf, and Collected in the Course of the Years of my Ministry there.'[8] Like most such compilations it is arranged by format: first folios [6], then quartos [29], finally octavos [42]. Most titles are in German, but enough are in Latin to suggest that Langepeter was at home in the learned tongue. By far the greatest part consists of books of practical use to a working clergyman; for example, only a small group touches related fields such as history. Langepeter owned only one classical author and seems to have evinced not much interest in secular subjects. Judging by his books, he thought about little but his work.

The Bible in German translation – Old and New Testaments – was present in two copies, one of them the illustrated Wittenberg edition of 1540, printed by Hans Lufft in folio. In addition to these, Langepeter owned three octavo New Testaments, all in German, and three editions of the Psalms, one of them in Latin. Paraphrases of the Bible occupied three additional volumes: they were useful in suggesting the plain, straightforward way of expounding Scripture (Erasmus had made the type popular in the 1520s), and their succinct interpretations are sure to have helped Langepeter over some of the difficult passages he was called on to expound. Written by pillars of the Lutheran establishment such as the Nuremberg theologian Veit Dietrich (*Summary of the Entire Bible*) and the Hamburg superintendent Christoph Vischer (*A Christian and Simple Explanation of the Passion, Death, Resurrection and Ascension of Our Lord*), these paraphrases bridged the gap between the rich metaphorical language of the Bible and the comprehension of the common man – including, of course, that of the preacher himself.

The same purpose was served, but more systematically, by *Postillen* (explanations of Scripture in the form of homilies), usually arranged to cover a year's pericopes and intended as guides and models for pastors still insecure in their understanding and insufficiently skilled in the art of preaching. In Langepeter's library, *Postillen* account for the largest section. He owned twelve altogether, including the archetype, Luther's *Kirchenpostillen*, published between 1522 and 1543 (Langepeter had this in three editions) and the *Hauspostillen*, sermons preached by Luther as head of his household to the family, disciples, guests and servants gathered at his table. Langepeter had the two earliest versions of the *Hauspostillen*, Veit Dietrich's of 1544 and Georg Rörer's – 'copied year after year from the Doctor's own mouth, and compiled faithfully without altering, taking away, or adding a word' – printed in Jena in 1559. Among his other *Postillen* – huge tomes, all of them – were Dietrich's own so-called *Kinderpostillen* of 1549 for children 'and other simple folk' (in the terminology of Lutheran pedagogy

8 *Verzeichnis meiner Johann Langepeter der Zeit zu Capellendorf pfarher eigener bücher, die ich die Zeit uber so ich im ministerio gewesen, gezeugett.* Staatsarchiv Weimar, Reg. Ii, No. 53, fols 21ʳ–24ᵛ.

all untutored lay people were addressed as *Kinder*), Caspar Huberinus's *German Postil On the Whole Gospel and Epistles*, Johann Spangenberg's *Explanation of the Epistles and Gospel throughout the Whole Year, for Young Christians*, a collection of gospel sermons by the Swabian reformer Johannes Brenz, and Erasmus Sarcerius's *Postillen* in three folio volumes.

So large a collection was justified not only by its immediate usefulness to a pastor looking to the masters for instruction, but also by the generally favourable responses auditors seem to have given to *Postillen* readings from the pulpit on Sundays and holidays. Indeed, interested church members seem more than occasionally to have demanded them. 'They say they would like to have a *Postille* read to them', visitors reported after sounding out congregations on the preaching of their pastors.[9] Churchmen like Dietrich and Spangenberg – not to mention Luther himself – were, of course, vastly more skilled than the ordinary, even the well-schooled parish curate, in gaining and holding the attention of town and village folk preoccupied with their mundane affairs. Especially in the task of relating Scripture to the plain, everyday world of human experience, their genius as theological popularizers really counted. In their intense effort to make people listen to the Gospel and open their consciences to its spirit, church administrators relied chiefly on the preacher's power to appeal and evoke. They realized, of course, that the average pastor fell far short of what was required for success in this endeavour, and they attempted to remedy the flaw by urging clergy to study the work of the experts. Hence the prevalence of model sermons in Langepeter's library.

Theology was not entirely missing from his shelves, but here, too, everyday concerns took precedence over intellectual matters. He had Melanchthon's *Commonplaces* in German translation, Johann Spangenberg's *Margarita theologica* (a book of theological topics in question and answer form) also in German, Luther's *Preface* to Daniel and the German exposition of Jonah written, so Luther said, to strengthen his own and his followers' spirits in their struggles against sectarianism from below and the ravages of power politics from above – struggles in which every conscientious village pastor in his own microcosm was fully engaged.

Apart from a couple of obscure tracts, Langepeter possessed no other work of academic theology. Sermons, on the other hand, abounded: not only the *Postillen* already mentioned, but also Luther's sermons on John 18–20 (1528–29), Matthew 5–7 (1532), and 1 Corinthians 15 (1534). These publications, of which Langepeter owned the first edition in each case, had a special pertinence to the dedicated preacher whose embattled position in the midst of a hostile populace was vividly described by Luther. As long as the devil lives and the world stands, the Reformer wrote in his *Preface* to Matthew 5–7, the Sermon on the Mount will be the chief bone of contention between true Christians and those –

9 Staatsarchiv Dresden Loc. 1997, fol. 127ᵛ.

163

schismatics and 'jurists' – who try to subvert it for their own purposes. Only the preacher can hold the line between truth and falsehood.[10] Pointing to Mary Magdalen as an example of one truly zealous in her piety and burning with the love of Christ, Luther portrayed his own contemporaries as indifferent, lazy, deaf and blind to God's truth. Men have been hearing the pure Word for ten years now, Luther wrote in 1529, but they act as though nothing had changed. Not long ago, under the papacy, there were indulgences, pilgrimages, bulls and much idolatry. Now eyes have been opened, but with what result? Ingratitude, apathy, indolence.[11] No country parson in 1570 needed to be convinced that these were in fact the attitudes determining the indifferent reception given his best efforts. He must have been encouraged, however, to learn that Luther himself, in his own state of deep disappointment, had held fast to the conviction that 'only the pulpit can keep the sacraments, the Apostles' Creed, and the worldly estates from falling into corruption.' Addressing himself to ministers and their recalcitrant congregations, Luther declared that only 'where there are right-thinking preachers will the doctrine remain pure and things go well'.[12] This message of reassurance was sorely needed by the working pastor who knew better than academic theologians and ecclesiastical bureaucrats how fragile was the hold of Christian doctrines and institutions on the loyalty of their nominal followers.

Langepeter's library contained other volumes of sermons: two collections of miscellaneous preaching by Luther, two sermons by Georg Major on the first chapter of John, and Cyriacus Spangenberg's sermons of 1562 on Luther as prophet. Prominent also among his volumes were consolation books and devotional guides: the *Book of Comfort for the Dying* by the prolific Urban Rhegius, Johann Pfeffinger's tract of the same title, a *Straight Path to the Eternal Life* by one Nicodemus Krämer, and several manuals on how to pray. Such books, written by senior theologians in the Lutheran Church (although representing diverging positions on matters of doctrine, as will be seen) were composed for the laity, but they must have been equally helpful to ministers trying to take the initiative in their task of giving evangelical direction to people's lives. A pamphlet called *The Holy, Cunning, and Learned Devil versus the First Commandment* suggested another approach apt to win the pastor some attention from his flock. Visitations revealed that ministers were easily confounded by adversary arguments against their articles of belief; as spoken by the devil in this popular pamphlet, such arguments were set out in extreme formulation, thus facilitating refutation.

Catechisms were, of course, the basic tool for giving sound Christian instruction. Every official directive from prince and consistory affirmed catechism

10 *Preface* to Sermons on Matthew 5–7, WA 32:299–301.
11 *Sermons* on John 20, WA 28:448–52.
12 From the seventeen Sermons on 1 Corinthians 15, WA 36:485.

teaching as the pastor's first duty and gravest responsibility. Langepeter had Luther's *Larger* and *Shorter Catechisms* as well as three other titles from among the huge number of available alternatives. So many variant catechisms were circulating in Saxony, as everywhere else in Germany, that in 1580 Duke August was to declare Luther's two catechisms the only legitimate ones in the land, in order – so his ecclesiastical constitution of that year stated – to put a stop to 'all kinds of trickery and deceit' and prevent further 'dangerous divisions' in the Lutheran church.[13] More than ten years before this law went into effect, Langepeter showed himself conservative in this respect. He used only Johann Spangenberg's question and answer version of Luther's *Larger Catechism*, as well as his *Digest of the Shorter Catechism*, and Sebastian Fröschel's *Catechism, as it has been Preached all these Years in the Church in Wittenberg* of 1559 – another faithful rendering of Luther's own catechetical work. Langepeter's formal duties required that he devote much of his own and his parishioners' time to catechism practice. He thus rehearsed the *Catechism* from the pulpit every Sunday morning, preached it with authoritative explanations to young people and hired hands on Sunday and holiday afternoons, and conducted regular mid-week examinations for the 'young and simple'. This was no easy undertaking. In fact, the sullen obstruction of congregations resentful of such regimentation (as they saw it), and unwilling to submit to it, made life wretched for many a devoted minister who regularly heard himself preaching to the bare walls on Sunday and Wednesday afternoons. Another aspect of the service seems to have met with a somewhat better response, however: church hymns set to popular tunes, their verses epitomizing in simple and emotionally-charged language the gist of the evangelical message. Langepeter owned three books of religious songs, one of them a collection sung in his own church in Kapellendorf. He also owned an *Agenda* more than usually explicit on the place of music in the divine service. This was the so-called *Heinrichs-Agende*, introduced by the duke of that name in Albertine Saxony of which territory he was the reformer. Again, visitation documents support the conclusion that congregations found the musical part of the service more to their liking, and the words of their hymns more comforting, than anything else in the liturgy.[14]

Another substantial component of his library indicates that Langepeter was deeply involved in a dominant aspect of the real life of a working clergyman: the doctrinal rivalries raging within Lutheranism in the second half of the sixteenth century. 1570, the year of Langepeter's library list, marked the beginning in Saxony of the most heated of these divisions, the quarrel over 'Crypto-calvinism', which pitted 'Philippists' against 'Lutherans', Wittenberg against Jena

13 From *Des durchlauchtigsten . . . Fürsten . . . Herrn Augusten, wie es in seiner churf. gnaden landen . . . mit der lehr und ceremonien . . . gehalten werden sol. 1580* in Emil Sehling, op. cit., I, i, pp. 359, 423. Actually, a visitation order of 1569 had stated the same principle, but seems to have been disregarded; ibid., p. 243.
14 See my *Luther's House of Learning*, pp. 233–4.

on the question of the Real Presence. But this controversy between the warring disciples of Luther and Melanchthon was only the latest and most heated of a series of disputes reaching back to the time of the reformers themselves: antinomianism, synergism, the Majorist controversy, the arguments over *adiaphora* and the opinions of Andreas Osiander. On all these matters there existed, at one time or another, both an orthodoxy and a heterodoxy, with frequent shifts of sides and abrupt changes of alignment to confuse simple pastors lacking the subtle understanding of a doctor of theology. In an age of bitter religious and ecclesiological contentions, Church authorities refused to let pastors work these matters out in the privacy of their own consciences. They held them accountable on every point of disputed dogma. When Langepeter, along with his fellow ministers, was obliged to answer in 1570 'whether or not the *Declaratio Victorini*, forced upon our churches eight years ago, accords with the Word of God and the writings of Luther',[15] he had, on pain of losing his living, to know what points of theology were touched by this declaration, and what he was expected to believe and disbelieve of them. Two polemical pamphlets in his library gave him the facts: *A Memorandum of Doctor Johann Wigand and Magister Mattheus Judex on Adiaphoric Falsifications*, and *News of the Dismissal of the Theologians of Jena*. Wigand and Judex were conservative theology professors at the University of Jena and partisans of Matthias Flacius there. Flacius, who in 1559 had persuaded Duke Johann Friedrich to issue the so-called Weimar *Book of Confutation* against Wittenberg and Philippist teachings on the roles of the human will and divine grace, fell out of favour when the Duke subsequently threw his support to the chief Philippist at Jena, Victorinus Strigel. The latter thereupon drew up a statement of his synergist position, and a number of Saxon ministers signed it. Flacius, Wigand and Judex refused to accept this solution and were dismissed from the Jena faculty – an event recounted in circumstantial detail in one of the pamphlets just mentioned. But a few years later everything changed. Strigel having gone to Heidelberg and apparently accepted the reformed confession there, his doctrine, as set out in the *Declaratio*, now smacked of Calvinism, the influence of which in Thuringia and Saxony was causing great concern among the authorities. Flacius was rehabilitated and all signatories of Strigel's document had to recant. Langepeter was required to confess to the Saxon visitors 'why he had signed it [if he had] and whether it now grieves him in the depth of his heart to have done so?'[16] To show him the proper way to recant past errors, he had a *Confession Submitted by Several Preachers in the Districts of Greiz, Gera, and Schönburg*, while the official *New Confutation of the Declaration of Victorinus* made it clear to him what he was now disaffirming.[17]

15 From Instruction by Duke Johann Wilhelm for visitation of 1569–70 in Thuringia, in Sehling, op. cit., I, i, p. 246.
16 Ibid.
17 The most complete record I have seen of the consequences of the *Declaratio Victorini* is in

Matching recantations were demanded, as needed, on the Majorist claim that good works are necessary for salvation and the antinomian taunt that 'laws are for City Hall only'.[18]

It is not known where Langepeter stood on these issues. Most likely he never had a position of his own. His books suggest that he was undiscriminating when it came to the fine points of grace, the Eucharist, freedom of the will, or the place of good works in the scheme of salvation. He did, of course, own copies of the official manifestoes of correct belief: the *Augsburg Confession* with its *Apologia*, the *Schmalkald Articles*, the *Saxon Confutation* (of synergism) of 1559, and a volume of 'Chief Articles of the Christian Faith'. He also had the Nuremberg–Brandenburg *Ecclesiastical Constitution* of 1533. Most of these books the ecclesiastical authorities required him to own.[19] Some other titles suggest the essentially uncritical posture he took toward the experts' fluctuating opinions. A volume by the Philippist Johann Pfeffinger and a book of sermons by the arch-synergist Georg Major stood beside a set of tracts by their vociferous opponent Nicolaus von Amsdorf. It appears, in fact, that Langepeter knew the great theological controversies of the day mostly from polemical literature. He had Flacius against Osiander on justification, and a pamphlet against the 'Swiss' on the Lord's Supper, also Flacius against the Heidelberg brand of Calvinism. A small book by Justus Menius furnished him with arguments against Anabaptists. He even had a Catholic harangue against Luther. In any case, the bitter in-fighting within his church does not seem to have shaken Langepeter's dedication to his calling. Less than five years before he submitted his library list, he acquired a treatise on the priestly vocation, *De vocatione ministrorum*, published in 1565 by Joachim Mörlin (another conservative controversialist and associate of Flacius), who counselled Lutheran pastors to 'work hard, remain true to your convictions, pray diligently, and God will bless your labours'.

Books on worldly subjects made a very small row on Langepeter's shelves, and each of his secular titles was of some relevance to the exercise of his profession. He had the Latin–German and German–Latin dictionary by the Strasbourg professor Petrus Dasypodius, a book of commonplaces with quotations from ancient authors, arranged topically for handy reference, and 'the Pandect book in German' – that is, a translation of excerpts from Justinian's digest of passages from the Roman jurists – a volume sure to have been useful at a time when legal procedure and, to some extent, substance were undergoing a steady

Staatsarchiv Coburg B 2461, fols 31–140, containing written recantations by ministers in the principality of Coburg who, seven years earlier in 1562, had been forced by the Coburg superintendent Maximilian Mörlin to sign the *Declaratio*. Maximilian was the brother of Joachim Mörlin mentioned later in this article.

18 Sehling, op. cit., I, i, p. 246. See also Franz Blanckmeister, *Sächsische Kirchengeschichte* (Dresden, 1899), pp. 156–62.

19 Cf. Visitation instruction 1569 in Sehling, op. cit., I, 1, 245.

process of romanization in Germany. Of greater interest to us is Langepeter's reading in history. He had three historical books, none of them strictly secular in author and subject. Josephus's *Jewish Antiquities* he owned in Caspar Hedio's German translation in a handsome folio published in Strasbourg in 1544, the only 'classic' in his collection. Closer to home, he had Johannes Sleidan's famous chronicle of the Reformation in Germany in the translation by Michael Beuter, published in 1567: this gave him the chronology and outline of events since 1517 – in the Protestant interpretation, of course. Another work suggested the place of these events, the most recent of which he had seen himself, in the grand design of universal history. *A Brief Description of the Four World Monarchies*, also by Sleidan, delineated the scheme of worldly affairs since earliest times as the unfolding of God's plan for mankind. Both books must have served to convince him that he had witnessed and, in his modest way, helped shape an extraordinary segment of time: 'The transformation having taken place in our days', Sleidan wrote in the preface to his chronicle of the Reformation, 'cannot be observed without great astonishment. It had a mean, almost contemptible, beginning. One man alone withstood the hatred and fury of the entire world when he could so easily have been silenced. . . . To allow such things to be forgotten by failing to immortalize them in books,' he added, 'would be a sin and a disgrace'. Sleidan's prose was uninspiring, but his story had immense drama. To have played even a trivial part in such a spectacle must have lifted the spirits of the humblest pastor in his ramshackle parsonage. More: his sense of the grand sweep of history must have suggested to him that there was meaning in the trials and frustrations of his life. Little but tribulation was to be expected by those who laboured near the end of the last of the great empires foretold in Daniel's prophecy to King Nebuchadnezzar. Sleidan stated this as a certainty on the final pages of his book on the four monarchies:

God's servants shall be persecuted all the world over and the godly shall be afflicted until the end of the world. This is what Daniel tells us, and his testimony offers no hope of a reconciliation or healing in the divisions that have arisen in our doctrine and religion – until Christ himself shall appear again. Let us, these our times being the most miserable, read most diligently in this prophet who preaches to us who are now acting out the last scene on the stage of this world.[20]

The final titles among Langepeter's books to be considered here indicate that their owner did indeed ponder Daniel most attentively. He had a commentary by one Johannes Chrysarus on the sixth chapter of Daniel's book (the lion's den). More important, he had Luther's *Preface* to the Book of Daniel in his German Bible of 1545 where the Reformer worked out Daniel's prophecies in concrete historical detail so as to demonstrate, first, that everything foretold had come true, the most recent events being the most precise fulfilments of

20 From an English translation of Sleidan's work, *The Key of Historie, or A most methodicall Abridgement of the foure chiefe Monarchies* . . . (London, 1627), pp. 373–5.

Daniel's signs and images; and secondly, that the visions and their interpretation were clear and obvious announcements of the impending reign of Christ as well as an accurate description of the brief time remaining before the Second Coming.[21] As Luther adumbrated these final days some among his readers must have felt a keen sense of recognition: 'heretics and false teachers', 'greed and Mammon', 'the church a poor remnant, remaining true to the Word while the world grows fat and epicurean, turning against Scripture'. 'For my part,' Luther concluded, 'I am sure that the Day of Judgement is just around the corner. It doesn't matter that we don't know the precise day'; and characteristically he adds: 'perhaps someone else can figure it out. But certain it is that time is now at an end.'[22]

Like Sleidan, Luther urged the reading of Daniel upon all who were suffering 'in these wretched days'. Daniel recorded his prophecies, he said, not in order to satisfy our idle curiosity about future events, but 'to console the pious and cheer them with the assurance that their misery will have an end.' 'Your redemption is near,' he asserted, confidently.[23] It is not difficult to imagine pastor Langepeter – overworked, poor, unappreciated, with few or no visible signs that the years of his labours had borne fruit – feeling his heart grow warm as he read these comforting words. That he saw the circumstances of his life and time as signs of the imminent end of the world, seems clear from his choice of three other eschatological books for his library: Andreas Musculus's *Of the Devil's Tyranny, Might, and Power, especially in These Last Days*, Nicolaus von Amsdorf's *Concerning the Five Momentous and Certain Signs to Occur Shortly Before Judgement Day*, and Jacob Frisch's *Book of Wondrous Signs*. Every recent and current calamity was shown by these authors to be a reliable indicator of Doomsday approaching, especially the false sense of security, the *Sicherheit*, from the impenetrable smugness of which people now ignored the Word of God and defied the warnings of his ministers.[24] Reading the dispirited reports given, year after year, by Langepeter and his colleagues of the ignorance and indifference of their people,[25] it is possible to grasp something of the force of persuasion exerted by a historical scheme that explained a dismal state of affairs which no human effort seemed powerful enough to correct.

No list of books should be used as a pass-key to a man's mind. Even as lengthy a catalogue as Langepeter's cannot reveal all about him. But it tells something, and by relating that to what can be learned elsewhere about the circumstances of his life and work, the historian can go some little way toward reconstructing the thought world of an obscure man at his humble post in a distant age. The image drawn from this exercise is certainly not without

21 Luther's *Preface* to Daniel, *WA Deutsche Bibel* 11:ii:11.
22 Ibid., 115, 117, 119, 125.
23 Ibid., 129.
24 Andreas Musculus, *Von des Teuffels Tyranney, Macht und Gewalt* ... (Worms, 1561), Cvii v.
25 Staatsarchiv Weimar Reg. Ii, Nos. 1–69, as well as my *Luther's House of Learning*, chapter 13.

interest to a student of the Reformation. Langepeter conformed better than most of his colleagues to the Lutheran paradigm of the good pastor. He was studious, a conscientious preacher, sound in what he believed and taught, serious – if not single-minded – about his duties. This much may be taken from his books. The rest is inference. It seems that the closer he came to the reformers' ideal, the greater was the gap separating him from his flock. If the Protestants' axiomatic equation of good preaching and sound Christianity did not work – and the evidence seemed to point to this conclusion – he laboured in vain. This painful reflection could not have passed through his mind without inflicting wounds that disturbed his mental balance. Many of his colleagues appear to have lapsed into indifference as they brooded on their lack of success. If his books are accepted as a guide to his thought, Langepeter did not. He knew the unpleasant facts of pastoral life but accepted the explanation of them given by his mentors. Knowing why, and how long, he kept up the good fight. For this he deserves to be remembered, perhaps as a Reformation counterpart of Professor A. G. Dickens's 'last medieval Englishman', Robert Parkyn, curate of Doncaster.[26]

26 A. G. Dickens, 'The Last Medieval Englishman', in Peter Brooks (ed.), *Christian Spirituality* (London, 1975), p. 143ff.

X

Cranbrook and the Fletchers: Popular and Unpopular Religion in the Kentish Weald

✤

PATRICK COLLINSON

I am particularly indebted to four institutions for permission to consult and make extensive use of documents, and to members of staff for their co-operation and assistance: Cathedral Archives Library Canterbury (CALC), Dr Williams's Library (DWL), East Sussex Record Office (ESRO), Kent Archives Office (KAO). I am grateful to Dr G. F. Nuttall and to Dr N. R. N. Tyacke for their comments on this essay.

In 1579 the churchwardens of Cranbrook returned a formal complaint against their vicar, Richard Fletcher, who had settled in the Wealden township early in the reign of Elizabeth and was to die there in 1586. Fletcher was the progenitor of a remarkable family: the father of the Richard Fletcher who ended his days as bishop of London and so the grandfather of the dramatist John Fletcher, eternally linked with Francis Beaumont. There was also a younger son, Dr Giles Fletcher, a distinguished civilian who served on an embassy to Muscovy and wrote one of the earliest and least diplomatic accounts of Russia in English and much else besides, including some verse. Giles Fletcher's sons were not insignificant literary figures: Giles Fletcher the younger, and Phineas Fletcher. Since both the vicar of Cranbrook's sons married local girls, there was Cranbrook blood flowing in these talented veins. In comparison with his descendants, Richard Fletcher the elder is almost unknown to history, even to the extent of being sometimes confused with his son and namesake.[1] But he was a familiar and even commanding presence in the Kentish Weald for a quarter of a century, appearing constantly in the act books of the archdeacon's court[2] as the moving force behind the detection of sexual crimes and other transgressions, publishing sentences of excommunication and more occasionally certifying the due performance of penance. These are doubtless but a selection of the scenes from a busy clerical life, an energetic round of preaching, treating wounded consciences, investigating sin, composing quarrels and making some of his own. Never before in almost twenty years had Fletcher himself been cited to appear in court.

The terms of the presentment were enigmatic: 'We present Mr Fletcher for that he preached that there were some of his paryshe that dyd sweare they would not come unto the church untyll such thinges were brought to passe that they had devysed.' This amounted to a charge that the vicar had defamed his parishioners as schismatics. On two successive court days Fletcher failed to appear. The innerness of the matter, which will become apparent in the course of this essay, may at first have eluded the archdeacon's officers. But on the third occasion, when Fletcher was again contumacious, the judge used his discretion to dismiss the case *ex certis causis* and no more was heard of it.[3] But whereas the interest of the court was not sustained, it will be seen that Fletcher's unhappy experience with his flock will open a path into a fruitful exploration of the uncertain terrain lying between two kinds of religion in Tudor England. Historians

1 The confusion occurs in John Strype, *Ecclesiastical Memorials* (Oxford, 1822), vol. ii, part I, pp. 402–3; and more recently in Roger B. Manning, *Religion and Society in Elizabethan Sussex* (Leicester, 1969), p. 76n.
2 A principal source for this essay: CALC, in the series X.1–10.
3 CALC, X.2.2, fol. 58ʳ.

of the English Reformation have long been concerned to understand the nature of the interface between the officially inspired Reformation of the national Church and what might be called the local and unofficial Reformation, with its ancient Lollard roots. And since no living historian has contributed more to our knowledge of these aspects of Reformation principle and practice than A. G. Dickens, it is appropriate that they should be investigated on this occasion. Another and related area of persistent interest concerns the bifurcation of English Protestantism towards, on the one hand, those conservative religious sentiments which approximated to our understanding of Anglicanism, and on the other through a transitional Puritanism to the Dissent of the later seventeenth century. The microcosm of Cranbrook, more especially in the time of the Fletchers, will serve to particularize both these large questions and to shed some light on them.

In this period Cranbrook was one of the largest parishes in Kent and possibly the most populous of all. Measuring eight miles by six it contained in 1557 three hundred households and 1,500 communicants. Forty years later there were said to be at least 2,000 communicants; in 1640 the vicar wrote of his labours among 'above 2000 soules'.[4] All these people, many of them dispersed in the distinct hamlets of Milkhouse Street (or Sissinghurst), Golford, Hartley, Glassenbury and Flishinghurst, as well as in isolated farms and cottages in the Wealden 'dens', were served by a single parish church, 'the cathedral of the Weald', the only subsidiary chapel of ease at Milkhouse having been suppressed in 1548.[5] Some parishioners must have lived as far as five miles from the church along by-roads which, even in the eighteenth century, were 'very bad in winter' and in summer 'offensive and painful'.[6] In the late sixteenth century it was the custom of the parish to stagger the obligatory Easter communion over the weeks between Easter and Whitsun and not to certify the archdeacon of absentees until this season was past.[7] When plague came to the district in 1597, those dying in the outlying hamlets were buried at their doors with no attempt made to carry them into Cranbrook.[8] Modern social historians have begun to ask whether such an entity as Cranbrook was a community at all, or in what sense it was a community.[9] Alexander Dence, the town's chief benefactor in the six-

---

4 *Archdeacon Harpsfield's Visitation, 1557*, ed. W. Sharp and L. E. Whatmore, Catholic Record Society, vols xlv, xlvi (1950, 1961), pp. 182–3; CALC, X.3.5, fol. 133ᵛ; Robert Abbot to Sir Edward Dering, 15 March 1640, BL, MS Stowe 184, fols 47–8.
5 C. C. R. Pile, *The Chapel of Holy Trinity Milkhouse*, Cranbrook Notes & Records no. 1 (n.p., 1951).
6 Edward Hasted, *History of Kent* (1972 edn), vol. vii, p. 91.
7 In 1592 the newly-installed vicar, William Eddy, presented the churchwardens for reporting this custom to him (CALC, X.3.5, fol. 133ᵛ). The dates for the purchase of bread and wine given in the churchwardens' accounts suggest staggering of the Easter communion in some years (KAO, P/100/5/1, fols 63ᵛ, 76, 78, 102ᵛ).
8 KAO, TR/1042/5 (typescript of earliest Cranbrook registers, without foliation or pagination).
9 Alan Macfarlane et al., *Reconstructing Historical Communities* (Cambridge, 1977).

teenth century, may have pondered the same question when he provided in his will for an annual Christmas dinner at the inns and taverns 'for all the honeste howseholders and fermors of the towne and parishe', explaining that he did not have in mind the rich or the poor, for whom he had made other provision.[10]

Much of this inflated population was sustained, directly or indirectly, by the industry which produced Cranbrook's famous and 'durable broad cloths with very good mixtures and perfect colours.'[11] It was a population as unstable and fluctuating as the cloth trade itself, the great variety of surnames in the parish registers[12] and much other circumstantial evidence suggesting that people were for ever coming and going. 535 individuals, presented in the archdeacon's court between 1560 and 1607, shared 369 surnames, while 283 of these family names occur once only in the presentments. And only fifty-one parishioners were cited on more than one occasion within these dates. The historian who studies the history of a parish in such flux over a period of a century may well wonder whether or in what sense he is contemplating the 'same' community. On the other hand, the leading clothing families show little variation throughout the sixteenth and early seventeenth centuries. At the end of this period, as at the beginning, the parish vestry was dominated by the names of Hendly, Dence, Sheaffe, Sharpy, Courthope, Cuchman, Brickenden and Hovenden, these wealthy clothiers yielding precedence only to the parish gentry, the Bakers of Sissinghurst and the Roberts family of Glassenbury. The bearers of these names dined together at the George, had ground broken for them inside the parish church, and formed a self-defining and self-perpetuating oligarchy. It was the custom for each churchwarden, at the end of his first year of office, to recruit the colleague with whom he would serve for his second year, 'with the consent of the parishioners'.[13]

Historians cannot agree whether to attribute the persistent reputation of places like Cranbrook for religious dissent to intractable geographical and demographical conditions, inimical to the pastoral interests of the established Church, or to some intangible, but sympathetic, connection between radical religion and the manufacture of cloth.[14] Both explanations are generalizations

10 PRO, PROB/11/56/20.
11 J. Philpot, *Villare Cantianum or Kent Surveyed and Illustrated* (1659), p. 98, quoted by Peter Clark in *English Provincial Society from the Reformation to the Revolution: Religion, Politics and Society in Kent, 1500–1640* (Hassocks, 1977), p. 463n. See C. C. R. Pile, *Cranbrook Broadcloth and the Clothiers*, Cranbrook Notes & Records no. 2 (n.p., 1951); C. W. Chalklin, *Seventeenth-Century Kent: A Social and Economic History* (1965), pp. 116–23.
12 KAO, TR/1042/5.
13 KAO, P/100/5/1.
14 Alan Everitt, 'Nonconformity in Country Parishes', in *Land, Church and People: Essays Presented to Professor H. P. R. Finberg*, ed. Joan Thirsk, *Agricultural History Review*, vol. xviii supplement (Reading, 1970); J. F. Davis, 'Lollard Survival and the Textile Industry in the South-East of England', *Studies in Church History*, vol. iii, ed. G. J. Cuming (Leiden, 1966), pp. 191–201.

which cannot help very much in understanding the religious history of a particular place. What is certain is that no later than the 1420s the Kentish Weald became a breeding-ground for Lollard heresy. The credit for this is usually given to the priest William Whyte who fled from Kent to Norwich and was burned there in 1428.[15] But for all that is known, anti-catholic and specifically anti-sacramentarian sentiment in the region may have had older, indigenous origins. Archbishop Warham's investigations of 1511 – the so-called *magna abiurata*[16] – uncovered a long-established heretical tradition in the clothing towns of Tenterden, Cranbrook and Benenden. Four inhabitants of Cranbrook were interrogated, among whom William Baker confessed how after 'communication ageynst pilgrimages and worshipping of sayntes and of offeryngs' he had altered his intention to offer money to the rood of grace 'and went not thyder but gave his offeryng to a poore man.' Villagers assisting the ecclesiastical judges in their enquiries identified the arch-heretic of the region as William Carder, a Tenterden weaver, who for many years had pursued his cryptic apostolate with ones and twos, sometimes at home, sometimes at alehouses or in church, communicating the doctrine that the sacrament of the altar was 'very bread and not Christ's body' and that the other sacraments were 'nothing profitable' for man's soul. It was forty years since Carder's mother had fled from Tenterden for fear of these opinions, and twenty since Carder had spoken of them to John Grebill of Tenterden as he sat at his loom, reading from 'a book of two evangelists'.

When, in 1511, William Baker of Cranbrook declared of St Matthew's Gospel that 'it was pitie that it might not be knowen openly', Richard Harman, a native of Cranbrook, may have already been living in Antwerp, where he later became William Tyndale's associate and factor, helping, as Queen Anne Boleyn later testified, 'both with his gooddis and pollicie . . . to the settynge forthe of the Newe Testamente in Englisshe.'[17] When Harman's papers were searched in 1528 they were found to include letters of pious exhortation from two Cranbrook men, one of them a clothier, both 'consernyng the New Testament in Yngliche.'[18] Perhaps they were carried to Antwerp by Thomas Hitton who,

15 J. A. F. Thomson, *The Later Lollards 1414-1520* (Oxford, 1965), pp. 173–6; *Heresy Trials in the Diocese of Norwich, 1428-31*, ed. Norman P. Tanner (1977), Camden ser. 4, vol. xx, passim.
16 Lambeth Palace Library, Archbishop Warham's Register, fols 159^r–75^v. See Thomson, op. cit., pp. 186–91, and Thomson's critique of Foxe's use of Warham's Register for his account of these trials, 'John Foxe and Some Sources for Lollard History: Notes for a Critical Appraisal', *Studies in Church History*, vol. ii, ed. G. J. Cuming (1965), pp. 251–7.
17 Quoted in *The Complete Works of St. Thomas More*, ed. Louis A. Schuster et al. (New Haven and London, 1973), vol. viii, p. 1182n. 'Robert Necton's Confession' (*Letters and Papers of the Reign of Henry VIII*, vol. iv, 4030) establishes that Simon Fish sold New Testaments which he received 'from one Harmonde, an Englishman beyond sea.'
18 *The Letters of Sir John Hackett 1526-1534*, ed. E. F. Rogers, Archives of British History and Culture vols i and ii (Morgantown, 1971), pp. 173–7, 207. I am grateful to Dr A. C. Duke of Southampton University for this reference.

after visiting his 'holy congregaccyons' in 'dyvers corners and luskes lanes', was taken at Gravesend in 1530 and burned at Maidstone. It provoked Sir Thomas More beyond measure that Hitton supplanted St Polycarp in the calendar published by the Protestant exiles as the new 'St Thomas of Kent'.[19] Nine years later a royal commission of enquiry into the sacramentarian heresy specified three localities: Calais, Bristol – and Cranbrook parish.[20]

'Sacramentarianism' (the denial of Christ's bodily presence in the sacrament of the altar) was still a touchstone of vernacular heresy in Kent in the 1550s, when once again the Wealden townships were of particular interest to the tribunal charged with the extirpation of heresy in the diocese of Canterbury.[21] At Cranbrook the vicar was enjoined not to bury any parishioner who had failed to confess or receive the sacrament and not to administer communion to any who refused to creep to the cross on Good Friday. Every household was to be represented, week by week, at procession and litany on Wednesdays and Fridays.[22] The town was to win notoriety in local Protestant folklore not for its two martyrs, William Hopper and William Lowick,[23] but as the place where many suspect persons were sent for questioning by Sir John Baker and other justices and detention in the room above the south porch of the church, 'Baker's Jail'.[24] The history of the Marian persecution in Kent, like the story of the Bristol martyrs,[25] suggests that as late as the mid-sixteenth century popular heresy, was expressed in categories which ostensibly owed very little to the new Protestant theologians. Far from assuming that dissenting circles readily submitted to the intellectual and pastoral leadership of university-trained divines, Dr J. F. Davis suggests that the academic reformers were themselves susceptible to popular heretical traditions, and particularly responsive to traditional Lollard sacramentarianism.[26]

Consequently, it is a question to what extent the Marian martyrs in Kent had embraced the officially-endorsed Edwardine doctrine, or were heretics in a more

19 *Complete Works of More*, vol. viii, pp. 13–16, 684, 1207, 1216; *The Acts and Monuments of John Foxe*, ed. G. Townsend and S. R. Cattley (8 vols, London, 1837–40) (hereafter, *A & M*), vol. viii, pp. 712–15. Peter Clark (op. cit., p. 34) calls Hitton 'the Maidstone curate'. But he is described in the signification of his relaxation to the secular arm (PRO, C/85/25/23) as 'Thomas Hitton laicus', and by his own confession he had lived 'by the joiner's craft' (*Works of More*, vol. viii, p. 15).

20 Lambeth Palace Library, Archbishop Cranmer's Register, fol. 68r. I owe this reference to Mr K. G. Powell.

21 J. F. Davis, 'Heresy and the Reformation in the South-East of England: 1520–1559' (unpublished Oxford D.Phil. thesis, 1966), pp. 67–8, 153–4, 433. I am indebted to Dr Davis's account of Kentish 'neo-Lollardy' and grateful for permission to cite his thesis.

22 *Archdeacon Harpsfield's Visitation*, pp. 182–3.

23 *A & M*, vol. viii, pp. 322, 326.

24 *Archdeacon Harpsfield's Visitation*, pp. 127, 129, 132, 177; William Tarbutt, *Annals of Cranbrook Church*, vol. i (Cranbrook, 1870), pp. 11–14.

25 K. G. Powell, *The Marian Martyrs and the Reformation in Bristol* (Bristol, 1972).

26 Davis, 'Heresy and the Reformation', pp. 445–50.

fundamental sense, or at least eclectic in their beliefs. Elizabethan Protestants, and John Foxe in particular, scouted the possibility that any of the martyrs could have been deviant from the godly Protestant consensus. Foxe was told that at Maidstone the turncoat curate John Day had been forced to confess, on the doorstep of his favourite alehouse, that he had lied shamelessly in condemning those who had died at Maidstone as 'heretykes most damnabelle', who had denied the divinity of Christ and the doctrine of the Trinity.[27] But there is evidence in documents which were in Foxe's own files that some of the Kentish martyrs were indeed heretics in precisely the sense that Day had alleged.[28] Such embarrassments were glossed over by the martyrologist with the formula: 'To these articles what their answers were likewise needeth here no great rehearsal, seeing they all agreed together, though not in the same form of words, yet in much like effect of purposes.'[29]

But perhaps the nature of the beliefs entertained in the village conventicles was less significant than the existence of the conventicles themselves, with their sense of brotherhood and their insistence on primary moral and social virtues to the extent of shunning those who were morally offensive. John Fishcock of Headcorn, seven miles from Cranbrook, one who 'had a good iudgemente of the Trynytie' and condemned 'yvill opynyon therein', told his judges that 'if there be anny that is a brother whiche is an adulterer, a fornicator, an extorcioner, a worshipper of images, he thought not to eate nor drinck with him, nether yet salute him.' John Plume of Lenham 'beynge emonge the congregation' had often heard it affirmed as a general doctrine that 'they oughte not to salute a synner or a man whome they knowe not.'[30] What John Philpot of Tenterden called, in contradistinction to the Catholic Church, 'Christ's congregation',[31] was no abstract theological principle but a social reality and a matter of intense experience. In a letter to Mrs Roberts, a gentlewoman of Hawkhurst included in Foxe's tally of near-martyrs, Richard Woodman, an iron-maker of Warbleton in Sussex, saluted 'all our brethren and sisters that are around about you', 'all the people of the household of God', 'all others of God's elect': 'Now is the Lord come with his fan in his hand, to try the wheat from the chaff.'[32]

Richard Fletcher was not a native of Kent,[33] but as a staunch Edwardine

27 BL, MS Harl. 416, fols 123-4.
28 Examinations of William Prowtynge of Thornham, John Syms of Brenchley and Robert Kynge of (East) Peckham; BL, MS Harl. 421, fols 94-5.
29 *A & M*, vol. viii, p. 300. See Davis, 'Heresy and the Reformation', pp. 423-4, Thomson, loc. cit., pp. 251-7.
30 BL, MS Harl. 421, fols 101, 103, 134ᵛ.
31 Ibid., fol. 92.
32 *A & M*, vol. viii, pp. 374-7.
33 His origins are problematical. His funerary monument (inscription in Tarbutt, op. cit., vol. ii (1873), p. 17) describes him as 'ex Eboracensi Provincia' and further states that he was ordained by bishop Ridley of London (confirmed by Strype from Ridley's Register, *Ecclesiastical Memorials*, vol. ii, part I, pp. 402-3) and served in his diocese. His son Giles was born at Watford in 1549 and he was vicar of Bishop's Stortford from 1551 until he was deprived in 1555,

Protestant he may have evaded the Marian persecution by concealing himself in the close, wooded country of the Weald. This is implied by his ability to supply Foxe with information about the troubles of Edmund Allin, the miller of Frittenden.[34] It is more certain that in June 1555,[35] in company with his son Richard, then a young boy of perhaps nine, he witnessed the burning at Dartford of the linen-weaver Christopher Wade, and, more than twenty years later, communicated to Foxe one of the most vividly circumstantial of all the narratives in the *Acts and Monuments*, with its details of fruiterers coming with horse-loads of cherries to sell to the crowd and the victim clad in a 'fair long white shirt from his wife', 'standing in a pitchbarrel'.[36] If only it was possible to measure the distance in mentality between the Cambridge graduate and Bishop Ridley's ordinand and the linen-weaver of Dartford! Perhaps the gap was far from unbridgeable? Foxe's brief account of the interrogation of Wade and the bricklayer Nicholas Hall suggests that Hall was the more radical and eclectic of the two; while according to Fletcher's narrative Wade died exhorting the people 'to embrace the doctrine of the gospel preached in King Edward's days.'[37] No doubt Fletcher's subsequent reputation with the godly fraternity rested on his known fidelity in the years of trial. According to the funerary monument erected in Cranbrook church by his sons, he had himself suffered hardship and imprisonment, 'adversa multa et vincula'.[38] As late as the 1570s, he was a vocal critic of John Day, the turncoat curate of Maidstone.[39]

With the renewed Protestant ascendancy under Elizabeth, the relationship between the dissenting Protestant minority and the parish churches was dramatically altered. Dr Peter Clark has found 'little evidence of any popular backlash in Kent against the Marian persecutors.'[40] To be sure, the martyrs were of less interest to most of their contemporaries than they were to Foxe, or to the contributors to this volume. At Cranbrook, the churchwardens reported, laconically, that 'one Hopper' had been burned and 'dyvers other imprisoned whose names we know not.'[41] But Dr Clark perhaps underestimates the

---

presumably as a married priest. But his son Richard was admitted in 1569 to one of archbishop Parker's Norfolk fellowships at Corpus Christi College, Cambridge, and was styled 'Norfolciensis' (*DNB*, art. Fletcher).

34 *A & M*, vol. viii, pp. 320-5. On the other hand Foxe was not in possession of this information in 1563. William Fuller reported in the seventeenth century that bishop Richard Fletcher was born in Cranbrook *c.* 1546. But the statement is unsupported.

35 Foxe's dating is corrected from the original signification of relaxation to the secular arm, which relates to Christopher Wade, Nicholas Hall and Margery Polleye (PRO, C/85/144/33).

36 *A & M*, vol. vii, pp. 319-21.

37 Ibid., pp. 318, 320. Davis however ('Heresy and the Reformation', pp. 291-4) regards both Foxe's summary of the examination and Fletcher's account of Wade's attachment to Edwardian orthodoxy as somewhat suspect.

38 Tarbutt, op. cit., vol. ii, p. 17.

39 DWL, MS Morrice B II, fol. 22r.

40 Clark, op. cit., p. 151.

41 CALC, X.1.2, fol. 32v.

strength of feeling which found expression in some parishes. At Littlebourne, near Canterbury, and at Maidstone, there were formal complaints against clergy who had defamed the martyrs in their preaching.[42] At Elmstead, near Wye, the wardens objected to their vicar as 'an open enemy to Godes worde' and begged the archdeacon: 'The Lorde move you by some meanes to rydd hym from us.'[43] Here and in other parishes there were clashes between Protestants and 'the enemyes of God', 'Kayne's children', when the rood-lofts were removed. At Throwleigh the ancients of the parish ordered a man to be present at the pulling down of the rood-loft 'for that he was an accuser in Queen Marys tyme.'[44] Ministers were denounced for failing to preach against popery, or in line with sound Protestant doctrine.[45] At Bethersden, the churchwardens thought it in order to present their vicar for preaching at Tenterden that 'yt was not lawfull for us to use the servyce used at Geneva', and that it was no more lawful to follow the Genevan church than the Roman church.[46] A lone Anglican voice crying in the wind!

But at Cranbrook, with the resignation (deprivation?) of the Marian vicar and the admission in October 1561 of Richard Fletcher,[47] Protestants had cause for satisfaction rather than complaint. Until this late date there had probably been no experience of a genuine Protestant ministry in the parish, and not much experience of a resident vicar. From 1534 until 1554 the incumbent had been Hugh Price, notable as the founder of Jesus College, Oxford, but also as a pluralist who was represented at Cranbrook by curates.[48] This tradition of absenteeism was not incompatible with a vigorous parish life, an active vestry and sacrificial expenditure on the fabric of the church and its goods, which suggests the continuing vitality of traditional Catholic sentiment. In 1530 eighty-eight parishioners had contributed £370 to the rebuilding of the south

42 CALC, X.1.2, fol. 9ᵛ; BL, MS Harl. 421, fol. 123ʳ.
43 CALC, X.1.2, fols 27ʳ-8ᵛ.
44 CALC, X.1.3, fol. 133ᵛ; another case, ibid., fol. 155ᵛ.
45 At Preston iuxta Faversham (CALC, X.1.2, fol. 42ᵛ) and Boughton Mallarde (X.1.3, fol. 68ᵛ).
46 CALC, X.1.2, fo. 34.
47 Various dates are given by local historians for the commencement of Fletcher's ministry at Cranbrook. There is no doubt that he was collated by archbishop Parker on 17 October 1561; *Registrum Matthei Parker*, ed. W. H. Frere, Canterbury and York Society (Oxford, 1928–33), p. 784. This is inconsistent with the details on Fletcher's funerary monument where it is stated that at the time of his death in February 1585(/6) he had had charge of the church for 26 years and 7 months (Tarbutt, op. cit., vol. ii, pp. 17–18). This is either a mistake or Fletcher had served as a curate before his collation. But in 1560 there was another curate, Robert Foster, who is mentioned in the churchwardens' accounts (KAO, P/100/5/1, fol. 11ᵛ) and for whom letters dimissory for ordination to the priesthood were issued on 2 June of that year, describing him as of Cranbrook (*Registrum Matthei Parker*, p. 346).
48 A. B. Emden, *A Biographical Register of the University of Oxford A.D. 1501 to 1540* (Oxford, 1974), p. 462. Dr Price was noted as non-resident from 1550 to 1554 in the earliest surviving visitation call books for this period (CALC, Z.3.6, fols 13, 40, 60, 76ᵛ). Three curates came and went within these four years.

aisle.[49] Consequently Dr Clark can identify Cranbrook (which he will soon call 'the Puritan town of Cranbrook') as 'an old Lollard centre' and (on the evidence of late Henrician will preambles) a 'major conservative stronghold'.[50] But now the outward symbols of religious conservatism were promptly erased. Before Fletcher's arrival, the rood-loft had been taken down and the altars removed (in accordance with the Injunctions), and a great quantity of Catholic ornaments and furniture sold or otherwise disposed of. In Fletcher's first year there was payment to the painter 'for blottynge owt of the ymagrye in the glass wyndowes.'[51]

Dr Clark has suggested that, once such external matters had been dealt with, the Protestant ascendancy in Elizabethan Kent became identified with 'ethical radicalism' and 'a growing preoccupation with social control', popery having proved 'something of a paper tiger'.[52] The criminal or 'office' business of the court of the archdeacon of Canterbury bears him out, with its copious documentation of a crusade against sin, and sin as defined by respectable Protestant opinion. It was sufficient to be 'a common minstrel' to be presented,[53] since as professional musicians[54] the minstrels played on Sundays in houses or inns where there might be 'half a hundred of youth', 'drinkyng of syder' or 'a firkyn of beere', 'fydling, pyping, and as we suspect dauncing' and perhaps outnumbering the people in church.[55] From Cranbrook, for example, Walter Mascall was presented in 1570 for 'keepynge daunsynge in his house apon the sabothe day whereby the people be styrred to wantonnes.'[56] In the 1560s and 1570s (but not thereafter) there were also many presentments from Wealden parishes for various forms of witchcraft and sorcery, most involving *maleficium*, but others not remote from vestigial Catholicism, as when Henry Clegate of Headcorn confessed that he helped bewitched people and cattle by repeating prayers and the creed, as he had been taught to do years before by a neighbouring priest and by his mother.[57]

For Dr Clark, such cases indicate that Protestantism was expressing itself

---

49 KAO, P/100/5/1, fol. 5. See also the inventory of church goods of 1509 (ibid., fols 1–2* printed in *Archaeologia Cantiana*, vol. xli, pp. 57–68) and the list of subsequent benefactions (P/100/5/1, fols 3ᵛ–6).
50 Clark, op. cit., pp. 30–1, 59, 62, 151.
51 KAO, P/100/5/1, fol. 10.
52 Clark, op. cit., pp. 157, 149, 152.
53 Examples in CALC, X.1.7, fol. 47ᵛ, X.1.12, fol. 136ᵛ.
54 There is a reference in 1581 to 'Henry Newman beinge a mynstrell . . . and his ii parteners' (CALC, X.1.14, fol. 44) and another to the hiring of minstrels 'to come to Ashford to play' and to 'divers' sharing in the payment of their wages (X.2.2, fol. 26ᵛ).
55 Details drawn from cases from Molash 1575 (CALC, X.1.12, fol. 151ᵛ) and Cranbrook 1606 (X.4.11, fol. 7ᵛ). It was the minister of Warden in Sheppey who complained in 1576 that 'John Herne the mynstrell . . . had more with hym then I had at the churche.' (X.1.13, fol. 80ᵛ.)
56 CALC, X.1.10, fol. 11.
57 *Acta* in Archbishop Parker's metropolitan visitation; CALC, X.8.5, fol. 72.

in an onslaught on the mores of a 'Third World' of the poor and spiritually ignorant, a world of 'the charmist, the church absenter and the tramp' – 'non-respectable society'. But the alluring 'Third World' analogy can be deceptive. By identifying Protestantism with advancing wealth and respectability it posits a polarity of culture which did not yet exist, as if only the poor and disreputable enjoyed a drink, or the children of the poor a romp on Sundays.[58] Likewise, it diverts attention from the fact that a high percentage of the sins which concerned the parochial and archidiaconal authorities were of a sexual nature: fornication, whoredom, adultery – 'incontinence' in all its forms. Such moral failings have rarely been confined to one social class. It must have been with respect to sexual transgression, and in measure as they were socially discriminatory in proceeding against it, that the new disciplines approximated to 'social control'.

Richard Fletcher's reign at Cranbrook began in a confrontation with unsympathetic elements in the town which was worthy of Geneva itself in its lack of respect for persons. Within weeks of his coming, the wife of Alexander Dence was presented as a noisy 'contemner of prests and ministers' and 'a talker in the church'. Alexander Dence would become the greatest of the town's benefactors when he wrote his will in 1573. But it was a conservative will which retained in its preamble the old kyries. Dence himself was presented on this same occasion for keeping suspicious company with the wife of another man of property, Stephen Sharpy, who at his death disposed of no less than seventeen houses. The suspicious goings-on had occurred in the house of Bartholomew Hendly, another man of substance, whose wife, 'an evell woman from her youth', was herself presented for 'bawdry'.[59] It was not every day that a Dence or a Sharpy or a Hendly was called to account for such matters.[60] In May 1562 a number of parishioners of lesser rank were brought to book as 'receivers of naughty and evil persons' and 'maintainers of evil rule'. One of these, a widow, was also accused of 'charminge, in measuring and fealing of sycke persons and telling howe things lost should be founde againe.'[61] In the following year the bawdy court (to use its popular name) met exceptionally in Cranbrook itself, as it did in other Wealden parishes, and in addition to the vicar and churchwardens, forty-two parishioners from the elite of the town were cited, with the intention that they should be sworn, and present any of their neighbours who had

58 Clark, op. cit., especially pp. 152, 180. See also Dr Clark's essay in Donald Pennington and Keith Thomas (eds), *Puritans and Revolutionaries: Essays in Seventeenth-Century History presented to Christopher Hill* (Oxford, 1978), pp. 47–72. These remarks are intended to engage with the concept of 'the reform of popular culture' launched by Dr Peter Burke in *Popular Culture in Early Modern Europe* (1978).
59 CALC, X.1.3, fol. 74ᵛ. Dence's will in PRO, PROB/11/56/20.
60 Walter Hendly, gentleman, was presented for adultery in 1597 (CALC, X.4.3, fol. 100ᵛ). Simon Dence was accused of fathering a bastard in 1605 but the case lapsed for lack of evidence (X.4.8, fol. 160). I know of no other cases involving these names.
61 CALC, X.1.4, fols 94ᵛ–6ᵛ.

offended within the terms of the visitation articles. The fact that only Fletcher, one churchwarden and nine other parishioners appeared doubtless reduced the value of this ambitious experiment. But Fletcher personally accused four of his flock of drunkenness, one of them being also 'a great swerer and blasphemer of God's name.' And he denounced a servant boy in the employ of one of the richest inhabitants, Richard Taylor,[62] 'for swearing together with other boys being and lyinge together on a night determyned who should or could best or most swear by the name of God.'[63] (The prize was later won by an older person, Alexander Warley, who appeared in court to answer for such blasphemous oaths as 'by the flesh of God, by the guttes of God.'[64])

It should not of course be thought that the vicar was solely responsible for bringing such matters to the attention of the authorities. Normally bills of presentment were drawn up by the churchwardens with the consent of the sidesmen and in response to articles published in the archdeacon's visitation. The detection of Mrs Dence's loquacity, for example, would have been prompted by some such question as 'whether there be enye that walketh, talketh or slepeth in tyme of divine service or sermon?'; and of the drunkards and swearers by the question 'whither ther be eny notorious dronkardes, great swearers or common skowldes and disquieters of ther neighboures?'[65] But the response to such questions, and with it the whole tone of the parish, depended to an immeasurable extent on the minister's interpretation of his pastoral functions. In the eighteen months before Fletcher's arrival there were only five presentments from Cranbrook. Within the next seven months there were thirty, all concerned with immoral or irreligious behaviour.

With the stabilization of the Protestant settlement, Fletcher continued to meet occasional defiance from certain intractable parishioners,[66] who may indeed have been provoked by his naming individuals from the pulpit, a practice known as 'personal preaching'.[67] But the detection of sin soon settled into a routine of which the outstanding and by no means unusual feature was passive non-compliance with ecclesiastical authority. The facts are best stated as statistics (see Tables 1 and 2). From Table 2 it will be seen that of all those parties cited, two-thirds, 66%, failed to appear in court. But of those cited under

---

62 Taylor himself, 'old Richard Taylor', 'a very riche and a welthy man' and a septuagenarian bachelor, was repeatedly presented for failure to pay his assessment towards parish expenses and was suspected of usury (CALC, X.1.5, fol. 168ᵛ, X.1.9, fol. 76ᵛ, X.1.11, fol. 68ʳ).
63 Details of the extraordinary 1563 visitation in CALC, X.1.5, fols 168ʳ-9ʳ. Seven other Wealden parishes were given the same special treatment: Benenden, Biddenden, Goudhurst, Hawkhurst, Headcorn, Rolvenden and Sandhurst. The court spent half a day in each parish.
64 CALC, X.1.11, fol. 67.
65 Articles in the visitation of exempt parishes by the archbishop's commissary, 1564; preserved in CALC, X.8.2, fol. 28.
66 Particularly in 1570; CALC, X.1.10, fols 11, 74.
67 Suggested by episodes in 1570, 1575, 1580; CALC, X.1.10, fol. 11; DWL, MS Morrice B II, fol. 22ʳ; CALC, X.2.2, fol. 58.

TABLE I
*Topical analysis of office cases from the parish of Cranbrook
in the corrective jurisdiction of the
Archdeacon of Canterbury, 1560–1607*

Incontinence as evidenced by bridal pregnancy	All other sexual and marital offences	Other disorderly offences against religion and morality
50	307	69
Working or trading on Sabbath or holidays	Non-attendance at church	Failure to receive communion
19	14	114
Usury	Failure to pay 'cesses', 'scots' or other dues	Catholic Recusancy
2	38	4*
Conduct symptomatic of Puritanism	Offences against ecclesiastical order and abuse of office	Stands Excommunicate
4† TOTAL 717	52	44

* Two individuals only: Mary Baker, wife of John Baker Esq., of Sissinghurst, and her maid servant.

† Only two individuals were presented under this heading in the entire history of the parish from 1560 to 1640: Robert Holden (on three counts) in 1585, and Peter Walker, servant to Richard Jorden, clothier, in 1591.

NOTE The record is not necessarily complete. There are apparent gaps in the series of act books covering the Deanery of Charing in 1569 and 1573 and there may be other omissions, less readily detected.

the category of 'All Other Sexual and Marital Offences', no less than 211 of 257, or 82%, proved contumacious. An even higher level of contumacy could be demonstrated if only one sex were counted, for in cases of simple fornication the man sometimes appeared and attempted to clear his name, or render satisfaction, but the unmarried woman almost never. On the other hand, of those cited to answer a charge of incontinence as evidenced by bridal pregnancy, 50% thought it in their interest to appear in court, usually to attest a contract of marriage undertaken before carnal knowledge took place. Presentments for bridal pregnancy increased towards the end of the period covered in these tables, outnumbering the presentments for all other sexual offences in 1592 and in 1606, when there were no less than twenty presentments under this heading. These presentments may reflect social anxiety in a time of economic hardship rather than any sense of moral outrage. For this reason the figures have been given up to 1607, by which date they suggest a new pattern, and a secular progression from

TABLE 2
Procedural analysis of cases, 1560–1607

Presentments	Citations	Individual cited appears in court or certifies to the satisfaction of the court
637	602	179
Respondent denies matter objected or objects to form or terms of citation	Respondent dismissed summarily	Respondent dismissed with monition
25	76	33
Respondent required to undergo purgation	Purgation successful	Court imposes penance
21	11	43
Court is certified that penance performed according to the schedule	Penance commuted	Individual cited fails to appear and is contumacious
28	2	396
Poena reservata in proximo	*In poena excommunicationis in scriptis*	Sentence of excommunication pronounced and recorded
44	25	328
Court is certified that sentence of excommunication has been denounced in parish church	Excommunication for cause other than contumacy	Excommunicate is subsequently absolved
230	2	44*
General pardon or *indulgentia regia* claimed	Court applies for writ *de excommunicato capiendo*	Case transferred to another court
5	10	7
Proceedings terminated by death of individual presented and/or cited		
10		

* The record of the court is likely to be incomplete. Many of those excommunicated may have removed themselves, for that or other reasons, to other parishes or jurisdictions. But many inhabitants of Cranbrook may have found it possible to live in a state of semi-permanent excommunication. In some instances excommunicate persons applied for absolution after an interval of as much as eight years. Not all these applications were successful. Many excommunications may have lapsed informally, with the passage of time. It is not known whether excommunicates were regularly denounced every six months, as the Canons required.

the urgent reformism personified by Fletcher in early Elizabethan days to the routinized procedures found in 1606: 'We the churchwardens . . . do presente for incontinent living before the time of their marriages as manifestly doth appear by publique fame . . .', followed by a list of names.[68]

Fletcher coped as best he could with what might seem to have been an intolerable disciplinary situation. Denunciations of those excommunicated for contumacy must have punctuated Morning Prayer with the same frequency as the calling of banns of marriage. The performance of public penance followed by the vicar's certificate to the archdeacon's court that it had been done penitently, according to the schedule, was a more occasional spectacle which may have been seen less than twenty times in Fletcher's twenty-four years in the parish. This is all that is normally seen of Fletcher's pastoral activity in the archdeaconry act books. But in 1566 the registrar made an unusually full record of a curious case which shows him briefly in a different light. Mrs Walter, the wife of the vicar of the neighbouring parish of Goudhurst, married for twenty years with seven children, was persuaded that the village tailor, whom she had been 'moved inwardly to love', was her husband before God. Following the advice of St James to seek wisdom of God, she resorted to prayer, whereupon it was revealed to her that the tailor 'in tyme to come' should be her husband. Either she took her problem to the vicar of Cranbrook or, more probably, the initiative lay with him, since it was a notorious fact that Mrs Walter was estranged from her husband. Either way here is a glimpse of Fletcher in the role of marriage-guidance counsellor, sixteenth-century style.[69]

Clearly to refer to 'Puritan Cranbrook' is not to suggest that the whole town reverberated with psalm-singing and godliness. Nor was morality and attendance at sermons enforced with the same credible sanctions which the magistrates employed in communities of a comparable size which were corporate towns – such as Rye, a subject to be discussed later in this essay. Early in the seventeenth century it was still a place where the barbers and butchers plied their trade on a Sunday morning.[70] When Paul Baines, the famous Puritan divine, married into the clothing family of Sheaffe, as Richard Fletcher junior had done before him, he found that Mrs Sheaffe, his wife's sister, and others of her family, spent their time playing cards 'and such like games'. Baines (whose only recreation was chess) converted his sister-in-law from her habits by preaching against them in a public sermon. ('It might not have been so well if he had spoken to her in private.'[71]) The visitation of the plague in 1597 was attributed by the vicar, William Eddy, to the sins of the town, especially 'that vice of drunkenness which did abownd heere', and to the recent deaths of 'many honest and good men and

68 CALC, X.4.11, fol. 4ᵛ.
69 CALC, X.1.8, fols 119ʳ–20ᵛ.
70 In 1606: CALC, X.4.11, fols 52ᵛ–3ᵛ, 64ʳ, 72ʳ; 1611: X.5.5, fols 49ʳ, 51ʳ; 1620: X.6.7, fol. 37.
71 'The Life of Master Paul Baines', in Samuel Clark, *Lives of Thirty-Two English Divines* (1673), pp. 23–4.

women'. But what distressed him most was that God's judgement, far from driving people to repentance, had hardened them in their sins, a conventional parsonical complaint.[72] But the historian can discover for himself that, of 122 Elizabethan and early Jacobean wills made by Cranbrook inhabitants, only eight include professions of faith (or 'religious preambles') which breathe an authentic and personal spirit of Calvinist piety.[73] This is less remarkable than it may seem since, until his own death in 1597, nearly all wills were drawn up by the parish clerk, Laurence Weller, and shared an identical preamble.[74]

What is more notable is that, with the exception of the generous and imaginative will made by Alexander Dence, only three out of 122 testators in this community of fluid and disposable wealth made any religious or charitable bequests whatsoever apart from the common form gift of a few shillings for distribution to the poor, sometimes in the form of bread.[75] This is not to count the prosperous carrier who left sixpence each to Canterbury Cathedral and the parish church, who was either a pleasant man, or anticlerical, or more probably both.[76] It should not be forgotten that the inhabitants of Cranbrook in their lifetimes were regularly and heavily assessed by the vestrymen for a variety of public expenses, from the two shillings paid annually to the man who whipped the dogs out of church to charges for repair of the fabric, payment of clerk, sexton and schoolmaster and the relief of the poor.[77] This for Cranbrook was the orderly, rational alternative to voluntary charity rather than a redirection of the philanthropic impulse of the kind imagined by Professor W. K. Jordan.[78] But for the present purpose, the important fact is that only two testators left sums of money to select groups of godly preachers, a practice much commoner in the clothing towns of the Essex–Suffolk border than in Cranbrook.[79] Only ten Cranbrook testators made provision for a funeral sermon, an institution with less appeal than the sociable 'drinking' paid for in many wills, 'for my neighbours',

72 KAO, TR/1042/5.
73 I have examined 85 wills proved in the archdeacon's court (KAO, PRC 17/36–60), 8 proved in the consistory court (KAO, PRC 32/30–39) and 29 proved in the Prerogative Court of Canterbury (PRO, PROB 11).
74 'First and principally I commend my soul to Almighty God my creator, saviour and redeemer, trusting and assuredly and steadfastly believing to be saved by and through the death and bloodshedding of our Lord and Saviour Jesus Christ.'
75 This would appear to have been a secularization of the pre-Reformation common form of leaving small sums to the high altar in respect of 'tithes neglygently forgotten' and other sums for 'alms deeds'. All these provisions invariably occur immediately after the religious preamble.
76 The carrier was Thomas Hollandes, who otherwise disposed of £60 and 'six of my best horses with the furniture belonging to them.' (KAO, PRC 17/47/400.)
77 KAO, P/100/5/1, passim.
78 W. K. Jordan, *Philanthropy in England, 1480–1660* (1959), and *Social Institutions in Kent 1480–1660: A Study of the Changing Pattern of Social Aspirations, Archaeologia Cantiana* (Ashford, 1961), vol. lxxv.
79 For the two testators, see p. 191. References to Suffolk wills will be found in my essay 'Magistracy and Ministry: A Suffolk Miniature', in R. Buick Knox (ed.), *Reformation Conformity and Dissent: Essays in Honour of Geoffrey Nuttall* (1977), p. 77.

or for 'them which go to church with me on the day of my burial' – the old 'good fellowship' rather than the new puritanism. To continue: out of 138 Cranbrook probate inventories covering the years 1565 to 1612 only twenty mention a Bible among the contents of the household.[80] Nine of the households possessing Bibles also had some other books, and five more inventories mention books other than the Bible. Admittedly this evidence is less than decisive, since Bibles and other books might have been given away by will, as when Elizabeth Jorden, after a distinctly Calvinist profession of faith, found a home for her 'whole booke of Martyrs'.[81] Richard Fletcher's own inventory values only the books 'lefte ungeven away'.[82] But the wills add only two more households which contained Bibles. If only 17% of modern English homes boasted a television set we should conclude that viewing was a sub-cultural activity. So no doubt was the pursuit of godliness in Cranbrook. Bibles are sometimes owned and never read. One of the twenty-two Bibles belonged to a man who in the year before his death was in trouble for allowing dancing in his house on the Sabbath and for calling the vicar a knave when he denounced him from the pulpit.[83]

So Cranbrook was Puritan merely in the sense that it contained a Puritan minority, in some measure set apart if only by the pastoral failure to correct and convert the rest of the community. It cannot be shown, and may not be worth asking, whether this minority was associated with a particular socio-economic group. It is an interesting suggestion that the tendency to Puritan exclusivism in late-Elizabethan Kent articulated the resentful alienation of 'small respectable folk' from hardening local oligarchies,[84] but it would be hard to demonstrate that this was the case in Cranbrook. To be sure, there is little evidence linking Puritanism especially with the wealthy clothiers, the customers of the mercer William Ruck whose shop contained hundreds of pounds worth of such merchandise as gloves, ribbons, silk buttons, drinking glasses, currants, raisins and playing cards.[85] Like Alexander Dence's Christmas diners, it is likely that Cranbrook's godly inhabitants were neither very rich nor very poor.

At first the godly may have depended upon Fletcher for inspiration, and later it would be conceded by a Puritan critic that some had assigned 'a great part of their conversion' to his teaching.[86] But if so their affections were increasingly alienated towards a godlier, or at least more radical style of discourse, still represented in early-Elizabethan Kent by itinerant preachers, following

80 The inventories are in KAO, PRC 10/1–33.
81 KAO, PRC 32/39/146. Mary Sheaffe, widow, mother-in-law to Dr Giles Fletcher and so the grandmother of Giles and Phineas Fletcher, left 'my Booke of Marters in two volumes' in her will of 1609 (PRC 17/58/375).
82 KAO, PRC 10/15, fols 172^v–3^r.
83 Walter Mascall's inventory (4 May 1571) is in KAO, PRC 10/5, fol. 180, and his presentment in court in 1570 in CALC, X.1.10, fol. 11^r.
84 Clark, op. cit., pp. 177–8.
85 KAO, PRC 10/25, fols 233^r–5^v.
86 DWL, MS Morrice B II, fol. 18^v.

in the steps of the Marian martyr John Bland, and perhaps supported by some of the gentry.[87] In 1661 it would be said that 'the wild of Kent is a receptacle for distressed running parsons.'[88] So it was perhaps in 1561. In that year a preacher called Thompson aroused conservative opposition in both Cranbrook and Frittenden, which in Cranbrook was offered by the formidable Mrs Dence.[89] Another preacher was a blind man called Dawes, of whom the historian catches a glimpse as he entered Headcorn, 'comyng through the streat with dyvers honest men with hym.' Dawes preached in many parishes on working days, and one Headcorn man thought it 'a shame that he is suffered soe to goe about a-preachinge.'[90] When Mr Ridley preached at Goudhurst in 1562 he had to compete with dancing at the market cross.[91] In Cranbrook such sporadic and irregular preaching later gave place to a weekly sermon on Saturdays, market day, and offered not by Fletcher but by the preachers of the surrounding country taking their turns: the device known in the early seventeenth century as a 'lecture by combination'.[92]

Towards 1580 numbers of godly preachers were settling down in the Wealden parishes, where they formed a brotherhood if not a *classis* of 'the ministers of Kent', soon to resist archbishop Whitgift and conformity in 1584.[93] Two of the more notable members of the group were Josias Nicholls, minister of the tiny parish of Eastwell from 1580 (72 communicants compared with Cranbrook's 2,000!)[94] and George Ely, vicar of Tenterden from 1571. The kind of ministry which was now almost the norm in such places is implied in the description accorded to the vicar of Benenden, never a member of the Puritan group, in a formal document, the inventory of his possessions: 'mynister and preacher of the worde to the congregation at Benenden.'[95]

Fletcher was not part of the brotherhood. Whether he would wish to have been is not known. But he was a conformable man and the practice in Cranbrook church was Protestant rather than Puritan. The surplice seems to have been worn throughout the 1560s and 1570s,[96] and communion was received kneeling,

87 Clark, op. cit., pp. 151–2. For Bland, see *A & M*, vol. vii, pp. 287–306. See also Davis, 'Heresy and the Reformation', p. 426.
88 *Victoria County History of Kent*, vol. ii, ed. William Page (1926), p. 100.
89 CALC, X.1.3, fol. 75ᵛ; X.1.4, fol. 86ᵛ.
90 CALC, X.1.9, fol. 66.   91 CALC, X.8.5, fol. 104.
92 KAO, P/100/5/1, fol. 58ᵛ; Thomas Wotton to Sir Francis Walsingham, 3 May 1579, *Thomas Wotton's Letter-Book 1574–1586*, ed. G. Eland (1960), pp. 24–5. Cf. P. Collinson, 'Lectures by Combination: Structures and Characteristics of Church Life in 17th-Century England', *Bulletin of the Institute of Historical Research*, vol. xlviii (1975), pp. 182–213.
93 Patrick Collinson, *The Elizabethan Puritan Movement* (1967), pp. 249–72. Documents in *The Seconde Parte of a Register*, ed. Albert Peel (Cambridge, 1915), vol. i, nos 132, 149, 150.
94 Peter Clark, 'Josias Nicholls and Religious Radicalism 1553–1639', *Journal of Ecclesiastical History*, vol. xxviii (1977), pp. 133–50.
95 Marten Sanders, who died in 1585: KAO, PRC 10/15, fols 120–1.
96 There are several references in the churchwardens' accounts to the making, washing and repairing of surplices (KAO, P/100/5/1).

in the chancel.[97] The organs were repaired, not destroyed.[98] This is no more than was to be expected of a client and perhaps a friend of archbishop Parker, who also became his son's patron.[99] Thanks to Parker, Fletcher was able to become a pluralist. In 1566 he was collated to the rectory of Smarden, a parish ten miles to the east of Cranbrook, and a better living.[100] In the words of a Puritan critic, there was no need for the vicar to complain of hard times, now that he had two strings to his bow and had 'put two haycockes into one.'[101]

So Fletcher was no Puritan. But between 1575 and 1585 he employed, in succession, three curate-preachers who were. Their presence may have been due to circumstances not entirely within his control in the form of financial and other inducements and pressures from the godly element in the surrounding country, some gentry included, who may have promised support for preachers of whom they approved.[102] For two at least of the three were already men of some notoriety. There is clear evidence of this element of voluntary support in the case of John Strowd, the first of a trinity to arrive on the scene. Strowd, a deprived minister on the run from the West Country, was one of the operators of the clandestine Puritan press of the early 1570s, and he arrived with recent experience of the Presbyterian church settlement in the Channel Islands.[103] Strowd was followed by Thomas Ely (or Hely), who first appeared as Fletcher's curate at Smarden: perhaps the brother of George Ely of Tenterden, and possibly the same man who, as minister of Warbleton, was later a leading Sussex nonconformist.[104] And last but far from least there came to Cranbrook the most erudite of the Puritan divines of his generation, the young prodigy Dudley Fenner, who arrived in 1583 to become a spokesman for 'the ministers of

97 'Payd for mattes to laye in the quyre to knele on', 1563; 'Payd for 12 yardes of mattynge for the communyon place', 1564 (KAO, P/100/5/1, fols 20ᵛ–23ʳ).
98 Ibid., fol. 23. But in 1568 the parish received 36s 8d for the sale of 75 organ pipes (ibid., fol. 34).
99 *DNB*, art. Fletcher.
100 *Registrum Matthei Parker*, p. 825.
101 DWL, MS Morrice B II, fol. 24ᵛ.
102 Fletcher seems to have employed an assistant curate from time to time. A will of 1566 was witnessed by 'Henry Wybarne, curatt of Cranbroke' (KAO, PRC 17/39/313). If Henry Wybarne was by any chance the brother of the well-known Puritan Percival Wiburn, at this time a prebendary of Rochester, this may add to the score of radical Cranbrook curates.
103 *Seconde Parte of a Register*, vol. i, pp. 112–14; A. F. Scott Pearson, *Thomas Cartwright and Elizabethan Puritanism 1535–1603* (Cambridge, 1925), pp. 87, 110–13. Strowd's recent visit to Guernsey is hinted at by both Richard Fletcher the younger and Thomas Good in DWL, MS Morrice B II, fols 9ᵛ, 22ʳ.
104 Ely's presence in Cranbrook has not previously been noticed. His curacies at Smarden (1576–7) and Cranbrook (1579–80) are recorded in the archdeaconry call books: CALC, Z.7.1, fols 14, 41ᵛ, 62ᵛ, 79ᵛ, 255; X.2.3, fols 32ᵛ, 67ᵛ, 103ᵛ. On Thomas Hely of Warbleton, see *Seconde Parte of a Register*, vol. i, pp. 209–20; and Manning, *Religion and Society in Elizabethan Sussex*, op. cit., pp. 201, 209n, 211. There was also Nathaniel Ely, son of George and later a preacher at Biddenden. He is mentioned in Cranbrook wills of 1582 and 1600 (KAO, PRC 17/44/40, 52/44.)

Kent' in their confrontations with archbishop Whitgift.[105] That Fletcher himself was not in this special sense a 'minister of Kent' is suggested by two Cranbrook wills of 1579–80. Both testators left sums of money to select preachers. Peter Courthope, a clothier employing four weavers, provided £20 for distribution among nine preachers, including Ely of Tenterden and Josias Nicholls and 'Mr Strowd'. The widow Rose Austen similarly remembered six preachers, including Nicholls and Mr Ely of Tenterden and 'Mr Ely of Cranebrooke, minister.'[106]

John Strowd was a provocation by his mere presence. His activities as a clandestine Puritan printer had made him well known to the ecclesiastical courts in both London and Rochester. But this did nothing to damage his reputation in the upper Medway valley and the Weald where he was regarded with great admiration by a cross-section of 'the country', including several ranking gentry, Walter Roberts of Cranbrook among them.[107] His arrival in Cranbrook as a kind of refugee from his previous base at Yalding in the diocese of Rochester (where Josias Nicholls replaced him) rapidly brought to a head the uneasy relations between Fletcher and a party in his parish. The story has to be disentangled from thousands of words of spirited but rancorous rhetoric exchanged between one of Strowd's protagonists, the Cranbrook schoolmaster Thomas Good, and Fletcher's son, the future bishop.[108]

According to Good, who was 'a special party' to bring him in, Strowd's arrival (probably in late May 1575) was initially welcome to Fletcher as 'a mutuall healpe', paid for by others. But since Strowd was still under excommunication, it seems more likely, as Fletcher's son alleged, that he thrust himself in with the encouragement of his local supporters. Strowd had undertaken not to preach in another man's charge without his good will but then in contempt of Fletcher's attempt to deny him the pulpit preached in his absence, twice on one day. Good could not see why Strowd should have held back 'for a froward man's fantasies'. One of the churchwardens had said 'we will have him to preach', and someone else remarked: 'The vicar of Cranbrook proposeth but God disposeth.' If Fletcher's son is to be believed, Strowd's doctrine was sufficiently inflammatory and 'popular'. Those who were not sent of the Spirit should never do good in the ministry. The bishops would be called gracious lords 'but you may call them ungracious knaves'. 'It is said credibelly in the countrie that he hathe preched that it is no greater a sinne to steal a horse on

105 *DNB*, art. Fenner.
106 KAO, PRC 32/34/64, PRC 17/44/134.
107 *Seconde Parte of a Register*, vol. i, pp. 114–16.
108 The controversy occupies fols 6–25 in DWL, MS Morrice B II and is calendared by Peel in *Seconde Parte of a Register*, vol. i, pp. 116–20. It consists, in order, of 'Evill coherences not without some errours gathered out of Mr Fletchers sonnes sermon made July 27th 1575'; 'An answere made by Mr Fletcher of Rye'; 'The answere unto a certayne pryvie reply of invective of Mr Fletcher of Rie'; and, finally, five tables prepared by Good, extracting 'scoffs' and uncharitable speeches from Fletcher's reply.

Munday then to sell him in fayre on the Sunday; that it is as ill to play at games as shootings, bowlings on Sundaye as to lye with your neybors wiffe on Monday.' Strowd was also active on another front in what Fletcher junior called conventicles. 'It is a common thinge now for every pragmaticall prentice to have in his hand and mouthe the government and reformation of the Churche. And he that in exercise can speak thereof, that is the man. Every artificer must be a reformer and a teacher, forgetting their state thei stand in bothe to be taught and to be reformed.' But Good insisted that what Fletcher called conventicles were 'honest and lawfull convencions', and some of the 'pragmaticall prentices' weighty clothiers. 'Your eyes dasill by tooting on Cranbrooke clothiers colours.'

On 12 June the vicar mounted his pulpit to preach of the necessity and dignity of church ceremonies and of obedience to the law. When, in his usual style, he attacked Strowd by name, there were 'open challenges' from the congregation, and one man was removed by the constable and subsequently punished by the magistrate, Sir Richard Baker. Good was present with his scholars, making notes ('pens walking at sermons'), and thought the interruptions an excusable disorder since Fletcher's defence of ceremonies had wounded tender consciences by repudiating the sound doctrine which he himself had delivered in the past. He had 'run headlong, to the eversion of many consciences, unless God's spirit prevent them'. That amounted to a declaration that Fletcher's revisionism threatened to drive the godly into separation.

On 27 July Fletcher's son was recruited to preach in his father's defence and 'for the staying or appeasing of error, dyvysyon or schism'. Richard Fletcher the younger had assisted his father in the Cranbrook ministry in the past but, since September 1574, he had been fully employed as preacher and minister of Rye,[109] a parish no less populous and demanding than Cranbrook.[110] He agreed with Thomas Good on one thing at least. There was schism, or the threat of schism, in his father's parish. But he attributed this to ingratitude and to Strowd's alienation of the people who had 'gone back from their first love' with 'great alteracion and hartburninge', making 'a new circumcision against their ancient and sufficient pastor'. Strowd was 'one of Austen's puritans' (the first

109 The likelihood is that Richard Fletcher the younger assisted his father between his marriage in Cranbrook in May 1573 and his engagement by the town of Rye in September 1574. Some books inaccurately describe Fletcher as vicar of Rye. The true situation was one of some complexity. In Fletcher's time the vicarage was leased and the fruits were a matter of litigation and for a time sequestered. Attempts by the mayor and jurats and by the bishop of Chichester to resolve this impasse were not successful. Fletcher was in receipt of some benefit from the fruits of the vicarage and of a further 'augmentation' or 'benevolence' from the town of £10, £5 of which was paid by the churchwardens and £5 by the town chamberlain. His normal style was 'preacher[or minister] of the word of God in the church at Rye' (ESRO, RYE MSS 47/12/6, 11 and 22/10; RYE MS 1/4, fols 171^v, 186^r, 252^v, 340; RYE MS 147/2; RYE MS 60/9, fols 54^r, 47^r).
110 There were alleged to be 1,800 or 1,900 communicants in June 1580 (ESRO, RYE MS 47/22/10).

recorded use of the word 'puritan' in the context of Cranbrook), his religion the disliking of religion. The usual charges of Anabaptism and Familism were thrown in for good measure. Pens walked at this sermon too, and a bitter exchange ensued between the younger Fletcher and Good, in which other issues made their appearance. Fletcher made the half-hearted charge that Strowd, the 'printing preacher', might be operating a press somewhere in the parish. Good retorted that Cranbrook, as a clothing town, was full of presses, 'but they will not nor cannot print'. At a time of worsening trade for the town the vicar was said to have pressed his claim to tithe and other dues with callous disregard of any interest but his own. 'His tythes must not faile howsoever the worlde goeth.' But Fletcher claimed that his father was more reasonable in his demands than his predecessors, and told Good that he was the unworthiest schoolmaster that had ever been seen in Cranbrook,[111] neglecting his scholars for religious agitation. True enough, Good would later be presented in the archdeacon's court for not using 'such diligence in teachyng as ought to be', and was duly admonished.[112] The controversy came to its climax when Strowd was again inhibited from preaching, by the archbishop of Canterbury. This caused great dismay in the country and widespread petitioning which was perhaps encouraged by the fact that the archbishop was now (1576) Edmund Grindal. According to a document subscribed by twelve ministers and 138 of their people, headed by Ely of Tenterden, 'our beloved neighbours of Cranebrooke' joined in with a testimonial to Strowd's worthiness. Naturally their vicar's signature is not to be found in this roll-call of the godly of the Weald and the Medway, which included twenty names of quality.[113] Strowd remained in Cranbrook as a private person, and was buried as a plague victim in October 1582.[114] No doubt he continued to be found in private 'exercises', and perhaps some were more willing to hear him in their homes than to be present at the public sermons in the parish church. Was this why Fletcher brought Thomas Ely over from Smarden in 1579, the same year in which he publicly accused some of his people of staying away from church?

---

111 There has been some discussion about the date when Cranbrook first acquired a school, given the complications arising from the application of bequests left by William Lynch (1539) and Alexander Dence (1574), although it is known that eventually the town enjoyed a grammar school and (the intention of Dence) a school for reading and writing in English. (Jordan, *Social Institutions in Kent*, pp. 80–1; Clark, op. cit., p. 444n.) There are references to the schoolmaster's wages in the churchwardens' accounts from 1564 (KAO, P/100/5/1, fol. 24) and in 1566 the effects were valued of Michael Halsall 'scole-master, late of Cranebrook' (KAO, PRC 10/1, fols 167–8).
112 CALC, X.2.4, fol. 53r.
113 *Seconde Parte of a Register*, vol. i, pp. 114–16; DWL, MS Morrice B II, fol. 5r. Clark discusses the significance of the names of some of Strowd's more notable supporters (op. cit., pp. 151–2, 165–6).
114 Strowd was named in Peter Courthope's will of 20 November 1579 (KAO, PRC 32/34/64) but not as a minister and not as 'of Cranbrook'. The John Strowd buried in October 1582 (KAO, TR/1042/5) was presumably the preacher, although he is not so described.

Thomas Good struck a shrewd blow when he told the younger Fletcher that in preaching against Reformation 'you speak against yorselfe.' For Fletcher's background, like his father's, was impeccably Protestant. Some historians, not too nice about terms, might call it Puritan. He had rallied to the defence of his father, not of some abstract 'Anglicanism', and not all of his invective against Good was in the currency of a Whitgift or a Bancroft. Some was drawn, no doubt with cunning, from the Puritans' own mint. It was good Presbyterian doctrine that the bond between a pastor and his flock was all but indissoluble. So Fletcher could state that unlike Strowd he 'drew noe love or lykinge of people from their pastor but preached it, maynteyned it.' In his Cranbrook sermon he admitted the existence of 'hurtfull ceremonys', even 'corruptions', while denying to private men the liberty to cut themselves off from a church where the word was truly preached and the sacraments duly administered.

In Rye the Protestant settlement had been enthusiastically enforced. The church had long since been whitewashed and adorned with Scripture texts, 'the great organs' in their turn 'taken asunder'.[115] Fletcher's predecessor as 'preacher of the word of God within the church of Rye' was John Philpot, a leading nonconformist in the London vestiarian troubles of 1566.[116] Still preserved in Rye church is a collection of sermons on the Decalogue, traditionally attributed to Fletcher, which are forthright in their condemnation of ecclesiastical imagery:[117] 'For surely if idolatry it selfe as a most execrable thinge be forbidden then all occasions and means leading thereunto are likewise prohibited and what stronger provocation to that spirituall whoredome then erecting images in the place of Godes worship and therfore without doubt the meaning of the Commaundment is to bind the Chirche from all such snares and allurements to sinne.' They were a scandal to 'the simple sort' and to 'them that cary idolatrous mindes'. With the same *topos* from 1 Corinthians in mind,[118] Good accused the Fletchers of wounding poor men's consciences with the defence of ceremonies admitted to be 'hurtful'.

Whether or not these sermons were preached by Fletcher,[119] they reflect the uncompromising Protestantism in which he participated as minister of Rye. Like his father he devoted himself with energy to the promotion of a godly order

---

115 ESRO, RYE MS 147/1, fols 162^v, 165^v, 211^r.

116 ESRO, RYE MS 1/4, fol. 186^r. On Philpot, see Collinson, op. cit., pp. 77–8, 82.

117 I am most grateful to the vicar of Rye, the Rev. Canon J. E. R. Williams, for allowing me to examine and partially transcribe the contents of this small paper book (5 inches by 3 inches) without cover, title, date or foliation and written in an Elizabethan hand. It was sight of this object in a display case in St Mary's church in Rye in February 1974 which first prompted the questions which have led to the writing of this essay.

118 John S. Coolidge, *The Pauline Renaissance in England: Puritanism and the Bible* (Oxford, 1970), especially chapter 2.

119 There is nothing in the MS itself to connect them with Fletcher. The only dateable reference is to 'this sickness of plague' which may refer to either of the terrible visitations of 1563 and 1579–80.

in what was often a disorderly seaport town.[120] Soon after returning from battle with the Cranbrook Puritans, he was invested with 'jurisdiction ecclesiastical' in Rye for 'the ponishment of synne and wickedness' and the securing of 'suche a civill and vertuous order of lyvinge as the worde of God dayly taught unto us doth require.' The effect of this arrangement, negotiated between the mayor and jurats and the bishop of Chichester, Richard Curteys,[121] was to unify civil and ecclesiastical government in the town. The correction of 'ill rule' was sometimes a matter for Fletcher by virtue of his own, delegated authority, but on other occasions he sat with the civil magistrates in a tribunal which resembled Elizabethan ecclesiastical commissions in its dual character but which presumably conformed to civil procedures and offered no threat to the secular magistracy.[122]

Thus fortified, Fletcher engaged with irreligion and disorder, and like his father met with his share of defiance: from the ruder sort in the taverns and market place, where one John Bennett with 'other reproches' inaccurately declared that he was as good a man as Mr Fletcher since his father was a butcher and Mr Fletcher's a weaver; and more insidiously in the 'indirect and sinester' approaches made to the bishop by Richard Abbot, a powerful and dangerous man living outside the town's liberties and jurisdiction and allegedly a maintainer of 'roges, incontinent persons, theves, pirates and all such lyke skumme of the world.'[123] So Fletcher was too distracted to give much thought to Cranbrook. His children were being born in quick succession: Nathaniel (1575), Theophilus (1577) (godly names both!), Elizabeth (1578) and the dramatist John (1579).[124] And in 1579 and 1580 he exercised joint responsibility with the magistrates for the enforcement of measures against the plague which, for the second time in a generation, carried off as much as a quarter of the town's population.[125] Not

120 There was a particularly spectacular occurrence of 'ill rule' in the town on the night of 26 September 1575 when among other acts of wanton destruction the lattice was torn down from Thomas Edolfe's window and deposited in the vicarage garden (ESRO, RYE MS 1/4, fols 214v–15v).
121 For the career of Curteys, see Manning, op. cit., passim.
122 Mayor and jurats of Rye to the bishop of Chichester, 20 September 1575; bishop to mayor and jurats, 26 September 1575; decision of the mayor and jurats to draw up 'an instrument in wrytinge' to be sent to the bishop, and draft of the 'instrument', 10 October 1575; mayor and jurats to bishop, 16 October 1575. (ESRO, RYE MS 47/12/5, 6; RYE MS 1/4, fol. 215v; RYE MS. 47/12/11v, 11r). The letters but not the draft 'instrument' are printed in *Historical Manuscripts Commission 13th Report*, Appendix IV, pp. 45-7. Cf. the letter written by bishop Parkhurst of Norwich to the bailiffs of Yarmouth, 12 November 1572, granting them 'that aucthoritie I may to punishe synne . . . All that I and you with all my officers can do is to little, synne doth so much abound and punishment therof is so slack.' But Parkhurst required the rights of his comissary to be respected. (*The Letter Book of John Parkhurst 1571-5*, ed. R. A. Houlbrooke, Norfolk Record Society (1975), vol. xliii, p. 215.)
123 ESRO, RYE MSS 47/12/29b and 47/13.
124 ESRO, PAR 467/1/1/2, fols 12v, 21r, 24v, 28v.
125 ESRO, RYE MS 1/4, fols 309v–10r, 310r–11v, 323v; RYE MS 47/22/3. 562 were buried in August–October 1563 and 627 between November 1579 and October 1580 (ESRO, PAR 467/1/1/1 and 2).

long after these terrible events Fletcher was gone, to reap his reward in a brilliant ecclesiastical career which, as dean of Peterborough, found him on the scaffold with Mary Stuart in February 1587; and took him from there in rapid order to the bishoprics of Bristol, Worcester and London. His last days drew out sadly in the Queen's displeasure at his second, unsuitable marriage and came to an end suddenly and incongruously, 'taking tobacco in his chair, saying to his man that stood by him, whom he loved very well, *Oh boy, I die.*' So departed at the age of about fifty the boy who in June 1555 had been obliged to watch Christopher Wade burn until 'altogether roasted'. Sir John Harington's epitaph was that 'he could preach well and could speak boldly, and yet keep *decorum*. He knew what pleased the Queen, and would adventure on that though that offended others.'[126]

It would be an oversimplification to imply that the events at Cranbrook in 1575 converted the future bishop and his father out of primitive Protestantism into a kind of Anglicanism. They were a step in that direction, but in the ten years of life remaining to him the relations of Richard Fletcher with the godly of his parish were neither broken off nor tidily resolved. In 1579, as already indicated, there were complaints against him for denouncing 'some of his paryshe that dyd sweare they would not come unto the church untyll such thinges were brought to passe that they had devysed.'[127] But from his side there was no attempt to make a case against the Puritans in the archdeacon's court. 'Such thinges' probably included the abandonment of the hated surplice; and by 1582 Fletcher seems to have worn it no longer.[128] It was only now that Foxe received Fletcher's account of the martyrdom of Wade.[129] Was the vicar of Cranbrooke concerned to hold his place in 'the English Protestant tradition', or to remind Foxe's readers in Kent that Wade's dying words were an endorsement of prayer-book religion? Some kind of *modus vivendi* with the Puritan preachers in the parish must have been achieved. They too were never presented for any offence, and if there were unseemly scuffles around the pulpit they were not made public. Fenner might seem to have been a formidable threat, with his precocious intellect, glowing reputation and private means.[130] But there is some

126 *DNB*, art. Fletcher; F. O. White, *Lives of the Elizabethan Bishops* (1898), pp. 308–16; John Harington, *A briefe view of the state of the Church of England* (written 1608, published 1653), pp. 29–32; *A & M*, vol. vii, p. 321.
127 CALC, X.2.2, fol. 58ʳ.
128 In December 1582 the churchwardens reported: 'The mynister weareth no surples' (CALC, X.2.4, fol. 52ᵛ).
129 The account of Wade's martyrdom appeared in *Acts and Monuments* for the first time in 1583 (pp. 1679–80), authenticated by 'Spectatores presentes, Richardus Fletcher pater, nunc Minister Ecclesiae Crambroke (*sic*); Richardus Fletcher filius, Minister Ecclesiae Riensis.' It must therefore have been communicated between the setting up of the 1576 edition, when Foxe still had 'no full certaintie when [Wade] suffered' (p. 1591), and the departure of Richard Fletcher the younger from Rye, apparently late in 1580 or in 1581.
130 According to a source quoted in the *DNB* (art. Fenner) he was 'heire of great possessions'. His personal contribution to the relief of Geneva in a collection organized in the diocese of

evidence that he employed these talents for the healing of old sores. When Reginald Scot, author of *The discoverie of witchcraft*, accused Fenner of making 'broile and contention' in Cranbrook he was told: 'If there were broile and contention in Cranbrooke he found it there and made it not, but rather he pacified some contentions and dislikinges which he found among them.'[131] Unless it was a later hand which embellished the entry, Fletcher described Fenner in an obituary notice in the parish register as 'a most worthy preacher'.[132] Dr Clark suggests that the basis of peaceful coexistence may have been that Fenner had unchallenged control of the Saturday lecture.[133] No doubt this market day occasion was a rallying ground for the Cranbrook saints, and for their friends living beyond the parish within riding distance.

It was Fenner who introduced to Cranbrook, without any apparent resistance from the vicar, the still novel and outlandish practice of baptizing with peculiar names. The apparent intention was to underline baptism as a true separation from the world and to God and his Church by the use of a name having 'some godly signification for that worke.'[134] The new fashion was first seen in March 1583 with the baptism of Joyagaine Netter and Fromabove Hendly (surnames of quality in the town), and continued at the end of the year with the christening of Fenner's own daughter Morefruit, sister of Freegift, who, having been brought to Cranbrook, died there in September 1583. Two years later, Faintnot Fenner was baptized; and in August 1588 Wellabroad Fenner was buried, after her father's death in voluntary exile in the Netherlands.[135] Only when Fletcher was almost on his deathbed was a Cranbrook man presented in the archdeacon's court for participating in the naming of John Bigge's son Smallhope.[136]

Canterbury in 1583 was £4. This was the largest contribution by any individual cleric with the exception of the archbishop himself and the archdeacon, and was surpassed by only five secular magnates (PRO, S.P. 12/161/21).

131 DWL, MS Morrice B I, fol. 426ᵛ. 'The defense of the mynisters of Kent' is calendared in *Seconde Parte of a Register*, vol. i, pp. 230–41.

132 The entry reads: 'Faint not Fenner, daughter of D. F. Concional. (*sic*) Digniss.' The surviving copy of the register for this period was made by William Eddy in 1598 (Tarbutt, op. cit., vol. ii, pp. 15, 20.)

133 Clark, op. cit., pp. 439–40n, following KAO, P/100/5/1, fol. 58ᵛ.

134 As Dr Tyacke has suggested, Fenner was most probably the inventor of a practice for which he supplied the rationale in *The whole doctrine of the sacramentes* (Middelburg, 1588), sig. C2, and *The order of householde* (Middelburg, 1588), sig. F5ᵛ: Nicholas Tyacke, 'Popular Puritan Mentality in Late Elizabethan England', in *The English Commonwealth 1547–1640*, ed. Peter Clark, Alan G. R. Smith and Nicholas Tyacke (Leicester, 1979). But if, as seems likely to me, Thomas Ely of Cranbrook and Thomas Hely of Warbleton in Sussex were one and the same, it is a curious and perhaps significant circumstance that Ely preceded Fenner at Cranbrook before proceeding to Warbleton where, as Tyacke has shown, more than half the children baptized between 1587 and 1590 received peculiar Puritan names. Since Fenner himself was apparently of Wealden stock, it strengthens the possibility that the notion of names with 'godly signification', like primitive sacramentarianism, was nurtured in the popular rather than highly educated mind.

135 KAO, TR/1042/5.

136 CALC, X.2.4, fol. 274. I am happy to report that the unfortunately-named Smallhope was

Smallhope Bigge was the fifth child to be given such a name, and there would be twenty more in the next nineteen years of whom the archdeacon would take no cognizance. Among them, the six children of Thomas Starr made their own little procession to the font: Comfort, Nostrength, Moregift, Mercy, Suretrust, and Standwell. Comfort Starr grew up to be a physician who later emigrated from Ashford to Massachusetts where he died in 1659, leaving to his son 'my large Book of Martyrs'. Other Starrs remained in Kent, and when in 1669 a later Comfort Starr preached in Cranbrook, this too was an echo of its Elizabethan past.[137]

Dr Tyacke has shown that the historian can use the evidence of peculiar baptismal names to identify and evaluate the distinctive Puritan element in the parishes where they occur.[138] The fact that relatively few Cranbrook children were made to suffer such names, compared with the mass movement in some Sussex villages, could suggest that the Puritan presence in the parish was neither large nor influential, but may only mean that successive vicars discouraged a practice which in any case was somewhat peripheral to the Puritan mainstream. Other fragments of evidence enable scholars to form vivid impressions of individuals, but not to measure, still less to characterize, the religious and social phenomenon which was Cranbrook Puritanism. The Reignold Lovell who christened his children Thankful and Faithful, buried them in the plague of 1597 and then named another Faithful in 1599,[139] was presumably the 'Lovell of Cranbrook', 'a good honest poore silly puritane', who aroused the admiration of a Kentish cousin of the diarist John Manningham. ' "O" said shee, "he goes to the ground when he talks in Divinitie with a preacher." '[140] Robert Holden, who was Smallhope Bigge's godfather, refused to let his wife be churched and often said of his own son that he would grow up to be a bishop, 'bycause that every day after dynner he will fall asleepe.'[141] But for a chance presentment, perhaps motivated by private circumstances still unknown, nothing would have been recorded of this man's obstinate but whimsical mind. There are no Puritan signals in the will which the parish clerk Laurence Weller wrote for Robert Holden, yeoman, in 1594,[142] unlike the clothier Richard Jorden's will, made a year later, which included an unusual prayer 'for the restauration of the churche instituted by the apostles of our Lord Jesus Christe

alive and well in 1615, when he was appointed executor to Richard Busse, clothier (KAO, PRC 17/60/85).
137 KAO, TR/1042/5; B. P. Starr, *A History of the Starr Family of New England* (Hartford, Conn., 1879), p. vii; G. F. Nuttall, 'Dissenting Churches in Kent Before 1700', *JEH*, vol. xiv (1963), p. 188.
138 Tyacke, loc. cit.
139 KAO, TR/1042/5.
140 *The Diary of John Manningham of the Middle Temple, 1602–1603*, ed. R. P. Sorlien (Hanover, New Hampshire, 1976), p. 44.
141 CALC, X.2.4, fol. 274.
142 PRO, PROB 11/91/17.

and prescribed in the word of God.'[143] Presbyterian in their prejudices some of the Cranbrook godly certainly were; Strowd and Fenner had seen to that.

But were some of them also schismatics, as the Fletchers had insinuated? Were such people even 'hereditary separatists', as Dr Clark has suggested?[144] This to be sure is the crucial question on which it is easier to adopt a position before, rather than after, undertaking grassroots research. On the one hand, there is the evidence of Strowd's conventicling, which seems to have amounted to the household religion familiar to students of Puritanism in other localities.[145] Were these gatherings separatist in their tendency by associating people otherwise unrelated for purposes which were not shared or tolerated by the majority? Or, on the contrary, did they relate to the given circumstances of settlement and kinship? If with further research it proved possible to place the Cranbrook puritans on the map it might emerge that they were concentrated in some of the outlying hamlets of the parish. It would be useful to know where Strowd lived, and Fenner. When a will like Rose Austen's is found to contain bequests to neighbouring preachers it can be assumed that this widow woman was in the habit of 'gadding to sermons' and that she had shared in the select society of the godly-minded. Yet, in the manner of widows, Mrs Austen also found room in her will for numerous kinsfolk, sharing twenty-two surnames.[146] No social shunning on her part. In his Presbyterian will Richard Jorden renounced, as might be expected from a man of his opinions, all the 'heretikes and scismatickes of this age', including, specifically, the Brownists.[147] But when it is discovered that in 1591 Jorden's servant Peter Taylor 'woulde by no perswasion come into the church' for a service which included the sacrament of baptism, but 'in contempt and ill example to others and dishonour to God made his refusall'.[148] Knowledge of Cranbrook's Baptist future poses a question. Nevertheless on the evidence available it is not possible to state that household religion in this community went beyond what a later vicar referred to approvingly in 1639 as 'the private communion of saints', in the same breath as he condemned the separatists of that later generation.[149]

'Private communion' may well have had a long ancestry in Cranbrook. There is an odour of it, a distinctly feminine odour, in the *obiter dicta* in which the vicar William Eddy indulged as he copied out the parish registers in 1598.

---

143 PRO, PROB 11/87/15.
144 Clark, op. cit., p. 177. Clark gives a generalized impression of widespread and rampant separatism in Kent at the turn of the sixteenth and seventeenth centuries. Reviewing *English Provincial Society* in the *Times Literary Supplement* (1.9.78), Professor Alan Everitt raised a cautious eyebrow.
145 Collinson, op. cit., pp. 372–82.
146 KAO, PRC 17/44/134.
147 PRO, PROB 11/87/15.
148 CALC, X.3.8, fol. 95ʳ.
149 Robert Abbot, *A trial of our church-forsakers. Or, a meditation tending to still the passions of unquiet Brownists* (1639), sig. aᵛ.

Most of his people were incorrigibly sinful. But this had been 'a good woman' and that 'a godly and good woman'. Bridget Sheaparde, a gentlewoman who boarded at the vicarage until her premature death, was 'a mayden and most godlie'.[150] Eddy wrote her will and placed in her mouth this touching Calvinist affirmation: 'Jesus Christ, in whome amongst many other daughters in Israell [God] hath elected mee before the foundation of the world unto eternall lyfe and salvation.'[151] Yet like Fletcher before him, and like his successor Robert Abbot, Eddy would have found schism, a separation of these saints, as grievous to bear as wickedness and vice.

If ever favourable conditions obtained for an outbreak of formalized separa-tion in Elizabethan Cranbrook, it was in the five years before Eddy became vicar in 1591. Archbishop Whitgift's policies had driven Dudley Fenner not only away from Cranbrook but out of England, and he was soon to die in Middelburg. The godly were orphaned. Nationally the reaction against Puritanism intensified; the cause of further Reformation was blighted and in London the consequent frustration led to a new separatist movement associated with the leadership of Henry Barrow and John Greenwood. After Richard Fletcher's death there was a reversion in Cranbrook to an impoverished pastoral situation. There were two brief incumbencies,[152] long periods of non-residence, the neglect of basic parochial duties and sometimes only the clerk or the sexton to read the services, or to bury the dead.[153] And with the hungry nineties there was more than spiritual deprivation to contend with. If separatism was a natural growth in areas of scattered settlement and pastoral neglect, still more if it is read as the expression of harsh and unsettling economic conditions, it might have been expected to flourish in this decade among a people sensitized by a generation of intensive Puritan indoctrination. Yet there is no reason to suppose that it did. Separatism in the proper sense of the gathering and covenanting of a separated people to form a new kind of church was a rare phenomenon before the mid-seventeenth century. Apart from any other favourable circumstances, it may

---

150 KAO, TR/1042/5.

151 KAO, PRC 17/52/44.

152 Robert Rhodes, 1586–90, and Richard Mulcaster, 1590–1, probably regarded Cranbrook more as a benefice than as a cure. Rhodes, who had been president of St John's College, Cam-bridge, was intermittently resident and in his will remembered 'the poorer sort that live nearest the vicarage' as well as an otherwise unknown curate, Mr Allen (PRO, PROB 11/75/21. See also CALC, X.2.4, fols 295, 307, 333, 346, 374, 379ʳ). The distinguished schoolmaster and educational theorist Richard Mulcaster was almost wholly non-resident, for which he was cited, but failed to appear to answer the charge on thirteen successive occasions. His resignation was perhaps enforced (CALC, X.3.5, fols 39ᵛ, 40, 47ᵛ–8ʳ, 50, 133ᵛ). William Eddy seems to have been a curate in the parish from as early as May 1586 and in November 1587 married a local girl. He was collated to the vicarage late in 1591 and remained until his death in 1616 (CALC, X.2.4, fol. 295, X.3.5, fol. 83ᵛ; Tarbutt, op. cit., vol. iii, pp. 16–21).

153 CALC, X.3.5, fols 39, 40, 47ᵛ–8ʳ, 133ᵛ. Griffith Bishop, the sexton, presented for churching women and burying the dead, appeared on 6 October 1590 to say that 'some four tymes at the request of Mr Moncaster their vicar in his absence' he had performed these offices.

have required a species of charismatic leadership which was lacking in Cranbrook in the 1590s, to overcome the strong inhibitions which held the separating urge in check.

The origins of the Dissent – Independent, and above all Baptist – for which Cranbrook was later noted,[154] are to be found in the 1630s, under the pressure of royal and episcopal policies which provoked a more profound alienation of the godly than any of the events of Elizabeth's reign. The beginnings can be observed through the eyes of Robert Abbot, vicar from 1616 until 1643,[155] whose experience replicated that of Richard Fletcher sixty years before but surpassed it in personal bitterness. Abbot was a divine in the moderate Calvinist tradition which his patron and namesake archbishop Abbot promoted in the Church at large. In his earlier years he was fiercely anti-Catholic and content to be known as 'preacher of God's word at Cranbrook.'[156] As a pastor he was earnest, warning his fellow ministers: 'We dwell like men under a Frigid Zone, our parishes Friezeland, our people frozen into the mud of the world and dregges of sinne; and will you not be hissing hot in spirit?'[157] He was exceptionally well-disposed to his flock, dedicating a published sermon in Pauline terms to 'my deare and loving parishioners . . . my brethren beloved and longed for, my ioy and my crowne.'[158] Where Fletcher might have denounced sin indifferently, Abbot could beg that a parishioner might be excused the trauma of public penance: 'I would willingly winne him by more gentle courses if I may.'[159] He stayed with an attempted suicide in the three days that it took her to die, persuading her into a repentant state of mind.[160]

But with Abbot's affection for his people went a sense of professional, clerical dignity which was typical of his generation, and a growing devotion to the institutional Church as 'my deare mother, the much honored, holy and blessed Church of England.' In the conditions prevailing in the diocese of Canterbury under William Laud's government, his unconcealed respect for the established polity of the Church won him the name of 'bishop's creature', with a pope in his belly. 'I have loved the godly, as such, though I have hated their indiscretions, as well as my owne . . . Onely, this is the truth, I have loved the Church of God amongst us, and the whole government ecclesiastical and

---

154 Hasted (op. cit., vol. vii, pp. 92–3) reported in the mid-eighteenth century that of some 3,000 inhabitants 'a great part' were dissenters and attached to five distinct religious societies. See C. C. R. Pile, *Dissenting Congregations in Cranbrook*, Cranbrook Notes and Records no. 5 (n.p., 1953). The facts relating to the formation of the earliest dissenting churches in Kent are supplied by Nuttall, loc. cit.
155 *DNB*, art. Abbot.
156 See Abbot's sermons *The danger of popery* (1625) and *Bee thankfull London* (1626).
157 Abbot, *Davids desires* (1623), sig. *₌*3.
158 Ibid., sig. A6.
159 CALC, X. 6.7, letter from Abbot to the archdeacon's official, 13 June 1621, loose between fols 35 and 36.
160 Ibid., fol. 185ᵛ.

temporal.' It was a fatal conflict of loves. 'I have loved and desired to spend and to be spent, though the more I love the lesse I am loved of some few.'[161] The schism which ensued was portrayed in letters to the parliamentarian Sir Edward Dering whose views on all matters Abbot was glad to share. 'They stick not onely at our bishops, service and ceremonies, but at our Church. They would have every particular congregation to be independent, and neither to be kept in order by rules given by king, bishops, councels or synods.'[162] This was a more serious matter than the old private communion of saints, and it prefigured the formation of a gathered and covenanted church which followed in 1648.[163] These people were proud to call themselves separatists, glorying in the Biblical resonances of the word 'separate', but Abbot unhesitatingly labelled them 'Brownists'. As he wrote in 1639: 'It is no small charge to unchurch a church, to unminister a ministry, and to unworship a worship.'[164] The probability is that this drastic course was not followed in Cranbrook before the stressful decade which preceded the Civil War. The sequel, the history of Cranbrook nonconformity, enjoys only superficial continuity with earlier traditions of dissent. Separate, in the sense of different, Cranbrook's 'hotter sort of protestants' may have always been. Separated they were not, until the 1640s.

This essay should end with a comment on the 'popular and unpopular religion' of its title. What was 'popular religion' in sixteenth- and seventeenth-century Kent? According to current usage it must be looked for in Dr Clark's 'Third World'. It has been demonstrated that, among the majority, Protestant and Puritan religion never enjoyed popularity. But there was a sense in which the religion of the godly was also 'popular': it was held against John Strowd that his preaching was seasoned 'to please the people'.[165] And to these people nothing could be more unpopular than the fatal, recidivist tendency of clerics like Fletcher and Abbot to align themselves with some of the more unpopular features of the established Church. In matters of religion, 'popular' and 'unpopular' are relative terms, and deceptive.

161 Abbot, *Trial of our church-forsakers*, sigs A8ᵛ, A6ᵛ. The circumstances are discussed by Clark, op. cit., pp. 364, 386; and by Alan Everitt, *The Community of Kent and the Great Rebellion* (Leicester, 1966), pp. 86–7.
162 Abbot to Dering, 15 March 1640; BL, MS Stowe 184, fols 27–30. Further letters, 5 July, 3 October 1641; ibid., fols 43–4, 47–8.
163 Nuttall, loc. cit., p. 182.
164 Abbot, *Trial of our church-forsakers*, sig. a2ʳ.
165 DWL, MS Morrice B II, fol. 10ᵛ.

XI

Priests into Ministers:
The Establishment of Protestant
Practice in the City of York
1530 – 1630

❧

CLAIRE CROSS

Until comparatively recently it has been assumed that when successive Henrician, Edwardine and Elizabethan governments secured parliamentary legislation separating the English Church from Rome and introducing various degrees of Protestant doctrine the English Church became Protestant almost overnight. Outwardly this may well have been the case. Churchwardens' accounts demonstrate that, with a surprising rapidity in individual churches throughout the country, priests and parishioners obeyed royal injunctions to dismantle newly-designated monuments of superstition, bought Bibles and other Protestant books, and replaced the Latin mass with the services prescribed in the various versions of the *Book of Common Prayer*. Yet exterior actions did not make men Protestant, though they may ultimately have predisposed them towards Protestantism. The example of the city of York, a church-dominated, while not necessarily a particularly religious, city, illustrates the obstacles which could lie in the way of achieving the active practice of Protestantism in sixteenth-century England.[1]

In the early sixteenth century the Church in York pervaded all aspects of civic life. The Minster with its archbishop, dean and chapter of thirty-six prebendaries, its vicars choral and many servants, functioned at least in theory both as the chief church of the city and as the focus of ecclesiastical administration for the whole of the northern province. Just outside the walls stood the great Benedictine abbey of St Mary, one of the richest monasteries in the north of England. Within a stone's throw of the Minster the extremely wealthy St Leonard's hospital, now more of a monastery than an institution for the care of the sick, continued in its ancient routine. The city housed three other monastic communities of a much smaller size: the Benedictines of Holy Trinity Priory in Micklegate, the canons of St Gilbert of Sempringham in Fishergate and the Benedictine nuns of Clementhorpe. The four convents of friars, the Franciscans, Dominicans, Austins and Carmelites, also maintained a positive presence in the city. Yet all these manifestations of institutional religion had remained to some extent peripheral to the lives of the majority of York's inhabitants, whose first loyalties belonged to their parish churches; and in 1530

1 I am much indebted to recent scholars for pioneering work on the ecclesiastical history of York in the sixteenth century, primarily to Professor Dickens for his many writings cited below, but also to D. M. Palliser, *The Reformation in York 1534-1553*, Borthwick Paper 40 (York, 1971); J. C. H. Aveling, *Catholic Recusancy in the City of York 1558-1791* (Catholic Record Society, 1970); and R. A. Marchant, *The Puritans and the Church Courts in the Diocese of York 1560-1642* (1960). This article, based on a study of the 72 wills of York clergy who served in the city between 1520 and 1600 and, for comparison, also on the 55 wills of aldermen who held the office of mayor between approximately the same dates, can only stand as a footnote to their research. I also acknowledge with gratitude the kindness of the archivists at the Borthwick Institute of Historical Research in York, and the sub-librarian of York Minster Library.

the city still contained about forty parish churches. This meant that York, with a declining population, now had approximately one church for every two hundred inhabitants. In their turn these churches did not usually content themselves with the services of a single priest. When, in the more affluent days of the earlier fifteenth century, a York merchant wanted to remember all the parish clergy in his will, he considered he needed to set aside a hundred shillings to give four pence to every rector and chaplain celebrating in the parish churches of the city and its suburbs, which suggests that he thought there were around 260 parochial clergy. The records of St Michael, Spurriergate, reveal what this superabundance of clergy signified in one city parish in the early sixteenth century.[2]

St Mary's Abbey owned the advowson of St Michael's and had in 1531 appointed Nicholas Atkinson to the living, valued four years later at a mere £11 derived entirely from personal tithes and casual offerings. Although the vicarage was poor, the parish had accumulated a considerable amount of house property which in a good year might produce £15 gross. In addition to the parson, the parish maintained a chantry priest, Thomas Worall, an ubiquitous member of the local community who, besides performing numerous extra masses, supervised the parish property and compiled the accounts. His many activities over the years earned their due reward: when he died in 1550 his goods were assessed at over £20, which included books in his study worth 2s., at least twice as much as some contemporary clergy actually beneficed in the city contrived to leave. The parish also made annual payments to its clerk and underclerk, one of whose many duties included singing 'A mind of me' every year. A woman who washed the vestments, the bell man, the organ blower and the children who assisted at the altars and perhaps also sang completed the church's pay roll. In 1537 the accounts specify by name those who participated in the nine obits established in the church, incidentally revealing the close links between St Michael's and the surrounding parishes. The parson himself usually attended these commemorations, sometimes accompanied by his priest, together with Worall, the chantry priest; Sir Richard Stubbs, probably already priest of St Katherine's chantry in the church of St John, Ousebridge; Sir John Bateman, who by the 1540s had gained the living of St Crux; Sir William Colte, an elderly chantry priest in St Mary, Castlegate; and a Grey Friar, Sir John Wickham. Other civic churches may not have benefited to quite the same extent from property rents; but in very many, wealthy citizens had also instituted annual memorial services, and the small payments made to the clergy at these obits must also have attracted priests from neighbouring parishes. Most York

---

2 G. E. Aylmer and R. Cant (eds.), *A History of York Minster* (Oxford, 1977), pp. 193–232; D. M. Palliser, 'The Unions of Parishes at York 1547–1586', *Yorkshire Archaeological Journal*, xliv (1974), pp. 87–102; R. B. Dobson, 'Foundation of perpetual Chantries by the Citizens of medieval York', in G. J. Cuming (ed.), *Studies in Church History*, vol. iv (1967), pp. 37–8.

churches seem to have closely resembled St Michael's both in the number of their resident clergy (perhaps two or three in each parish), and in the priests they drew to special services. On the eve of the Reformation, York had this great array of beneficed and stipendary parish priests who, if the conditions pertaining at St Michael's are an adequate guide, had a reasonable chance of augmenting their normally meagre incomes with additional priestly offices and clerical and accounting work.[3]

In 1535 archbishop Lee made his well known pronouncement on the quality of the parish clergy in the northern province, asserting that, because of their poverty, no learned men would consider accepting northern livings, and that in consequence the bishops had no choice but to ordain all the men who presented themselves, so long as they appeared to be of honest behaviour, could understand what they read, and had the capacity to minister the sacraments and sacramentals according to the proper form. Preaching had been left to the friars, and the archbishop could recall scarcely any secular clergy capable of undertaking that duty. Lee's generalizations certainly applied to the York civic clergy. In 1535 only two graduates, William Martin and Henry Joy, continued to hold parish livings, though there had recently been two others, John Marshall, LL.B., incumbent of St Michael, Spurriergate for about eight years from 1523, and Henry Carbott, also LL.B., vicar of St Maurice's for a time earlier in the 1530s. Martin served the cure of St Crux in conjunction with livings outside the city and, such was its indigence, probably regarded it as an incidental perquisite in a career pursued largely outside the parish: he had apparently gone from York by 1540. The case of Joy seems to have been rather different. A theology graduate and just possibly a former monk, he took the very poor living of All Saints, North Street, in August 1535, and there is record of him in the city ten years later. He remained the only theologian and, after 1540, one of the only two graduates in the city churches for almost two decades. At a time when opportunities for graduates were expanding rapidly at the national level, York parishes offered few inducements for university-trained men since much more lucrative posts existed elsewhere.[4]

The parish clergy formed without doubt the lowest stratum of the York clerical hierarchy, recruited locally and educated locally. William Simpson graphically exemplifies this insularity. A chantry priest at the altar of St Katherine in All Saints, Pavement, when he died in 1528, Simpson had apparently only come the very short distance along Walmgate from his birthplace in the parish of St Lawrence (and there, indeed, he wished his body to return for

3 Minster Library, MSS Add 220/1, fols 123b–7a; Borthwick Institute of Historical Research Parish Records York/Michael Spurriergate 3, fols 28ᵛ, 28ᵛ–36ʳ; Dean and Chapter Original Inventory 1550; *Victoria County History, Yorkshire: the City of York* (1961), pp. 396–7.
4 J. Strype, *Ecclesiastical Memorials*, vol. i (1721), pp. 189–90; Borthwick Probate Register 13, fol. 51ʳ⁻ᵛ.

burial beside his mother and father). William Coca, chantry priest of Mr Nelson's chantry in Holy Trinity, Micklegate, may never have left his native parish, seeking similarly to be buried near his parents in Holy Trinity church in 1537. In 1541 Robert Hill, parson of St Mary, Bishophill, Junior, had already set up an obit for his dead sister, Ellen, in his church; his mother and surviving brother lived close at hand, perhaps also within the city. Another chantry priest in the same church, and an erstwhile Dominican, Brian Godson, had moved into York from the nearby village of Newton on Ouse; when he came to make his will his thoughts too turned to his birthplace and he arranged at some length for his friends to carry his body back to Newton for burial. Almost all the testaments of York city clergy who died in the 1520s and 1530s give this impression of localism, of clergy who had never left their original environment, and who, throughout their lives, showed great interest in the ramifications of their families, keeping in the closest contact with their brothers and sisters, nephews, nieces, cousins, and even step-parents.[5]

As might be expected, the religious practices of these very local priests seem to have been of a very traditional kind. With hardly a variation in terminology, all at their death consigned their souls 'to Almighty God, our blessed Lady St Mary, and all the celestial company of heaven'; and then, according to their means, asked for wax candles to be burnt about their body at the mass and dirge on the day of their burial, making bequests to the poor and the friars in return for prayers. Gregory Woodall, chantry priest in St John's, Ousebridge, had sufficient resources to provide 10s. 'to cause thirty masses to be done the day of my burial for my soul and all Christian souls, if it can be conveniently.' Stereotyped though this piety may have been, it still clearly had great significance for these priests, and could even attain a certain eloquence when a priest appeared somewhat more articulate than his fellows. Richard Oliver, parson of All Saints, North Street, writing his last will and testament in his own hand in June 1535, transformed the preamble of his will into a heartfelt declaration of faith:

First I commend my soul to Almighty God, my creator and saviour and my redeemer and my great judge for to come on the dreadful day of doom, trusting to his great mercy and in the merits of his blessed, glorious and painful passion to be one of the number that shall be saved, to reign evermore to see the face of my saviour *in terra viventium*, beseeching his blessed mother, Mary, evermore virgin, and St Anne, and all the saints in heaven to pray for me and obtain the same.

On the day he died he wished his corpse to be brought to lie in his parish church, the lamp to be lit, and to be surrounded by seven great tallow candles. He asked his executors to provide bread and ale for all who came to the church while his body remained there, and left 4d. for two or three poor scholars to say

5 Borthwick Archbishop's Register 27, fol. 161ᵛ; Prob. Reg. 11, fol. 225ʳ⁻ᵛ; Minster Lib., D & C Prob. Reg. 2, fols 196ᵛ, 198ᵛ–199ʳ.

David's psalter. To prevent his wake degenerating into unseemly revelry, he required all his parishioners to leave the church by nine at night, except for sober widows who might stay on to watch by his body. Then, the following day, he wanted to be carried up the hill to Holy Trinity Priory in Micklegate, and, after dirge and mass, buried there at the entry to the west choir door.[6]

Oliver stands out among York parish clergy not only for the freshness and practicality of his piety but also for his interest in education; indeed, he may possibly himself have been a part-time schoolmaster. He bequeathed a little money for the scholars in the Clee, the boarding house run by St Mary's Abbey for the boys at the Minster school, and hoped that they with their usher might be allowed to attend his obsequies. He owned a *Calepinus* (the most modern Latin and Greek dictionary of that date), Erasmus's *Adages*, and the *Epistles* and *Offices* of Cicero. Here his interests outdistanced those of other York parish priests, but, so far as can be gathered from the evidence of their wills, were not altogether different from theirs. Thomas Barton, vicar of St Lawrence, in 1523 left a popular medieval book of sermons, *Sermones Discipuli*, the *Precepts* of Nicholas of Lyra, a volume of *Institutes* (not particularized further) and several service books. A decade later the chantry priest of St John's, Ousebridge, Gregory Woodall, also had a copy of *Sermones Discipuli*, and a dictionary, *Ortus Vocabularum*. Lawrence Hall, priest of St Michael-le-Belfrey, as well as Oliver, possessed the late-medieval handbook for priests, *Rationale Divinorum*; while a clearly more prosperous chantry priest at the Minster, John Hickson, included among his books the sermons of Vincent [Ferrar] in three volumes, the *Pupilla Oculi*, another popular medieval guide for parish priests, *Ortus Vocabularum*, certain unspecified works of Hugh of St Victor and Sulpicius, a book of the Ten Commandments of the Law in English together with a breviary and other old written books. More typically, if they mentioned any books at all, York priests bequeathed the tools of their trade, their service books, processioners, glossed psalters, legends, breviaries and mass books of the York use. Some clergy in addition thought it necessary to gain a smattering of canon law, at least in so far as it concerned the security of their benefices. Lawrence Hall passed on to George Cooke, the parson of the very poor living of St Margaret's, his copy of *Constitutiones Othonis* and *Constitutiones Legantines*, as well as *Pupilla Oculi*. Perhaps a minority of these York priests had slightly wider intellectual horizons than archbishop Lee supposed.[7]

In the 1520s and 1530s some lay people in areas like East Anglia, Kent, the

---

6 Minster Lib., D & C Prob. Reg. 2, fols 155^r–6^r; Borthwick Prob. Reg. 11, fols 168^r–9^r; Archbp. Reg. 28, fols 168^r–9^r.
7 Borthwick Archbp. Reg. 28, fols 168^r–9^r; D & C Orig. Inv. 1523; Prob. Reg. 11, fols 368^v–9^r; D & C Orig. Inv. 1547; Minster Lib., D & C Prob. Reg. 3, fol. 20^r: even if Oliver's library is set aside as exceptional, the variety of books in the possession of other York civic clergy compares rather favourably with those mentioned in the wills of Norfolk clergy for the same period; P. Heath, *The English Parish Clergy on the Eve of the Reformation* (1969), pp. 86–90.

Chilterns, Coventry and London reacted strongly against the conventional piety of priests such as these, first showing a new enthusiasm for Lollardy, and later seizing upon the earliest examples of Protestant literature being brought into England from the Continent. In York, however, the citizens seem to have been overwhelmingly content with their priests and their theology. Although the leaders of the community no longer had the resources to found chantries as they had done in the late fourteenth and fifteenth centuries, they nevertheless went on adding to already existing chantries right up to the dissolution. Others arranged for annual prayers for their souls by establishing obits. York people believed no less ardently than their monarch in the efficacy of prayers for the dead. When he died during his year of office as mayor in 1521 Thomas Backus provided for a parson to sing masses for his soul for a year after his death, as did alderman Paul Gillour in the next year. Alderman Norman of All Saints, Pavement, commissioned a priest to sing for his soul for three years and in addition left an annuity of 40s. to augment the chantry in his parish church served by Sir Nicholas Ben. After his wife's death, Thomas Drawswerd intended part of his estate should go towards the finding of a chantry priest. In very much the same way as their priests, although usually on a considerably more lavish scale, members of the city's governing class gave precise directions for the performance of their funerals. In 1538 John Shaw, mayor and merchant of Fossgate, wished six aldermen, preceded by the four orders of friars, to bear his body to its resting place in the high choir of his parish church, St Crux. On the day of his burial, he left the large sum of £13 13s. 4d. to be spent on a dirge, on the poor and on a dinner for all the parish, and bequeathed a vestment to the church and money to the church works, the rood light and the All Hallows' light. In the ostentation of their last rites, other aldermen fell little short of Shaw.[8]

These citizens demonstrably lived on the most friendly terms with their priests. Both alderman Norman and alderman Jackson had brothers in orders. Many remembered their parish priests and chantry priests in their wills, William Harrington giving Sir Richard Trepeland, a chantry priest of Holy Trinity, King's Court, a grey trotting nag, while the more usual bequest of £1 or 10s. must have been a welcome gift to an incumbent or chantry priest who might have received £5 (or even less) from his living a year. Almost always, in this period, the priest witnessed the wills of his parishioners and gained a nominal sum in return. At least in the hour of their death, the chief citizens of York felt very close to their local priests, a fact that sometimes went a little way towards improving clerical living conditions. They showed no sign at all of wanting to alter the state of religion in the city. Any changes to be made in the life of the Church in York had in consequence to be imposed upon the parish

8 Dobson, 'Foundation of perpetual Chantries', pp. 22–38; Borthwick Prob. Reg. 9, fols 195[r], 283[v]–4[v], 327[r]–[v], 448[v], 435[r]; Prob. Reg. 11, pt I, fols 1[r], 276[r]–[v]; Prob. Reg. 11, pt II, fol. 497[r]–[v].

priests and the citizenry from outside. The five or six inhabitants who appeared before the ecclesiastical courts on charges of heresy and, in the person of the Dutch immigrant Valentine Freez, even suffered death for religion, seem to have been highly exceptional. They were in all cases 'foreigners', and in no sense constituted an indigenous lay movement for reform.[9]

The dissolution of the four monastic houses for men, and the little convent of nuns in York and its immediate suburbs, had the unintended effect of actually strengthening the conservative, unadventurous nature of the city's religious life, since a number of monks found parish livings as did some friars when their four convents a little later fell to the Crown. One monk of St Mary's, Thomas Baynes, acquired the rectory of St Mary, Castlegate, and another, John Thompson, became the last rector of St Wilfred's and subsequently, after its merger with St Michael-le-Belfrey, curate of St Michael's. Thomas Clint, *alias* Staveley, B.D., although he seems not to have had a formal cure, settled in St Martin's, Micklegate, the parish adjoining Holy Trinity Priory, and asked to be buried in St Martin's on his death in 1550. Yet another St Mary's monk retired to his family at Escrick, making provision of a shilling in his will for each of his 'brethren of the house of religion' who attended his funeral. Taking into account the one or two other monks known to have obtained Yorkshire livings, it seems possible that as many as ten from the complement of fifty left in St Mary's Abbey in 1539 may have remained in York or its vicinity.[10]

The much smaller priory of Holy Trinity definitely maintained some sort of presence in Micklegate for two decades after its closure. William Gryme, a Triniter, had been instituted rector of the former priory church of Holy Trinity, Micklegate, by 1537, and stayed there till his death in 1556, when he bequeathed two great books of the Bible and an ordinary in Latin to his parish church. Richard Stubbs, another monk from Holy Trinity, secured a chantry in the Minster which he served in conjunction with another chantry in St John's, Ousebridge, only yards away from his conventual church. The former prior of Holy Trinity, Richard Speght, *alias* Hudson, managed to continue as a priest in Holy Trinity church and, on his death there in 1545, left small sums for any of his fellow monks who might come to his funeral. He appointed Henry Joy, the parson of All Saints, North Street, to oversee his will. Since the presentation of All Saints had belonged to the priory, and since Joy, a graduate in theology, received the living in 1535, it seems possible that he too had once been a monk of Holy Trinity, or had otherwise been closely associated with the house. There is much less uncertainty over the identity of Richard Collinson, named as a monk of Holy Trinity in 1536. He like Speght stayed on in York as an

9 A. G. Dickens, 'Tudor York', *V C H Yorks.: the City of York*, pp. 142–3.
10 For this and the two following paragraphs I have depended heavily on Palliser, *The Reformation in York*, pp. 13–14; *Letters and Papers of Henry VIII*, vol. xv, p. 552; Borthwick Prob. Reg. 13, fol. 683ʳ; Prob. Reg. 11, fol. 640ʳ.

unbeneficed priest, and in his will made in 1558 asked to be buried in St Margaret's.[11]

Fewer monks from the other two religious houses, St Andrew's and St Leonard's, gained a foothold in the city churches. Robert Acred, who in 1548 had a chantry in St Saviour's church, and also ministered in the impecunious parish of St Helen-on-the-walls, may once have been a canon of St Andrew's. Another canon, John Hodgson, was curate of St Mary, Bishophill, Junior, from at least 1541 till he died in 1551. One of the brothers of St Leonard's, William Shute, went on to be a vicar choral in the Minster; another, Edward Smith, probably succeeded in getting the living of St Denys in Walmgate, where in 1546 Robert Hall, also a brother of St Leonard's, definitely followed him. A fourth brother, John Grayson, though unbeneficed, seems also to have remained around York and in 1548 was remembered in the will of the parson of St John, Ousebridge.[12]

Friars, unlike monks, had not been permitted to accept appropriated rectories among their endowments and consequently York friars had fewer opportunities of moving into livings locally, but some nevertheless managed to establish themselves in the city churches. George Bellerby, rector of St Wilfred's from 1544 to 1546, may have been an Austin friar. Peter Glenton, a chantry priest in both the Minster and St Helen's, Stonegate, almost certainly also an Austin, witnessed Bellerby's will. In addition, two other Austin friars, John Ask, the prior, and William Watson, may have acquired chantries in York, while a fifth, William Mottey, probably became a stipendiary priest in St Martin's, Coney Street, where he was still serving in 1557. The three other orders of friars seem to have been rather less well treated. The Franciscan, Ralph Clayton, obtained a chantry in St Mary, Castlegate, and his colleague, John Wickham, assisted at obits in St Michael's, Spurriergate, until 1542. A Dominican, Brian Godson, held a chantry in St Mary, Bishophill, Junior, till his death in 1541, when he left a bequest to a fellow York Dominican, William Bradfurth, who does not seem to have had any living in the city. A third Dominican, John Wilson, may possibly have been the chantry priest of the same name in Holy Trinity, King's Court, from 1538 to 1548. Lastly two Carmelites may have settled in York, John White perhaps as a chantry priest in St Crux and later as curate there, and James Johnson just possibly as vicar of St Lawrence from before 1558 until 1582.[13]

11 D. S. Chambers, *Faculty Office Registers 1534–1549* (Oxford, 1966), pp. 76, 87; Borthwick Prob. Reg. 15, pt I, fols 64^v–5^r; Prob. Reg. 13, fol. 51^{r-v}; Prob. Reg. 17, pt II, fol. 767^{r-v}; J. Solloway, *The Alien Benedictines of York* (Leeds, 1910), pp. 304–18.

12 *Eighth Report of the Deputy Keeper of the Public Records* (1847), appendix 2, p. 51; W. Page (ed.), *The Certificates of the Commissioners appointed to survey the Chantries . . . in the County of York*, Surtees Society, xci, xcii (1894–5), p. 472; Minster. Lib., D & C Prob. Reg. 2, fol 198^v–9^r; D & C Prob. Reg. 3, fol. 31^v–2^r; Borthwick Archbp. Reg. 29, fol. 81^v.

13 *Eighth Report*, appendix 2, p. 51; Borthwick Archbp Reg. 29, fol. 99^v; Archbp. Reg. 30, fol. 45^{r-v}; PRY/MS3.

The dissolution of the chantries in 1548, even more than the dissolution of the monasteries in the previous decade, added to the number of priests in York city parishes. When the chantry commissioners visited York first in 1546, and then in 1548, they listed some hundred chantry priests in the Minster and the civic churches. Eleven of these priests never had to leave the Minster since they combined their chantry duties with those of vicars choral; two former chantry priests, James Crosthwait and Denis Heckleton, continued as vicars choral in the cathedral without a break until their deaths in 1579. Other chantry priests in city churches went on living in or near the parish churches where their chantries had been, presumably managing to exist on their pensions. Christopher Painter, already more than seventy years old in 1548, did not have to face the problem of finding other employment for long, since he died early in 1549, only a few months after his chantry in All Saints, Pavement, had come to an end. Painter opted to be buried in St Mary, Bishophill, Senior. Several of his younger fellow priests, however, stayed in their parishes, some for ten, some even for a further twenty years. Miles Walshforth, who had held chantries in both St Crux and St Nicholas, Micklegate, mentioned twice in clerical wills in the 1550s, left bequests to St Nicholas's church when he died in 1558. Somewhat more fortunate in that he had at least gained an exiguous chaplaincy at St Thomas's Hospital, William Pinder, once a chantry priest at St Crux and St John, Hungate, died in York in 1558 and wished to be buried near the hospital in All Saints, Pease-holm. Two more priests may never have left the parishes where they had once performed their requiem masses: Christopher Petty, formerly chantry priest in St Mary, Bishophill, Senior, asked his executors to bury him there in 1557; while, almost eight years later, in 1565, William Foster, who had served a chantry in St Saviour's, sought also to be buried where his chantry had been. Edward Sandall was more footloose, and certainly more obstreperous; aged forty-four in 1548, and priest of the chantry in the chapel of St Agnes on Foss bridge, he reappeared as an unlicensed teacher in the parish of Holy Trinity, Micklegate, in the 1560s.[14]

In general rather less well provided for than the vicars choral who could remain in the Minster, but certainly better off than their fellows who seem to have had only their pensions on which to live, were the large numbers of priests, well over twenty of them, who eventually obtained parish livings in York. Even before the Reformation some vicars choral had added to their income by taking a city church. Now that they no longer had the option of acting as a chantry priest, this practice increased; and whenever they could, they moved into one of the poorer city advowsons belonging to the dean and chapter or the vicars

14 *Yorkshire Chantry Surveys*, pp. 5–84, 248–473; Borthwick Prob. Reg. 13, fol. 703ʳ; Minster Lib., D & C Prob. Reg. 3, fol. 31ᵛ–2ʳ; Borthwick Prob. Reg. 15, pt III, fols 2ʳ⁻ᵛ, 85ʳ⁻ᵛ; Prob. Reg. 13, fol. 703ʳ; Prob. Reg. 17, pt II, fol. 493ᵛ; Visitation 1567–8 Court Book 2, fols 83ʳ⁻ᵛ, 211ʳ⁻ᵛ; Aveling, *Catholic Recusancy*, pp. 166–9.

choral. In particular, St Michael-le-Belfrey and St Sampson's contributed a little towards augmenting the stipends of several vicars choral throughout the sixteenth century and beyond. Edward Swaine, chantry priest at the altar of St John the Evangelist in the Minster in 1548, acquired the living of St Mary, Bishophill, Junior, and Copmanthorpe in the reign of Elizabeth and died, still a vicar choral, in 1586 or 1587. He outlived by a few months Anthony Iveson, another vicar choral and priest at the altar of the Holy Trinity in the Minster in 1548. Iveson, too, became an Elizabethan pluralist, and died in 1586, rector of St Cuthbert's and of Burgwallis. Some of the less privileged chantry priests in civic churches contrived to gain the living of the church where their chantry had once been or another parochial living in York. John White, priest of Our Lady's chantry in St Crux, was still curate of St Nicholas beyond the walls, and clerk in St Crux, at the time of his death in 1572. Wilfred Archer went on from being curate in St Peter-the-less, where he had once served a chantry, to the slightly better-paid parish of St Olave in about 1550. He died there nine years later. Richard Barwick, chantry priest in St Saviour's, died in 1558 as rector of St Saviour's. John Walker, one of a handful of priests who held a chantry in the Minster and in a parish church (also St Saviour's), became rector of St Margaret's from 1550 until his death in 1555; and similarly Robert Mell, who alternated between a chantry in the Minster and one in St Crux, was rector of All Saints, Peaseholm, from 1567 to 1573, as well as being rector of Withernsea in the East Riding and a vicar choral. Beginning his religious life as a canon of Newburgh Priory, Thomas Grayson first found refuge as a chantry priest in the Minster after the dissolution of his house; and then, after holding parish cures at Fulford and St Lawrence's, ended his life in 1578 as vicar of St Martin's, Coney Street, and curate of Stillingfleet. At least seven former chantry priests lived on as York parish incumbents into the first, second or even third decades of Elizabeth's reign.

The one change engineered by the citizens of York, and not inflicted upon them by the central government at the time of the Reformation, was the amalgamation of certain York parishes. This, to a very limited extent, improved the financial position of some of these former chantry priests by adding a few pounds annually to the permanent endowment of their cures. Although the scheme did not get formal ratification until 1586, the corporation sponsored a local Act of Parliament, passed in December 1547, to reduce the forty parishes of York to twenty-three with two further churches surviving non-parochially. Some fifteen parish churches seem to have gone out of use in the reign of Edward VI, their revenues being combined with a neighbouring parish, making the cures thus augmented slightly more capable of supporting an unambitious local priest. Yet even after these unifications of parishes, the best city living did not exceed £11 per annum on the *Valor* estimates, and many still did not come up to the bare minimum of £5 a year. Despite the continued poverty of York parishes because of the glut of priests seeking cures, caused first by the dissolution of the monasteries and then by that of the chantries, most managed to get one or more priests to carry out parochial duties without undue difficulty until about the time of Elizabeth's accession.[15]

During the crucial twenty years between 1533 and 1553, therefore, when Protestant doctrines should have been implemented, the ecclesiastical authorities had no real problem over the supply of clergy in York, but grave reservations over both their capacity and will to fulfil their task adequately. In 1535 archbishop Lee had considered that the vast proportion of northern parishes were too badly financed to attract university-educated men; and the subsequent amalgamation of some York livings had been on far too modest a scale to alter the situation materially. The dispersal of the monks and chantry priests may admittedly have brought one or two graduates like Henry Joy and William Garnett to city parishes; but only one graduate, Thomas Nelson, LL.B., appears to have come to York from outside during this period. Perhaps drawn by the opportunity to practise in the church courts, Nelson accepted the living of St Martin's, Coney Street, in November 1551, dying there a little more than a year later. An Oxford graduate, and also rector of Winterslow in Wiltshire, his will revealed connections with the 'south country' and mentioned a kinswoman in Essex. In addition, the inventory of Nelson's goods disclosed that he possessed more than eighty-one (unnamed) books valued at 52s., far more than any other city incumbent is known to have had at any time during the sixteenth century. Had he lived longer, he might possibly have introduced some of the new ideas emanating from London and the universities to his fellow York priests. The city of York at this period seems to have had singularly few natural contacts with centres of Protestant reform. Unlike some towns in southern Lancashire, no young men from civic families appear to have been studying at Oxford or Cambridge, and the town thus lacked those with the inspiration to launch Protestant evangelizing missions to their birthplace. It was only much later in the century, if the wills are a reliable guide, that York merchants began systematically to think of a university education for some of their sons. In marked contrast to some southern towns, there seems to have been no readiness in York to anticipate Protestant changes. In consequence, such innovations had to be imposed from above, and the chief driving force behind this movement was Robert Holgate who became archbishop of York in 1545 on the death of the conservative Lee.[16]

Holgate clearly realized that he had on his hands the daunting task of re-educating almost all the parochial clergy. Those he could most easily influence in York were the vicars choral, several of whom also held city livings. His

15 Palliser, 'Unions of Parishes at York', pp. 87–102.
16 Minster Lib., D & C Prob. Reg. 3, fol. 41ᵛ; Borthwick D & C Orig. Inv. 1552; C. Haigh, *Reformation and Resistance in Tudor Lancashire* (Cambridge, 1975), especially chapter 11.

injunctions, issued to the dean and chapter in 1552, directed especial attention to the vicars, ordering all those under forty to learn, by heart, every week, a chapter of St Paul's epistles in Latin, beginning with the book of the New Testament most cherished by Luther, the Epistle to the Romans. Holgate required every vicar choral to equip himself with an English New Testament, which he made strenuous efforts to see that he actually read. He seems to have made some impact; as early as 1540 one vicar choral, William Crosby, died owning a Bible and other unspecified books worth the considerable sum of 9s. Edward Smith, parson of St Denys, in 1546 bequeathed a Latin New Testament to the vicar of St Margaret's. At St Michael-le-Belfrey's, under the eye of the Minster, Lawrence Hall also owned a New Testament which he left to the parson of St John-del-Pike. Holgate, nevertheless, must have found the overall response to his initiative disappointing, for it continued to be far more usual for York city priests, if their wills and inventories mentioned any books at all, to concentrate on breviaries, song books and legends.[17]

Nowhere does the conservatism of the generality of York priests emerge more clearly than in their attitude to clerical marriage. Although Holgate himself led the way (and none too happily as it proved), the clergy of York, in contrast to the clergy of Essex and some other parts of the country, showed themselves exceedingly reluctant to follow the archiepiscopal example. Of all the parish clergy in York, only four definitely married during the reign of Edward VI. Three of these were vicars choral: Robert Cragges, Walter Lancaster and Peter Walker. Cragges had also been rector of All Saints, Pavement, since 1544. The Marian authorities deprived Cragges on account of his marriage from both his benefices, and he does not seem subsequently to have regained any ecclesiastical office in York. Yet immediately he had set his wife aside, Walker was restored to his functions in the Minster. Lancaster received similar treatment, and in 1557 went to be incumbent of St Michael's, Spurriergate, in succession to Ralph Whiting. Whiting himself had been the fourth priest in York to marry, but he also agreed to separate from his wife, and was allowed to continue as rector of St Michael's.[18]

This same conservatism appears equally pronounced in the wills the civic clergy made between 1540 and 1560. Even in the Edwardine period, the clergy almost without exception commended their souls to God, the Virgin Mary and all the celestial company of heaven. In 1550 Thomas Clint, the former monk of

17 A. G. Dickens, *Robert Holgate, Archbishop of York and President of the King's Council in the North*, Borthwick Paper 8 (York 1955); W. H. Frere (ed.), *Visitation Articles and Injunctions*, Alcuin Club Collection, XV (1910), II, pp. 310–21; Borthwick D & C Orig. Inv. 1540; Archbp. Reg. 29, fol. 77ᵛ; Minster Lib., D & C Prob. Reg. 3, fol. 20ʳ.
18 H. E. P. Grieve, 'The Deprived Married Clergy of Essex, 1553–61' *Transactions of the Royal Historical Society*, 4th series, xxii (1940), pp. 141–69; A. G. Dickens, *The Marian Reaction in the Diocese of York, Part I, The Clergy*, Borthwick Paper 11 (York, 1967), pp. 23–9.

St Mary's, gave a far more explicit indication of his beliefs. He yielded his soul 'both in my life, and especially in the hour of death, into the hands of Almighty God, my creator and redeemer', trusting 'by the merits of his passion to be partaker of his infinite merciful salvation.' Then, referring to 'the glorious thankful prayer of our blessed Lady', he besought her 'and all the saints in heaven to pray with me and for me.' Thomas Nelson, the one new graduate recruit to the York clergy, while he also placed emphasis on 'Our blessed Lady, St Mary and . . . the holy church triumphant', stood alone in stressing the unique nature of Christ's passion 'which did pay a sufficient ransom for the redemption of all mankind', hoping 'that the same passion being sufficient may work effect in me by him, which my only trust is and shall be.' More typical of the local clergy was Richard Rundall, who, in 1550, requested thirty priests to sing masses for his soul and left £5 to be spent on a dirge. When, soon after her accession, Mary once more formally authorized prayers for the dead, the city's priests apparently had no theological objection to obeying the royal command. In June 1556 Lawrence Harrison, who held the cure of St George's in conjunction with that of Naburn, provided for a trental of masses for his soul, and gave £3 to the poor to pray for him. William Gryme, the former monk of Holy Trinity Priory, bequeathed beads to hang before the sacrament in Holy Trinity church; while William Bate, vicar choral and vicar of St Lawrence, requested an elaborate funeral with lights, mass and dirge attended by his fellow vicars. Whereas scarcely any priests who died in the reign of Edward VI mentioned any books at all in their wills, few died in York in the Marian period without leaving mass books, breviaries, missals, psalters, processioners or hymnals.[19]

All the evidence suggests that the ruling class of York shared their civic clergy's preference for the old ways in religion. Even under Edward VI so long as it remained possible, aldermen like Peter Robinson continued to commission funerals of the customary kind, arranging for poor men with torches to surround the corpse, for a dirge and a lavish dinner on the day of their burial. Then, very quickly after Mary came to the throne, they brought their old traditions back. Alderman Richard White founded an obit in St Michael-le-Belfrey on the Friday after St Matthew's day and, in addition, provided an annuity of £4 for a priest to say mass for his soul every Wednesday and Friday at the common altar in the Minster. As late as September 1558, alderman William Holme also wished to establish an obit in his parish church of St Denys though, anticipating further changes in religion, he took the precaution of saying that, if the law should not permit obits to be celebrated, the money should instead be distributed to the poor of the parish. In 1556 alderman George Gale of Holy Trinity, Goodramgate, gave a front cloth to the high altar of the Minster in return for prayers,

19 Borthwick Prob. Reg. 13, fol. 683ʳ; Minster Lib., D & C Prob. Reg. 3, fol. 41ᵛ; Borthwick Archbp. Reg. 29, fol. 142ʳ; Prob. Reg. 15, pt I, fols 64ᵛ–5ʳ; D & C Orig. Will 1557/8; Prob. Reg. 15, pt III, fols 2ʳ–ᵛ, 23ʳ, 25ʳ–ᵛ, 126ᵛ–7ʳ.

disclosing incidentally that his sister had once been prioress of Wilberfoss, a property now in his possession. The connections between these citizens and their clergy continued to be close. As he divided up his estate among his children, William Holme took account of the fact that one of his sons, Peter, might decide to take orders. Almost without exception, all used the local incumbent to witness their will. While there was very little indication of reformed Catholic thinking in York either among the civic clergy or the laity apart from the refoundation of St Peter's school, which in any case was carried out by the dean and chapter under the direction of the absentee archbishop Heath, the local clergy and their leading parishioners seem to have been eager to take up again the old religious practices they had so much cherished in the 1520s.[20]

The death of Mary abruptly halted this revival of conservative Catholicism, as alderman Holme had feared might happen. York's Catholic archbishop refused to recognize Elizabeth as Supreme Governor of the Church and was deprived; the same fate awaited something like half the largely non-resident chapter of the Minster, thus making possible the appointment of a Protestant archbishop in the person of Thomas Young and of some committed Protestant prebendaries. In the city, however, only one cleric, Henry Moore, a graduate recently instituted as rector of St Martin's, Micklegate, would not swear to the royal supremacy, and he subsequently conformed and became a convinced Protestant. When Young reached York in 1561, he, together with the three or four resident prebendaries, confronted the same problem, which Holgate had earlier without much success attempted to solve, of bringing the conservative clergy and laity of York to an active acceptance of Protestantism. Men such as Richard Barnes, who was made chancellor in 1561, and Matthew Hutton, who replaced Nicholas Wotton as dean on the latter's death in 1567, did not doubt that this could only be achieved through an abundant supply of Protestant preaching.

From early in the 1560s the Minster dignitaries began a systematic course of instruction; but it seems to have taken an exceptionally long time for this academic Protestantism to affect the conservatism of the local clergy and laity. For decades the subject of clerical marriage aroused an instinctive aversion in some inhabitants. After attending a Minster sermon in which Ralph Tonstall had attacked the Catholic tradition of clerical celibacy, alderman William Allen remarked to John Myton, rector of St Crux and Holy Trinity, Goodramgate, that he considered that Myton and the preacher were lying if they claimed that the apostles lived with their wives after Christ had called them. Allen later found himself before the northern High Commission Court to answer for his opinions. Some of the older aldermen had little choice but to learn to overcome their prejudices. Alderman Robert Heckleton had a son, Richard, who was a priest

20 Borthwick Prob. Reg. 13, pt II fol. 604^v; D & C Prob. Reg. 5, fols 14^r–18^r; Prob. Reg. 15, pt III, fol. 229^{r-v}; Prob. Reg. 15, pt I, fol. 62^{r-v}.

and had acquired the living of All Saints, North Street. He must have been one of the first locally recruited parish clergy to marry; by the time of his father's death in 1568 he already had two daughters. Judging from their wills, most of the Elizabethan civic clergy still abstained from marriage, in contrast to their Jacobean successors; and dislike of married clergy lingered in the city for many years. In 1580 Mrs Barton, herself the wife of a vicar choral, was presented for voicing her distaste for ministers, their wives and godly religion; and when she died the next year, some of her women friends went so far as to place lighted candles about her body, according to a 'superstitious order'.[21]

It is scarcely surprising that old Catholic customs persisted when so few in the city felt any call to stand against them. A somewhat expurgated version of the Corpus Christi plays continued to be acted annually throughout the 1560s with, it appears, the positive cooperation of the corporation. In 1568 dean Hutton intervened to try to get the council to oppose the staging of the plays; and apparently won over one or two aldermen. The majority, however, still supported the continuation of the plays, albeit performed in a further emasculated form. Only with the coming of archbishop Grindal had the Church the strength to forbid the Corpus Christi plays in their entirety, condemning in addition the annual ride of Yule and Yule's wife at Christmas, which, like the plays, had 'drawn a great concourse of disorderly people and diverted multitudes from divine service and sermons'. Even after the decision had been made, a minority of the corporation tried to revive the plays in the 1570s, this time with no success.[22]

Nostalgia among the civic leaders for the old ways seems also to have been shared by those of their clergy who, like many of the aldermen, had memories of religious life in York going back at least to the 1530s. Thomas Grayson, one-time canon of Newburgh Priory and later a former chantry priest, who by the beginning of Elizabeth's reign had obtained the cure of St Martin's, Coney Street, appeared before the High Commission Court in 1567 on a charge of receiving Catholic books from a county recusant family. He weathered the proceedings, nevertheless, and retained his living until he died in 1578. Another former chantry priest, Edward Sandall, now maintaining himself as best he could by teaching (without a licence) in the parish of Holy Trinity, Micklegate, had openly defended praying to saints and boasted that he trusted to see the day when he would have under his girdle twenty of the heads of the heretics 'now in authority'. Despite his braggado he ultimately took the oath of supremacy in 1568, only to be suspended from his clerical function by the Court of High Commission in 1573 for 'vile filthiness not to be named'. Two other York priests acted more discreetly during their lives, but both left distinctly Catholic

21 Borthwick High Commission Act Book 4, fol. 190; Aveling, *Catholic Recusancy*, p. 169; Borthwick Prob. Reg. 18, fol. 33ᵛ–4ʳ; HCAB 10, fols 59ᵛ, 105ᵛ.
22 Aveling, *Catholic Recusancy*, p. 31; Borthwick HCAB 7, fol. 41ʳ⁻ᵛ.

wills. In February 1567 Thomas Layther, rector of St Saviour's, still commended his soul 'to Almighty God my creator and redeemer and to our blessed Lady, St Mary, and to all the holy company of heaven'; and he seems to have been a close friend of several other city clergy. Five years later Robert Norham, vicar of St Mary, Bishophill, Junior, since 1541, and subsequently also vicar of Lofthouse in plurality, expressed his trust in 'our blessed Virgin, our Lady St Mary'. These conservatives slowly disappeared from the scene, but, to the dismay of those who, like archbishop Grindal and dean Hutton, wanted active teaching of Protestantism in the parish churches, their places were either not filled at all, or only filled by clergy incapable of preaching.[23]

Such was the poverty of even the best of the York city livings that they continued to offer absolutely no inducement to university-trained clergy, and only two graduates served in the city's parishes in the first part of Elizabeth's reign. John Bateman, vicar of Holy Trinity, King's Court, from 1550 until his death in 1569, vicar also of Burghwallis in the West Riding from 1564, held in addition the offices of succentor of the vicars choral, and rural dean of Christianity. Only it seems by pluralism on this scale, could an able and committed Protestant be retained in the city. The one other graduate incumbent, Henry Moore, who took a law degree at Cambridge in 1563, and was known to have been active in teaching Protestant doctrine in his city parish in the 1560s, appears to have been tempted into pluralism on an even greater scale. Earlier in the 1560s his attacks on Catholic abuses had been making a forcible impression on his auditory in Micklegate; but in 1568 the churchwardens of St Martin's began complaining that 'the youth of the parish have not sufficiently been instructed and taught since the said Mr Moore went from them', that he exercised no oversight over the curate, and that many Sundays and holy days the parish had no service at all. As Elizabeth's reign progressed, this tendency towards pluralism and non-residence among the civic clergy went unchecked. The churchwardens of St Michael's, Ousebridge, reported to Grindal in 1575 that their parson was also vicar of Askham Richard, and ministered at St Michael's by sequestration. At All Saints, Peaseholm, Anthony Iveson, parson of Burghwallis, in addition to being a vicar choral in the Minster, had not shown his dispensation for combining the offices. The churchwardens at St Sampson's stated explicitly that they had not heard the Homilies in their church because their vicar was also a curate in the Minster, and lacked the time to read them. The vicar of St Lawrence's ran his parish in conjunction with that of Heslington, a village a mile or so away. At least pluralism of this kind involving two adjoining parishes could be justified in a time of clergy shortage. The fairly common

---

23 Borthwick HCAB 3, fols 126ʳ, 131ʳ, 142ᵛ; D & C Prob. Reg. 5, fol. 90ᵛ; V 1567-8 CB 2, fols 83ʳ⁻ᵛ, 115ʳ, 150ʳ, 211ʳ, 225ᵛ; HCAB 4, fols 6ʳ, 14ʳ, 21ʳ, 34ʳ; HCAB 7, fols 100ʳ, 101ʳ, 105ᵛ, 106ʳ, 110ʳ, 127ʳ; Aveling, *Catholic Recusancy*, pp. 166–8; Borthwick Archbp. Reg. 30, fols 45ʳ⁻ᵛ, 178ᵛ⁻9ʳ.

practice of holding a city cure with a living miles away in one of the Ridings, or even further afield, was far less satisfactory. At All Saints, North Street, the new parson, Simon Blunt, seems to have been permanently absent, having substituted a mere reader, Henry Wilson.[24]

The custom of vicars choral taking a city living became more than ever entrenched at this period. Robert Burland, a vicar choral continuously from 1534 until his death in 1585, worked in a succession of York parishes – St Michael-le-Belfrey, St Helen's, Stonegate, Holy Trinity, King's Court – while also rector of Angram. In 1572 he acquired the rectory of Brayton near Selby, and no longer had the financial need to minister to a city parish. A bachelor, he used one of his nephews, Thomas Tomlinson, as his curate at Brayton and placed another nephew, John Tomlinson, among the vicars choral. Edward Bowling, vicar choral and the Elizabethan rector of St Crux, also held the living of Sherburn in Elmet. A rather younger man, John Richardson, vicar choral in 1556, was still a vicar choral in addition to being rector of St Saviour's and of Thornton in Pickering Lyth, when he made his will in 1608. New vicars, as they took up their office in the Minster, followed exactly the same pattern. Like Burland, Henry Hooke had a Yorkshire living, in this case Angram, in addition to his York living of Holy Trinity, Goodramgate, from 1567 to 1605; and John Hunter served at St Sampson's, St Cuthbert's, St Michael-le-Belfrey's, and lastly, All Saints, Pavement, from the 1570s till his death in 1601.[25]

The example set by the generality of these vicars choral fell considerably below the standard expected by the Minster dignitaries, and successive archbishops continued to enquire minutely into the education of the vicars just as Holgate had done. Grindal ordered all vicars to be present at the daily divinity lecture in the Minster, and arranged for them to be examined monthly by the chancellor or some other senior cleric. He commanded them to receive the communion whenever it was celebrated; and wished them to read systematically both the Latin and English Bible, beginning with St Paul's Epistle to the Romans. In 1577 archbishop Sandys instituted investigations into the conduct of the lesser clergy in the Minster, enquiring whether any officers or ministers had spoken 'against the word of God', or were 'known in their hearts to be against the religion publicly received'; and the incidents concerning Barton's wife confirm that he had some foundation for this suspicion of conservatism in Minster circles. Some vicars choral, too, could in no sense be seen as leading lives of Protestant sobriety. In 1590 the High Commission Court took the unprecedented and severe step of summoning Hugh Hookes, John Howell and John Richardson, almost a third of the complement of vicars choral, to face a charge of excessive drinking. The Commissioners prohibited them from patronizing York alehouses in the future, and went so far as to imprison their ringleader,

24 Borthwick V 1567/8 CB 2, fols 211^{r-v}, 81^v; V 1575 CB 1, fol. 3^v–7^v.
25 Borthwick D & C Prob. Reg. 5, fol. 117^v–118^r; Orig. Chancery Will 1608.

Howell, who had been observed lurching and staggering in the city streets.[26]

These pluralists, often at least partially-absentee clergy, not surprisingly enjoyed far less friendly relations with the aldermanic class than their predecessors had done in the earlier decades of the century. From soon after Elizabeth came to the throne, very few aldermen, in contrast with their previous attitudes, made bequests to their local incumbents, and now it was less and less usual for ministers to witness their wills. The majority of the governing class appears to have been apathetic rather than hostile towards the new Protestant Church, but, especially in the 1570s, a minority of the City Council certainly inclined towards Catholic recusancy. Both alderman Dineley and alderman Cripling had recusant wives; and Cripling went over to out-and-out recusancy himself after his term of office as mayor had come to an end. The scandal of Cripling using his position as mayor to shield York Catholics from the rigours of recusancy fines highlighted the problem of implementing Protestantism in York. Since 1560 the citizens had supposedly been listening to Protestant preaching in the Minster; and from 1570, according to a corporation order, two members of every household should have been attending Minster sermons Sunday by Sunday. Despite these regulations, none of the civic hierarchy personally displayed any active reforming zeal, in marked contrast to their counterparts in the cities of London, Bristol or Coventry, or in much smaller towns like Leicester or Bury St Edmunds. In 1579 the Earl of Huntingdon, a committed Protestant who, since his arrival in York as President of the Council in the North late in 1572, had done all in his power to aid Grindal in his design to advance informed Protestantism in the northern province, determined to take action to overcome the lethargy of both the civic clergy and the governing elite. Earlier injunctions issued at episcopal visitations bidding congregations without preaching ministers to go to the Minster to hear sermons had clearly not worked. Huntingdon, therefore, decided to try the different tack of bringing preaching to the people, and wrote to the York corporation urging them to create and finance a civic lectureship, a post which had already been set up at his prompting in his own town of Leicester almost twenty years previously. The city aldermen showed the greatest reluctance to gather the necessary funds, but at least agreed in principle in 1580 to the scheme, and Huntingdon refused to let the matter rest until he had procured a preacher for the city. This lecturer received a salary of £30, raised a few years later to £40, an amount far more than any city cleric who was not a considerable pluralist could ever have hoped to achieve. The first civic preacher provided by the Lord President did not stay in York long; but in 1585 his successor, Richard Harwood, a Cambridge graduate, gave years of devoted service to the city, and at last members of the corporation seem to have discovered the positive attractions of Protestantism. Early in 1597 alderman Robert Askwith asked Harwood

---

26 Frere, *Visitation Articles and Injunctions*, pp. 345–54; Minster Lib. Collection 1906; Borthwick HCAB 11, fol. 224[r].

to preach his funeral sermon; in June 1599 alderman Beckwith left Harwood 20*s*. to perform the same office for him; and this marks the beginning of a practice which soon became customary at least among the city's governors. When their lecturer died in 1615, an enthusiast went so far as to compose an epitaph to commemorate the exceptional nature of Harwood's ministry:

> Noah's faithfulness, Abraham's obedience,
> Phineas' strong zeal, Job's praised innocence,
> St Jerome's love, Chrysostom's diligence,
> Augustine's labour and experience
> Lie buried with Harwood in this tomb . . .

It is difficult to conceive of such sentiments being expressed about any city cleric in the Elizabethan period.[27]

By the later 1580s and 1590s the leading citizens of York were also beginning, for the first time, to make strongly Protestant assertions of faith. Alderman Christopher Maltby died in 1585 'most faithfully believing and firmly trusting and hoping to be a member of our Lord and Saviour Jesus Christ and partaker of that redemption and justification that was made by his most glorious passion, death and resurrection.' In 1599 alderman Robert Brook set out his very individual beliefs in much detail in the preamble to his will. His only hope lay in Christ's 'right cruel death and blood shedding' which had appeased

the wrath of God the father that he had against mankind for the disobedience of our forefather Adam, so that my trust is that only by this sacrifice of Christ his body once offered upon the altar of the cross I shall be saved and my sins and offences put out of God's remembrance and not imputed unto me, for Christ's obedience shall satisfy God the father's wrath for my disobedience.

He then went on to consign his children to his wife Jane, in the sure confidence that she would continue their education 'in the fear of the Lord and true knowledge of his word.' In 1600 alderman Birkby exuded a similar trust to be saved 'by the death and blood of his son Jesus Christ . . . and by no other merits or ceremonies.' Elsewhere among convinced English Protestants such statements may have been almost common form a generation or more earlier, but in York, where less than twenty years previously alderman Bean had been hoping 'that at the departure of my body and soul all the holy angels of God may be present with me and to receive my soul', they signify a real and decided break with the past.[28]

The last decade of Elizabeth's reign in fact seems to have been the time when the members of York corporation, until 1580 passive if not actively hostile

27 A. Raine (ed.), *York Civic Records*, vii, Yorkshire Archaeological Society, Record Series CXV (1950), 13; York City Archives Housebook 1577–80, fol. 189; Housebook 1581–5, fols 54, 184; Housebook 1585–7, fol. 10; F. Drake, *Eboracum* (1736), p. 296; Borthwick Prob. Reg. 27, pt I, fol. 25^{r-v}; Prob. Reg. 27, pt II, fol. 722^{r-v}.
28 Borthwick Prob. Reg. 22, pt II, fols 673^v–4^r; Prob. Reg. 27, pt II, fols 596^r–7^v; Prob. Reg. 31, pt. I, fols 267^v–8^v; Prob. Reg. 21, pt II, fols 414^v–15^r.

towards the new settlement of religion, finally started to take the initiative in the development of civic Protestantism. Whereas aldermen had earlier continued the old custom of indiscriminate almsgiving to the poor on the day of their burial – as in 1571 when Percival Crawforth desired 1,000 halfpenny loaves to be distributed to the poor on his death – by the 1590s their bequests had become much more purposeful. Alderman Robert Askwith gave the mayor and corporation £20 to lend out to the poor in perpetuity; and alderman Brook did the same with a smaller sum, a trend which ultimately led to alderman Agar's bequest in 1631 of £100 to the corporation to set the poor of the city on work. By around 1600 the city began benefiting from the nation-wide increase in the numbers of university graduates entering the Church. Henry Hoyle, B.A., came to St Crux from Peterhouse, Cambridge, in 1595, and stayed for nine years, establishing a considerable name for himself as a preacher before moving to a better living in the county. With men like Hoyle in a city living, and aldermen such as Herbert and Brook sending their sons to the university, the leaders of civic society were being brought more in touch with academic influences. Gradually some aldermen came to realize that, if they were to keep men of the stature of Hoyle in their parish churches, they had themselves to subsidize their grossly inadequate endowment.[29]

There can be no doubt that, by the beginning of the seventeenth century, members of the corporation placed a very high value on the civic lectureship. In 1612, this time without any outside interference, they created a second lectureship. As the century progressed, these lectureships were linked to the central parish of All Saints, Pavement, and when held by the incumbent, a lectureship could prove an important supplement to his stipend. Individual aldermen again began to remember clerics in their wills. In 1616, for example, alderman Robinson left Roger Bellwood, the graduate vicar of St Crux, £5, Mr William Sadler, preacher, 20s., Mr Rogers, preacher, 20s., Mr Collingwood, preacher, 20s., and the readers, that is, the non-preaching ministers, of St Olave's and St Michael-le-Belfrey a mere 10s. – a nice economic distinction of their relative worth. At the end of James I's reign alderman Moseley's benefactions had become even more wide ranging: he left to Mr White, the incumbent of St Michael's, Spurriergate, and to his successors, an annuity of £4 for 'holy and sacramental sermons and religious exercises'. As with the bequests to provide work for the poor, these voluntary attempts, by leading laymen to improve the financial standing of approved civic clergy, increased in the 1630s, culminating in the will of Elias Micklewaite, who in 1633 not only gave 40s. for five years to Mr Cudworth, if he should remain so long at Holy Trinity, Micklegate, and left bequests to other favoured preachers, but laid aside £40 towards buying up impropriate livings 'to be paid when there is feoffees appoin-

29 Borthwick D & C Prob. Reg. 5, fol. 59[r-v]; Prob. Reg. 27, pt I, fol. 25[r-v]; Prob. Reg. 41, pt I, fols 447[v]-9.

ted in this city'. Given that 1633 was the very year in which Laud had broken the organization of the London Feoffees for Impropriations, archbishop Neile and his supporters at the Minster cannot have failed to grasp the significance of a gesture such as this.[30]

By the time of the accession of Charles I, if not by that of his father, York had become an avowedly Protestant city. Both the members of the corporation and the civic clergy, now much more frequently graduate, had explicitly committed themselves to Protestantism. The question remains why in York this transformation had taken the better part of a century, when in many other urban centres the transition from Catholicism to active Protestantism seems to have been accomplished very much more rapidly. Undoubtedly the hold of the institutional Church on the city made for conservatism: the vicars choral in the Bedern went on living much like their Catholic predecessors well into the third quarter of the sixteenth century, while the presence of former monks, friars and chantry priests in civic churches until the second half of Elizabeth's reign also seems to have inhibited any wide-scale movement for fundamental change among the parish clergy. Had the amalgamations of York churches in 1547 been much more drastic, and the number of parishes been reduced not to twenty-five but to eight, as was indeed contemplated in 1650, the income of a city living could have been brought up from an average of £5–£10 to perhaps £30, and then active Protestant preachers might have come to the city earlier. Much of the responsibility, nevertheless, for the slowness in implementing Protestantism must rest with the corporation. Until the creation of the civic lectureship there was no one city preacher of sufficient standing to inspire the members of the ruling elite with an enthusiasm for propagating Protestantism. There was indeed no particular minister whose presence and continuance in the city the chief inhabitants could control. This absence of local lay initiative in furthering Protestantism for most of the Elizabethan period, in direct contrast with the attitude of the governing classes in some towns (especially in the south and the midlands), and also in direct contrast with the attitude of York corporation itself early in the following century, is the factor most difficult to explain. The city fathers do not seem to have had contacts with university Protestantism in the 1530s, 1540s and 1550s; indeed, all their ties lay with the representatives of 'the old religion', the monks and chantry priests. Only such intangibles as these can perhaps help to account for the length of time it took to achieve the active practice of Protestantism in the city of York.[31]

30 Borthwick Prob. Reg. 34, pt I, fols 170ᵛ–2ᵛ; Prob. Reg. 38, pt I, fols 238ᵛ–40ʳ; Prob. Reg. 42, pt I, fols 109ʳ–10ᵛ; I. M. Calder, *Activities of the Puritan Faction of the Church of England, 1625–33* (1957), pp. xi–xxiv.

31 The lack of success of Protestant preaching in Elizabethan Lancashire, where there was also little support from influential lay people in the later sixteenth century, has been discussed in a recent article: C. Haigh, 'Puritan Evangelism in the Reign of Elizabeth I', *English Historical Review*, xcii (1977), pp. 30–58.

XII

The Heart of
The Pilgrim's Progress

❦

GEOFFREY F. NUTTALL

The list of books licensed for publication issued on 18 February 1678 looks much like any other of that period. It consists, as usual, of books of divinity, history, physick, mathematicks, miscellanies, law, plays and poems, with other kinds of literature. The order in these lists is not inflexible, but divinity always comes first. In this issue divinity claims fifteen titles, ranging from a *Sermon preached before the Honourable the House of Commons* and an *Exposition of the Catechism of the Church of England* to *The Young Man's Calling, or The Whole Duty of Youth* and *The Seaman's Spiritual Companion, or Navigation Spiritualized*. Tucked in amongst them is *The Pilgrim's Progress from this World to that which is to come; delivered under the Similitude of a Dream: wherein is discovered the manner of his setting out, his dangerous Journey, and safe arrival at the desired Country*. By J. Bunyan. In Octavo. Price, bound, 1s. 6d. Printed for N. Ponder at the Peacock in the Poultry.[1]

1678 is a long time ago: 1980 was then unimaginably far ahead. Had he known that, three hundred years later, his book would not only still be read but would be discussed in lectures and sermons and published pieces, would Bunyan have been surprised? I hardly think so. Before his death ten years later his book had already run into as many editions, or more. He must have learned to live with at least the beginnings of the popularity which, in time, has carried his book not simply into innumerable editions but into more languages, it is said, than any other book but the Bible.

Today the standard edition of *The Pilgrim's Progress* – as also of *Grace Abounding*, and, it is intended, of all his other writings – is a splendid volume published in 1960 by the Clarendon Press at Oxford, under the care of Professor Sharrock of King's College, London, the general editor of the whole series.[2] This, I think, *would* surprise Bunyan. What, one cannot help wondering, would he think of having his books published by what was to him an excluding and (in his terms) almost pagan university, and under the editorship of a papist?

Now I saw in my Dream, that at the end of this Valley lay blood, bones, ashes, and mangled bodies of men, even of Pilgrims that had gone this way formerly: And while I was musing what should be the reason, I espied a little before me a Cave, where two Giants, Pope and Pagan, dwelt in old time, by whose Power and Tyranny the Men whose bones, blood, ashes, &c., lay there, were cruelly put to death. . . . but I have learned since, that Pagan has been dead many a day; and as for the other, though he be yet alive, he is by reason of age, and also of the many shrewd brushes that he met with in his younger dayes, grown so crazy, and stiff in his joynts, that he can now do little

1 *Term Catalogues*, ed. E. Arber, vol. i (London, 1903), p. 299.
2 John Bunyan, *The Pilgrim's Progress*, ed. J. B. Wharey, 2nd edn revised by Roger Sharrock (Oxford, 1960).

more than sit in his Caves mouth, grinning at Pilgrims as they go by, and biting his nails, because he cannot come at them.

What is this? Prejudice – offensive, or merely comical? Or is it more? For it is followed by these lines:

> O world of wonder! (I can say no less)
> That I should be preserv'd in that distress
> That I have met with here! O blessed bee
> That hand that from it hath delivered me! . . .
> Yes, Snares, and Pits, and Traps, and Nets did lie
> My path about, that worthless silly I
> Might have been catch'd, intangled, and cast down:
> But since I live, let JESUS wear the Crown.[3]

To class pope and pagan, Rome and the (Gentile) world, together was then in a respectable Reformed tradition.[4] Bunyan returns to it later.[5] More remarkable here, and a clue to much else, is the reference to Christ.

Today *The Pilgrim's Progress* is studied mainly as great imaginative literature, as the work of imaginative genius. What would Bunyan make of this? So far as words go, probably not much. To Bunyan 'imagination' denoted what was 'made up', fantastic, not true, and, where religion was concerned, therefore, what was dishonouring to God. In this he was at one with his age as a whole:

> The lunatic, the lover and the poet
> Are of imagination all compact.

> And my imaginations are as foul
> As Vulcan's stithy.

> The imagination of man's heart is evil from his youth . . .
> He hath scattered the proud in the imagination of their hearts:

so the Bard and the Authorized Version. The recovery of the word, as denoting the power 'to create . . . to idealize and to unify',[6] what is now termed creative imagination, is no older than Coleridge, whose words these are, except that he still so far reverenced God alone as the Creator that the most he allows imagination is to recreate. This Bunyan would understand. The sound, the sane Christian will do no more, and will aim to do no more, than to think God's thoughts

---

3 *Pilgrim's Progress*, pp. 65–6.
4 Cf. the title *Les trois conformités; assavoir l'harmonie et convenance de l'Eglise Romaine avec le Paganisme, Judaisme . . .*, by François de Croy (?Amsterdam, 1605), translated by W. Hart in 1620 as *The three conformities, or the harmony and agreement of the Roman Church with Gentilisme, Judaisme . . .* (London, 1620); also William Greenhill, *Exposition continued upon the nineteen last chapters of the prophet Ezekiel* (London, 1662), epistle to reader: 'Do not Judaize, do not Gentilize, do not Romanize, but see you Christianize.'
5 *Pilgrim's Progress*, p. 89, of Vanity Fair: 'the Ware of Rome and her Merchandize is greatly promoted in this fair.'
6 S. T. Coleridge, *Select Poetry and Prose*, ed. S. Potter (London, 1933), p. 246.

and feel God's feelings after him; and the pictures, or images, on which the Christian will dwell will be those which God provides; and provides, not solely but predominantly, in the Bible. This is the meaning of all those Biblical references in *The Pilgrim's Progress* which Professor Sharrock dutifully reproduces in the margin. Bunyan's images may be so far transmuted by his genius that they can be called his own, can even be recognized as characteristically his; but they have a source, a basis, for they are all well pegged, in the one book with which his contemporaries were familiar, the Bible. 'During our golden seventeenth century the Bible worked as a midwife to bring forth a whole great literature. It enabled a tinker of Bedford to write *The Pilgrim's Progress*.'[7] 'I will use similitudes', states the titlepage of the first edition. Bunyan knew what he was doing, and did what he intended; but he also provides the reference for the words, even here, namely Hosea 12:10. In fact Bunyan's manner is consistent metaphor, not a succession of similes. But to the purpose to use images to describe experience, and to use them so powerfully as to evoke experience – to this Bunyan was no stranger, so long as it is accepted that the experience was not imaginary but real. What follows is offered as tribute to one who has not only attended to institutions in all their detail and shown a readiness to assess the issues arising, but who treats of the Reformation as affecting generations of ordinary people and making a difference to them.[8]

In the seventeenth century self-consciousness was coming to birth: in Descartes' *cogito, ergo sum*; in Rembrandt's innumerable paintings of his own face; in the great number of diaries and autobiographies. Some years before the Civil War a poem called *Self Civil War* appeared.[9] In the ethical sphere a number of words are coined which are compounded with 'self'.[10] What Bunyan does is, within this new self-consciousness, to place Christ firmly. 'For a more clear discovery of themselves to themselves', he writes, men come to Christ.[11]

For himself it started on that day when, as he recounts the story in *Grace Abounding*,

the good providence of God did cast me to Bedford, to work on my calling; and in one of the streets of that town, I came where there was three or four poor women sitting at a door in the Sun, and talking about the things of God; and being now willing to hear them discourse, I drew near to hear what they said. . . . They talked how God had visited their souls with his love in the Lord Jesus. . . . And me thought

---

7 A. G. Dickens, *The English Reformation* (London, 1964), p. 136.
8 It is illuminating to read Professor Dickens's study of his 'old friend of more than forty years' standing', Robert Parkyn, in Peter Brooks (ed.), *Christian Spirituality, Essays in Honour of Gordon Rupp* (London, 1975), pp. 141–81, in the light of his critical remarks on the historian's 'externalizing habit' at the expense of religious impulse in an essay on Sleidan in R. Buick Knox (ed.), *Reformation Conformity and Dissent* (London, 1977), pp. 17–43.
9 Cf. my *Holy Spirit in Puritan Faith and Experience* (Oxford, 1946), pp. 7–8.
10 W. Franz, *Der Wert der engl. Kultur für Deutschlands Entwicklung* (1913), pp. 4–5, cited by K. Müller, *Kirchengeschichte*, II, ii (Tübingen, 1919), p. 443, n. 1.
11 John Bunyan, *Works*, ed. G. Offor (London and Edinburgh, 1862), vol. i, p. 225.

they spake as if joy did make them speak: . . . they were to me, as if they had found a new world.[12]

This was only the beginning; but gradually, as he states more than once, 'God led me into something of the mystery of union with Christ'; and all the way his experience was vivid and real. On one occasion he writes, 'With joy I told my Wife, O now I know, I know! . . . that night was a good night to me, I never had but few better; . . . I could scarce lie in my Bed for joy, and peace, and triumph, thorow Christ.' On another occasion, 'I could not be contented with saying, I believe, and am sure; methought I was more then sure.' At last he gave himself up utterly and for ever:

Wherefore, thought I, the point being thus, I am for going on, and venturing my eternal State with Christ, whether I have comfort here or no; if God doth not come in, thought I, I will leap off the Ladder even blindfold into Eternitie, sink or swim, come heaven, come hell; Lord Jesus, if thou wilt catch me, do; if not, I will venture for thy Name.[13]

This is from *Grace Abounding*; but his imagination is involved, no less than in *The Pilgrim's Progress*. It is the same man writing, here or there: it is imaginative writing and it is also real. And ever after, whatever he was doing – preaching, writing, or simply lying in prison year after year – Christ was at the centre of his consciousness, controlling and colouring his imaginative genius and powers of expression. 'Hast thou not sometimes as it were the very warmth of his wings overshadowing the face of thy soul . . . ?',[14] he asks. Henri Talon draws attention to what, in a Kierkegaardian phrase, he calls Bunyan's '*contemporanéité*' *avec Jésus*.[15] 'Me thought', Talon quotes from Bunyan, 'I was as if I had seen him born, as if I had seen him grow up, as if I had seen walk thorow this world, from the Cradle to his Cross'.[16] Behind the path of Christian in *The Pilgrim's Progress* is the path of the greater pilgrim, 'from the Cradle to his Cross'; and the 'reality' of *The Pilgrim's Progress*, its extraordinarily convincing power, so that a reader fortunate enough to have read it or had it read to him in childhood has scenes that stay with him all his life, is rooted in the reality, however mysterious it remained, of Bunyan's own 'union with Christ'. What he wrote was not something imagined *ab extra*, an outer varnish or an escape-mechanism to conceal or to avoid what was real, it *was* real, he was writing of what he knew; just as he preached and prayed what he knew, and only that. In preaching, for instance, he notes, 'I never endeavoured to, nor durst make use of other men's lines': 'I preached what I felt, what I smartingly did feel.'[17]

12 John Bunyan, *Grace Abounding to the Chief of Sinners*, ed. R. Sharrock (Oxford, 1962), pp. 14–15.
13 Ibid., pp. 73, 86, 82, 87, 101.
14 John Bunyan, *Works*, vol. i, p. 299.
15 Henri Talon, *John Bunyan: l'homme et l'oeuvre* (Paris, n.d.), p. 89.
16 *Grace Abounding*, p. 38.
17 Ibid., pp. 87, 85.

Likewise with prayer. 'Those prayers in the Common Prayer book', he writes, 'was such as was made by other men, and not by the motions of the Holy Ghost.'[18] 'There is in Prayer', rather, 'an unbosoming of a man's self': 'the whole man is engaged': 'right Prayer bubbleth out of the heart . . . as blood is forced out of the flesh.'[19] Though obviously this has its limitations, the implication of it is vital for understanding *The Pilgrim's Progress*. Awareness of, contact with, Christ, immediate and direct, is at the heart of the book. By every artistic means at his disposal and by the cumulative effect of an unselfish and single-minded purpose, Bunyan will share this with his reader, and in the sharing will convince him that it is real and may be as controlling and all-important in his reader's life as he has proved it to be day after day in his own life.

Through Bunyan's artistry the figure of Christ is present throughout *The Pilgrim's Progress* in a variety of ways. Though he may not be aware of it, the reader can never turn more than a page or two without, in one way and another, being reminded of him. To begin with, there are the sayings and actions of Jesus as reported in the gospels for Bunyan to lift (neat) and then comment on or illustrate within the structure of his story. It would be of no small interest to list and classify the logia recorded in *The Pilgrim's Progress* and to observe the use to which Bunyan puts them. As an example, take the 'surround' of the wicket-gate. Right at the beginning of the story Evangelist asks Christian, 'Do you see yonder Wicket-gate?' 'No,' Christian replies, but sets out hopefully, only to be diverted, almost at once, by Mr Worldly-Wiseman. When Evangelist comes to his rescue a second time, almost the first question Evangelist puts to him is 'Did I not direct thee the way to the little Wicket-gate?'; and here, in the middle of a severe dressing-down, interspersed with words of encouragement and hope, Evangelist quotes the saying of Jesus, 'The Lord says, Strive to enter in at the strait gate, . . . for strait is the gate that leadeth unto life, and few there be that find it.' 'So in process of time', we read a page or two later, 'Christian got up to the Gate.'[20] Of course, in making so much of the strait gate/wicket-gate motif, Bunyan displays his Puritanism. He is always in earnest, always one of those who would 'go further', very different from that earlier writer concerned with pilgrims whom Dom David Knowles described as 'the typical easy-going *croyant* who . . . sits loose to moral standards through life but makes his peace with God as years advance.'[21] The present point is that the motif springs from a logion: 'the Lord says . . .' And Evangelist goes on with another: 'the King of glory hath told thee, that he that will save his life shall lose it.' 'The Lord', 'the Governour of that Countrey', 'the King', 'the Law-giver', 'Master', 'the King of glory', 'the Son of the Blessed': all these titles, and there are probably others,

18 Ibid., p. 114.
19 John Bunyan, *The Doctrine of the Law and Grace unfolded* and *I will pray with the Spirit*, ed. R. L. Greaves (Oxford, 1976), pp. 240, 239, 237.
20 *Pilgrim's Progress*, pp. 10, 20, 22, 25.
21 D. Knowles, *The Religious Orders in England*, vol. ii (Cambridge, 1955), p. 112, of Chaucer.

come in the first twenty-five pages of the book. Even in this way the reader is all the time being referred to Christ and reminded of him. Occasionally, though not often, he is referred to by name. When the Interpreter shows Christian first 'a Fire burning against a Wall, and one standing by it always, casting much Water upon it to quench it: Yet did the Fire burn higher and higher'; and then had Christian 'about to the back side of the Wall, where he saw a Man with a Vessel of Oyl in his hand, of the which he did also continually cast, but secretly, into the fire'; and Christian asks the Interpreter, 'What means this?' The Interpreter replies, 'This is Christ, who continually, with the Oyl of his Grace, maintains the work already begun in the heart; ... And in that thou sawest, that the Man stood behind the Wall to maintain the fire; this is to teach thee, that it is hard for the tempted to see how this work of Grace is maintained in the soul.'[22]

A similar pattern, if this is not too sophisticated a word, may be observed in the following twenty-five pages, which include a still more famous scene, where Christian

came at a place somewhat ascending; and upon that place stood a Cross, and a little below in the bottom a Sepulcher. So I saw in my Dream, that just as Christian came up with the Cross, his burden loosed from off his Shoulders, and fell from off his back; and began to tumble; and so continued to do, till it came to the mouth of the Sepulcher, where it fell in, and I saw it no more.

Then was Christian glad and lightsom, and said with a merry heart, He hath given me rest, by his sorrow; and life by his death:

'He', note; indeed

Christian gave three leaps for joy, and went on singing.

> Blest Cross! blest Sepulcher! blest rather be
> The Man that there was put to shame for me.[23]

'The Master' now becomes 'My Master', 'the Lord' now becomes 'My Lord'; and the personal reference is made explicit in Christian's answer to a question put to him in the house 'built by the Lord of the Hill ... for the relief and security of Pilgrims.' 'What is it that makes you so desirous to go to Mount Zion?' he is asked; and he replies, 'Why, there I hope to see him alive, that did hang dead on the Cross. ... For to tell you truth, I love him, because I was by him eased of my burden.'[24] In these few words Bunyan connects the death of Jesus in history, the present experience of benefits gained from it, and the beatific vision at the end of time – three things which came similarly together for him in the observance of the Lord's Supper. I think he means to suggest this when he goes on to relate, shortly afterwards:

Now I saw in my Dream, that thus they sat talking together until supper was ready.

22 *Pilgrim's Progress*, pp. 22, 32–3.
23 Ibid., p. 38.
24 Ibid., pp. 46, 50.

So when they had made ready, they sat down to meat; Now the Table was furnished with fat things, and with Wine that was well refined; and all their talk at the Table was about the Lord of the Hill: As namely, about what he had done, and wherefore he did what he did, and why he had builded that House: . . . And besides, there were some of them of the Household that said, they had seen, and spoke with him since he did dye on the Cross; and they have attested, that they had it from his own lips, that he is such a lover of poor Pilgrims, that the like is not to be found from the East to the West, . . . and that they had heard him say and affirm, That he would not dwell in the Mountain of Zion alone.

No wonder that in the 'large upper Chamber, whose window opened towards the Sun rising' and whose name was Peace, Christian 'slept till break of day. And then he awoke and sang,'

> Where am I now? Is this the love and care
> Of Jesus, for the men that Pilgrims are?
> Thus to provide! That I should be forgiven!
> And dwell already the next door to Heaven![25]

This introduces another kind of awareness of Christ. He is constantly brought before the reader not only in references to his words and his death as recorded in Scripture, he is also in some sense mystically present: as when Hopeful tells Christian how 'suddenly, as I thought, I saw the Lord Jesus look down from Heaven upon me', and goes on to describe a conversation between Christ and himself which Christian at once acknowledges 'was a Revelation of Christ to your soul indeed'; or when Christian tells Hopeful, ' 'Tis good also that we desire of the King a Convoy, yea that he will go with us himself. . . . O my Brother, if he will but go along with us, what need we be afraid of ten thousands that shall set themselves against us . . .'[26] Bunyan would surely understand what Gerard Manley Hopkins means in his poem 'The Blessed Virgin compared to the Air we Breathe', when he writes

> I say that we are wound
> With mercy round and round
> As if with air –

only for Bunyan, of course, the subject would not be the Virgin, but Christ –

> My more than meat and drink,
> My meal at every wink;
> This air, which, by life's law,
> My lung must draw and draw . . .
> And men are meant to share
> Her/His life as life does air.[27]

But the form in which, for Bunyan, Christ is mystically present is, mainly, the

25 Ibid., pp. 52–3.
26 Ibid., pp. 143, 132.
27 G. M. Hopkins, *Poems*, ed. R. Bridges (London, 1943), pp. 57–8.

lives of those whom Christian meets and in whom, by his holy and loving Spirit, Christ is unmistakably active. And this in two ways. First, there are all the people who prove so helpful to Christian along the way. The person in charge of the wicket-gate is named Good-will; he not only opens the gate but gives Christian a pull over the threshold; and he tells Christian (even without a marginal reference to the words of the Spirit of Christ in Revelation) 'An open Door is set before thee, and no man can shut it.' There is the Interpreter, who shows Christian the picture of the 'Man, whom the Lord of the Place whither thou art going, hath Authorized, to be thy Guide in all difficult places.' There are the maidens in the house built for the entertainment of pilgrims, who say, 'Come in thou blessed of the Lord'; who assure him 'how willing their Lord was to receive into his favour any, even any, though they in time past had offered great affronts to his Person and proceedings'; who urge and persuade him to stay on for an extra day; and who, when the time does come for him to leave, 'would accompany him down to the foot of the Hill.'[28] All along the way, Christian meets with these people who are loving to him, and in their kindness Christ's love shines through. It cannot but do so, because what they say and offer to Christian Bunyan himself is saying through them to the reader, as he was accustomed to say it when he went preaching – as, in fact, he does say it in some of his other published pieces, such as the little book entitled *Come and Welcome to Jesus Christ*:

But, saith another, I am so heartless, so slow, and, as I think, so indifferent in my coming, that, to speak truth, I know not whether my kind of coming ought to be called a coming to Christ . . .
   Poor coming soul, thou art like the man that would ride full gallop, whose horse will hardly trot! . . . But be of good comfort, Christ judgeth not according to the fierceness of outward motion, but according to the sincerity of the heart and inward parts. . . . Hadst thou seen those that came to the Lord Jesus in the days of his flesh, how slowly, how hobblingly, they came to him, by reason of their infirmities; and also how friendly, and kindly, and graciously, he received them, and gave them the desire of their hearts, thou wouldest not, as thou dost, make such objections against thyself, in thy coming to Jesus Christ.[29]

Here Bunyan can be heard preaching; how understandable that one of his hearers, Agnes Beaumont, could write, 'Oh, I had such a sight of Iesus Christ yt brake my heart to peeces' – 'it was like death to me to bee kept from such A meeting.'[30] Preaching or not, it has the same style, and the same purpose, as *The Pilgrim's Progress*.

To return to this: in some moods it seems natural to compare it with the *Divine Comedy*. Yet paradoxically, in the medieval work, where the sense of the Church might be expected to be all-pervasive, Dante, while also Everyman,

28 *Pilgrim's Progress*, pp. 25–6, 29, 47, 53–5.
29 John Bunyan, *Works*, vol. i, pp. 251–2.
30 Agnes Beaumont, *Narrative*, ed. G. B. Harrison (London, n.d.), pp. 17, 11.

is himself and himself alone, and in a sense is also alone, in that, while he meets crowds of other people, he alone persists throughout the poem; whereas in *The Pilgrim's Progress*, written in the century when the individual is coming to self-consciousness, one has much more the sense of company, of Christian *with* Faithful and *with* Hopeful, and of their being joined by friends and companions along the way. The reason is this: whereas Dante was both a solitary by tempera-ment and a political exile by circumstance, Bunyan, whether in prison or not, was the leader and friend, and eventually the minister, of a congregation of Christ's people in Bedford.

These people, Bunyan's fellow-Christians in life, are mostly anonymous – or, to be more precise, since the records containing their names are actually still extant, their names are mostly no more than names. But in a deeper sense we *know* them, because Bunyan has put them into his book. They were men and women with the usual doubts and fears, anxieties and weaknesses; and in *The Pilgrim's Progress* Bunyan paints them to the life, and with a marvellous tender-ness and gentleness. I do not mean Mr Stand-fast or Mr Great-heart; I mean Mr Despondency and his daughter Much-afraid, Mr Feeble-mind and Mr Ready-to-halt. They are part of the church life which was Bunyan's life, the people who would pray for him when he was in prison and perhaps get a present through to him, when they dared not venture to come and visit him themselves. Here is Mr Feeble-mind:

I am a man of no strength at all, of Body, nor yet of Mind, but would, if I could, tho' I can but craul, spend my Life in the Pilgrims way. When I came at the Gate that is at the head of the Way, the Lord of that place did entertain me freely. Neither objected he against my weakly Looks, nor against my feeble Mind; but gave me such things that were necessary for my Journey, and bid me hope to the end. . . . because the Hill Difficulty was judged too hard for me, I was carried up that by one of his Servants. . . . they bid me be of good Chear, and said that it was the will of their Lord, that Comfort should be given to the feeble minded, and so went on their own pace. . . . this I have resolved on, to wit, to run when I can, to go when I cannot run, and to creep when I cannot go. As to the main, I thank him that loves me, I am fixed; my way is before me, my Mind is beyond the River that has no Bridg, tho I am as you see, but of a feeble Mind.[31]

And in the end 'the Post sounded his Horn at his Chamber Door' and 'came in and told him, saying, I am come to tell thee that the Master hath need of thee'; and in a little 'he entered the River as the rest. His last Words were, Hold out Faith and Patience.'[32] In this passage the love of Christ shines through, not only in Bunyan's tenderness towards Mr Feeble-mind in the *book*, but because in Mr Feeble-mind in the church in Bedford Bunyan had joyfully recognized the

31 *Pilgrim's Progress*, pp. 267–8.
32 Ibid., pp. 307–8. See further, G. F. Nuttall, 'Church Life in Bunyan's Bedfordshire', *Baptist Quarterly*, xxvi, pp. 305–15.

transforming spirit of Christ, not despising the least member for whom Christ died. Christ is mystically present here too.

This must surely get through to, and move, any but a hard-hearted reader. The reader with theological interests may ask: is it not all rather one-sided? Is Bunyan a Marcionite? Or like Blake in one of his mischievous moments? 'Thinking as I do that the Creator of this World is a very Cruel Being, & being a Worshipper of Christ, I cannot help saying: "the Son, O how unlike the Father!" First God Almighty comes with a Thump on the Head. Then Jesus Christ comes with a balm to heal it.'[33] But Bunyan is not like this. His theology is single, like himself. 'In my preaching of the Word . . .,' he writes, 'the Lord did lead me to begin where his Word begins with Sinners', with the Law; for 'the terrours of the Law, and guilt for my transgressions, lay heavy on my Conscience.' Sin was real to him, so real that he had a gospel to preach, the gospel of Christ's love; and 'I found', he says, 'my spirit leaned most after awakening and converting Work.' 'Sound conviction for Sin, especially for Unbelief', and then 'an heart set on fire to be saved by Christ, with strong breathings after a truly sanctified Soul: that was it that delighted me; those were the souls I counted blessed.'[34]

> Jesu, Thou art all compassion,
> Pure, unbounded love Thou art . . .

So Charles Wesley, and Bunyan would agree; but no one would call Wesley a Marcionite. In any case, Christian meets many people who, though they are not among the better-known rascals and rapscallions of Vanity Fair, are still living under judgement and the Law. Bunyan's position may be schismatic, but it is not heretical; and at bottom the schism is between the Church and the World. By implication *The Pilgrim's Progress* is a powerful plea for separatism. If there was a case for separating from the Roman Church, there was also a case for separating from a worldly Church. Mr Formalist and Mr Pliable might find a place in it, but they could not be members of the Church of Christ in Bedford, who in principle are already translated from death to life because they love the brethren, with a love greater than their own. This is another way of saying that for Bunyan ecclesiology has its roots in Christology and in awareness of Christ.

Yet where did Bunyan get the title of his book? *The Pilgrim's Progress* seems an odd sort of title for a Puritan or Nonconformist. Pilgrims and pilgrimages were papistical, and had long been done away with. The fuller title, however, provides the clue: *The Pilgrim's Progress from this World to that which is to come.* The pilgrimage is a pilgrimage to heaven. 'These all died in faith, not having received the promises, but having seen them afar off, and were persuaded of them, and embraced them, and confessed that they were strangers and pilgrims

33 William Blake, *Poetry and Prose*, ed. G. Keynes (London, 1927), p. 844.
34 *Grace Abounding*, pp. 85, 89.

on the earth.' This is the source (Hebrews 11:13): we are back with the Bible. *The Pilgrim's Progress* is, in fact, eschatological and teleological throughout, concerned with the End in both senses (*telos* as well as *eschaton*). There are few more vivid scenes in it than when in the Delectable Mountains the Shepherds have Christian and Hopeful to the top of an high hill called Clear, and put a perspective glass to their eye, which they had difficulty in holding steady, 'yet they thought they saw something like the Gate, and also some of the Glory of the place. Then they went away, and sang':

> Thus by the Shepherds, Secrets are reveal'd,
> Which from all other men are kept conseal'd:
> Come to the Shepherds then, if you would see
> Things deep, things hid, and that mysterious be.[35]

At this point Bunyan joins hands with his older contemporary, the royalist Sidney Godolphin, who was killed in the Civil War at the age of thirty-three.

> There is no merit in the wise
> But Love, (the shepherds' sacrifice)
> Wise men, all ways of knowledge past,
> To the shepherds' wonder come at last.[36]

'All ways of knowledge past'; but one of Bunyan's Shepherds is *called* Knowledge! For their 'names were, Knowledge, Experience, Watchful and Sincere.'[37]

'Whose delectable Mountains are these?' the pilgrims ask the Shepherds. 'And whose be the sheep that feed upon them?' Shepherds: 'These mountains are Immanuels Land, and they are within sight of his City; and the sheep also are his, and he laid down his life for them.'[38] The attraction of *The Pilgrim's Progress* has always lain in its appeal to simplicity and wonder: the shepherds' wonder and the simplicity that is in Christ. 'Whither I go ye know, and the way ye know. Thomas saith unto him, Lord, we know not whither thou goest; and how can we know the way? Jesus saith unto him, I am the way.' The book is certainly a work of supreme imaginative genius; but its power is as a book of 'the way': the way to Christ, the way of Christ and the way with Christ. This is its theme, the manifold reality of Christian experience; and in this Bunyan continued a long tradition. Truly, as Professor A. G. Dickens notes of some earlier Reformers, John Bunyan has his place beside those whose 'desire . . . to bring men nearer in love to the real person of the Founder . . . lies at the heart of their message for our own century.'[39]

35 *Pilgrim's Progress*, p. 123.
36 Sidney Godolphin, 'Hymn', in *Minor Poets of the Caroline Period*, ed. G. Saintsbury (Oxford, 1906), vol. ii, p. 247.
37 *Pilgrim's Progress*, p. 120.
38 Ibid., p. 119.
39 A. G. Dickens, *The English Reformation* (London, 1964), p. 340.

Bibliography

BOOKS, ARTICLES AND PRINCIPAL REVIEWS BY A. G. DICKENS
(*to 1979*)
[*All books were published in London unless otherwise stated*]

1935–1939

Historical and general articles, theatre reviews and poems (some unsigned) in the *Oxford Magazine* (Oxonian Press), *passim*.

1937

'St Bernard's College: the Cistercian ancestor of St John's', *Oxford Magazine*, 21 October 1937, pp. 52–4.

'New records of the Pilgrimage of Grace', *Yorkshire Archaeological Journal*, 33, pp. 298–308.

'The marriage and character of Archbishop Holgate', *English Historical Review*, 52, pp. 428–42.

'A new prayer of Sir Thomas More', *Church Quarterly Review*, 124, pp. 224–37 (subsequently attributed to St John Fisher: see *Tudor Treatises* [below, 1959], p. 19).

1938

'A seventeenth-century don: Griffin Higgs and his friends', *Oxford Magazine*, 3 February 1938, pp. 350–2; 10 February 1938, pp. 378–80.

'The Yorkshire submissions to Henry VIII, 1541', *EHR*, 53, pp. 267–75.

'A versatile Oxford Elizabethan: Sir Francis Verney and his tragedy Antipoe', *Oxford Magazine*, 28 April 1938, pp. 539–43.

'The Northern Convocation and Henry VIII', *CQR*, 127, pp. 84–102.

'Royal pardons for the Pilgrimage of Grace', *YAJ*, 33, pp. 397–417.

1939

'Some popular reactions to the Edwardian Reformation in Yorkshire', *YAJ*, 34, pp. 151–69.

'Sedition and conspiracy in Yorkshire during the later years of Henry VIII', *YAJ*, 34, pp. 379–98.

Review of Brian Magee, *The English Recusants: a study of the post-Reformation Catholic survival and the operation of the recusancy laws*, in *Journal of Theological Studies*, 40, pp. 301–3.

1940

'An Elizabethan defender of the monasteries', *CQR*, 130, pp. 236–62.

'The Edwardian arrears in augmentation payments and the problem of the ex-religious', *EHR*, 55, pp. 384–418.

Review of J. Charlesworth (ed.), *The Wakefield Manor Book, 1709*, Yorkshire Archaeological Society, Record Series, 101 (1939), in *EHR*, 55, p. 684.

1941

'The first stages of Romanist recusancy in Yorkshire, 1560–1590', *YAJ*, 35, pp. 157–82.
'Archbishop Holgate's apology', *EHR*, 56, pp. 450–9.

1945

Fifteen Poems (privately printed, Lübeck).
'A municipal dissolution of chantries at York, 1536', *YAJ*, 36, pp. 164–74.

1947

'Robert Parkyn's narrative of the Reformation', *EHR*, 62, pp. 58–83.
Lübeck Diary (Victor Gollancz).

1948

'The extent and character of recusancy in Yorkshire, 1604', *YAJ*, 37, pp. 24–49.
'Student Life in Finland. An Oxford visit to Helsinki and Turku', *The Times*, 6 January.

1949

'Robert Parkyn's MS books', *Notes and Queries*, 194, pp. 73–4.
'Two Marian petitions', *YAJ*, 37, pp. 376–84.
Review of E. G. Rupp, *Studies in the making of the English Protestant tradition – mainly in the reign of Henry VIII*, in *JTS*, 50, pp. 106–7.

1950

'Yorkshire clerical documents, 1584–1586', *Bodleian Library Record*, 3, pp. 34–40.
'South Yorkshire letters, 1555', *Transactions of the Hunter Archaeological Society*, 6, pp. 278–84.
'John Parkyn, Fellow of Trinity College, Cambridge', *Cambridge Antiquarian Journal*, 43, 21–9.

1951

Editor, *The register or chronicle of Butley Priory, Suffolk, 1510–1538* (Warren and Son, Winchester).

1952

'Robert Parkyn's Life of Christ', *Bodleian Library Record*, 4, pp. 67–76.
'Aspects of the intellectual transition among the English parish clergy of the Reformation period: a regional example', *Archiv für Reformationsgeschichte*, 60, pp. 51–9.
'Norman and Angevin York: some suggested revisions', *Yorkshire Architectural and York Archaeological Society Report 1952–1953*, pp. 34–5.

1953

'The "shire" and privileges of the Archbishop in eleventh-century York', *YAJ*, 38, pp. 131–47.
Review of 'Calendar of ancient deeds, letters and miscellaneous documents' [Corporation of Hull], in *YAJ*, 28, pp. 122–3.

1954

The East Riding of Yorkshire, with Hull and York: A Portrait (A. Brown and Sons; reprinted 1958).
'Peter Moone, the Ipswich gospeller and poet', *Notes and Queries*, 199, pp. 513–14.

1955

Robert Holgate, Archbishop of York and President of the King's Council in the North, St Anthony's Hall Publications No 8.
'High School and College in American society', *Studies in Education* (University of Hull), 2, pp. 207–17.
'Further light on the scope of Yorkshire recusancy in 1604' (with John Newton), *YAJ*, 38, pp. 524–8.

1956

A guide to the regional studies on the East Riding of Yorkshire and the city of Hull (with K. A. MacMahon), Departments of Adult Education and History, University of Hull.
'The Tudor Percy emblem in Royal MS 180 D ii', *Archaeological Journal*, 112, pp. 95–9.
'Wilfred Holme of Huntington: Yorkshire's first Protestant poet', *YAJ*, 39, pp. 119–35.
'Estate and household management in Bedfordshire, *circa* 1540', *Bedfordshire Historical Record Society*, 36, pp. 38–45.
Reveiew of York Civic Records, viii, ed. A. Raine, *Yorkshire Archaeological Society, Record Series*, 119, in *EHR*, 71, pp. 152–3.

1957

Contributions to *The Oxford Dictionary of the Christian Church*, ed. F. L. Cross (Oxford University Press).
'The purposes of historical study at the university', *Occasional Papers of the Institute of Education, University of Hull*, 1, pp. 1–12. (Finnish translation 'Historia ja luentosali', *Suomalainen Suomi* 5, pp. 265–71, Helsinki.)
The Marian reaction in the Diocese of York, St Anthony's Hall Publications, 11 and 12 (two parts).

1958

'Britannia ja Mannermaa' [Britain and Continental Europe], *Suomalainen Suomi*, 8, pp. 491–9, Helsinki.
Editor, *Tudor Treatises*, for the *Yorkshire Archaeological Society Records Series*, 125.
Thomas Cromwell and the English Reformation (English Universities Press; 5th impression, 1972; 6th impression, Hodder and Stoughton, 1977; American edition, Perennial Library [P 144], Harper and Row, New York, 1969).
Lollards and Protestants in the Diocese of York, 1509–1558 (Oxford University Press for the University of Hull).

1960

Review of H. C. Porter, *Reformation and Reaction in Tudor Cambridge*, in *EHR*, 75, p. 347.
Review of R. S. Sylvester (ed.), *George Cavendish, life and death of Cardinal Wolsey* (*E.E.T.S.*, 1959), in *EHR*, 75, pp. 723–4.
Review of W. J. Brown, *Life of Rowland Taylor*, in *Journal of Ecclesiastical History*, 11, p. 270.

1961

Chapters in *Victoria County History: The City of York:* (1) 'York before the Norman Conquest', (2) 'Tudor York', (3) 'Anglo-Scandinavian antiquities' (Oxford University Press for the Institute of Historical Research).

Editor, *Clifford Letters of the Sixteenth Century*, Surtees Society, 172 (Andrews, Durham and Quaritch, London, for the Society).

Review of R. A. Marchant, *The Puritans and the Church courts in the diocese of York, 1560–1642*, in *EHR*, 77, pp. 331.

Review of Clare Talbot (ed.), *Miscellanea: Recusant records* (Catholic Record Society, 1961), in *JEH*, 13, p. 267.

1963

'The writers of Tudor Yorkshire', *Transactions of the Royal Historical Society*, 5th series, 13, pp. 49–76.

Review of Walter C. Richardson, *History of the Court of Augmentations*, in *JEH*, 14, pp. 99–101.

1964

'Heresy and the origins of English Protestantism', in J. S. Bromley and E. H. Kossmann (eds), *Britain and the Netherlands*, 2, pp. 47–66 (J. B. Wolters, Groningen).

The English Reformation (Batsford; reprinted 1965; 3rd impression, 1966; 4th impression, 1971; 5th [revised] impression, 1972; 6th impression, 1973; American edition, Schocken Books, New York, 1964; Collins Fontana editions [revised], 1967 and 1972).

Review of Robert Peters, *Oculus Episcopi: administration in the archdeaconry of St Albans, 1580–1625*, in *JEH* 15, pp. 258–9.

Review of G. H. Williams, *The Radical Reformation*, in *Past and Present*, 27, pp. 123–5.

Review of John Addy, *The Archdeacon and ecclesiastical discipline in Yorkshire 1598–1714*, in *JEH*, 15, pp. 258–9.

1965

'The Reformation in England', Chapter 4 in Joel Hurstfield (ed.), *The Reformation Crisis* (Edward Arnold; American edition, Harper Torchbook [1267 G], Harper and Row, New York).

'The English Reformation and religious tolerance', *Comité International des Sciences Historiques*, Rapports 1, Grandes Thèmes, XIIth International Congress of Historical Sciences. See also 'Religious toleration and liberalism in Tudor England', in *Congregational Historical Society Transactions*, 20, pp. 58–73.

Review of Hugh Aveling, *The Catholic recusants of the West Riding of Yorkshire*, in *JEH*, 16, p. 130.

1966

Review of W. Haller, *Foxe's Book of Martyrs and the Elect Nation*, and Helen C. White, *Tudor Books of saints and martyrs*, in *EHR*, 80, pp. 389–91.

Reformation and Society in Sixteenth-Century Europe (Thames and Hudson; French translation *La réforme et la société du XVIe siècle*, J. Hall and J. Lagrange for Flammarion, Paris, 1969; Dutch translation *Een nieuw Europa: de zestiende Eeuw*, S. L. Verheus for Ten Have, Amsterdam; Portuguese translation *A reforma na Europa do seculo XVI*, Antonio Gonçalves Mattoso for Editorial Verbo, Lisbon, 1971).

Introduction to A. F. Pollard, *Henry VIII* (Harper Torchbook, Harper and Row, New York), pp. ix–xxiii.

Introduction to A. F. Pollard, *Wolsey* (Harper Torchbook, Harper and Row, New York), pp. xiii–xxix.

Articles on 'Albigenses', 'Lollards', 'Wyclif, John' and 'York' in *Chambers' Encyclopaedia* (Pergamon Press).

Review of W. A. Clebsch, *England's earliest Protestants, 1520–1538*, *JTS*, 17, pp. 227–9.

1967

Martin Luther and the Reformation (English Universities Press; 3rd impression, Hodder and Stoughton, 1977; American edition, (Perennial Library [P 136], Harper and Row, New York, 1969).

Introduction to Macaulay's *History of England to the Death of William III*, vol. i, pp. vii–xi (Heron Books).

Articles on 'Lollards' and 'Wycliffe, John' in *Encyclopaedia Britannica*.

'Secular and religious motivation in the Pilgrimage of Grace', *Studies in Church History*, 4, ed. G. J. Cuming (E. J. Brill, Leiden), pp. 39–64.

Editor (with Dorothy Carr), *The Reformation in England to the Accession of Elizabeth I*, volume in the series *Documents of Modern History* (Arnold).

Review of J. A. F. Thomson, *The later Lollards, 1414–1520*, in *Medium Aevum*, 36, pp. 299–301.

'Some first fruits of the Luther-Anniversary', *JEH*, 18, pp. 233–5.

Review of J. K. McConica, *English Humanists and Reformation politics under Henry VIII and Edward VI*, in *History*, 52, pp. 77–8.

Review of John P. Dolan, *History of the Reformation: a conciliatory assessment of opposite views*, in *JEH*, 18, pp. 102–3.

Review of J. E. Oxley, *The Reformation in Essex to the death of Mary*, in *EHR*, 82, pp. 82–3.

1968

The Counter Reformation (Thames and Hudson; French translation *La Contre-Réforme*, H. Seyrès for Flammarion, Paris, 1969; Dutch translation *De Contra-Reformatie*, S. L. Verheus for Ten Have, Baarn, 1971; Portuguese translation *A Contra Reforma*, Antonio Gonçalves Mattoso for Editorial Verbo, Lisbon, 1972).

'Recent books on Reformation and Counter Reformation', *JEH*, 19, pp. 219–26.

1969

Three supplementary chapters in the Purnell Part-Works edition of Winston Churchill, *History of the English Speaking Peoples:* (1) 'The Lollards', 2, part 25, pp. 814–16; (2) 'The English Church before the Reformation', 3, part 35, pp. 1117–21; (3) 'The Reformation on the Continent', 3, part 35, pp. 1130–6.

1971

Review of Glanmor Williams, *Reformation views of church history*, in *The Welsh History Review*, 6, pp. 403–4.

Review of Heinz Otto Burger, *Renaissance, Humanismus, Reformation*, in *European Studies Review*, i, pp. 399–400.

'The Reformation', in *Perspectives on the European Past: Conversations with Historians*, ed. Norman F. Cantor (Macmillan, New York), pp. 252–4.

1972

The Age of Humanism and Reformation: Europe in the Fourteenth, Fifteenth and Sixteenth Centuries (Prentice-Hall, Engelwood Cliffs, New Jersey; revised edition for the Open University, Prentice-Hall International, 1977).

Foreword to Derek Wilson, *A Tudor Tapestry: Men, Women and Society in Reformation England* (Heinemann).

1973

Review of J-P. Massaut, *Josse Clichtove, l'humanisme et la réforme du clergé*, in *JEH*, 24, pp. 207–9.

1974

The German Nation and Martin Luther (Edward Arnold; American edition, Harper and Row, New York; Collins Fontana edition [revised], Glasgow, 1976).

'The Ambivalent English Reformation', in J. B. Trapp (ed.), *Background to the English Renaissance* (Gray–Mills Publishing), pp. 43–56.

'The Elizabethans and St Bartholomew', in Alfred Soman (ed.), *The Massacre of St Bartholomew: Reappraisals and Documents* (Martinus Nijhoff, The Hague), pp. 52–70.

Foreword to V-L. Tapié, *France in the Age of Louis XIII and Richelieu*, trans. and ed. D. McN. Lockie (Macmillan).

1975

Revisions of historical sections in Sir Banister Fletcher's *A History of Architecture*, 18th edition, revised by J. C. Palmes (Athlone Press).

'The last medieval Englishman', in Peter Brooks (ed.), *Christian Spirituality: Essays in Honour of Gordon Rupp* (S.C.M. Press), pp. 141–82.

1976

Review of Steven E. Ozment, *The Reformation in the Cities: the Appeal of Protestantism to sixteenth-century Germany and Switzerland*, *JEH*, 27, pp. 200–1.

Review of Mark U. Edwards, *Luther and the False Brethren*, in *Times Literary Supplement*, 2 April, p. 401.

Preface to *The Anglo-Dutch Contribution to the Civilization of Early Modern Society. An Anglo-Netherlands Symposium* (Oxford University Press for the British Academy).

'The rôle of cities in the German and English Reformations', in K. Friedland (ed.), *Frühformen Englisch–Deutscher Handelspartnerschaft* (Bohlan Verlag, Cologne and Vienna, for the Hansische Geschichtsverein), pp. 1–8.

'Intellectual and social forces in the German Reformation', in *Friends of Lambeth Palace Library, Annual Report*, pp. 9–17.

'The Lutheran Reformation' (with G. R. Elton), in P. Wells (ed.), *European History 1500–1700* (Sussex Publications).

'The German Historical Institute', in *Times Literary Supplement*, 5 November, p. 1403.

1977

Editor, *The Courts of Europe: Politics, Patronage and Royalty, 1400–1800* (Thames and Hudson, with McGraw-Hill, New York). Contributor: 'Introduction', p. 7; 'Monarchy and cultural revival. Courts in the Middle Ages', pp. 8–32; 'Epilogue', pp. 325–7.

'Johannes Sleidan and Reformation History', in R. Buick Knox (ed.), *Reformation*

Conformity and Dissent: Essays in Honour of Geoffrey Nuttall (Epworth Press), pp 17–43.

'Vivian Hunter Galbraith, 1889–1976', in *Bulletin of the Institute of Historical Research*, 50, pp. 1–3.

Speech at the opening of the German Historical Institute, London, in P. Kluke and P. Alter (eds), *Aspekte der deutsch-britischen Beziehungen im Laufe des Jahrhunderts* (*Veröffentlichungen des Deutschen Historischen Institute*, Klett-Cotta, Stuttgart), Band 4, pp. 7–10 [German text in *Geschichte in Wissenschaft and Unterricht, Jahrgang* 28, *Heft* 3, *Marz* 1977.]

'S. T. Bindoff: an appreciation', in E. W. Ives, R. J. Knecht and J. J. Scarisbrick (eds), *Wealth and Power in Tudor England: Essays presented to S. T. Bindoff* (Athlone Press), pp. xvii–xxi.

'Neville John Williams, 1924–1977', in *Proceedings of the British Academy*.

1979

'Joel Hurstfield: a memoir', in Peter Clark, Alan G. R. Smith and Nicholas Tyacke (eds), *The English Commonwealth, 1547–1640* (Leicester University Press, Leicester).

'La réforme Protestante en Angleterre et en France,' in D. W. J. Johnson (ed.), *Britain and France* (Dawson Publishing for *Conseil Franco-Britannique, Section Français*, Paris).

Contemporary Historians of the German Reformation. The 1978 Bethell Memorial Lecture. Institute of Germanic Studies, University of London, 1979.

'Intellectual and Social Forces in the German Reformation' in Mommsen, J. (ed.), *Stadtbürgertum und Adel in der Reformation.* Klett-Cotta, Stuttgart, 1979.

'La Réforme en Angleterre et en France' in *Ten Centuries of Franco-British History.* Éditions Albin Michel, Paris, 1979 (for *Conseil Franco-Britannique*).

Index*

* The Editor gratefully acknowledges assistance in the compilation of this index from Mr Paul Ayris, Mr Gareth Hayward, Mrs. P. N. Brooks and Miss Jenny Brooks.

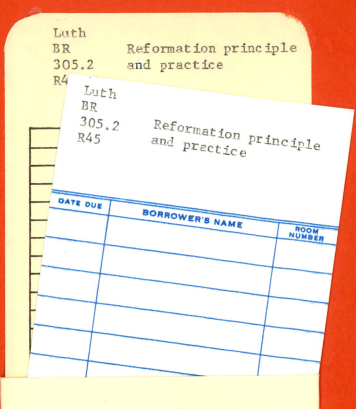